Creation Through Evolution

Creation Through Evolution

New Perspectives in Thomistic Philosophy and Theology

NICANOR PIER GIORGIO AUSTRIACO, OP
EDITOR

THE CATHOLIC UNIVERSITY OF AMERICA PRESS
WASHINGTON, D.C.

Copyright © 2025
The Catholic University of America Press
All rights reserved
The paper used in this publication meets the minimum requirements of
American National Standards for Information Science—Permanence of Paper
for Printed Library Materials, ANSI Z39.48-1992.
∞
Cataloging-in-Publication Data is available from the Library of Congress

ISBN: 978-0-8132-3925-5
eISBN: 978-0-8132-3871-5
Paperback ISBN: 978-0-8132-3870-8

ThomisticEvolution.org

Contents

Chapter 1: Introduction 1
Nicanor Pier Giorgio Austriaco, OP

Chapter 2: Essentialist and Hylomorphic Notion of Species and Species Transformation 11
Mariusz Tabaczek, OP

Chapter 3: Thomas Aquinas on the Proportionate Causes of Living Species 43
Brian Carl

Chapter 4: *Nihil dat quod non habet*: Thomist Naturalism Contra Supernaturalism on the Origin of Species 65
Daniel D. De Haan

Chapter 5: Is Thomistic Ethics Compatible with Evolutionary Biology? 93
Raymond Hain

Chapter 6: The Teaching of the Catholic Church and the Evolution of Humanity 115
Simon Francis Gaine, OP

Chapter 7: What if "Adam" Had Not Sinned? Explorations on How Human Vulnerabilities Might Have Been Overcome in the First Human Beings and Their Descendants 143
Richard Conrad, OP

Chapter 8: The Transmission of Original Sin in Light of Evolution 177
Robert Barry

Chapter 9: What Kind of Death? Romans 5 and Modern Science 205
Isaac Augustine Morales, OP

Chapter 10: Defending a Historical Adam and Eve after Darwin 225
Nicanor Pier Giorgio Austriaco, OP

Chapter 11: "You Prepared a Body for Me" (Heb 10:5):
           The Eschatological End of Evolution   237
           Daria Spezzano

Select Bibliography   263

Biographies   271

Index   275

CHAPTER ONE

Introduction

NICANOR PIER GIORGIO AUSTRIACO, OP

According to a Pew Research Center survey undertaken in the United States that was published in 2019—one hundred and sixty years after the publication of Charles Darwin's *On the Origin of Species* in 1859—87% of the Catholic respondents affirmed that human beings had evolved.[1] This was several points higher than the percentage of adult respondents (81%) who had answered in the same way.

And yet, my professional experience as a priest-biologist has revealed to me that a significant number of Catholics are unsure about how they can reconcile their religious faith with the theory of evolution that they learned in school. They often compartmentalize and distinguish the scientific narrative of the origins of life on the planet from their theological affirmations that God created the world and all that is in it. Moreover, in the United States, there has been a recent emergence of Catholic groups who are deeply suspicious of the possibility that an evolutionary worldview may be compatible with the Catholic faith.[2] In contrast to their Protestant counterparts who ground their anti-Darwinian views on the incompatibility of an evolutionary timeline for creation in a literalist reading of the opening pages of Genesis, these Catholic creationists also include arguments that appeal to philosophical principles, alleging that evolutionary change is impossible. Their arguments also include magisterial citations from the writings of the Church Fathers who held to a six-day account of creation.[3]

In this volume, the scholars of ThomisticEvolution.org have written a series of essays to continue the ongoing task of thinking through some of the

---

1. Cary Funk, "How Highly Religious Americans View Evolution Depends on How They're Asked About It," Pew Research Center, February 6, 2019, https://www.pewresearch.org/fact-tank/2019/02/06/how-highly-religious-americans-view-evolution-depends-on-how-theyre-asked-about-it/.

2. Brett Salkeld, "Catholic Creationism as a Conspiracy Theory," *Church Life Journal*, May 13, 2020, https://churchlifejournal.nd.edu/articles/catholic-creationism-as-a-conspiracy-theory/.

3. For one example of this strategy, see the website "Aquinas and Evolution": http://aquinasandevolution.org/.

apparent tensions between Catholic and Darwinian accounts of the origins of life. These chapters articulate a view of evolutionary creation that takes as a starting point the foundational philosophical and theological principles undergirding the *Catechism of the Catholic Church*. They take as a given the words of Pope St. John Paul II, who in his letter to the Pontifical Academy of Sciences on October 22, 1996, declared:

> I am delighted with the first theme that you have chosen, which is the origin of life and evolution, an essential theme that is of great interest to the Church, since Revelation contains, for its part, its own teachings concerning the nature and origins of man. How may the conclusions reached by the various scientific disciplines and those contained in the message of Revelation come into mutual concord? And if, at first glance, it may seem that these are opposed to each other, in what direction should we look for their resolution? We know that the truth cannot contradict the truth.[4]

Moreover, these chapters are motivated by the conviction that the Thomistic intellectual tradition begun by St. Thomas Aquinas (1225–1274) can still provide insightful and compelling responses to disputed questions in science and religion. From our pastoral experience, my Dominican brothers and I have discovered that Catholics and other Christians are frequently surprised by the novelty and brilliance the Thomistic intellectual tradition can bring to conversations about God and evolution. This is often the case because these answers transcend and reconcile the dichotomies—for instance, the oft-cited dichotomy between chance and design —that shape the contemporary science and religion debate. Instead, St. Thomas can say, "God designs with chance!" In the same light, by making distinctions and clarifying arguments, the chapters that follow reveal the power and sophistication of a Thomistic approach to resolving the apparent conundrums at the intersection of faith and reason.

Finally, a brief word about the title of this anthology: *Creation Through Evolution*. Properly speaking, God creates simply by giving being to creatures. However, evolution is not just about the transformation of one species into another. It is also about innovation. It is about how novel adaptive traits arise because of natural selection. In this sense, the evolutionary process is creative. It generates novelty where novelty did not exist. The title of our work reflects this view. It proposes that God used and continues to use an evolutionary process to create the novelty and diversity that adorn the living things that populate our universe.

---

4. John Paul II, "Address to the Pontifical Academy of Sciences (October 22, 1996)," in *Papal Addresses to the Pontifical Academy of Sciences 1917–2002* (Vatican: Pontifical Academy of Sciences, 2003). English translation from the French is my own.

1. Philosophical Issues

In the first half of this volume, four philosophers of ThomisticEvolution.org address three disputed questions that are often raised by those critical of the idea that God created through evolution. The first objection involves the reality of biological species and natural kinds; the second interrogates the metaphysics of biological speciation or the natural process whereby individuals of one biological species can give rise to progeny that belongs to a different biological species; and the third deals with the implications of evolutionary theory on a classical ethical account, which holds to moral absolutes grounded in the natural law.

First, there is a consensus among modern biologists and philosophers of biology that evolutionary theory has rendered a natural-kind essentialism (i.e., the view that organisms have underlying natures or essences that sort them into natural kinds) obsolete.[5] This has led Christian theologians to question the traditional narrative of human origins that specifies a distinct moment for the beginning of our kind: "According to the scientific version of genesis, on the other hand, the arrival of the first humans is not marked by sudden bursts or clear boundaries. . . . There are no faint lines, no lines at all, in fact, that mark the advent of the human, unambiguously distinguishing our kind from other kinds or announcing our arrival."[6] According to this view, Adam or Eve did not exist because there was never such a thing as a "first" human being.

In his chapter, Fr. Mariusz Tabaczek, OP (Pontifical University of St. Thomas Aquinas, Rome) surveys the debate surrounding the species concept and discusses the work of philosophers of biology who have challenged orthodoxy by claiming that a realist account of biological species that affirms the existence of biological essences and biological kinds is a more robust explanation than its nominalist counterpart. With the resurgence of essentialism among analytic philosophers, Christians can once again affirm with intellectual coherence that "God made every kind of wild animal, every kind of tame animal, and every kind of thing that crawls on the ground. God saw that it was good" (Gen 1:25 NABR).

Next, a common objection to evolution among Catholic skeptics is the philosophical claim that the evolution of new biological species is metaphysi-

---

5. For a representative of the consensus view, see Philip Kitcher, "Species," *Philosophy of Science* 51 (1984): 308–33.

6. Ron Cole-Turner, *The End of Adam and Eve: Theology and the Science of Human Origins* (Pittsburgh: TheologyPlus Publishing, 2016), 69. For my response to Cole-Turner, see Nicanor Pier Giorgio Austriaco, OP, "Defending Adam After Darwin: On the Origin of *Sapiens* as a Natural Kind," *American Catholic Philosophical Quarterly* 92, no. 2 (2018): 337–52.

cally impossible.[7] This argument appeals to the principle of proportionate causality (PPC), which affirms that an effect cannot "exceed" its cause, be "more powerful" than its cause, or "be more perfect" than its cause. More popularly, this principle is often expressed as "nothing can give what it does not have." According to critics who deploy the PPC to counter evolution—often accompanied by an appeal to the authority of St. Thomas Aquinas—it is metaphysically impossible for lizards to evolve into snakes with their own distinctive traits not found in lizards (which is the standard Darwinian account) because two lizards, by definition, do not have any "snakeness" to give to their progeny.[8]

In their chapters, Brian Carl (University of St. Thomas, Houston) and Daniel De Haan (University of Oxford) respond to critics who have used the PPC to anathemize evolutionary theory. First, Dr. Carl notes that for St. Thomas, it cannot be that the generation of a new organism only follows when like gives birth to like, since the Dominican Master, like his peers, believed that some living things are spontaneously generated from nonliving things, like flies from rotting flesh or oysters from slimy mud. Instead, for Aquinas, biological reproduction is best understood as a remote universal cause that uses the instrumental causality of mediating instruments (i.e., the breeding pair or inanimate decaying flesh or mud) to produce more powerful effects that are manifest in the progeny. As Dr. Carl affirms, the PPC seems entirely reconcilable with evolutionary change as well.

In a complementary chapter, Dr. De Haan convincingly shows that the anti-Darwinian view that the PPC renders evolutionary change impossible fails to appreciate that natural systems of interacting substances in creation have potentialities and actualities that can explain biological speciation.

---

7. For one example of this view, see Fr. Chad Ripperger, "The Metaphysical Impossibility of Human Evolution," The Kolbe Center for the Study of Creation, September 26, 2015, https://www.kolbecenter.org/metaphysical-impossibility-human-evolution-chad-ripperger-catholic-creation/.

8. For discussion on the standard Darwinian account, see Philip J. Bergmann and Gen Morinaga, "The Convergent Evolution of Snake-Like Forms by Divergent Evolutionary Pathways in Squamate Reptiles," *Evolution* 73, no. 3 (2019): 481–96. In my view, it is striking that philosophical critics of evolution are not willing to deploy their argument to propose that spontaneous chemical reactions where two unlike chemical substances are able to generate a third unlike substance are also metaphysically impossible. For example, the reaction of baking soda ($NaHCO_3$), which is a solid, with vinegar (CH_3COOH), which is a liquid, gives rise to sodium acetate (CH_3COONa), which is a solid, carbon dioxide (CO_2), which is a gas, and water (H_2O). According to a strict reading of the PPC, a solid and a liquid should not be able to produce a gas, since neither original substance is a gas. As such, they cannot give "gasness" to the products of the reaction. And yet, this chemical reaction actually occurs! This example suggests that the PPC is not an absolute philosophical principle that can be used to rule out scientific phenomena a priori.

According to this alternate view, systems of hylomorphic substances in the cosmos created by God can generate novel ontological species without special intervention. Dr. De Haan concludes his essay by demonstrating that his systems construal of the PPC is a superior Thomistic account to the atomized view embraced by scholastic critics of evolution.

Finally, there is the old charge among proponents of an evolutionary worldview that Darwin has ruled out any form of classical ethics that is eudemonistic in character.[9] There are two challenges to a specifically Thomistic account of ethics. First, there are contemporary ethicists who have disqualified a Thomistic approach to moral reasoning because it presupposes a stable human nature that provides the content and justification for a natural law ethics that promotes human flourishing. Second, there are critics who have attacked the classical Thomistic strategy of moving from theoretical knowledge of human nature to practical knowledge of human action because evolutionary biology can only tell us how things are and not how things ought to be.

In his chapter, Raymond Hain (Providence College) provides a comprehensive response to those who argue that evolutionary biology has made a Thomistic ethics untenable. He proposes that an ethical strategy, which acknowledges that an analysis of human nature and an analysis of first-person practical reasoning are entangled where neither is ultimately epistemologically prior to the other, can still justify a natural law ethics that is ordered toward human flourishing. As such, Dr. Hain concludes, "Thomistic ethics is indeed compatible with evolutionary biology, but any confidence we might have that this will continue to be the case requires ongoing critical engagement with the methods, results, and implications of both."

2. Theological Issues

In the second half of this volume, six scholars address several theological questions that are often raised by Catholics who are struggling to reconcile evolutionary biology with the Church's account of our origins that is sketched out in the *Catechism of the Catholic Church*.[10] Not surprisingly, in my view, most of these questions revolve around the implications of human evolution on the Church's teachings of the origin and destiny of the *imago Dei*.

Fr. Simon Gaine, OP (Pontifical University of St. Thomas Aquinas, Rome) opens the theological section with a magisterial chapter that lays out

---

9. For a historical summary and analysis of the engagement between evolutionary theory and ethics, see Paul Lawrence Farber, *The Temptations of Evolutionary Ethics* (Berkeley: University of California Press, 1994).

10. *Catechism of the Catholic Church*, 355–421.

the Catholic Church's doctrinal account of human origins to answer the question: How did God create the human species? His narrative includes a detailed and critical analysis of the provenance of Pope Pius XII's encyclical, *Humani Generis*, which addressed the question of biological evolution for the first time. Importantly, Fr. Gaine's work has been informed by Church documents that were released by the Archives of the Dicastery for the Doctrine of the Faith at the Vatican. He concludes that the Church's ordinary magisterium has tolerated some versions of polygenism (i.e., the view that human beings today are descended from more than one original couple) since the late 1960s but remains committed to monogenism (i.e., the contrasting view that we are all the children of an original couple).

Moving now to specific disputed questions in origins theology, the *Catechism* proclaims, "The Church, interpreting the symbolism of biblical language in an authentic way, in the light of the New Testament and Tradition, teaches that our first parents, Adam and Eve, were constituted in an original 'state of holiness and justice.'"[11]). This affirms an ancient Christian belief inherited from the opening paragraphs of Genesis that God created human beings good (see Gen. 1:31) because he is a good God who would never have created anything, let alone anyone, broken. But what would this original state of holiness and justice look like in an evolving creation?

In his contribution, Fr. Richard Conrad, OP (Blackfriars Hall, Oxford) defends this doctrine of an original state of holiness and justice by exploring how human vulnerability might have been overcome in the first humans. Drawing on St. Thomas's nonmythical account of "the state of innocence," he notes what elements in the Dominican Master's portrait of "the first man" do not square with the consensus today that the first human beings were descended from prehuman ancestors in Africa. He then explores how the first unfallen human beings and their offspring might have known God, how grace might have affected their moral lives, and how social structures might have remained relatively unmarked by sin. Finally, Fr. Conrad asks how the physical vulnerabilities of unfallen human beings might have been remedied.

The *Catechism* then moves to the initial corruption of the first human beings. It summarizes Catholic doctrine as follows, "The account of the fall in Genesis 3 uses figurative language, but affirms a primeval event, a deed that took place at the beginning of the history of man. Revelation gives us the certainty of faith that the whole of human history is marked by the original fault freely committed by our first parents."[12] Many Catholic theologians remain skeptical of this magisterial teaching because of evolutionary theory. Fr. Jack

---

11. *Catechism of the Catholic Church*, 375.
12. *Catechism of the Catholic Church*, 390.

Mahoney, SJ, wrote, "I argue that with the acceptance of the evolutionary origin of humanity there is no longer a need or a place in Christian beliefs for the traditional doctrines of original sin, the Fall, and human concupiscence resulting from that sin."[13]

In their chapters, Robert Barry (Providence College) and Fr. Isaac Morales, OP (Providence College) address the question of the fall and its consequences. How can we understand these historical realities in an evolving creation, especially one that includes a polygenic origin of modern human beings? In his essay, Dr. Barry turns to St. Thomas to begin thinking through a coherent account of original sin that can be reconciled with a polygenetic origin of our species. He proposes that what Adam confers on his descendants is a nature that is "stained" by original sin through not being suited to the immediate reception of the grace of original justice as it would have been if Adam had not sinned. Dr. Barry notes that if someone was "generated from a principle of human nature other than Adam's, and not given a gift of grace productive of original justice, that person would exist in a condition identical to the condition of original sin." In both these scenarios, the fitness of human nature for receiving sanctifying grace is not a biological property, but a moral property accounted for by divine justice and divine punishment.

In his contribution, Fr. Morales turns to the key biblical text found in Romans 5:12–21 that is at the heart of the Christian doctrine of original sin and its relation to death.[14] Young earth creationists, who are critical of evolutionary theory, have argued that this scriptural text affirms that death—not only human death but death in general—only entered the world after the fall, a claim that seems to fly in the face of scientific evidence that our planet has witnessed both life and death for billions of years.[15] Fr. Morales shows that a proper understanding of the text reveals that the death St. Paul speaks of applies only to human beings and not to the natural world at large. Moreover, even in the case of human beings, the death referred to in Romans does not refer to the cessation of biological life (i.e., physical death), but rather to alienation from God and the consequences that follow from that alienation (i.e.,

---

13. Jack Mahoney, *Christianity in Evolution: An Exploration* (Washington, DC: Georgetown University Press, 2011), 71.

14. Romans 5:12–17: "Therefore, just as through one person sin entered the world, and through sin, death, and thus death came to all, inasmuch as all sinned . . . For if, by the transgression of one person, death came to reign through that one, how much more will those who receive the abundance of grace and of the gift of justification come to reign in life through the one person Jesus Christ" (NABR).

15. For one example, see Ken Ham, "Young Earth Creation & The Gospel," Answers in Genesis, September 28, 2019, https://answersingenesis.org/age-of-the-earth/does-the-gospel-depend-on-a-young-earth/.

spiritual death). Therefore, this biblical pericope cannot be used to argue that evolutionary theory contradicts divine revelation.

Next, as noted earlier, though the *Catechism* does not embrace a literalist reading of the opening pages of Genesis, it presupposes the historicity of "our first parents" who committed the original fault.[16] This reflects the Catholic Church's enduring commitment to monogenism despite, as Fr. Gaine shows well, their recent openness to some forms of polygenism. As one example of this openness, the International Theological Commission (which is a Vatican advisory panel of theologians selected from around the world) concluded in its 2004 document "Communion and Stewardship: Human Persons Created in the Image of God": "While the story of human origins is complex and subject to revision, physical anthropology and molecular biology combine to make a convincing case for the origin of the human species in Africa about 150,000 years ago in a humanoid population of common genetic lineage."[17] But the Church's openness to polygenism raises a question: Can we still defend monogenism after Darwin?

In the penultimate chapter of this volume, I synthesize a handful of my previously published essays that have defended the historicity of Adam in light of the most recent discoveries of contemporary evolutionary biology. To weave a theological narrative of our origins, I make a crucial distinction between our biological species and our natural kind by proposing that the first member of our natural kind was the first member of the biological species who had the capacity for language—*Homo sapiens*. This human being—to whom divine revelation gives the name Adam—was the first rational animal. All of us are descended from this individual because all of us are born with the capacity for language, which we have all inherited from him. I conclude by turning to Eve, proposing that a fittingness argument can be made for her existence. Eve is the mate of the first speaking primate; she herself was also able to speak, and therefore was able to know and love God.

Finally, we turn to the end. The *Catechism* teaches: "At the end of time, the Kingdom of God will come in its fullness. After the universal judgment, the righteous will reign forever with Christ, glorified in body and soul. The universe itself will be renewed."[18] It continues, "The visible universe, then, is itself destined to be transformed, 'so that the world itself, restored to its orig-

---

16. *Catechism of the Catholic Church*, 390.
17. International Theological Commission, "Communion and Stewardship: Human Persons Created in the Image of God," in *International Theological Commission: Texts and Documents 1986–2007*, ed. Michael Sharkey and Thomas Weinandy (San Francisco: Ignatius Press, 2009), 319–51.
18. *Catechism of the Catholic Church*, 1042.

inal state, facing no further obstacles, should be at the service of the just,' sharing their glorification in the risen Jesus Christ."[19]

In the last chapter, Daria Spezzano (Providence College) responds to those who believe that evolution excludes any supernatural destiny for our species other than further evolution or extinction. Instead, she relies on St. Thomas to show how in God's providence, human evolution from the beginning was directed toward an eschatological end, anticipated in the state of original justice of our first parents. More specifically, Dr. Spezzano contends that God used an evolutionary process to prepare the human body for the infusion of a rational soul capable of grace and deification, and so with the potential for incorruptibility and the ultimate destiny of the resurrection. According to Christian revelation, though human evolution began with innocence and continued with life and death, it will end with glory.

Conclusion

The essays included in this volume are intended for Catholics who are struggling with questions that relate evolution to their Christian faith as it is summarized in the *Catechism of the Catholic Church*. They should also be of interest, however, to Christians who belong to other ecclesial communities who face similar vexing questions about the evolutionary origins of life—especially of human life—on our planet, and who are similarly working their way forward in fear and trembling.[20] Clearly, the task of explaining God's creative work through evolution is an ongoing effort of faith and reason that will continue for the foreseeable future.

Finally, I would like to conclude by acknowledging a handful of individuals who have helped me with this volume: Andrew Kubick and Sharifa Mejasmine Sawadjaan for their editorial expertise, John Martino of The Catholic University of America Press for his encouragement and support, and the John Templeton Foundation for a grant to ThomisticEvolution.org. Last and certainly not least, I am grateful to God and His Beloved Mother for my academic colleagues who made this task an intellectually stimulating and fruitful collaboration.

---

19. *Catechism of the Catholic Church*, 1047.
20. For examples, see Deborah B. Haarsma and Loren D. Haarsma, *Origins: Christian Perspectives on Creation, Evolution, and Intelligent Design* (Grand Rapids, MI: Faith Alive Christian Resources, 2011); and J. B. Stump, ed., *Four Views on Creation, Evolution, and Intelligent Design* (Grand Rapids, MI: Zondervan Books, 2017).

CHAPTER TWO

Essentialist and Hylomorphic Notion of Species and Species Transformation

MARIUSZ TABACZEK, OP

One of the many concerns of logical positivism in the first half of the twentieth century was the final dismissal of typological thinking in biology and the philosophy of biology—a logical consequence of the commitment to mechanism encouraged by the Scientific Revolution, the statistical treatment of natural selection in population genetics, and the modern evolutionary synthesis. The idea that organisms have intrinsic underlying natures (i.e., essences) and belong to natural kinds—an idea thought to arise from a naïve and uninformed view of biology—was replaced by relational and "population" thinking, which was commonly considered as more fitting with the modern evolutionary synthesis. Hence, referring to the essence of an organism as an explanatory principle was perceived for decades as indicative of dogmatic entrenchment in scholasticism and detachment from the advancements of contemporary science.

The rejection of essentialism in evolutionary biology and biological taxonomy had repercussions among Catholic philosophers and theologians. The Aristotelian-Thomistic school of thought, which defines species in reference to hylomorphically understood essences of living things, was questioned. The new evolutionary cladistic approach inspired the processual vision of Pierre Teilhard de Chardin and led to the conviction that essentialism is an obstacle on the way to reconcile the doctrines of creation and evolution. A notable proponent of this critical opinion was Joseph Ratzinger. In his 1964 course on creation theology taught in Münster, Ratzinger emphasized that opposition to evolutionary thinking comes not so much from Christian ideas, but from the enclosure in the matter-form scheme and the essentialism that it implies. He referred to the Christian notion of "Being as Becoming," saying that it seems to be more clearly expressed in evolution than in the traditional matter-form scheme. Ratzinger sided with the popular opinion that forms are fixed, which makes essentialism incapable of properly dealing with being as becoming.[1]

However, this radically anti-individualistic and antiessentialist orthodoxy has been recently challenged by a number of thinkers who claim that the relational approach in defining species should be supplemented with the complementary, classical view—the one that acknowledges the reality of the intrinsic natures/essences of individual organisms. Several suggestions have been made for what should constitute nature defined in essentialist terms, including genetic, phenetic, and relational/historical properties, along with fundamental dispositions, developmental programs, and substantial forms.

The aim of this chapter is to present the reemergence of biological essentialism and its interpretation within the context of the complex and multidimensional contemporary debate concerning biological species and taxonomy. In addition, the most recent versions of the essentialist definition of species will be supplemented with the reintroduction of the hylomorphic grounding of essentialism. Consequently, I will argue that the classical Aristotelian-Thomistic school of thought offers a plausible background for developing an ontological and causal view of speciation that remains in conversation with contemporary evolutionary biology.

My argumentation will proceed as follows: in section 1, I briefly refer to the controversy concerning nominalism versus realism regarding the category of species. Section 2 introduces the three levels of inquiry in the debate over species concepts and offers—as a heuristic device—a graphic classification depicting the concepts that are discussed in the text. Section 3 concentrates on relational species concepts. After listing their types (3.1), I refer to their ontological qualification of species as spatiotemporally restricted individuals with parts (3.2), discuss the issue of pluralism of the species concepts (3.3), and point toward the main challenges of the relational approach in defining species (3.4). In section 4, I examine intrinsic species concepts. Apart from more detailed analysis of the reemergence (4.1) and contemporary variants/aspects of the essentialist definition of biological species (4.2), I refer briefly to homeostatic property cluster and phenetic species concepts (4.3) and answer two major arguments against the compatibility of intrinsic species concepts (and essentialist species concepts in particular) with evolutionary biology (4.4).

---

1. See Francisco J. Novo, "The Theory of Evolution in the Writings of Joseph Ratzinger," *Scientia et Fides* 8, no. 2 (2020): 324–25. Novo refers to Santiago Sanz Sánchez, "Joseph Ratzinger y la doctrina de la creación: los apuntes de Münster de 1964 (y III). Algunos temas debatidos," *Revista Española de Teología* 74 (2016): 453–96.

1. Nominalism Versus Realism Regarding the Category of Species

Darwin's theory of evolution was undoubtedly revolutionary for the entire enterprise of biology. Moving it beyond mere description and an analysis of the intrinsic natures and extrinsic relationships of countless animate entities within their ecological niches, his theory boldly suggested that it is the same scientific inquiry undertaken by biologists that enables us to specify and describe if not the ultimate/primary cause, then at least the proximate/secondary causes of the origins of the profuse variety of lifeforms on earth.[2] However, a more careful scrutiny of Darwin's undertaking, implemented and reinterpreted within the context of the modern evolutionary synthesis, raises an important question concerning the scale of his revolution. On the one hand, one might think Darwin did not only aim at explaining the origin of species but in fact dismissed the very concept of "species" altogether, thus opening the way to contemporary "population thinking" in biology.[3] In support of such a thesis, one could refer to the often-cited passage from chapter 2 of *On the Origin of Species*, where we find Darwin saying:

> I look at the term species as one arbitrarily given, for the sake of convenience, to a set of individuals closely resembling each other.... [I]t does not essentially differ from the term variety, which is given to less

---

2. Toward the end of the final chapter of his seminal work, Darwin famously states: "To my mind it accords better with what we know of the laws impressed on matter by the Creator, that the production and extinction of the past and present inhabitants of the world should have been due to secondary causes, like those determining the birth and death of the individual." Charles Darwin, *On the Origin of Species by Means of Natural Selection, or the Preservation of Favoured Races in the Struggle for Life* (London: John Murray, 1859), 488, http://en.wikisource.org/wiki/On_the_Origin_of_Species_(1859).

3. The idea is that neither individual organisms with their putative intrinsic dispositions and features, nor universal categories such as the category of "species," play any explanatory role in evolutionary biology. What explains the abundance of living forms is genetic variation and the distribution of traits among organisms within populations. As Stephen Boulter notes, "In the population thinking characteristic of evolutionary biology, to determine the effects of evolutionary mechanisms one need[s] only advert to statistical laws about the interactions of the individuals in a population. One needs no knowledge of the particular properties of particular individuals. It is only properties of populations that are truly explanatory." Stephen J. Boulter, "Can Evolutionary Biology Do Without Aristotelian Essentialism?" *Royal Institute of Philosophy Supplements* 70 (2012): 92. See also a critical evaluation of this idea in David S. Oderberg, *Real Essentialism* (New York: Routledge, 2007), 207–8; and Denis Walsh, "Evolutionary Essentialism," *The British Journal for the Philosophy of Science* 57, no. 2 (2006): 426. I will explain below how "population thinking" inspires the "population structure" species concept.

distinct and more fluctuating forms. The term variety, again, in comparison with mere individual differences, is also applied arbitrarily, for convenience's sake.[4]

On the other hand, portraying Darwin as an ardent enthusiast of radical nominalism about species begs the question. Despite his struggle to specify the unit and subject of evolutionary transformations reflected in the above quoted passage Darwin says in chapter 13 of the same work that the classification he offers—based "on the view that the natural system is founded on descent with modification," that is, "that the characters which naturalists consider as showing true affinity between any two or more species, are those which have been inherited from a common parent"—"is evidently not arbitrary like the grouping of the stars in constellations."[5] In chapter 6, we find him saying that "all organic beings have been formed on two great laws—Unity of Type, and the Conditions of Existence," where the former law, "explained by unity of descent," should be understood in terms of "organic beings" belonging to "the same class."[6]

---

4. Darwin, *On the Origin of Species*, 52. This constatation by Darwin might be treated as an incentive to abandon the Linnaean taxa and develop an alternative to his system. He analyzes some candidates.

5. Darwin, 420, 411.

6. Darwin, 206. The latter law ("Conditions of Existence") "is fully embraced by the principle of natural selection" (Darwin, 206). Marc Ereshefsky thinks this only proves that Darwin was a realist about taxa (including taxa called "species") while he remained an antirealist about the species category, based on his uncertainty whether it might be distinguished from the category of "variety." See Marc Ereshefsky, "Darwin's Solution to the Species Problem," *Synthese* 175, no. 3 (2010): 405–25. Hence, Ereshefsky himself suggests abandoning the system of Linnean taxa and developing an alternative one, which would, nonetheless, keep the "hierarchy of categorical ranks." Marc Ereshefsky, "Species and the Linnean Hierarchy," in *Species: New Interdisciplinary Essays*, ed. Robert A. Wilson (Cambridge: MIT Press, 1999), 299. Brent D. Mishler goes still further and advocates developing a "rank-free taxonomy." Brent D. Mishler, "Getting Rid of Species?" in Wilson, *Species*, 307–15. For further debate on Darwin's notion of "species" concept, see Michael T. Ghiselin, *The Triumph of the Darwinian Method* (Chicago: University of Chicago Press, 1969); Ernst Mayr, *The Growth of Biological Thought: Diversity, Evolution, and Inheritance* (Cambridge, MA: Harvard University Press, 1982); John Beatty, "Speaking of Species: Darwin's Strategy," in *The Darwinian Heritage*, ed. David Kohn (Princeton, NJ: Princeton University Press, 1985), 265–82; David N. Stamos, *Darwin and the Nature of Species* (Albany: SUNY Press, 2007); James Mallet, "Mayr's View of Darwin: Was Darwin Wrong about Speciation?" *Biological Journal of the Linnean Society* 95, no. 1 (2008): 3–16; David Kohn, "Darwin's Keystone: The Principle of Divergence," in *The Cambridge Companion to the "Origin of Species,"* ed. Michael Ruse and Robert J. Richards (Cambridge: Cambridge University Press, 2008), 87–108; and John S. Wilkins, *Species: A History of the Idea* (Berkeley: University of California Press, 2009).

Hence, when one of the founding fathers of the modern evolutionary synthesis, Ernst Mayr, entered the conversation about the reality of the universal category of biological species, he stated categorically—in reference to the popular nominalist interpretation of Darwin's position on this matter—that "whoever, like Darwin, denies that species are non-arbitrarily defined units of nature not only evades the issue but fails to find and solve the most interesting problems of biology."[7] Further, Mayr states that "without speciation there would be no diversification of the organic world, no adaptive radiation, and very little evolutionary progress. The species, then, is the keystone of evolution."[8] What we find in this assertion is Mayr's fundamental, metaphysical intuition that without universal categories taken as ontological (and not merely epistemological) units, we would be unable to specify the outcomes of changes occurring in the world of living creatures over time.[9]

2. Debate over Species Concepts

However, if we decide to follow Mayr's argument in favor of the reality of the universal category of "species" and the necessity of its application in biology, we face the complexity of the debate on the proper definition of biological species. This debate has been going on for decades and its subject remains probably the most controversial issue in contemporary biology and the philosophy of biology.[10] I believe it contains at least three important levels of inquiry; the first one refers to the general character of the definition in question. Here we encounter two rival schools: one (I) claiming that the definition we are looking for should be entirely relational (i.e., outlined in terms of relations among organisms in space and time); and the other (II) advocating for

---

7. Ernst Mayr, *Animal Species and Evolution* (Cambridge, MA: Harvard University Press, 1963), 29.

8. Mayr, *Animal Species and Evolution*, 621.

9. David N. Stamos compares and contrasts nominalism and realism about species (as classes) in *The Species Problem, Biological Species, Ontology, and the Metaphysics of Biology* (Lanham, MD: Lexington Books, 2004), chapters 2 and 3.

10. "The species problem is one of the oldest controversies in natural history." Robert J. O'Hara, "Systematic Generalization, Historical Fate, and the Species Problem," *Systematic Biology* 42, no. 3 (1993): 231. It is "one of the thorniest issues in theoretical biology." Philip Kitcher, *In Mendel's Mirror: Philosophical Reflections on Biology* (Oxford: Oxford University Press, 2003), xii. What indicates the scale of the controversy is certainly the fact that we have around two dozen species concepts in philosophy of biology, and as claims Ereshefsky, "at least seven well-accepted ones." Marc Ereshefsky, "Species Pluralism and Anti-Realism," *Philosophy of Science* 65, no. 1 (1998): 103. See also Richard A. Richards, "Species and Taxonomy," in *The Oxford Handbook of Philosophy of Biology*, ed. Michael Ruse (Oxford: Oxford University Press, 2008), 161–88. Richards defines at least sixteen species concepts.

a definition that is at least partially outlined in terms of the intrinsic features of particular organisms.

Once we make our choice between (I) relational species concepts (RSCs) and (II) intrinsic species concepts (ISCs), we enter the second level of inquiry, where one faces various attempts by members of both schools striving to provide an adequate definition of the category of "species." At this stage, the discussion proliferates in a number of definitions that I will try to introduce and classify below.

Finally, the third level of inquiry undertakes the task of classifying species under higher taxa, including genera, families, and several other steps up the ladder of the Linnaean hierarchy. At this stage, one encounters at least four competing schools of biological taxonomy, which include: phenetic, evolutionary, cladistic, and the classical Porphyrian school of taxonomy. I briefly analyze their main assumptions in the extended version of this chapter contained in my latest monograph on theistic evolution.[11] In what follows, I will concentrate on the controversy over species concepts. In order to help the reader navigate through the complexity of the subject matter, I offer a graphic classification that covers all the major species concepts that I am about to discuss. Although imperfect and limited since some species concepts go beyond the general distinction between I and II, I believe figure 1 will serve as a helpful heuristic device.

3. Relational Species Concepts (RSCs)

Entering the second of the proposed three levels of inquiry concerning species concepts, we shall begin with an analysis of RSCs (I). Although definitions falling into this group are much younger than the historically predominant and commonly accepted intrinsic or essentialist definitions of species as natural kinds, RSCs quickly gained popularity in the post-Darwinian milieu and are considered by many as a new orthodoxy in the philosophy of biology. Hence, we shall treat them first.

The point of departure and a common presupposition of all species concepts falling within this group (I) is the conviction that "the property in virtue of which a particular organism belongs to one species rather than another is a relational rather than an intrinsic property of the organism."[12] In other words, species should be defined in terms of spatiotemporally grounded relations among organisms rather than in terms of the intrinsic properties of par-

---

11. See Mariusz Tabaczek, *Theistic Evolution: A Contemporary Aristotelian-Thomistic Perspective* (Cambridge: Cambridge University Press, 2024), 88–91.

12. Samir Okasha, "Darwinian Metaphysics: Species and the Question of Essentialism," *Synthese* 131, no. 2 (2002): 201.

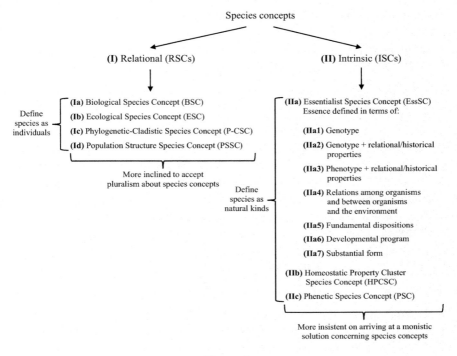

Figure 1.

ticular organisms analyzed in themselves.[13] What differentiates RSCs is the nature of the relation that plays the central role in the definition.

3.1. Types of RSCs

The most popular option is the (Ia) biological species concept (BSC) developed by Mayr, who claimed that "species are groups of actually or potentially interbreeding natural populations which are reproductively isolated from other such groups. . . . Isolating mechanisms are biological properties of individuals which prevent the interbreeding of populations that are actually or potentially sympatric."[14] Note that this definition takes into account present

---

13. "Two organisms are conspecific in virtue of their historical connection to each other, not in virtue of their similarity." Elliott Sober, *Philosophy of Biology* (Boulder: Westview Press, 1993), 150. "If species are interpreted as historical entities, then particular organisms belong in a particular species because they are part of that genealogical nexus, not because they possess any essential traits. No species has an essence in this sense." David L. Hull, "A Matter of Individuality," *Philosophy of Science* 45, no. 3 (1978): 358.

14. Mayr, *The Growth of Biological Thought*, 273–74.

causal and relational situations rather than the historical context of common ancestors.

Another concept within the group of RSCs defines species as a lineage "which occupies an adaptive zone minimally different from that of any other lineage in its range and evolves separately from all lineages outside its range."[15] It is commonly classified as the (Ib) ecological species concept (ESC) and is distinguished from the entire group of species concepts classified as (Ic) phylogenetic-cladistic (P-CSC). Concentrating on the historical connections, the latter defines species as "a lineage (an ancestral-descendant sequence of populations) evolving separately from others and with its own unitary evolutionary role and tendencies."[16] Okasha says that on this view we "identify species in terms of evolutionary history . . . [with] particular chunks of the genealogical nexus. . . . Species come into existence when an existing lineage splits into two . . . and go extinct when the lineage divides, or when all members of the species die."[17]

One more RSC was proposed by Ereshefsky and Matthen, who called it the (Id) "population structure" species concept (PSSC). In reference to trait distribution among organisms within populations and taking into account both the similarity and dissimilarity (polymorphism) of these characteristics, they define species genealogically as an "inter-population structure" and claim that species are "lineages of populations."[18] As such, PSSC follows the consensus among philosophers of biology who welcomed the shift from typological toward the population thinking introduced by Darwin.[19]

---

15. Leigh Van Valen, "Ecological Species, Multispecies, and Oaks," *Taxon* 25, no. 2/3 (1976): 233. Discussing this species concept, Okasha offers a more concise definition that assumes that species "exploit the same set of environmental resources and habitats" ("Darwinian Metaphysics," 200).

16. George Gaylord Simpson, *Principles of Animal Taxonomy* (New York: Columbia University Press, 1961), 153.

17. Okasha, "Darwinian Metaphysics," 200. Kim Sterelny and Paul E. Griffiths claim that "something like a consensus emerged in favor of a *cladistic* of systematics." See Kim Sterelny and Paul E. Griffiths, *Sex and Death: An Introduction to Philosophy of Biology* (Chicago: University of Chicago Press, 1999), 194. On another occasion, Sterelny defines species as "evolutionary linked metapopulations" or "ecological mosaics"—effects of "the relationship between evolutionary unit[s] and ecological forces." Kim Sterelny, "Species as Ecological Mosaics," in Wilson, *Species*, 120.

18. See Marc Ereshefsky and Mohan Matthen, "Taxonomy, Polymorphism, and History: An Introduction to Population Structure Theory," *Philosophy of Science* 72, no. 1 (2005): 1–21.

19. See Ernst Mayr, "Typological Versus Population Thinking," in *Evolution and Anthropology: A Centennial Appraisal*, ed. Betty J. Meggers (Washington, DC: Anthropological Society of Washington, 1959), 409–12; Ernst Mayr, *What Evolution Is* (London: Phoenix, 2002), 83.

3.2. Species as Individuals

What remains crucial about RSCs (and is thought to distinguish them ontologically from ISCs) is a deep conviction of their advocates that instead of perceiving species as spatiotemporally unrestricted natural kinds that may emerge at any place and at any time in the history of the universe, we should think of them as spatiotemporally restricted individuals with parts, having their beginning and end. David Hull explains:

> By "individuals" I mean spatiotemporally localized cohesive and continuous entities (historical entities). By "classes" I intend spatiotemporally unrestricted classes, the sorts of things which can function in traditionally defined laws of nature. The contrast is between Mars and planets, the Weald and geological strata, Gargantua and organisms.[20]

In other words, if we take species as units of Darwinian evolution, we must acknowledge that hereditary relations (genetic or otherwise), require generations of a given species to be causally and thus spatiotemporally connected. This, notes Ereshefsky, has a number of important implications:

> For one, the relationship between an organism and its species is not a member/class relation but a part/whole relation. An organism belongs to a particular species only if it is appropriately causally connected to the other organisms in that species. The organisms of a species must be parts of a single evolving lineage. If belonging to a species turns on an organism's insertion in a lineage, then qualitative similarity can be misleading. Two organisms may be very similar morphologically, genetically, and behaviorally, but unless they belong to the same spatiotemporally continuous lineage they cannot belong to the same species.[21]

3.3. Pluralism of Species Concepts

One of the vexing questions concerning RSCs is their plurality and variety. What are we to make of such diversity? Whereas practicing systematists referring to RSCs are more committed to the search for a monistic solution, many

---

20. Hull, "A Matter of Individuality," 336. See also Michael T. Ghiselin, "A Radical Solution to the Species Problem," *Systematic Zoology* 23, no. 4 (1974): 536–44.
21. Marc Ereshefsky, "Species," in *Stanford Encyclopedia of Philosophy*, ed. Edward N. Zalta, https://plato.stanford.edu/archives/sum2022/entries/species/. See section 2.2. See also Stamos, *Species Problem*, chapter 4.

philosophers signing up with (I) are willing to turn to pluralism.[22] In its pragmatic and epistemological version, species pluralism builds on the acknowledgment of the limitations of our cognitive capacities when facing the exceeding complexity of the world.[23] Those who embrace ontological pluralism about species concepts argue that it is an outcome of the fecundity of biological material and forces rather than a paucity of scientific information. At the same time, while some ontological pluralists side with Ereshefsky, who argues that "the tree of life is segmented by different processes into different types of species lineages," which are captured by different species concepts that cannot be reconciled, others remain more optimistic and join Michael Ruse, who speaks about a developing "consilience." According to Ruse, this might eventually lead to a monistic solution: "There are different ways of breaking organisms into groups, and they *coincide!* The genetic species is the morphological species and the reproductively isolated species is the group with common ancestors."[24]

In response to Ruse's optimism, Ereshefsky notes that it does not look as if the consilience in question is really forthcoming: "Groups of organisms that have the most overall genetic similarity are not necessarily groups of interbreeding organisms. . . . Some groups of interbreeding units are not monophyletic taxa. . . . And some groups of organisms that form ecological units are not interbreeding units." This makes the idea of reaching a monistic position in the debate on species concepts very unlikely.[25]

Richard Mayden strives to face the same difficulty and proposes a hierarchical version of pluralism, which introduces a division of labor. He suggests treating P-CSC (Ic), which is classified by many as an evolutionary species concept (EvoSC), as the main definition of species. This is based on its accommodating both sexual and asexual organisms, as well as those that hybridize. He sees other concepts within the category of RSCs as secondary and operational.[26]

---

22. Hull complains about the approach according to which "indefinitely many species concepts are needed for indefinitely many contexts." He adds that "the great danger of pluralism is 'anything goes.'" David L. Hull, "On the Plurality of Species: Questioning the Party Line," in Wilson, *Species*, 24.

23. See Alexander Rosenberg, *Instrumental Biology, or the Disunity of Science* (Chicago: University of Chicago Press, 1994).

24. Ereshefsky, "Species," section 3.1; Michael Ruse, "Biological Species: Natural Kinds, Individuals, or What?" in *The Units of Evolution: Essays on the Nature of Species*, ed. Marc Ereshefsky, 343-361 (Cambridge: A Bradford Book, 1992), 356.

25. Marc Ereshefsky, *Poverty of the Linnaean Hierarchy: A Philosophical Study of Biological Taxonomy* (Cambridge: Cambridge University Press, 2001), 146.

26. See Richard L. Mayden, "A Hierarchy of Species Concepts: The Denouement in the Saga of the Species Problem," in *Species: The Units of Biodiversity*, ed. M. F. Claridge, A. H. Dawah, and M. R. Wilson (London and New York: Springer, 1997), 418–22.

In a somewhat similar vein, Kevin de Queiroz claims that various species concepts agree on one thing; namely, that species are "separately evolving metapopulation lineages."[27] He suggests that this fact defines a conceptual (i.e., a "single, more general") concept of species, which allows us to treat other properties over which we tend to disagree (e.g., being reproductively isolated or occupying a unique niche) as secondary, evidential (methodological), and "operational criteria" for "inferring the boundaries and numbers of species."[28] Richards suggests the division of conceptual labor, whereby various species concepts are useful in different theoretical and operational concepts.[29]

Ereshefsky notes that some of the pluralists who generally side with RSCs are actually willing to extend their list of viable species concepts to embrace not only those that require species to be individuals but also those based on the structural similarities among organisms sharing theoretically significant properties. Such is the view of Philip Kitcher, who defines the latter in terms of spatiotemporally unrestricted sets of organisms. He distinguishes between proximate ("structural") and ultimate ("historical") types of explanation in biology and claims that while the former characterizes species in reference to structural similarities (genetic, phenotypic, and developmental), the latter sees them as lineages and thus individuals. By accepting both types of species concepts, Kitcher crosses the boundary between RSCs and ISCs.[30]

One other ontological pluralist, John Dupré, suggests going even further than Kitcher. According to his promiscuous realism about species—apart from concepts listed under RSCs and implemented by Kitcher's spatiotemporally unrestricted sets of organisms—we should also pay attention to nonbiological classifications, as "there are many sameness relations that serve to distinguish classes of organisms in ways that are relevant to various concerns . . . [and] none

---

Richards believes in the possibility of finding "a single, primary concept that colligates facts via a set of correspondence rules (not concepts) that serve to bridge the theoretical concept to the observable data" ("Species and Taxonomy," 185). He finds the EvoSC proposed by Mayden as promising as any other option among RSCs to play the role of the main species concept.

27. Kevin de Queiroz, "Different Species Problems and Their Resolution," *BioEssays* 27, no. 12 (2005): 1263.

28. Kevin de Queiroz, "Species Concepts and Species Delimitation," *Systematic Biology* 56, no. 6 (2007): 880, 882; de Queiroz, "Different Species Problems," 1264. See also Kevin de Queiroz, "The General Lineage Concept of Species and the Defining Properties of the Species Category," in Wilson, *Species*, 49–90.

29. See Richard A. Richards, *The Species Problem: A Philosophical Analysis* (Cambridge: Cambridge University Press, 2010).

30. See Philip Kitcher, "Species," *Philosophy of Science* 51, no. 2 (1984): 308–33; Ereshefsky, "Species," sections 2.3 and 3.1.

of these relations are privileged."[31] He gives examples of carpenters grouping cedars on account of their aromatic timber or gastronomists grouping garlic and onions.[32] However, his view is criticized as leading to relativism and amphibolic pragmatism, which ends up being antirealistic about universal categories.[33]

3.4. Difficulties of RSCs

Despite the fact that RSCs have become virtual orthodoxy in the philosophy of biology, each one of them faces some critical challenges. One major weakness of BSC (Ia) is that it does not allow our classification to cover all forms of living entities we distinguish. In particular, when choosing it, we exclude all asexual organisms from forming species. This is a serious drawback once we realize that the group in question is not limited to some rare examples of reptiles, amphibians, and insects that are reproducing through cloning and vegetative means of self-fertilization. Indeed, asexual reproduction is rampant in plants, fungi, and bacteria, which makes it the predominant form of reproduction of living beings on earth. Therefore, by choosing BSC, we agree that most organisms do not form species.[34] This shows the arbitrary and opera-

---

31. John Dupré, *Humans and Other Animals* (Oxford: Clarendon, 2002), 33. In chapter 2, we find him saying: "Classification in biology has a life of its own. Biologists in areas only tangentially connected to evolutionary theory, such as ecologists, ethnobotanists, or ethologists, need to classify organisms, as do foresters, conservationists, gatekeepers, and herbalists . . . for many, perhaps even most groups of organisms, evolutionary considerations are of little or no use for classificatory purposes" (82).

32. See Dupré, *Humans and Other Animals*, 29, 34.

33. See P. D. Magnus, *Scientific Enquiry and Natural Kinds: From Planets to Mallards* (London: Palgrave Macmillan, 2012), 130–33. The editors of a volume on scientific pluralism acknowledge that "promiscuous realism is hard to distinguish from radical relativism." Stephen H. Kellert, Helen E. Longino, and C. Kenneth Waters, eds., *Scientific Pluralism* (Minneapolis: University of Minnesota Press, 2006), xiii.

34. Ereshefsky acknowledges that much of the debate over species concepts (and species pluralism) focuses on multicellular organisms, while most organisms in the world are single cell microbial organisms, which do not reproduce sexually and exchange genes laterally within the same generation. He notes that microbiologists have their own species concepts, as not only BSC but also other RSCs are inadequate in case of microorganisms. He lists four microbial species concepts: (1) recombination species concept that defines species as groups of microbes whose genomes can recombine (i.e., groups that form gene pools of organisms connected by recombination); (2) ecological species concept that defines bacterial species as evolutionary lineages bound by ecotype-periodic selection; (3) phylophenetic species concept that aims at obtaining stable classifications of bacterial species for medical research; and (4) phylogenetic species concept that strives to assign microbes to species according to their phylogenetic relations. See Ereshefsky, "Species," section 3.3. For further discussion, Ereshefsky refers his readers to Maureen A. O'Malley and John Dupré, "Size Doesn't Matter: Towards a More Inclusive Philosophy of Biology," *Biology*

tional character of this species concept, which also makes it difficult to apply to organisms that have died. Another criticism of BSC is that it might be confusing cause (speciation) with effects (reproductive isolation) when saying it is the latter that affects the former.[35] Finally, an important feature of BSC is the assumption of smooth transitions between closely related populations. This suggests the possibility of the existence of individuals in separate species that can cross the reproductive barrier. Consequently, the reproductive barrier serves only as an approximate criterion for distinguishing biological species, which once again proves the operational and pragmatic character of BSC, thus revealing its considerable ontological limitation.

Next, concerning ESC (Ib), we realize that it is difficult to apply it to large populations of organisms that often occupy various ecological niches while remaining one species (e.g., the red fox, *vulpes vulpes*). Other organisms belonging to the same species (e.g., cichlids) can adapt to a new ecological niche within one generation, which according to ESC should qualify as a speciation event. Another difficulty is posed by microorganisms, in particular by bacterial biofilms, which bring into close cooperation many types of bacteria occupying a particular ecological niche. Such biofilms might be classified as a unified species according to ESC, which seems to be counterintuitive.

Even if (I) brings together several species concepts, the one among them that became predominant is P-CSC (Ic). Building on Darwin's position, cladism strives to base all classification explicitly on the phylogenesis of organisms. It defines species as "particular chunks of the genealogical nexus."[36] David Oderberg lists at least five important difficulties of P-CSC:

1. Mere being part of a chunk of the phylogenetic tree bounded by a pair of speciation events (or splitting and extinction events) does not seem to be sufficient for conspecificity. In other words, cladism cannot define what a species is since it relies on the very concept of speciation.[37]

---

and Philosophy 22, no. 2 (2007): 155–91; L. R. Franklin, "Bacteria, Sex, and Systematics," *Philosophy of Science* 74, no. 1 (2007): 69–95; Marc Ereshefsky, "Microbiology and the Species Problem," *Biology & Philosophy* 25, no. 4 (2010): 553–68; Maureen O'Malley, *Philosophy of Microbiology* (Cambridge: Cambridge University Press, 2014).

35. See Mayden, "A Hierarchy of Species Concepts," 390–91. In reference to and apart from the main argument mentioned here, BSC has been the subject of extensive criticism. For an extended list of works questioning its adequacy and usefulness in taxonomy, see Michael Devitt, "Resurrecting Biological Essentialism," *Philosophy of Science* 75, no. 3 (2008): 356n25.

36. Okasha, "Darwinian Metaphysics," 200.

37. Oderberg dismisses the idea of supplementing the diachronic character of P-CSC with the synchronic aspect of species grasped by BSC and ESC (see Okasha, "Darwinian

2. P-CSC may entail counterintuitive, if not absurd, classifications based on the traits of the most recent common ancestor while ignoring the actual behavior and forms of organisms. Oderberg gives an example of *Reptilia* which, according to P-CSC, includes lizards, snakes, tortoises, and turtles, as well as birds and mammals. Simultaneously, P-CSC would treat two molecule-for-molecule identical organisms as members of different species.[38]
3. P-CSC suffers from a regress problem. For if classification is by descent, then what about the very first organism that did not have any ancestor? One might go down to the evolution of inanimate or even inorganic entities and still face the same question.
4. P-CSC makes species identity an extrinsic matter; as in, not having anything to do with the organism itself (its behavior, morphology, how it functions, etc.). Oderberg claims that the P-CSC is not much more operative than a Platonic form in explaining what factor or characteristic defines a particular organism.
5. Finally, some cladists strive to save (or reintroduce) an essentialist aspect of P-CSC by claiming that historical relations among organisms define the essences of species. However, invoking the Aristotelian typology of causes, Oderberg notes that identifying essence with descent confuses efficient and formal causes. In other words, it is true that we may say a lot about an organism's form and properties by knowing where it came from. Yet where it came from is not equal to what it is.[39]

The last argument might be summoned against PSSC (Id) as well. The fact that an organism is a part of a lineage of populations tells us quite a bit about its properties and form. But knowing its place in an interpopulation structure is not equal to knowing what it is. Approaching the same difficulty from another perspective, genetic variation within a population always depends on the behavior of particular organisms. Hence, Oderberg says, "the biologist might be able to form hypotheses about populations without identifying which member behaves in which manner, but he still needs to know how individuals behave in order to frame any meaningful hypothesis about

---

Metaphysics," 201). Oderberg says a definition of species should have only one determinant. When one tries to supplement P-CSC with BSC or ESC, P-CSC drops out of the picture, remaining merely as an historic representation of the way the real criterion applies across space and time (see *Real Essentialism*, 216–17).

38. One way to deal with the counterintuitive groupings under P-CSC is to accept a paraphyletic exclusion of some of the descendants of a common ancestor. However, advocates of this species concept ardently strive to perceive them as monophyletic.

39. See Oderberg, *Real Essentialism*, 214–24.

what population is like."[40] If this is true, population thinking needs to be implemented with individualistic thinking.

Apart from the difficulties of particular RSCs, an objection has been raised to species pluralism. It seems to be an overly liberal position, which may easily lead to virtually unlimited promiscuity about the species concept (remember the view of Dupré mentioned above). This may turn against the entire undertaking of biologists and philosophers of biology who try to define species by questioning the reality of species category as such.[41] Pluralists may try to provide some criteria for judging the legitimacy of a given species concept, such as empirical testability of its theoretical assumptions, its internal consistency, or its theoretical coherence. But the question remains of whether some commonly agreeable set of criteria might be established.

The version of the hierarchical solution offered by de Queiroz raises an objection on the side of the proponents of various types of RSCs who might argue that disagreements among them are not merely over evidence for the numbers and boundaries of the species. For it seems that advocates of BCS, ESC, and P-CSC believe that after all, they are identifying different types of lineages as constitutive for their classifications of species.[42]

4. Intrinsic Species Concepts (ISCs)

The alternative group of species concepts builds upon the conviction that what is decisive about identities of biological taxa are intrinsic features of particular organisms. Their advocates believe species are natural kinds and claim that species concepts should, therefore, be, at least partially, intrinsic. Similar to RSCs, there are several types of ISCs. However, they are much closer to one another in their presuppositions than RSCs, which justifies the tendency among those who develop and support them toward a monistic solution to the species problem.

4.1. Essentialist Species Concept (EssSC)

The most popular among ISCs is the (IIa) essentialist species concept (EssSC). Commonly accepted in ancient and medieval science and philosophy,

---

40. Oderberg, *Real Essentialism*, 208.
41. See Elliott Sober, "Sets, Species, and Evolution: Comments on Philip Kitcher's 'Species,'" *Philosophy of Science* 51, no. 2 (1984): 334–41; Michael T. Ghiselin, "Species Concepts, Individuality, and Objectivity," *Biology and Philosophy* 2, no. 2 (April 1, 1987): 127–43; and David L. Hull, "Genealogical Actors in Ecological Roles," *Biology and Philosophy* 2, no. 2 (April 1, 1987): 168–84.
42. See Ereshefsky, "Species," section 3.2.

essentialism was rejected in modernity. More recently, it was reintroduced by Kripke and Putnam in general philosophy and metaphysics, where it is considered one of the major theories of material entities.[43] However, this new essentialism was not welcomed among philosophers of biology who claim it is inadequate in reference to evolving organisms. Hull famously established the consensus on this matter, saying that essentialism was responsible for two thousand years of stasis in systematics.[44] Rosenberg expresses the same position, stating that "the proponents of contemporary species definitions are all agreed that species have no essence."[45] Sober follows him by saying that "biologists do not think that species are defined in terms of phenotypic or genetic similarities."[46] Sterelny and Griffiths agree, stating bluntly that "no intrinsic genotypic and phenotypic property is essential to being a member of a species."[47] Dupré accompanies them and says "it is widely recognized that Darwin's theory of evolution rendered untenable the classical essentialist concept of species."[48] Their view is followed by many other philosophers of biology, including Ghiselin, Mayr, de Queiroz, Matthen, Millikan, Ereshefsky, and Okasha.[49]

At the same time, however, the received antiessentialist consensus has been more recently challenged by a number of thinkers who claim that a reference to intrinsic dispositions, structures, or constitutions of organisms is necessary to formulate a viable species concept. A default version of their argument in reference to P-CSC (the most popular among the RSCs) is suitably expressed by Crawford Elder:

---

43. See Saul A. Kripke, *Naming and Necessity* (Cambridge, MA: Harvard University Press, 1980); Hilary Putnam, "The Meaning of 'Meaning,'" in *Mind, Language, and Reality: Philosophical Papers* (Cambridge: Cambridge University Press, 1975), 2:215–71.

44. David L. Hull, "The Effect of Essentialism on Taxonomy—Two Thousand Years of Stasis," pt. 1 and 2, *The British Journal for the Philosophy of Science* 15, no. 60 (1965): 314–26; 16, no 61 (1965): 1–18.

45. Alexander Rosenberg, *The Structure of Biological Science* (Cambridge: Cambridge University Press, 1985), 203.

46. Sober, *Philosophy of Biology*, 148.

47. Sterelny and Griffiths, *Sex and Death*, 186.

48. John Dupré, "On the Impossibility of a Monistic Account of Species," in Wilson, *Species*, 3.

49. See Ghiselin, "A Radical Solution"; Mayr, *The Growth of Biological Thought*; Kevin de Queiroz, "Systematics and the Darwinian Revolution," *Philosophy of Science* 55, no. 2 (1988): 238–59; Mohan Matthen, "Biological Universals and the Nature of Fear," *The Journal of Philosophy* 95, no. 3 (1998): 105–32; Ruth Garrett Millikan, *On Clear and Confused Ideas: An Essay about Substance Concepts* (Cambridge: Cambridge University Press, 2000), 19; Ereshefsky, *Poverty of the Linnaean Hierarchy*; Okasha, "Darwinian Metaphysics," 196.

If descent from certain ancestor organisms is part of what unites the members of a given species, then, the ancestor organisms in question must qualify for that crucial role by virtue of phenotypic (or perhaps genotypic) properties that they possessed—by virtue of their nonhistorical properties. Viewing biological species as "historical kinds" does not absolve us from the task of identifying nonhistorical properties that are diagnostic of membership in that species.[50]

Hence,

> *opponents* of the idea that biological species are natural kinds are . . . in much the same position as *proponents* of that idea. Each side must hold that some descent-involving property essentially characterizes any biological species. And each side must allow that there is some plurality of nonhistorical properties . . . that, one way or another, essentially characterize that species as well.[51]

In other words, according to Elder, even if we agree to define species as spatiotemporally restricted individuals, we need to refer to "its *structural* properties." This is necessary "to avoid the consequence that all organisms belong to just a single species." Consequently, we need to acknowledge that "operationally, the 'species as individuals' view must treat species as natural kinds."[52]

Based on this line of reasoning, defenders of ISCs formulate a contemporary version of EssSC, which Christopher Austin, invoking the name of Aristotle, defines as follows: "Aristotelian essence is (a) comprised of a *natural* set of *intrinsic* properties [some claim it might be just one property] which (b) constitute *generative mechanisms* for particularized morphological development which (c) are shared among groups of organisms, delineating them as members of the same 'kind.'"[53] Species are thus spatiotemporally unrestricted natural kinds.

---

50. Crawford L. Elder, "Biological Species Are Natural Kinds," *The Southern Journal of Philosophy* 46, no. 3 (2008): 350.

51. Elder, "Biological Species," 350.

52. Elder, "Biological Species," 349, 353–54. Travis Dumsday offers a similar reflection in "Is There Still Hope for a Scholastic Ontology of Biological Species?" *The Thomist* 76, no. 3 (2012): 371–95. Dumsday further develops his position in "A New Argument for Intrinsic Biological Essentialism," *Philosophical Quarterly* 62, no. 248 (2012): 486–504. Many other authors mentioned below agree with the basic line of this argument as well.

53. Christopher J. Austin, "Aristotelian Essentialism: Essence in the Age of Evolution," *Synthese* 194, no. 7 (2017): 2540. A strong contemporary advocate of essentialism, Brian Ellis, defines essences in terms of universal intrinsic properties, in virtue of which entities obey universal laws of nature. However, due to the complexity of living organisms, he restricts essentialism to lower levels of organization of matter. See Brian D. Ellis, *Scientific Essentialism* (Cambridge: Cambridge University Press, 2001); *The Philosophy of Nature: A Guide to the New Essentialism* (Montreal: McGill-Queen's University Press, 2002).

While the majority of the proponents of biological essentialism would most likely accept this definition, they seem to differ in their opinions on whether its main emphasis falls on (a) or (b) and in their answer to the question concerning particular intrinsic property (or properties) that defines essence of a given natural kind. Consequently, we find several variants of EssSC, which are listed in figure 1. Nonetheless, I would argue that, taken together, they form a consistent and thorough notion of species, one that takes into account both structural and historical—as well as purely empirical and metaphysical—aspects of this most basic biological taxon.[54]

4.2. Variants/Aspects of EssSC

4.2.1. (IIa1) Genotype

The (IIa1) genotype variant/aspect of EssSC is probably the most intuitive contemporary proposition of defining essences, which grounds them in the necessary and sufficient genetic disposition of organisms. David B. Kitts and David J. Kitts share their conviction that "the property which all the organisms of a species share and which ultimately accounts for the fact that they cannot be the parts or members of any other species is not some manifest property such as the pigmentation of a feather. It is an underlying trait."[55] They add that "since the discovery of the structure of genetic material it has been possible to get at this underlying trait not only through the manifest properties and the reproductive behavior of organisms, but more directly by means of chemical techniques."[56]

---

54. On the margin of my analysis, I would like to acknowledge the stark difference between biologists and philosophers of biology on the question of whether species should be treated as individuals or natural kinds. As Devitt notes, the study pursued by a group of researchers from Zagreb, which was based on a survey of the opinions of one hundred and ninety-three practicing biologists from one hundred and fifty biology departments in the United States and the European Union, shows that the position supporting individualism about species is among them "utterly marginal" (only 2.94 percent). Most of the respondents side with the notion of species as natural kinds. The opinion among philosophers of biology is quite the opposite. The majority of them think species are spatiotemporally extended (i.e., scattered) individuals. See Bruno Pušić, Pavel Gregorić, and Damjan Franjević, "What Do Biologists Make of the Species Problem?" *Acta Biotheoretica* 65, no. 3 (September 2017): 179–209; Michael Devitt, "Individual Essentialism in Biology," *Biology & Philosophy* 33, no. 5 (2018): 4n7.

55. David B. Kitts and David J. Kitts, "Biological Species as Natural Kinds," *Philosophy of Science* 46, no. 4 (1979): 617. They note that "No one would deny that '. . . to be a horse one must be born a horse' [Hull, "A Matter of Individuality," 349]. But that is not the end of it. The fact that all horses are begot by horses is something to be explained" (Kitts and Kitts, "Biological Species," 618). They bring this argument in support of essentialism.

56. Kitts and Kitts, "Biological Species," 622.

Rieppel speaks about "essentialism underlying species identification by means of a DNA bar code [which] results from the claim that phylogenetic background knowledge is not needed to identify gene species that are based on nothing but bar coding gaps (discontinuities of DNA variation among contemporaneous populations)." He adds that "with bar coding, . . . the typical DNA sequence becomes the underlying (intrinsic) essence of a species in the sense of Mayr's nondimensional species concept, that is, a contemporaneous time slice through a locally restricted population."[57]

4.2.2. (IIa2) Genotype and Relational/Historical Properties

Closely related to (IIa1) is the view that, apart from genotype, takes into account the relational/historical properties of organisms. Helping to provide for the maintenance of genotype, these properties may be considered important for the definition of biological taxa. Crossing the boundary between (I) and (II), this variant/aspect of essentialism about species finds explication and strong support in a series of articles by Michael Devitt. He says that "for most organisms the essential intrinsic properties are probably largely, although not entirely, genetic."[58] At the same time, however, it is "together perhaps with some historical ones" that the genetic properties "constitute the essence" of a given species.[59] Adopting Kitcher's terminology, Devitt distinguishes between structural and historical types of explanation in biology and finds both at least potentially important for defining species.[60]

---

57. Olivier Rieppel, "New Essentialism in Biology," *Philosophy of Science* 77, no. 5 (2010): 666. Rieppel also offers a short description of the historical development of the "bar coding initiative" (665).

58. Devitt adds that "sometimes those properties may not be genetic at all but in 'the architecture of chromosomes,' 'developmental programs,' or whatever" ("Resurrecting Biological Essentialism," 347).

59. Devitt, "Resurrecting," 353. Devitt says that what constitutes a species is necessarily at least partly intrinsic and possibly partly historical. Hence, the intrinsic aspect is crucial (i.e., essential) while the historical is not. He further develops his analysis of the historical component of species concept in "Historical Biological Essentialism," *Studies in History and Philosophy of Biological and Biomedical Sciences* 71 (2018): 1–7.

60. See Kitcher, "Species," 121; Devitt, "Resurrecting," 353. Devitt introduces a crucial distinction, saying that we need to set aside the task of distinguishing species from other taxa from the task of specifying why a given organism belongs to a particular species. He names the former (1) "the category problem" and the latter (2) "the taxon problem." He argues that although Okasha seems to be saying that RSCs answer to (1), while Sterelny and Griffiths, together with Wilson, claim they are concerned with both (1) and (2), the truth is that RSCs concentrate mainly on (1) and throw little light on (2), due to their ignorance of the intrinsic aspect of species definition. See Devitt, "Resurrecting," 356–58; Okasha, "Darwinian Metaphysics," 201; Sterelny and Griffiths, *Sex and Death*, 211; Robert

4.2.3. (IIa3) Phenotype and Relational/Historical Properties

Another variant/aspect of EssSC concentrates more on the phenotype and some crucial relational/historical properties that help explain its maintenance and stability across time and space. Once again crossing the boundary between (I) and (II), Elder thinks, "organisms possess the phenotypic and genotypic properties that they do simply in virtue of how matters stand during their own existences: these are nonhistorical properties. But historical properties may be crucial as well." Hence, "it would follow that the members of a biological natural kind must share not only certain phenotypic properties but also the common historical property of being descended from the same sorts of ancestors, under the influence of the same sorts of selectional pressures."[61]

4.2.4. (IIa4) Relations Among Organisms and Between Organisms and the Environment

An alternative and somewhat unorthodox variant/aspect of EssSC defines species in terms of relations among organisms and between organisms and the environment that are necessary and sufficient for the membership in a particular taxon. This variant is classified as relational, historical, or origin essentialism. Underlying the concept of monophyly, it defines essences as relational and extrinsic rather than intrinsic: "From the point of view of a phylogenetic taxonomy . . . being descended from a particular ancestral population may seem to be the essential property of a particular taxon."[62]

4.2.5. (IIa5) Fundamental Dispositions

In reference to the Aristotelian distinction between potency and act, Stan Wallace suggests that "the properties which are essential to the entities' existence

---

A. Wilson, "Realism, Essence, and Kind: Resuscitating Species Essentialism," in Wilson, *Species*, 191–92. Devitt further develops and defends his view in "Individual Essentialism in Biology," "Defending Intrinsic Biological Essentialism," *Philosophy of Science* 88, no. 1 (2021): 67–82; and most recently in a monograph entitled *Biological Essentialism* (Oxford University Press, 2023). See also Rieppel, "New Essentialism," 669.

61. Elder, "Biological Species," 347.

62. Dupré, *Humans and Other Animals*, 43. Similarly, Sterelny and Griffiths state that "the essential properties that make a particular organism a platypus . . . are historical or relational" (*Sex and Death*, 186). This view is also discussed by Paul E. Griffiths, "Squaring the Circle: Natural Kinds with Historical Essences," in Wilson, *Species*, 209–28; Ruth Garrett Millikan, "Historical Kinds and the 'Special Sciences,'" *Philosophical Studies: An International Journal for Philosophy in the Analytic Tradition* 95, no. 1/2 (1999): 45–65; Okasha, "Darwinian Metaphysics"; and Joseph LaPorte, *Natural Kinds and Conceptual Change* (Cambridge: Cambridge University Press, 2004).

cannot be genotypic or phenotypic." Rather, "an essentialist may reasonably define these essential properties as 'dispositional properties.'" Wallace defines them as "tendencies or proclivities for the organism to exist in certain ways. In other words, they are dispositions of the organisms to exemplify realized, or first-order, properties and functions."[63]

Austin further develops this idea and states that "in the framework of Æ [Aristotelian essentialism], organisms are ontologically sorted into natural kinds in virtue of sharing sets of causal properties which both generate and subsequently shape their morphological development . . . these 'powerful' properties are *dispositional properties*." Thus, he thinks that "evo-devo is a framework in which morphological variation is derived from invariant, functional causal mechanisms which serve as highly conserved 'deep homologies,' underwriting a vast array of organismal diversity."[64] Speaking about the modular character of development—in reference to components operating by their own intrinsically determined principles—he suggests calling these components "phenmodulatory dispositions," which are "ontological switches" that ground the phenomenon of phenotypic plasticity (morphological variation).[65] Austin concludes by saying that "in a notable shift from the neo-Darwinian perspective, evo-devo favors a 'structuralist' approach":

> An essence of a natural kind must be comprised of a nested, scalar set of a number of phenmodulatory dispositions. . . . [It] cannot be identified with a set of particularized morphological structures, but must instead be defined by a set of discrete morphogenetic developmental units, each individually responsible for the potential production of a unified gradient of an interrelated set of quantitative and qualitative permutations on a general architectural theme.[66]

4.2.6. (IIa6) Developmental Program

Austin's suggestion is related to yet another variant/aspect of EssSC, which emphasizes the importance of kind-specific developmental programs, which are goal-directed dispositions of organisms to produce viable offspring of their own kind. Stephen Boulter suggests that biological essences "are found not

---

63. Stan W. Wallace, "In Defense of Biological Essentialism," *Philosophia Christi* 4, no. 1 (2002): 34–35.
64. Austin, "Aristotelian Essentialism," 2544–45.
65. Austin, "Aristotelian Essentialism," 2546–47.
66. Austin, "Aristotelian Essentialism," 2547, 2549, 2550. Note that according to Austin, "natural kinds [being more inclusive] *cannot* be identified with *species*, but rather must be considered on analogy with the conceptual middle of the taxonomic tree" ("Aristotelian Essentialism," 2551).

in the genotype or the phenotype but in the species specific developmental programs that map genotypes onto phenotypes." He thinks "that (i) only a portion of an organism's genome determines its species (not all of it); (ii) that developmental control genes (i.e., genes that control the expression of other genes) determine the developmental pattern of an organism; and (iii) that these developmental patterns are 'lineage specific,' i.e., shared by individuals of the same biological species understood as a smallest diagnosable cluster of organisms related by ancestry and descent."[67] He concludes by saying that "on this suggestion two organisms belong to the same species and have the same essence if they share the same developmental programme regardless of how else they might differ."

Recognizing the tension between developmental stability and phenotypic plasticity in reference to evolutionary developmental biology (evo-devo), Dennis Walsh introduces the concept of evolutionary essentialism. He refers to Mary Jane West-Eberhard and her idea of adaptive evolution based on phenotypic and genotypic accommodation, which she explains as a consequence of the compartmentalization of organisms to developmental modules (local processes described as morphogenetic fields).[68] He says that "the ultimate source of variation within a population may be random genetic mutation, as the modern synthesis insists. But the *adaptiveness* of adaptive evolution seems also to require that the phenotypic variation that is visible to selection is non-random. It is regulated by the plasticity of organisms and biased by the requirements that organisms maintain viability in the face of perturbations." He thinks the latter disposition is grounded in a given species' essential features, which "should overturn the anti-individualist bias inherent in modern synthesis biology."[69]

4.2.7. (IIa7) Substantial Form

Finally, one more crucial variant/aspect of EssSC reaches toward more fundamental ontology by asking the question that—as notes Dumsday—"any essentialist philosophy of biology will be faced with," that is, "the question of what, if anything, grounds and unifies the collection of intrinsic properties generally taken to be definitive of 'organism.'" Dumsday is convinced

---

67. Boulter, "Can Evolutionary," 100.
68. See Mary Jane West-Eberhard, *Developmental Plasticity and Evolution* (New York: Oxford University Press, 2003).
69. Walsh, "Evolutionary Essentialism," 440. Like Austin, Walsh states that "in Aristotle's essentialist biology the nature of an organism is manifested as a goal-directed disposition to produce and maintain a living thing capable of fulfilling its vital functions in ways characteristic of its kind" ("Evolutionary Essentialism," 427).

that "this issue is often left wholly unaddressed in the existing literature on the nature and origin of life, and constitutes one possible opening for the introduction of substantial form into the discussion (an introduction that would in turn help draw out the tight connection between classification and explanation that is such a prominent feature of Scholastic philosophy of nature)."[70]

Although Dumsday is not himself "aiming at the more ambitious target of a distinctively hylomorphic account" of species, he does note that it is not the case that properties, be they genetic, phenetic, or dispositional, define the essence of a given type.[71] Rather, it is the essence that grounds the properties associated with a given biological natural kind and determines the range of behaviors of its individual members.[72] At the same time, the hylomorphic account of EssSC has already been developed within the analytic philosophical tradition by Oderberg, who says that essences are mixtures of actuality and potentiality, where the former is defined as substantial form (SF) and the latter as primary matter (PM). Echoing Aristotle, he states SF is a metaphysical principle "*by virtue of which* the substance is what it is." As such, it actualizes its complementary metaphysical principle, the purely passive potentiality of wholly receptive PM, which (underlying sensible, secondary, or proximate matter) individualizes SF in a particular entity, which is further specified by its accidental properties.[73] In this account, PM and SF are regarded as causes. This idea is based on the assumption that causal principles, going beyond physical interactions, are understood as metaphysical principles explaining essences of natural kinds. Thus, they are closely related with efficient and final causes, as well as with the quasi (*per accidens*) causal character of chance and fortune.[74] Taken together, they ground all types of

---

70. Dumsday, "Is There Still Hope," 394–95. The received answer to the question mentioned by Dumsday, popular among analytic metaphysicians, is usually based on the modal distinction of necessary (essential) and contingent (accidental) features, where the former are thought to define a given species in every possible world. Avoiding the complexity and challenges of hylomorphism, this view faces the need of embracing an already existing or developing a new ontology of possible worlds. See Michael Gorman, "Essentiality as Foundationality," in *Neo-Aristotelian Perspectives in Metaphysics*, eds. Daniel D. Novotný and Lukáš Novák (New York: Routledge, 2014), 122–23.

71. Dumsday, "Is There Still Hope," 390.

72. See Dumsday, "Is There Still Hope," 371.

73. See Oderberg, *Real Essentialism*, 62–81.

74. Note that the reference to efficient causes in causal description of an organism introduces a historical aspect to the hylomorphic variant/aspect of EssSC. Yet, as Oderberg notes, "It does not follow from the fact that a substance or species has a certain historical origin that its *essence* is to have that origin, even if it has its origin necessarily" (*Real Essentialism*, 101).

genetic, phenetic, or dispositional properties of organisms mentioned in other variants/aspects of EssSC.[75]

This account of the hylomorphic theory is crucial. Understood in this way, the hylomorphic aspect of EssSC clearly provides a necessary ontological and metaphysical ground and rationale that unifies and consolidates all other aspects proposed, discussed, and defended by the advocates of this species concept. It thus endows EssSC with plausibility and intrinsic coherence, making EssSC a consistent and viable option in the most recent debate over species. At the same time, it proves that the reintroduction of the classical categories of SF and PM (act and potency, respectively) within the context of contemporary evolutionary biology is not an arbitrary and forced move by the stubborn minority of classically oriented Aristotelian-Thomistic thinkers who ignore the mainstream research in this field. Quite the contrary, it shows that their metaphysical and ontological agenda becomes a logical conclusion of the multifaceted research conducted by those who suggest that a good candidate for a species concept should be, at least partially, intrinsic.

In conclusion, we should attempt to provide an essentialist definition of species that is hylomorphically grounded. I claim that species can be defined as a common nature expressed in and abstracted from concrete living beings that are determined by a particular type of essence. The latter is constituted by a specific kind of SF that—as a metaphysical principle of actuality—actualizes its correlative metaphysical principle of pure potentiality (i.e., PM). Causing thus an organism to be what it is, SF grounds a range of essential and accidental, intrinsic and extrinsic dispositions and properties, characteristic for a given type of living creature. A provisional list of these dispositions and properties includes particularized kind-specific morphological and physiological developmental programs and a variety of genotypic and phenotypic traits that find their distinctive expression in historical relationships of organisms that belong to a given species.

4.3. Homeostatic Property Cluster (HPCSC) and Phenetic Species Concept (PSC)

Apart from various types of EssSC, we can list at least two other ISCs that treat biological species as natural kinds. The first is the (IIb) homeostatic prop-

---

75. In reference to the hylomorphic notion of EssSC, Oderberg argues in favor of ISCs and notes that RSCs confuse essences and properties. Properties are founded on the essence of an organism and emanate from it, determining further its nature. But essence as such is always intrinsic. Hence, while the properties of species members might be relational (e.g., the power to act in a certain way in an ecological niche or to interbreed with some other organisms), what enables a given organism to have such relational properties is its essence. See Oderberg, *Real Essentialism*, 223.

erty cluster species concept (HPCSC), which builds on the conviction that natural kinds are groups of organisms across which some delimited phenotypic properties cluster together. Given evolutionary forces, none of these properties are essential for membership in a given species. At the same time, homeostatic causal mechanisms (e.g., interbreeding, sharing similar developmental programs, being exposed to similar selection regimes) provide for the similarity of members of a given species. Nevertheless, even if genealogical connectedness is important for HPCSC, it is similarity that plays the role of the final arbiter of species sameness.

On the face of it, HPCSC appears to be more flexible than EssSC, as it easily allows for variations of traits within clusters that define biological species. At the same time, however, HPCSC faces the difficulty of defining borders between them. This challenge becomes all the more acute once we realize that homeostatic mechanisms may also vary over time and space (across geographic regions).[76]

One more type of ISC is the (IIc) phenetic species concept (PSC), which assumes that a group of organisms forms a genuine natural kind due to the same phenotypic traits cropping up in each one of them. One might assume—as does the classical formulation of the PSC—that such properties must recur across literally all organisms that belong to the same species. However, species under PSC might be defined as statistical and not discrete. On such interpretation, we might think of "dense regions" representing relatively high statistical correlations of attributes shared by a number of living beings.[77] The price of this liberalization of PSC is that it ceases to crave clear-cut boundaries between species, as it is no longer defined by necessary and sufficient conditions. It also does not provide unambiguous borders between natural kinds. Probably the oldest among species concepts, PSC (often classified as morphology species concept, or MSC) has a strong operational flavor to it, as it

---

76. See Richard Boyd, "Homeostasis, Species, and Higher Taxa," in Wilson, *Species*, 141–85; Wilson, "Realism"; and Ereshefsky, "Species," section 2.4. Günter Wagner sees Boyd's HPCSC as "an important liberalization to the classical notion of natural kinds which was and is often expressed in fairly absolute terms." Günter P. Wagner, "Characters, Units, and Natural Kinds," in *The Character Concept in Evolutionary Biology*, ed. Günter P. Wagner (San Diego: Academic Press, 2001), 8. Elder, offers a critical evaluation of HPCSC, showing that it needs to treat one or more properties in a given cluster as essential for a particular species (see "Biological Species," 355–57).

77. Gerry Webster and Brian Goodwin state that each species by nature occupies a place within a possibility-space (i.e., a "morphological field"), in which certain adaptations (and not others) are available. See Gerry Webster and Brian Goodwin, *Form and Transformation: Generative and Relational Principles in Biology* (Cambridge: Cambridge University Press, 1996).

concentrates mainly on phenotypic and morphological features of organisms. It does not refer to their phylogenesis and mechanisms of speciation. As such, it seems to suffer from the difficulty of providing the general algorithm of similarity of properties. It may also be unable to distinguish between polymorphism (e.g., hierarchical and functional differences among organisms in one population) and speciation, as well as between homologies and cases of parallel and convergent evolution.[78]

At the same time, because morphology is in fact the basis of all recognition and classification—Oderberg notes that "it finds its way into ecological tests, reproductive criteria, cladistic analysis, genetic identification, mate recognition, and more"—it might be treated as an indispensable aspect of all other species concepts, even if it does not stand as a single and unique method of carving nature at its joints.[79] Undeniably, morphology (meaning the study of form [*morphē*]) seems to be a close ally of the hylomorphic (*hulē* + *morphē*) variant/aspect of EssSC, which defines essences in reference to substantial forms of particular types.

4.4. Compatibility of ISCs with Evolutionary Biology

Unlike RSCs, which were developed as grounded in the modern evolutionary synthesis, all ISCs (and EssSC in particular) are still considered by many as incompatible with evolutionary biology. It is this conviction in particular that makes many contemporary philosophers of biology suspicious and skeptical about any attempt to reintroduce essentialist thinking in life sciences. I will now present and answer two major arguments in support of this skeptical view of ISCs:

1. EssSC implies species fixism, which is in principle inconsistent with the view that species evolve. In other words, variation—which is crucial for natural selection and Darwinian evolution—clashes with the unchangeability of species and the Aristotelian "Natural State Model."[80] On this interpretation of essentialism variation, being a result of the action of

---

78. As an example of a polymorphism, we may think of different kinds of ants or bees in a colony. Homological properties occur in two or more organisms having a common ancestor (e.g., eyes in various mammals) and is differentiated from homoplasy, which refers to a similar trait that occurs in two or more organisms and was passed down from different ancestors (e.g., octopus' and mammalian eyes), in the processes of parallel or convergent evolution.

79. Oderberg, *Real Essentialism*, 235.

80. Okasha, "Darwinian Metaphysics," 197. Wilson rejects genetic essentialism because "the inherent biological variability or heterogeneity of species with respect to both morphology and genetic composition is, after all, a cornerstone of the idea of evolution by natural selection" ("Realism," 190).

"interfering forces," takes an organism away from its "natural stage," making it thus "the result of imperfect manifestations of the idea implicit in each species."[81] Sober finds this view contrasting Darwin's, for whom "individual differences are not *the effects* of interfering forces confounding the expression of a prototype; rather they are *the causes* of events that are absolutely central to the history of evolution."[82] Hence, adds Jody Hey, "that variation among organisms is the crucial stuff of changing life and of life's progress" is thought to be "devastating to essentialism."[83]

2. EssSC implies clear, nonbridgeable boundaries between species, but no set properties (genotypic or phenotypic) have been identified as jointly necessary and sufficient for defining such boundaries for any biological species.[84] Moreover, a fair number of species are characterized by regularized dimorphism (especially sexual dimorphism) or polymorphism of essential properties, while others seem to show similar traits despite the fact they do not share the same evolutionary history. This further contradicts the argument in favor of there being packages of properties defining species.[85] In addition, evolution between species with clear boundaries would only be possible if nature proceeded by jumps (saltations).[86]

To answer the first objection, we must note that it is based on Mayr's popular and overly Platonic phrasing of EssSC, in which he states that according to this concept "there are a limited number of fixed, unchangeable 'ideas' underlying the observed variability [in nature], with the *eidos* (idea) being the only thing that is fixed and real, while the observed variability has no more

---

81. Ernst Mayr, *Populations, Species, and Evolution: An Abridgment of* Animal Species and Evolution (Cambridge, MA: Harvard University Press, 1970), 11. Griffiths says variation makes an organism belonging to intrinsically defined species to be "deviation" from an "ideal." Paul E. Griffiths, "What Is Innateness?" *The Monist* 85, no. 1 (2001): 78–79.

82. Elliott Sober, "Evolution, Population Thinking and Essentialism," *Philosophy of Science* 47, no. 3 (1980): 371. Sober adds that "the Natural State Model presupposes that there is some phenotype which is the natural one *which is independent of a choice of environment*" (374).

83. Jody Hey, *Genes, Categories, and Species: The Evolutionary and Cognitive Cause of the Species Problem* (New York: Oxford University Press, 2001), 62.

84. Sober claims that "no genotypic characteristic can be postulated as a species essence; the genetic variability found in sexual populations is prodigious" ("Evolution," 380).

85. Referring to this argument against EssSC, Elder also mentions "members [of species] that are abnormal or aberrant" ("Biological Species," 346–47). Their existence introduces variations in a given population.

86. See Boulter, "Can Evolutionary Biology," 92.

reality than the shadows of an object on a cave wall."[87] However, one must not forget that, contrary to this view, on Aristotle's scheme, essences or natures are not transcendent, fixed "ideas" but "goal-directed capacities immanent in the nature of the organism." In other words, they exist as realized in concrete, temporal, individual, and contingent organisms. Hence, Walsh adds, "It certainly isn't inconsistent with Aristotelian essentialism to suppose that natures could change over time in just the way we have come to think that species do. Individual organisms may well vary in their formal and material natures, in such a way that over time some variants become more common than others."[88]

In reference to the hylomorphic variant/aspect of EssSC (IIa7), we may speak about two levels of potentiality inherent in the very fabric of the cosmos: (1) pure potentiality of PM, which can be actualized by all possible types of substantial forms and is proper for both inanimate and animate natural kinds; and (2) potentiality of primary matter underlying each and every instantiation of secondary (proximate and sensible) matter, which is specified (qualified) by the SF and accidental forms characteristic of a particular natural kind it belongs to. The actualizing principles dispose PM that is underlying entities classified as instantiations of secondary matter in a particular way, enabling thus—in the way of substantial change—an eduction of particular types of new substantial forms (typical of other natural kinds) from its potentiality. This allows for introducing the idea of evolutionary changes and transitions within the framework of the Aristotelian philosophy of biology.[89]

---

87. Ernst Mayr, *Evolution and the Diversity of Life: Selected Essays* (Cambridge, MA: Harvard University Press, 1976), 27.

88. Walsh, Evolutionary Essentialism," 431. In support of his argument, he refers to David Balme who says that "there is nothing in Aristotle's theory to prevent an 'evolution of species,' i.e. a continuous modification of the kinds being transmitted. But he had no evidence of evolution" (David M. Balme, "Aristotle's Biology Was Not Essentialist," in *Philosophical Issues in Aristotle's Biology*, ed. Allan Gotthelf and James G. Lennox [Cambridge: Cambridge University Press, 1987], 97). An expert in Aristotle's biology, James Lennox, says that "Aristotle's essentialism is not typological, nor is it in any way 'anti-evolutionary.' Whatever it is Darwin was up against, it was not Aristotelian essentialism." James G. Lennox, *Aristotle's Philosophy of Biology: Studies in the Origins of Life Science* (Cambridge: Cambridge University Press, 2001), 162. I believe that Walsh's suggestion of natures changing over time should be interpreted in terms of accidental changes affecting concrete organisms belonging to a given type (and thus changing the disposition of PM that underlies them), rather than in terms of gradual changes of the type of SF proper for the natural kind in question. The latter idea would be rather foreign to the Aristotelian-Thomistic metaphysics.

89. See Mariusz Tabaczek, "The Metaphysics of Evolution: From Aquinas's Interpretation of Augustine's Concept of *Rationes Seminales* to the Contemporary Thomistic Account of Species Transformism," *Nova et Vetera* 18, no. 3 (2020): 969–70.

Hence, concludes Dumsday, "essentialism not only allows for evolution but is plausibly required for it."[90] He notes that a similar argument was already made in 1934 by the scholastic scholar Richard Phillips. In his textbook on the philosophy of nature, Phillips writes: "Considering, then, natural species in the strict sense, do our principles allow us to say that they could be transformed? There seems to be nothing in them to render it impossible for we should only have a striking example of substantial change."[91]

Moving to the second objection, some advocates of nonhylomorphic variants/aspects of EssSC (IIa1–6) are willing to follow the consensus grounded in RSCs and say that, ontologically speaking, "essences are a bit indeterminate."[92] Thus, Devitt states that "the evolution of *S2* [species 2] from *S1* [species 1] will involve a gradual process of moving from organisms that determinately have [intrinsic essence or genotype] *G1* to organisms that determinately have [intrinsic essence or genotype] *G2* via a whole lot of organisms that do not determinately have either."[93] Walsh stipulates that "[a] shared nature (*genos*) does not determine any specific features of what we now call 'phenotype' (or, for that matter, genotype). Instead, it imposes a set of constraints upon the range of phenotypes that organisms sharing that nature might possess."[94] Leaning toward HPCSC, Elder states that "while there is, for a typical species, no fixed collection of properties that are individually necessary and jointly sufficient for membership in the species, it nevertheless is true that the members of the typical species are bound to present some shifting subset—some shifting majority—of the properties on a common list."[95]

However, according to the hylomorphic variant/aspect of EssSC (IIa7), ontological indeterminacy of species is not acceptable. If the essence of an organism is ultimately grounded in its SF, it must be emphasized that each SF either actualizes a "portion" of designated matter or it does not, there is no middle ground here. Hence, it is entirely unclear what a vague possession of form would amount to.[96] Consequently, notes Oderberg, we should acknowledge that:

---

90. Dumsday, "Is There Still Hope," 390.
91. Richard Percival Phillips, *The Philosophy of Nature*, vol. 1 of *Modern Thomistic Philosophy: An Explanation for Students* (Heusenstamm: Editiones Scholasticae, 2013), 342.
92. Devitt, "Resurrecting," 373.
93. Devitt, "Resurrecting," 373.
94. Walsh, "Evolutionary Essentialism," 429.
95. Elder, "Biological Species," 347. The level of similarity of organisms might be defined in reference to a particular part of the underlying structure that causes in its "normal" environment the distinctive phenotypic features of the species.
96. The tendency to treat species as ontologically indeterminate leads to a nominalist conclusion that they can be defined only in terms of a network of multilateral relationships

> Essence is not given by properties but by *form*, more precisely substantial form. Properties are indicators of essence, allowing fallible and provisional judgement as to the essence of an organism. . . . Given the complexity of even the simplest creature, the list of necessary characteristics will be incredibly large, possibly infinite. . . . The same goes for sufficient properties: it may be that, for even the apparently simplest organism, listing all of the sufficient characteristics essential to it will be either technically or metaphysically impossible. . . . Still, the essentialist sees no cause for concern, since all the systematist should be looking for is not an exhaustive list of necessary and sufficient characteristics, but enough characteristics to enable at least a provisional judgement as to the substantial form of an organism, followed by an accumulation of characteristics to increase the well-foundedness of the judgement.[97]

If it is true that properties do not define but merely reveal the essence of an organism, which is defined as such by the SF of a given type, then all difficulties and doubts concerning classification and demarcation of species boundaries based on their empirically verifiable features are epistemological and not ontological. In other words, the uncertainties faced by practicing biologists in classifying forms of living beings need not necessarily mean that the essences of organisms are vague metaphysically. Conversely, clarity at the level of the metaphysical classification of a given species may not translate into a clear and unanimously agreeable description of its empirical properties.

As to the argument that clear boundaries between species only allows for saltations and not for steady and gradual evolutionary changes, we must not forget that these boundaries are most likely marked by sparse, if not singular mutations (changes), which bring to fulfillment complex processes of changes that are extended in space and time and effected by a matrix of causes. In other words, the clarity of metaphysical boundaries between evolutionary-related species does not make them radical, empirically speaking. As long as our metaphysics allows for gradual changes affecting the dispositions of successive generations of offspring in a given lineage, it should welcome the possibility of an evolutionary transformation that is not saltational. Classical Aristotelian-Thomistic metaphysics certainly allows for such minute and grad-

---

and interactions between processes, within which it is impossible to distinguish any natural types. A species understood as a taxonomic group would simply be the result of the practical application of the species category (understood as one of the taxonomic ranks, defined in relation to selected criteria—e.g., genetic) based on a partially arbitrary decision of the researcher-systematist. Arbitrariness here is the result of fluid genetic and ecological boundaries as well as imperfect criteria for the use of species categories.

97. Oderberg, *Real Essentialism*, 212.

ual changes, disposing PM to be actualized at some point (in a particular transition from one generation to the next) by an SF of a new type, which marks the origin of a new species. Once again, such a clear metaphysical boundary between natural kinds may not easily translate or coincide with their empirical demarcation. Indeed, the latter may remain epistemologically vague. But this should not discredit our ontological assessment, at least not by default.

Conclusion

Although the anti-individualistic and antiessentialistic orthodoxy is most likely still predominant among philosophers of biology, I hope to have shown that there is a growing group of philosophers of science and of biology who think that the received consensus defining species as spatiotemporally extended (scattered) individuals needs to be at least supplemented with the classical view that acknowledges the reality of intrinsic natures (essences) of individual organisms. Moreover, I have argued that when considered in the context of its different variants or aspects—as in, referring to genetic and phenetic properties of organisms, historical relations among them, and their fundamental dispositions, developmental programs, and metaphysical (hylomorphic) constitution—EssSC becomes a viable and comprehensive proposition that belongs in the age of evolution. Moving forward the conversation, what I offered toward the end of section 4.2 is a comprehensive, hylomorphically informed essentialist definition of species, which builds upon earlier developments provided by Oderberg and Dumsday.

Hence, in conclusion, I want to acknowledge and emphasize that the strong resurgence of essentialism among analytic philosophers with a taste for metaphysics gradually finds its manifestation in the contemporary philosophy of biology, proving that Ereshefsky's pronouncement of its death was premature and most likely ill-conceived.[98] This transition is crucial for the classical school of thought, as it enables it to develop an ontological and causal view of speciation that remains in conversation with contemporary evolutionary biology. Based on both intrinsic (i.e., hylomorphic) and extrinsic (i.e., historical and relational) aspects of living creatures, the contemporary Aristotelian-Thomistic version of species essentialism grounds the model of discrete transitions from one species to another through the process of numerous accidental changes that have an impact on the disposition of PM, which underlies organisms that belong to a given species S_1. Consecutive substantial changes accompanying the generation of offspring within an evolutionary lineage that contains S_1 may reach the point where PM underlying an ovum and a sperm of the parental organisms

---

98. See Ereshefsky, "Species," section 2.1.

belonging to S_1 is disposed to be actualized by an SF of the new type (i.e., the SF of an organism belonging to the new species S_2).

My answer to the objections concerning the compatibility of intrinsic essentialist species concepts—including a hylomorphically-informed essentialist species concept—with contemporary evolutionary biology, offered in section 4.4, proves that this model becomes a viable position in the current conversation concerning the metaphysics and ontology of biological speciation that must not be dismissed or neglected.[99]

---

99. I develop such a model in greater detail in Tabaczek, "The Metaphysics of Evolution," 964–68, and my monograph *Theistic Evolution: A Contemporary Aristotelian-Thomistic Perspective*, chapter 1.

CHAPTER THREE

Thomas Aquinas on the Proportionate Causes of Living Species

BRIAN CARL

It is a frequently cited principle within the works of St. Thomas Aquinas that an effect cannot "exceed" its cause, be "more powerful" than its cause, or be more perfect than its cause.[1] In numerous texts, Thomas also asserts that "nothing acts beyond its species," often indicating that this is so because no effect can be more powerful than its agent cause.[2] As it is now often called, the principle of proportionate causality (or, the PPC) is also frequently expressed in the form that "nothing gives what it does not have."[3] Such a principle is, understandably, a source of concern about the reconcilability of a theory of biological evolution with Thomistic philosophy.[4]

I offer my thanks to the Thomistic Evolution project, led by Nicanor Austriaco, OP, with funding from the John Templeton Foundation, for opportunities to present and discuss earlier versions of this study and for support that made research for this project possible. I also owe my gratitude to David Cory, Brandon Zimmerman, Philip Neri Reese, OP, Robert C. Koons, Daniel De Haan, Mariusz Tabaczek, OP, Nicanor Austriaco, OP, Richard Conrad, OP, Raymond Hain, and Elliot Polsky for helpful comments and feedback. An earlier version of this chapter appeared in *Scientia et Fides* 8.2 (2020): 223–48.

    1. *SCG* 1.67; *ST* 2-2.24.6 s.c.; and *De pot.* 3.16 ad 8. *In Sent.* 4.23.2.2 qc. 1 ad 3; *SCG* 1.41, 3.120; *ST* 1.95.1, 1-2.66.1; and *De spir. creat.* 11 ad 11. *ST* 1-2.63.2 obj. 3.

    2. *In Sent.* 2.18.2.3; *De ver.* 24.14; *Quodl.* 9.5.1; *SCG* 3.84; *De pot.* 3.9; and *ST* 1-2.112.1. *In Sent.* 2.18.2.3 obj. 3. Cf. *De pot.* 3.8 obj. 13; *ST* 1-2.112.1; and *Comp. theo.* 1.93.

    3. This formulation only appears explicitly in Thomas's writings in objections. See, for example, *In Sent.* 4.15.2.6 qc. 1 obj. 2; *ST* 1-2.81.3 obj. 2, 3.64.5 obj. 1. See section 1, this chapter, for discussion. Alternatively, as a character in a story by Ralph McInerny memorably puts it, "*Nemo dat quod non got.*" See Ralph McInerny, *The Prudence of the Flesh* (New York: St. Martin's Press, 2006), 231.

    4. Fr. Michael Chaberek has pointed to the principles that "no being can convey more act than it possesses," that "no effect can exceed the power of its cause," and that "the perfection of the cause cannot be lesser than the perfection of the effect" as incompatible with the evolutionary emergence of novel genera of living things. See Michael Chaberek,

Like Aristotle, Thomas does in fact hold that there are some animal species whose members can only be generated through reproduction by already existing members of the same species. If this is so, then the emergence of such animals through any natural evolutionary process is impossible. That horses beget horses and human beings beget human beings might seem to be the most obvious application of the principle that "nothing gives what it does not have," that the actuality in an effect must be preceded by the same actuality in the cause. This is in fact the sort of example given by Aristotle in *Metaphysics* 9 in his discussion of the temporal priority of actuality in the universe, even if potentiality precedes actuality in the individual (*Metaphysics* 9.8).

As Aristotle's discussions of the generation of living substances (both in *Metaphysics* 7 and in his biological works) indicate, however, matters are somewhat more complicated, given his commitment to the claim that some living things are spontaneously generated, like flies from rotting flesh or oysters from slimy mud. For Aristotle or Thomas, it cannot be that the requirement for a generator of the same species, in cases like the horse or the human being, is simply a consequence of a general principle that "something cannot give what it does not have"; otherwise, spontaneous generation would seem to be ruled out. Matters are similarly complicated by Aristotle's discussion of another topic in the same texts; namely, animals that arise from hybridization, such as the mule, which is the offspring of a horse and a donkey. There is little hope of fully understanding Aristotle's assertion of the temporal priority of actuality, or Thomas's principle that an effect cannot exceed its cause, without an examination of their views about spontaneous generation and hybridization. I would propose that it is necessary to understand something of their biological and cosmological views in these cases, which are presumably consistent with their metaphysical principles if one wishes to raise the question of how their principles might bear on the contemporary question of biological evolution.

This chapter will examine the notion of "proportionate causality" as discussed by Thomas, followed by an examination of what the proportionate causes are for Thomas (and for Aristotle, insofar as Thomas follows him) of spontaneously generated animals and of reproduced animals, including hybrids like the mule. This will allow us to clarify why Thomas holds that some animals can only arise through univocal generation. I will show that Thomas does not reach this conclusion merely by reasoning from something like the principle of proportionate causality. Rather, Thomas's reasons for

---

Aquinas and Evolution (Leicester: The Chartwell Press: 2017), 48; "Classical Metaphysics and Theistic Evolution: Why Are They Incompatible?" *Studia Gilsoniana* 8, no. 1 (2019): 56.

asserting the need in some cases for a (univocal) generator of the same species are grounded in physical and biological doctrines that he receives from Aristotle and in his understanding of the causal hierarchy in which changes in the sublunary depend on the motions of the celestial bodies.

I will show that Thomas's understanding of the role of instrumental causality in univocal generation should undercut any use of the principle of proportionate causality to argue that biological evolution is irreconcilable with his metaphysical principles. In brief, Thomas does not in fact hold that any individual animal "has" its own nature in such a way that it is sufficient to "give" that nature to something else, for in his view, an individual animal is an instrumental cause in the generation of another individual of the same species. I will also document that there is a general principle about the causal hierarchy that Thomas invokes in his discussions of the need for univocal generators—that more mediating causes are required for the constitution of what is more perfect—but I will argue that this principle is far from irreconcilable with biological evolution. I will conclude with some suggestions about implications for the debate about the reconcilability of Thomistic metaphysics with biological evolution.

1. "Proportionate Causality" in Thomas's Thought

Like the claim that "there is nothing in the intellect that is not first in the sense," the formulation that "nothing gives what it does not have" only appears explicitly in Thomas's writings in objections. As Therese Cory has recently shown, the formulation "there is nothing in the intellect that is not first in the sense" is in fact difficult to reconcile with many of the details of Thomas's understanding of human intellectual knowledge about incorporeal realities.[5] The truth to which Thomas is committed to that is at issue with this well-known formula—the dependence of human intellectual cognition upon sense cognition—is better and more precisely expressed in other ways. I would suggest that in a similar way the formulation "nothing gives what it does not have" might easily mislead when one considers Thomas's views about animal generation and the requirement for a univocal generator in what Thomas calls perfect animals.

When Thomas's recent interpreters who speak of the principle of proportionate causality offer an interpretation of what this principle means in practice in Thomas's thought, they say that the principle amounts to the claim that something's efficient cause must possess the form/perfection that it causes,

---

5. Therese Scarpelli Cory, "Is Anything in the Intellect That Was Not First in Sense? Empiricism and Knowledge of the Incorporeal in Aquinas," in *Oxford Studies in Medieval Philosophy* 6, ed. Robert Pasnau (Oxford: Oxford University Press, 2018), 100–143.

by having that perfection formally (i.e., by actually having the same form in the same way), or by having it in a more eminent way, or by having it virtually, where to have it virtually is just to "have it" in such a way that it is able to cause it in something else.[6]

Such a principle, so understood, will have some implications concerning something identified as an absolute first efficient cause. A first efficient cause of everything other than itself will have to possess all perfections at least virtually. This in turn would be a reason for saying that an absolute first cause is superior to its effects, if it is also supposed, with Thomas, that virtual possession of some actuality can be a more perfect mode of possessing that actuality.[7] But apart from this further claim, the principle that "nothing gives what it does not have," in its application to a given efficient cause, amounts only to the claim that an efficient cause must at least be able to cause whatever perfection it causes, even if its ability to cause that perfection is not due to its own formal possession of the perfection. It turns out to be a principle that doesn't tell us very much on its own.

Thomas does occasionally use the language of proportion between effects and causes, although typically not as a way of expressing the principle that an effect cannot exceed its cause.[8] In several cases where Thomas speaks of a necessary proportion between effects and causes, he says (1) that *per se* effects are proportioned to *per se* causes, while *per accidens* effects are proportioned to *per accidens* causes; and (2) that particular effects are proportioned to particular causes, while universal effects are proportioned to universal causes.[9] As we will see below, the distinctions between *per se* and *per accidens* causes and between universal and particular causes are both centrally involved in

---

6. Ed Feser, *Five Proofs for the Existence of God* (San Francisco: Ignatius Press, 2017), 33.

7. *ST* 1.4.2: "Manifestum est enim quod effectus praeexistit virtute in causa agente, praeexistere autem in virtute causae agentis, non est praeexistere imperfectiori modo, sed perfectiori."

8. In one text he does offer as a principle that an effect must be proportionate to its cause: he argues that there must be something infinite about the object of supernatural hope, because it is caused by the infinite helping power of God. *ST* 2-2.17.2.

9. *In Meta*. 6.2. *De ver.* 2.5; *De sub. sep.* 10; and *SCG* 2.21. In the last of these texts, Thomas also asserts that potential effects are proportioned to potential causes, while actual effects are proportioned to actual causes. These claims about the necessary proportions between effects and causes are ultimately indebted to Aristotle's discussion of the modes of causality in *Physics* 2.3 and to a claim made by Aristotle at the conclusion of this chapter. See *In Phys*. 2.6 #197: "Et est, quod causis debent proportionaliter respondere effectus, ita quod generalibus causis generales effectus reddantur, et singularibus singulares; puta, si dicatur quod statuae causa est statuam faciens, et huius statuae hic statuam faciens. Et similiter causis in potentia respondent effectus in potentia, et causis in actu effectus in actu."

Thomas's account of the generation of living things, along with the distinction between principal and instrumental causality. As noted above, Thomas does with some frequency assert that an effect cannot exceed or be more powerful than its cause, but he recognizes that such a restriction does not apply to the relationship between instrumental causes and their effects.[10] He adds this same qualification to his claim that nothing acts outside of its species.[11]

2. Thomas on Novel Species After the Sixth Day: On the Mule

Before turning to some of the details of Thomas's understanding of the proportionate causes of the species of living things, I want to make clear that considering topics like spontaneous generation and hybridization will be directly relevant to thinking about the reconcilability of biological evolution with Thomistic metaphysics. In articulating his interpretation of the first book of Genesis in the *Summa theologiae*, Thomas considers the question of whether the work of creation is truly complete on the seventh day. The third objection in this article notes that many things of new species appear even today, through spontaneous generation—this is the view of Aristotle. In Thomas's reply, he points both to spontaneous generation and to hybridization as possible sources of novel species:

> Nothing entirely new was afterwards [i.e., after the seventh day] made by God; rather, [all things] in some way preceded [as already made] in the works of the six days. . . . Also new species, if these appear, preexisted in certain active powers, just as animals generated from putrefaction are produced by the powers of the stars [i.e., the heavenly bodies] and of the elements, which [powers] they received at the beginning, if new species of such animals should also be produced. Certain animals of a new species sometimes also arise from the connection of animals of diverse species, as when from a donkey and a horse there is generated a mule, and this [species] too previously existed causally in the works of the six days.[12]

Concerning this text, the question might be raised as to whether the mule is in fact a distinct species of animal in Thomas's or Aristotle's mind. In some well-known remarks about mules in *Metaphysics* 7, Aristotle indicates that

---

10. *ST* 3.79.2 ad 3: "Nihil autem prohibet causam instrumentalem producere potiorem effectum, ut ex supra dictis patet."
11. *In Sent.* 4.12.1.2 qc. 2 ad 2: "Ad secundum dicendum, quod propria virtute nihil agit ultra suam speciem: sed virtute alterius, cujus est instrumentum, potest agere ultra speciem suam, sicut serra agit ad formam scamni."
12. *ST* 1.73.1 ad 3.

although the mule is neither a horse nor a donkey, it is nevertheless of the same genus as its parents. In his commentary on this text, Thomas supplies as a name for this genus "beast of burden" (*iumentum*).[13] Some interpreters fill in the gaps in a way that would deny that the mule is a genuine species, by suggesting that the mule is somehow an imperfect member of a genus but not a member of a genuine species. This is not what Aristotle says, however, and it would seem impossible to square with Aristotle's understanding of genera and species to suppose that some individual could exist that was merely of a genus without belonging to a species.[14]

In any event, Thomas plainly asserts in another text from the *De potentia* that the mule is of a species distinct from both the horse and the donkey, a species as it were in the middle between them.[15] Thomas's position in *ST* 1.73.1 ad 3 is clear: there can be new species of living things that emerge after the work of the six days, so long as they are present in the active powers of things already created. That is, there must exist created things capable of causing their generation. Although this text concerning the seven days of creation is theological in character insofar as it expresses Thomas's interpretation of the creation narrative in Genesis 1, the view that novel species might arise from the active powers of already existent natural agents is strictly philosophical in character.

With respect to the mule, some interpreters also assume that Aristotle thinks that the mule is sterile simply because it is generated through hybridization, and that its sterility is a consequence and sign of its imperfection, or of its failure to be of a genuine species. Aristotle discusses the mule at some length in *De generatione animalium* 2.7–8. We do in fact find in c. 8 an argument along the lines just suggested. In attempting to explain the sterility of mules with what he calls an "abstract" and "general" proof of the sterility of mules, Aristotle suggests that perhaps their sterility is simply due to the fact that the mule arises from the copulation of two animals different in species, and it is different in kind from each of its parents.

Immediately after presenting this apparent proof, however, Aristotle proceeds to say that "this account is too general and empty, since theories not based on the appropriate principles are empty, appearing to be connected with the facts without really being so. . . . The basis of this particular account is not true, for many animals produced from different species are fertile, as was

---

13. My thanks to Michael Chaberek for pointing out that in an earlier version of this chapter, I mistakenly attributed to Aristotle rather than to Thomas the naming of this genus as "beast of burden." See Michael Chaberek, "Creation Is Not Generation: A Response to Brian Carl," *Studia Gilsoniana* 10, no. 1 (2021): 21–22.

14. See *De anima* 2.3.

15. *De pot.* 3.8 ad 16.

said before."[16] In fact, earlier in the *De generatione*, Aristotle lists numerous fertile hybrids of which he is aware, and he claims that as far as he knows, the mule alone is sterile among hybrid animals. Why then is this particular species sterile, in Aristotle's view? He proceeds to suggest that it has to do with the limited fecundities of the horse and the donkey. Each species typically gives birth to singletons, and it often takes repeated mating for conception to occur. The donkey has a colder nature than most quadrupeds, and the mare produces less menstrual blood than most female animals. That a colder nature makes for lower fertility is because Aristotle thinks that semen causes the generation of a new animal through vital heat, and he also thinks that menstrual blood is the matter from which the new animal is formed. Putting all of these factors together, Aristotle tells us that when a cross-breeding contrary to nature "is added to the difficulty they have in producing a single one when united with their own species, the result of the cross-breeding . . . will need nothing further to make it sterile."[17] Aristotle's fascination with the mule is not because it is not of a genuine species, but rather that there should exist any genuine species that is nevertheless by its nature sterile. But the explanation is to be found, he thinks, not in an abstract principle, but in the natures of the horse and the donkey from which the mule is descended.

3. Reproduction and Spontaneous Generation in Aristotle

The Aristotelian theory of animal generation—and Thomas's reception and understanding of that theory—cannot be properly understood without Aristotelian cosmology and elemental theory. Aristotle conceives of the cosmos as a concentric series of incorruptible celestial spheres rotating eternally around the earth. The lowest of these spheres is that bearing the moon; everything below that sphere is made of the four simple, elemental bodies of earth, air, fire, and water. These simple bodies make up the sorts of physical substances that are subject to generation and corruption. The celestial spheres are, by contrast, incorruptible, and so must not be composed of these simple bodies; the matter of the heavenly spheres is subject only to rotational locomotion, but to no other sort of change.

The four elemental bodies in the sublunary are understood by Aristotle fundamentally in terms of certain active and passive qualities—heat, coldness, moisture, and dryness—and each of his elemental bodies combines a pair of these contrary qualities, as fire is the hot and dry, water is the cold and wet, and so on. The celestial spheres, and in particular that bearing the sun, are causes of heat in

16. *De gen. anim.* 2.8 748a8–13 [Barnes 1160].
17. *De gen. anim.* 2.8 748b16–19 [Barnes 1161].

the sublunary: the sun heats the sublunary as its sphere rotates around the earth. The dependence of all substantial generation and corruption in the sublunary domain upon the rotation of the heavenly spheres is grounded in the claim that the primary active quality in all sublunary substances is heat, which is caused by the sun. In what follows, I will briefly present some basic theses from Aristotle's understanding of animal generation that are appropriated by Thomas.[18]

On the Aristotelian theory of the generation of living things, it is through heat that matter is qualitatively disposed to the generation of the new living substance, just as it is also through heat that an individual animal digests and assimilates food into itself through the hot blood that is concocted from food. In the case of reproduction among animals, the semen that comes from the father is itself concocted, purified blood.[19] The close relation between blood and semen in Aristotle's theory of reproduction is important to note: Blood is that through which the animal ultimately assimilates nutrients into itself, growing and healing by generating its homogeneous parts, such as flesh and bone, in an organized fashion. Semen is thoroughly concocted blood, endowed with a power similar to blood (i.e., a power to produce such things as flesh), but ordered to do so in the conception of a new individual, from the matter provided by the female.[20] As Thomas puts it, semen has a "formative virtue" derived from the soul of the parent.[21]

Aristotle compares semen to the tool of a carpenter, endowed with the movements given by the carpenter, as if a tool could be endowed with a tendency to move in the way necessary to form a table, even once separated from the hands of the carpenter.[22] But whereas the saw's movements are locomotions, semen acts through qualitative alteration by heating in a structured way.[23] And just as the saw does not become part of the table, so too Aristotle thinks of semen as an extrinsic agent that acts upon the passive matter—such as menstrual blood—supplied by the female.[24] Just as many of the individual

---

18. I am indebted to James Lennox, "Aristotle's Theory of Spontaneous Generation," in *Aristotle's Philosophy of Biology* (Cambridge: Cambridge University Press, 2001), 229–49, esp. 230–33; and to Daryn Lehoux, *Creatures Born of Mud and Slime* (Baltimore: Johns Hopkins University Press, 2017), 13–31.

19. *De gen. anim.* 1.18 726a26, 1.19 726b2–12.

20. *De gen. anim.* 2.4 740b24.

21. *ST* 1.71 ad 1; *De pot.* 3.9 ad 16.

22. *De gen. anim.* 1.22 730b9–24.

23. This is not to preclude cases in which human artifice involves qualitative alteration or even produces a substantial change. See the latter part of section 6 below for bread baking as an example of an artificially produced substantial change, in St. Thomas's view.

24. For the claim that the semen does not become part of the newly generated living thing, see *De gen. anim.* 2.3 737a12.

characteristics of a table are due to the characteristics of the wood upon which the saw acts (perhaps even contrary to what the carpenter intends through the movements of his tools), so too many individual characteristics of the generated animal are due to the mother, as she provides the proximate matter from which the animal is generated.

At this point, we should note that our contemporary understanding of sexual reproduction is quite different: the process of sexual reproduction is such that neither parent aims at a perfect copy of itself in all its individual characteristics, as the process is ordered *per se* toward some combination of traits of the parents or of the parents' own ancestors. In Aristotle's view, that the offspring should be anything but the spitting image of the father is always *praeter naturam*, apart from what the natural process of sexual reproduction intends. In contrast, with the modern understanding of sexual reproduction as a process that aims *per se* at a novel combination of traits, there is already more room for the notion of descent with modification.

4. Instrumental Causality in Thomas's Account of Generation

Because all heat in the sublunary depends on the activity of the sun, all reproductive generation also depends ultimately upon the sun. As Aristotle observes in *Physics* 2.2—an observation that is tremendously important for Thomas— "man and the sun generate a man." Thomas cites this observation frequently, and he takes it to mean that the sun and the individual animal are related to one another as (1) a universal, principal agent; and (2) a particular, instrumental agent. Just as a carpenter might use a tool—an instrument—to produce some effect by a motion that the carpenter imparts to the instrument, so Thomas thinks that all generative activity by individual animals depends on the heating action of the sun. The sun, as it were, uses the individual male animal as an instrument through which it produces new instances of the same species.

As noted above, in asserting the need for a proportion between causes and effects, Thomas distinguishes between universal causes and universal effects and particular causes and particular effects, asserting that universal effects must be proportioned to universal causes. Consider the following from c. 10 of Thomas's treatise *De substantiis separatis*:

> A twofold cause is found of some nature or form: one which is *per se* and absolutely the cause of such a nature or form; but another which is the cause of this nature or form in this [individual]. Indeed the necessity of this distinction is clear, if one considers the causes of things that are generated. For when a horse is generated, the generating horse is the cause

that the nature of a horse begins to exist in this [individual], but [the generating horse] is not the *per se* cause of the nature of horse. For in order for something to be the *per se* cause of some specific nature, it is necessary that it be its cause in all things having that species. Since therefore the generating horse has the same specific nature, it would need to be its own cause, which cannot be the case. It remains therefore that there must be, superior to all those things participating in the nature of horse, a universal cause of the entire species. Such a cause the Platonists held to be a species separate from matter, in the manner that the principle of all artificial things is the form in art [i.e., the artist's knowledge], not existing in matter. But according to the opinion of Aristotle, it is necessary to place this universal cause in some heavenly body: whence distinguishing these two causes, he said that man and the sun generate man.

In addition to the previously mentioned text from *Physics* 2.2, Thomas almost certainly has in mind here the discussion of the generation of living substances in *Metaphysics* 7, in which Aristotle rejects the theory of Platonic forms as causes of generation. In commenting on this part of *Metaphysics* 7, Thomas says that Aristotle intends to show, against Plato, that the natures and forms existing in individual sensible things need not be and could not be generated by forms existing outside of matter, but that they are generated "by forms which exist in matter" (*In Meta.* 7.6 #1381). (Here I would recall Thomas's assertion that if novel species arise after the work of the six days, they do so from active powers found among already existing species.) Furthermore, Aristotle does not, in Thomas's view, do away with a single universal cause of generation, a universal *per se* cause of the generated nature, but he places this cause too within the material universe, in a heavenly body, the sun. As Thomas puts it elsewhere, endorsing what he takes to be Aristotle's view, "whatever causes generation in these lower [bodies] moves [its patient] to a species as the instrument of a heavenly body."[25]

Here we come to a crucial point: it is not in fact Thomas's view that the individual generating animal is on its own a sufficient agent cause of the generation of a new animal within its own species, since the generating animal depends on its being moved by a higher agency in order to cause a thing's nature. The individual animal does not have a nature, on its own, in such a manner that it is able to give that nature to something else; it has that nature in such a manner that it can be used instrumentally by a superior cause. It also bears repeating that on Thomas's construal of Aristotelian metaphysics, against Platonic metaphysics, one needs to place the active causes for the generation of natural substances within the material universe. I will return to this point at the end of this study.

25. *ST* 1.115.3 ad 2.; cf. *SCG* 3.69 and *ST* 1.45.8 ad 3.

5. Spontaneous Generation and the Univocal Generation of Perfect Animals

Because the vital heat through which semen generates a new animal is itself ultimately from the sun, Aristotle and Thomas think that the phenomenon of spontaneous generation can be readily explained by the activity of heat present in nonliving matter acting upon matter that happens to have become disposed in such a way that something living can be generated from it (such as putrefying flesh or slimy mud). There is some indeterminacy about what results from spontaneous generation, as what results depends on how the matter happens to have been disposed, rather than on the sort of structured heating by semen that aims at educing a specific form with certain individual traits.

Spontaneous generation (or generation by chance) involves *per accidens* causation, as the activity of the proximate causes is not for the sake of producing a specific result. Thomas explains this in his *Commentary on the Metaphysics 7.6*:

> Nothing prohibits some generation from being *per se* when referred to one cause, which is nevertheless *per accidens* and by chance when referred to another cause, as is clear in the very example given by the Philosopher. For when health follows from a rubbing, outside the intention of the one rubbing, the health [that results], if it be referred to the nature that regulates the body, is not *per accidens*, but is intended *per se*. But if [the health that results] be referred to the mind of the one rubbing, it will be *per accidens* and by chance. Similarly too the generation of an animal generated by putrefaction, if it be referred to particular causes, the inferior agents, will be found to be *per accidens* and by chance. For the heat that causes decay does not intend by natural appetite the generation of this or that animal that arises from putrefaction in the way that the power which is from the semen does intend the production in a certain species. But if [the generation from putrefaction] be referred to the heavenly power, which is the universal regulative power of generations and corruptions in these inferior [bodies], it is not *per accidens*, but intended, since it is of the intention [of the heavenly body] that there be educed into actuality all the forms which exist in the potency of matter.[26]

The "proportionate causes" of spontaneously generated organisms include, for Thomas, both the incidental (*per accidens*) proximate cause and a *per se* remote, universal cause. In the case of generation through reproduction, the proximate cause acts as a *per se* cause whose causal activity is ordered

---

26. *In Meta.* 7.6 #1403.

toward a specific result, albeit still as a particular instrument of a universal, principal agent.

Aristotle in fact thinks that entirely new kinds of spontaneously generated animals may arise constantly, but he also holds that no spontaneously generated animal successfully reproduces in kind. On this point, we encounter a range of views in the later Peripatetic tradition. Thomas takes up this point in his commentary on *Metaphysics 7*, asserting (seemingly as an empirically observed fact) that there are species of plants that can be spontaneously generated and then go on to produce seed, thereby reproducing in kind. This is a rather tame position compared to that of Avicenna, who (as Thomas reports) asserts that any living species that can reproduce in kind—up to and including human beings—can also be produced, under the right material conditions, by spontaneous generation.[27]

Thomas, by contrast, draws the line at what he calls perfect animals. Plants and imperfect animals may arise by spontaneous generation, but the generation of perfect animals requires the instrumental contribution made by the animal reproducing within its species.[28] Where Thomas indicates what he means by "perfect animals," he points to the organic complexity of higher animals in comparison to lower animals and plants, telling us that "perfect animals have a supreme diversity in their organs, but plants a minimal [diversity]."[29] This is so because a perfect animal must have a wider range of powers, perhaps by having all of the senses, or more precisely, by having the internal-sense power of memory, in addition to imagination.[30]

It is essential to the notion of instrumental causality that an instrumental cause produces an effect that exceeds its own independent power, by virtue of its being moved by a principal agent, as the saw used by the carpenter produces a bed. But it is necessary to distinguish between those cases of instrumental causality in which the principal agent's own power is not augmented by the instrument and those in which the instrument does augment the power of the principal agent. All of the cases in which created agents act as instruments of divine agency are instances of the former sort, as a created instrumental cause never augments the power of the divine cause: God can produce immediately by his own power whatever he can also bring about through instrumental causes. But in many cases, a principal agent using an instrument is able to produce an effect that exceeds its power without the use of that instrument. Just as the tools of a carpenter also augment what the carpenter

---

27. *In Meta.* 7.6 #1399–1401.
28. *SCG* 3.69; *QDdA* 5.
29. *SCG* 2.72. Cf. *ST* 1.76.5 ad 3, *ST* 1.76.8, *QDdA* 10 ad 15.
30. *In Meta.* 1.1 #9. *In Meta.* 1.1 #14. Cf. *ST* 1.78.4.

can accomplish through his hands, so in Thomas's view the heavenly body needs the contribution made by the reproducing animal in order to produce another instance of the animal species.[31]

Why should the instrumental contribution made by a univocal generator be necessary in the case of perfect animals, whose organic complexity surpasses plants and imperfect animals? Given his commitment to the view that animals like flies are spontaneously generated from rotting flesh, it is not that Thomas thinks that it is beyond the power of heat from the sun to educe the form of an animal with powers for sensation and locomotion. Thomas thinks, however, that the "structured" heating accomplished by semen is necessary in order to account for the formation of the more complex bodies of higher animals. By what principle does Thomas reach this conclusion? Thomas asserts that "the power of a heavenly body suffices for generating certain less perfect animals from disposed matter, for it is obvious that more [things] are required for the production of a perfect thing than for the production of an imperfect thing."[32] This principle that "more things" are required for the production of what is more perfect would seem to find some explanation in a text from *De malo* 16.9, which examines a question we will discuss below; namely, whether a created immaterial substance (or more specifically, in *De malo* 16.9, a demon) can cause a qualitative or substantial change in a bodily thing.

In addressing this question in *De malo* 16.9, Thomas asserts that generally, a more remote agent—he must mean a created agent rather than the divine agent—produces a weaker effect immediately, while needing a mediating agent to produce a more powerful effect. In the same text, he offers the following to illustrate his point:

> For we see among sensible things that a weak effect is produced by a remote agent, but a strong effect requires a nearby agent; for something can be heated by fire, even if it is remote from the fire, but it cannot be ignited unless it is close to the fire, so that someone who wishes to ignite a thing that is remote from a fire in a lit furnace accomplishes this by means of a candle. And similarly the generation of perfect animals is caused by the heavenly bodies by means of proper active [causes], but the generation of imperfect animals [is caused by them] immediately.[33]

I would highlight here Thomas's explanation of why the heavenly body needs the instrumental contribution made by the univocal generator. The general

---

31. *In Meta.* 7.6 #1401.
32. *ST* 1.91.2 ad 2. Cf. *In Sent.* 2.18.2.3 ad 5; *De pot.* 3.11 ad 12; and *In Meta.* 7.6 #1401.
33. *De malo* 16.9.

principle employed is not a version of the principle of proportionate causality; it is instead a principle about the need for mediating instrumental causes in order for a created remote cause to produce a more powerful effect. This principle hardly seems irreconcilable with a theory of biological evolution.

Separate Substances as the Living, Intelligent Movers of the Heavenly Spheres

I argued above that the instrumental causality of a univocal generator, in Thomas's account, should impact how we understand the applicability of the principle of proportionate causality to the generation of living things. But there is a serious objection with which I must contend, which is grounded in how Thomas himself replies to a series of objections motivated by something like the principle of proportionate causality.

In *De pot.* 3.11, Thomas considers the question of whether the sensitive or vegetative soul is transmitted through semen in the generation of an animal, a question to which he gives an affirmative answer (albeit with the qualification, consistent with what we have seen above, that the sensitive and the vegetative soul are in the semen virtually rather than actually). The twelfth objection argues, contrary to Thomas's view, that the soul of a spontaneously generated animal must be created because in this case there is no agent similar in species to the animal by which it might be produced. Even more, the objection insists, it must be that the souls of animals generated by semen must also be created. The thirteenth objection begins with a likely response (a *sed dices*) to the twelfth objection, followed by a *sed contra*:

> But you will say that the sensitive soul is produced, in animals generated out of decay, by the power of a celestial body, just as [it is produced] in other [animals] by the formative power in semen. On the contrary, as Augustine says, a living substance is preeminent in comparison to every non-living substance. But a celestial body is not a living substance, since it is inanimate. Therefore a sensitive soul, which is a principle of life, cannot be produced by its power.[34]

Here the counterobjection does appeal implicitly to something like the principle of proportionate causality. This is then followed in the fourteenth objection by another *sed dices* and *sed contra*:

> But you will say that a heavenly body can be the cause of a sensible soul, insofar as it acts in the power of the intellectual substance which moves

34. *De pot.* 3.11 obj. 13.

it. On the contrary, what is received in another is in it [i.e., the recipient] in the mode of the recipient and not in its own mode. If therefore the power of an intellectual substance is received in a non-living heavenly body, it will not be [received] there as a vital power which can be a principle of life.[35]

In replying to this series of objections and counterobjections, Thomas begins by citing the principle we have already discussed, that "the more imperfect something is, the fewer are [the things] required for its constitution."[36] The power of a heavenly body is sufficient to produce the sensitive soul in an imperfect animal, but the heavenly body needs the contribution made by the reproducing animal in the case of perfect animals. Even though the heavenly body is not similar in species to a spontaneously generated animal, "there is nevertheless a likeness insofar as the effect preexists virtually in [its] active cause."[37] So far, this is consistent with what I have said above.

In replying to the thirteenth objection and counterobjection, which had raised the concern that a heavenly body cannot be the cause of something living because it is not itself living, Thomas replies by noting that "even if a heavenly body is not alive, it nevertheless acts in the power of the living substance by which it is moved, whether this be an angel or God; but a heavenly body is regarded as animated and alive according to the philosophers."[38] Here we do find Thomas replying to an objection motivated by something like the principle of proportionate causality by noting that although a heavenly body is not alive, the separate substance in whose power it acts is alive. The dialectical character of his reply is rather clear, given that he cites what he takes to be Aristotle's opinion—that the heavenly bodies are in fact animated—as an alternative reply that would satisfy the objector, but he does not commit to whether it is the divine agent or a created separate substance that moves the heavenly bodies.

In any event, there is no question in Thomas's mind that the divine cause must be intelligent and living, and that God is known to be so based on the presence of such pure perfections in creatures; Thomas is absolutely clear that all perfections must be found preeminently in the first cause. The objector is right to hold that what is living cannot be generated without the agency of something that is living; the question is whether the created agent possessing the proper power through which generation is caused must itself be living. Thomas's reply is that it suffices to answer the concern of the objector (i.e.,

---

35. *De pot.* 3.11 obj. 14.
36. *De pot.* 3.11 ad 12.
37. *De pot.* 3.11 ad 12.
38. *De pot.* 3.11 ad 13.

that some principal agent be living), but this has to be maintained along with the claim that the celestial body is an instrument without which a created separate substance could not generate a living thing.

The reply to the fourteenth objection and counterobjection illuminates the causal relationship between a created separate mover and the heavenly bodies in the generation of living things:

> The power of the living substance moving [the heavenly body] remains in the heavenly body and its motion not as a form having complete existence in a nature, but in the mode of an intention, just as the power of art is in the instrument of the artisan.[39]

I would suggest that Thomas's comparison of the agency of a human artisan using an instrument to produce an artifact and the agency of a separate substance moving a heavenly body in order to generate living things is quite exact, particularly if we think about a case in which human artistry produces a substantial change by using the natural powers of some instrument.

Let us take the case of a baker producing bread through a fire in an oven. Thomas explicitly maintains that bread is a substance, and that the form of bread is a substantial form. In replying to an objection (in his discussion of transubstantiation) against the status of bread as a substance, appealing to the fact that bread is an artifact, Thomas replies that "nothing prohibits something being made by art whose form is not an accident but a substantial form." Here he offers a somewhat surprising example that frogs and snakes can be produced by art.[40] So, in Thomas's view, baked bread is a substance

---

39. *De pot.* 3.11 ad 14 [Marietti 75]: "Ad decimumquartum dicendum, quod virtus substantiae virtualis moventis relinquitur in corpore caelesti et motu eius, non sicut forma habens esse completum in natura, sed per modum intentionis, sicut virtus artis est in instrumento artificis." The Parma edition (1859) has *spiritualis* in place of *virtualis*, which would make better sense; I have opted to read *virtualis* here as *vitalis*.

40. *ST* 3.75.6 ad 1. In addition, Thomas refers to the "substantial form of bread" in the body of this article. As for frogs and snakes generated by art, Thomas makes clear elsewhere that he has in mind the art practiced by magicians, such as those of Pharaoh, and that this art involves the cooperation of demons. For texts concerning the generation of frogs by such an art, see *SCG* 3.104; *ST* 1.114.4 ad 2, 2–2.178.1 ad 2; *De malo* 16.9 ad 10. In any case, Thomas is clear that the magician and the demon make use of the powers of nature to produce frogs, which Thomas includes among kinds that can be spontaneously generated (see *ST* 1.114.4 ad 2). For recent discussion of the status of bread as a substance in Thomas's thought, see Michael Rota, "Substance and Artifact in Thomas Aquinas," *History of Philosophy Quarterly* 21, no. 3 (2004): 241–59; Christopher Brown, "Artifacts, Substances, and Transubstantiation: Solving a Puzzle for Aquinas's Views," *The Thomist* 71, no. 1 (2007): 89–112; and Anna Marmodoro and Ben Page, "Aquinas on Forms, Substances, and Artifacts," *Vivarium* 54, no. 1 (2016): 1–21.

that is produced by a human artisan using the natural power of fire as an instrument (*In Sent.* 4.11.1.1 qc. 3 ad 3).

Although there is no natural process ordered *per se* toward the generation of bread, bread is produced *per se* by a baker, who uses the natural power of fire to heat the appropriate mixture of blended constituents in order to generate bread. Nothing would preclude bread being produced *per accidens* within nature: if wheat happened to be ground into flour by falling stones, which happened to be moistened by light rain into dough, which then happened to be heated by a brushfire (as improbable as the conjunction of these events might be), then bread would be naturally produced *per accidens*. But the preparation of dough as matter and the efficient causality of fire are intentionally ordered by a human baker, who intends bread as an effect and is a *per se* cause of the generation of bread. This is an instance in which the instrument augments the power of the principal agent, as the baker needs the oven in order to make the bread.

The causal relationship between (i) the baker, (ii) the fire in the oven, and (iii) the bread produced is, importantly, equivalent to the causal relationship between (i) a created immaterial mover, (ii) the heavenly body, and (iii) a living thing spontaneously generated in the sublunary. Just as the baker cannot produce the form of bread except through fire, for Thomas, created separate substances are unable to directly cause any formal transmutation of bodily substances; they are limited to causing changes of place. If a separate substance wishes to cause any transmutation of a bodily substance, it must use a mediating body, "just as a man can heat something through fire."[41] Just as the baker is the *per se* cause of the bread because he knows and intends the effect and employs fire as an instrument to bring about this effect, so the separate substance that causes the rotary locomotion of the heavenly sphere intends the generation of living things and employs the heavenly body as its instrument in the production of this effect. And just as bread could in principle be produced in nature *per accidens*, however improbable that might be, so too I would suggest that in Thomas's cosmology if (*per impossibile*) there were any way for the heavens to undergo their circular rotation other than by the agency of separate movers, then the heavens would cause corruptions and generations, including spontaneous generations, in the sublunary.

That is, there is nothing in Thomas's account of the role of created separate substances as intelligent principal agents whose instruments are the heavenly bodies that would suggest that the natural power of the celestial

---

41. *De malo* 16.9.

body for causing generation in the sublunary in any way depends on the intellectual or volitional acts of the separate substance, any more than the power of fire to generate bread from flour depends on the baker's intellectual or volitional acts. The power of the fire and the power of the celestial body are only moved to produce bread and living things as *per se* effects by an intelligent principal agent, but in neither case does the intelligent principal agent give the power for generation to the instrument. Again, both the oven and the heavenly body augment the powers of their created principal agents.

If this account of the causal relationship between a created separate substance and an animal generated in the sublunary is correct, then Thomas's reply to the objection motivated by the principle of proportionate causality need not undercut what I have argued above. Even if Thomas is willing to grant that some principal agent—whether this be a created immaterial mover or God—must be living in order for something living to be generated, it nevertheless remains that the nonliving heavenly body is for Thomas the agent with the natural power to educe the forms of spontaneously generated animals and, through the instrumentality of animals within the sublunary, to bring about reproduction within a species.

7. Universal Causes and Contemporary Cosmology

My presentation of Thomas's understanding of the proportionate causes of living species invites questions about how one might adapt his views to contemporary cosmology and biology. Perhaps the most pressing question is this: Can we identify anything that might play a similar role as the sun in Thomas's account; as in, as a universal, principal *per se* cause of generated living things?

To be clear, if we were to construct an account in which the role played by the celestial bodies was simply removed, leaving living things themselves to be identified as principal *per se* causes of their offspring, we would be departing greatly from Thomas's views concerning the proportionate causes of living things. In such a case, if one wished to otherwise maintain continuity with Thomas's views, only the divine agent could be identified as a universal cause of generation or as the *per se* cause of the generation of a novel species. But as we have seen, this too would represent a significant departure from Thomas's views, given his commitment to the claim that all generation has a *per se* cause that is a material agent.

In the Aristotelian cosmology accepted by Thomas, the celestial bodies among which he places the principal *per se* cause of generation are also more generally identified as prior movers with respect to all sublunary motions, whose own activity must causally depend on the divine first mover.[42] It is a commonly held view among many recent interpreters of Thomas that the argument from motion for God's existence is concerned with *per se* ordered series of moved movers rather than *per accidens* ordered series. This is so because the argument from motion employs the premise that a regress to infinity in moved movers is impossible, but Thomas would seem to acknowledge in some texts that there can be an infinite regress in a *per accidens* ordered series of movers or causes. It is also a commonly held view that every *per se* ordered series of movers or causes must be synchronic, such that the activity of the first mover in such a series is simultaneous with the motion of the last thing moved. On this view, if a series of movers or causes is diachronic, then it must be ordered only *per accidens*. If such a reading of Thomas's views about series of moved movers is correct, then it would seem to follow that anything identified as a universal *per se* cause of generation—something that would be a principal cause using an individual animal as an instrument, like the sun in Thomas's account—must be something whose existence and activity as a mover is temporally simultaneous with the activity of the reproducing animal.

Without attempting to identify any particular bodily substance as a universal *per se* cause of generation, I would suggest that Thomas's views would permit us to expand the range of bodies that could be regarded as playing something like the role of the sun, beyond the restriction imposed by the claim that a *per se* ordered series is always synchronic. This is so because Thomas denies that a principal, *per se* cause that uses something posterior as an instrument must act simultaneously with that instrument. As noted above, Thomas characterizes an animal's semen as an instrument of that animal, which acts in virtue of that animal's reproductive power. But in Aristotle's and Thomas's view, semen's effect is not produced all at once, and it should be apparent that semen can continue to produce its effect even if the animal that produced it dies. Thomas makes this point explicitly in response to an objection from *De pot.* 3.11. The objection is as follows:

> But you will say that the power that is in the semen, although it is not the sensible soul in act, it nevertheless acts in virtue of the sensible soul that was in the father, from whom the semen was derived. On the contrary, that which acts in the power of another acts as the instrument of that [other]. But an instrument does not move unless [it be] moved; but mover and moved must be together [*simul*], as was proved in *Physics*

---

42. For one indication of this, see the version of the argument from motion contained in *Comp. theo.* 1.3, in which Thomas begins the argument from motion by pointing to the celestial bodies as the movers of the elemental bodies, before proceeding to argue that a divine first mover must exist.

7. Since therefore the power which is in the semen is not joined to the sensible soul of the generating [animal], it seems that it cannot act as its instrument nor in virtue of it.[43]

In replying to this objection, Thomas offers the following:

> An instrument is understood to be moved by a principal agent so long as it retains the power impressed by the principal agent; whence the arrow is moved by the one projecting it so long as the power of the projector's impulse remains [in it], just as among heavy and light [bodies] the generated is moved by the generator so long as it retains the form given to it by the generator. Whence semen is also understood to be moved by the soul of the generating [animal] so long there remains in it the power impressed by the soul, even though it is separated bodily [from it]. For it is necessary for the mover and moved to be together [*simul*] at the beginning of the motion, but not for the entire motion, as is clear with projectiles.[44]

This text might have important implications for how interpreters of Thomas ought to think about *per se* ordered series and the impossibility of infinite regress in moved movers, but I will set these possible implications aside only to note that this text is clear on one point: for Thomas, something can be identified as a principal agent with respect to some instrument, even if the activity of the instrument is temporally posterior. If we were to look to identify something physical as a principal *per se* agent with respect to the generation of living things, we would not need to restrict our consideration to things that exist and act now.[45]

Conclusion

As I have noted above, although he places restrictions on which living things can arise by chance from the activity of ambient vital heat, in general, Thomas sees no difficulty with spontaneously produced organisms reproducing in turn. As we have also seen in Thomas's and Aristotle's discussion of the mule, there is no prohibition against two animals reproducing in such a way that what

---

43. *De pot.* 3.11 obj. 5.
44. *De pot.* 3.11 ad 5.
45. Here, by way of example, I would note a suggestion made by Robert C. Koons, that one should likely think of the initial state of the cosmos in Big Bang cosmology as a single substance. [I heard a lecture in which Koons made this suggestion.] In such a case, we might identify this single physical substance as the *per se* principal generative cause of everything produced in time.

results is something different in species from either of the parents; and the sterility of the mule is not, for Aristotle, a consequence of its being a hybrid. It should be clear that such claims, taken together, might provide grounds for optimism about the reconcilability of Thomistic philosophy with biological evolution. Furthermore, as we have seen, the only general metaphysical principle that Thomas invokes in order to argue for the need for the instrumental contribution of a univocal generator is not the principle of proportionate causality. Instead, it is the principle that a remote, created universal cause needs the instrumental contribution of mediating instruments to produce more powerful effects. This principle seems reconcilable with evolution as well—although to articulate this reconciliation would require much further work.

If it is the case that metaphysical principles like the principle that effects cannot exceed their causes can only be understood in their concrete application in the biology and cosmology of Aristotle and Thomas, then we should exercise due caution when bringing such principles to bear in thinking through problems posed by contemporary biology, chemistry, and physics. The preceding arguments have been offered in the hope of giving some flesh and bones to the somewhat abstract metaphysical claims that the potential is preceded by the actual, and that whatever is in the effect must first be virtually in the cause. To understand these metaphysical principles as Aristotle and Thomas do requires that one think through the causal claims involved in their physics and biology. No principle in Aristotle or Thomas regarding "the perfect not arising from the imperfect" precludes the generation of new kinds of living things by chance. The requirement for univocal generators for higher animals is not a consequence of a metaphysical principle of proportionate causality; it is grounded more in physical and biological views about the difference between ambient vital heat and the structured heating performed by semen. If there were some disposed matter that could be acted upon in the necessary way by some physical agent other than sperm concocted from the blood of a male horse, there would be for Thomas no metaphysical prohibition against a horse arising by chance. Whether an account of reproduction grounded in biochemistry and genetics makes more room than the account grounded in the Aristotelian elemental theory for the *per accidens* generation of new species that go on to reproduce in kind is a question for the biologist—metaphysics does not preclude an affirmative answer.

Finally, I would emphasize that it is no accident that spontaneous generation and the generation of the mule through hybridization are discussed by Aristotle and Thomas in their argumentation against the need for Platonic separate forms as principles of generation. Their purpose is to show that causes they identify in the natural world—the reproducing animals, even if they are of different species, the sun and the heat that it causes—are adequate for explaining the generation of all living things. In an Aristotelian cosmos, the active powers that generate living things are the powers of physical agents. In many recent discussions of how to possibly reconcile Thomistic metaphysics with biological evolution, contemporary authors have made direct recourse to the causality of the divine agent, who would be able to infuse the form of a new species into the first member of a new kind whenever the matter apt for that form has arisen by chance. Perhaps this is the metaphysical conclusion one needs to arrive at; but if so, we will have left Aristotelian or Thomistic metaphysics behind on one of its central conclusions about natural substances. It is ironic, but understandable, that some have been led to do this, from a version of the principle of proportionate causality derived from the very discussion in which Aristotle and Thomas have argued against Plato. But perhaps we should instead be optimistic with Thomas that it pertains to the goodness of the divine to endow creation with the power to act as a genuine cause of anything moved or generated.

CHAPTER FOUR

Nihil dat quod non habet:
Thomist Naturalism Contra Supernaturalism on the Origin of Species

DANIEL D. DE HAAN

quod ex quo omne quod generatur, generatur ex materia,
et iterum generatur a suo simili, impossibile est aliquid esse factum,
nisi aliquid praeexistat, sicut dicitur communiter.
Communis enim philosophorum naturalium sententia erat,
quod ex nihilo nihil fit.[1]

Many Thomists believe that the principle "nothing can give what it does not possess" is contravened by hylomorphic explanations of the natural evolutionary origins of biological species. Inanimate substances cannot generate animate substances and vegetative substances

---

1. *In VII Meta.* lect. 6, §1412. See *QDSC* 3 obj. 16; *SCG* 3.66. All citations from Thomas Aquinas are taken from the following editions, unless noted otherwise. *Scriptum super libros sententiarum*, ed. P. Mandonnet and M. F. Moos, 4 vols. (Paris: Lethielleux, 1929–1947) (= *In Sent.*); *Summa theologiae* (Rome: Editiones Paulinae, 1962) (= *ST*); *Liber de veritate catholicae Fidei contra errores infidelium seu Summa contra Gentiles*, t. 2–3., ed. P. Marc, C. Pera, and P. Caramello (Rome: Marietti Editori, 1961) (= *SCG*); *In Duodecim Libros Metaphysicorum Aristotelis Exposito*, ed. M.-R. Cathala and R. M. Spiazzi (Rome: Marietti Editori, 1950) (= *In Meta.*); *Quaestiones disputatae*, t. 2, *Quaestiones disputatae de potentia dei*, (= *QDP*), ed. P. M. Pession (Rome: Marietti Editori, 1965); I have used the following editions of the Leonine, *Sancti Thomae de Aquino Opera omnia*, Leonine ed. (Rome, 1882 –), vol. 22.1–3, *Questiones disputatae de veritate* (= *DV*); vol. 23, *Questiones disputatae de Malo* (= *De malo*); vol. 24.2, *Quaestio disputata de spiritualibus creaturis* (= *QDSC*); vol. 42, *Compendium theologiae* (= *CT*); vol. 43, *De mixtione elementorum*; vol. 50, *Super Boetium De Trinitate* (= *In Boet. de Trinitate*). Unless noted otherwise, English translations are from Thomas Aquinas, *Disputed Questions on the Power of God*, translation by English Dominican Fathers (Westminster, MD: Newman Press, 1952); Thomas Aquinas, *Summa theologica*, translated by Fathers of the English Dominican Province (Westminster, MD: Christian Classics, 1981); Thomas Aquinas, *Summa Contra Gentiles, Book III: Providence*, translated, with an introduction and notes, by Vernon Burke (Notre Dame, IN: University of Notre Dame Press, 1975); Thomas Aquinas, *Commentary on the Metaphysics of Aristotle*, translated by John P. Rowan (Chicago: Henry Regnery, 1961).

cannot generate sensitive substances because they both lack the ontological perfections required to generate these "ontologically superior" substances. I shall argue that this construal of what is called the "principle of proportionate causality" (PPC) presupposes two mistakes. The first is an atomized hylomorphism that overlooks the potentialities and actualities of the natural systems of interacting hylomorphic substances within the cosmos. The second is the mistaken assumption that this ontologically superior construal of the PPC is the most plausible and defensible Thomist version of the PPC. My major contribution to debates over the PPC is twofold. First, I demonstrate that this construal is in fact the more problematic, implausible, and less defensible version of the PPC. Second, I show why Thomists should instead endorse the "sufficiently powerful" construal of the PPC, which is compatible with Thomist naturalistic explanations of evolution. Clearing away these obstacles will open a pathway forward to more complete Thomist naturalistic explanations of how systems of hylomorphic substances do possess the powers required to generate new ontological species within the cosmos.

In the first section, I introduce and contrast Thomist naturalism with Thomist supernaturalism. Thomist supernaturalism maintains that God needs to intervene within the cosmos to engender major ontological leaps in nature, because creatures or secondary causes are insufficient to generate novel ontological species. Thomist naturalism holds that systems of hylomorphic substances in the cosmos created by God can generate novel ontological species without special divine intervention. In the second section, I sketch the explanatory framework presupposed by Thomist naturalism's account of eductive speciation as a distinct kind of substantial change. I draw attention to the error of hylomorphic atomism and how the finality of the cosmos underlies the *per se* and *per accidens* effects of systems of co-manifesting hylomorphic substances. In the third section, I explain why Thomist naturalism does not violate the PPC, and I present counterarguments that show how Thomist supernaturalism's rival construal of this principle leads to an insurmountable dilemma and entails the absurd result that special divine intervention is required to educe the requisite substantial forms in every instance of natural sexual reproduction.

1. Thomist Naturalism and Supernaturalism on the Origin of Species

Thomist naturalism and Thomist supernaturalism hold two different positions on the evolutionary origins of species within the cosmos, but they both hold in common the following understanding of reality: God creates, conserves, and governs the cosmos, which is the totality of all created hylomorphic physical beings. God is *qua* omnipresent primary cause the eternal Creator, Conserver, and Orderer of all creaturely acts of all created entities within the cosmos. These creaturely acts *qua* secondary causes are the creaturely operations performed by created hylomorphic beings. God alone is the Creator acting *qua* Creator. God does not act *qua* creature, for it is the created beings that are the creaturely agents acting as they do in creaturely ways according to the creaturely natures and powers God created them to be and to manifest. God is the Creator, universal cause, and ultimate source of the *ratio* (or nature) of every creature that comes into being via creation or adornment.² For example, God is the Creator and exemplar source of the *esse* and *essentia* (or nature) of an oak tree, but God *qua* Creator does not perform creaturely operations like photosynthesis; it is the creaturely agent, the oak tree, whose natural powers enable it to photosynthesize. It is a category mistake to suppose that Creator and creature are in competition for a single causal slot or that Creator and creature cooperation results in a problematic overdetermination. Aquinas teaches us to distinguish the way the creature is a real creaturely agent actualizing creaturely phenomena insofar as this is precisely what the Creator *qua* primary cause brings into existence and sustains in existence by creating. Miracles require another explanation, for they are unique ways in which divine providence has ordained to intervene in a distinct fashion within the governmental execution of creation via secondary causes.

According to Thomist naturalism, the cosmos is endowed with all of the secondary causal potentialities required *qua* interacting secondary causes to eventually bring about, via adornment (*opus ornatus*), the generative eduction of all fundamental particles, atoms, and molecules, galactic, stellar, and planetary systems, along with the abiogenesis and evolution of all living organisms, including the emergence of sentient animals.³ The principled exception is the

---

2. Andrew Davison, "'He Fathers-Forth Whose Beauty Is Past Change,' but 'Who Knows How?': Evolution and Divine Exemplarity," *Nova et Vetera* 16, no. 4 (2018): 1067–102; Mariusz Tabaczek, "The Metaphysics of Evolution: From Aquinas's Interpretation of Augustine's Concept of *Rationes Seminales* to the Contemporary Thomistic Account of Species Transformism," *Nova et Vetera* 18, no. 3 (2020): 945–72.

3. For other presentations of Thomist naturalism on evolutionary transformism similar to my own, see Bernard Lonergan, *Insight: A Study of Human Understanding* (Toronto: University of Toronto Press, 1997); Benedict Ashley, "Causality and Evolution," *Thomist* 36 (1972): 199–230; Mariusz Tabaczek "What Do God and Creatures Really Do in an Evolutionary Change? Divine Concurrence and Transformism from the Thomistic Perspective," *American Catholic Philosophical Quarterly* 93, no. 3 (2019): 445–82; Ernan McMullin, "Introduction: Evolution and Creation," in *Evolution and Creation*, ed. Ernan McMullin (Notre Dame, IN: University of Notre Dame Press, 1985), 1–56; and James F. Ross, "Christians Get the Best of Evolution," in McMullin, *Evolution and Creation*, 223–51.

immaterial rational soul of humans that cannot be educed from any totality of hylomorphic secondary causes, because there is no material potentiality for a *per se* subsisting immaterial form or rational soul.[4]

According to Thomist supernaturalism, God's created cosmos does not have sufficient secondary causal efficacy to generatively educe some or all hylomorphic substances. God's miraculous interventions into His created cosmos are therefore required to supply the novel substantial forms and ontological species that the order of created secondary causes within the cosmos are incapable of educing by their own powers from the potentialities latent in other hylomorphic substances.

My focus shall be the major disagreements between Thomist naturalism and supernaturalism on the evolutionary origins of species. In order to defend Thomist naturalism against the philosophical objections raised by Thomist supernaturalism, I need to develop at length the basic commitments of Thomist naturalism that pertain to the eductive generation of novel species. The major objection raised against Thomist naturalism is that its explanation of the origin of substantial forms for novel biological species violates the PPC, which states that "whatever perfection exists in an effect must be found in the effective cause."[5] How can secondary causes educe substantial forms for biological organisms when none of these secondary causes seem to possess these forms formally, virtually, or eminently?

The major objection against Thomist supernaturalism I shall present is that its construal of the PPC entails that the secondary causes of the cosmos are insufficient to generate many or all wholly hylomorphic substances. Avicenna defends a view like this. He argues that an immaterial substance outside of the cosmos, called the "Giver of Forms" (*dator formarum*) or agent intellect, is what beams down the exigent substantial forms whenever the occasions for substantial generation arise among the accidental causal commerce of already existing substances. Aquinas rejects Avicenna's *dator formarum* theory of generation along with its attendant occasionalism. I dub this error

---

4. "Although the rational soul has matter for its subject, it is not educed from the potentiality of matter, since its nature is raised above the entire material order, as is evidenced by its intellectual operation. Moreover, this form is a self-subsistent thing that remains when the body dies." *QDP* 3.8 ad 7 (trans. English Dominican Fathers). See *QDP* 3.4 ad 7; 3.9; *ST* 1.90.2 ad 2. Note that the rational soul is distinctive in being a *per se* subsistent immaterial form, whereas the substantial forms for all other hylomorphic substances are only immaterial in the sense of not being the material principle. It is better to say their forms are "nonmaterial" and reserve the term "immaterial" for separable or separate *per se* subsisting forms like the rational soul.

5. *ST* 1.4.2. See Ed Feser, *Scholastic Metaphysics: A Contemporary Introduction* (Editiones Scholasticae, 2014), 171–76.

dator-formarumism. Aquinas argues instead that secondary causes are sufficient to educe from matter the substantial forms needed to generate hylomorphic substances. Later I shall argue that the very arguments Thomist supernaturalism employs—both to reject Thomist naturalism's explanation of evolved novel species and to defend the supernatural origins of all novel substantial forms—entail a problematic form of *dator-formarumism*.

Thomist naturalism and supernaturalism, as I have characterized them, both acknowledge that if their respective positions have these fundamental problems, then there is something mistaken about their antecedent theses. So, both Thomist positions have clearly delineated conditions for their falsification, or at least for the exigency to substantively revise their positions.

2. Hylomorphism and Eductive Speciation

It will be helpful to start with how hylomorphism provides an *explanans* for, among other *explananda*, the *explanandum* of real change in nature. Physical things change in two basic ways. First, they change their attributes while remaining the same kind of thing. A dog can walk around, grow larger, shed its winter fur, and become a parent in relation to its offspring. These are accidental changes. Second, a substance, for example a dog, can change in a more fundamental way as well, insofar as it can cease to be what it is fundamentally. If the dog corrupts, the material components of its corpse become or generate a conglomeration of decaying organic material substances. Common to all these forms of change are three *explanantia*, two of which designate real or ontic explanatory factors; namely, the subject of change and its actual formal determination. The third *explanans* is a privation; that is, some potential alternative formal determination. Water with the actual form of being cold has the potential to become hot; the dog has the potential to corrupt and to become a corpse.

This Aristotelian explanation of accidental and substantial change provides the basis for the doctrine of hylomorphism, wherein matter (*hyle*) is the ontic *explanans* that is the subject of substantial change, and form (*morphe*) is the ontic *explanans* for the actual substantial determination of that subject of change. A substantial form actualizes the matter and thereby generates, organizes, unifies, and stabilizes a substance and its integral parts, and grounds its panoply of powers and other attributes. The essence or nature of any hylomorphic substance is comprised by this union of formal actuality and material potentiality. A substance's substantial formal actuality never exhausts all the potentialities of its matter. Some of these unactualized potentialities are more proximate and so more likely than others to be actualized through the perpetual bombardment by sundry contrary formal determinations (the *explanans* called a privation or privative form) that hylomorphic substances are subjected to.

Many Thomists assume there is only one kind of substantial change; namely, the generation of a substance by the eduction of a substantial form from the material potentialities of other hylomorphic substances corrupted by this generation. But (a) generation and corruption is distinct from other kinds of substantial change, such as (b) substantial ontogenesis (e.g., organogenesis and the developmental changes from an embryo to a fetus, to an infant, to a child, to an adolescent, and so on); (c) substantial mereological change (e.g., when a substance's integral parts are transformed by impairment, as with lesioned organs, or are entirely separated as with severed limbs); and (d) substantial fusion (e.g., the "virtual presence" or appropriation without corruption of retrievable elements, molecules, and other attributes into a substance). Recognizing how rich and varied the notion of substantial change is sets aside pseudo-objections against evolutionary substantial changes based on the mistaken assumption that generation and corruption is the only kind of substantial change. To these varieties of substantial change Thomist naturalism proposes another: (e) "eductive speciation." Eductive speciation consists in the generation of a novel species of hylomorphic substance by the total, proximate, and equivocal secondary causes actually educing a novel substantial form from the proximate potentialities of a nexus of interacting hylomorphic substances. Eductive speciation takes place in the generation of novel inanimate species, like the nucleosynthesis of gold or platinum from rapid process neutron capture, and it occurs in the generation of novel animate species, like the evolution of various species of cetaceans from artiodactyls. Unpacking and then defending a preliminary account of eductive speciation will be my main focus in this chapter.

2.1 Systems of Interacting Hylomorphic Substances

The first piece of the eductive speciation puzzle presupposes the Thomist distinction between univocal and equivocal causes and effects.[6] The effects of univocal agents have the same species as their causes, like hot fire causing heat in a patient or two horses begetting horse offspring; they actually possess the forms or attributes they cause.[7] Equivocal causes do not actually exhibit the forms they cause in their effects, but equivocal agents can possess these forms virtually; that is, they can have the power to contribute to the production of these forms. Furthermore, an equivocal cause of generation need not virtually

---

6. See Christopher A. Decaen, "An Inductive Study of the Notion of Equivocal Causality in St. Thomas," *The Thomist* 79, no. 2 (2015): 213–63.
7. See *In VII Meta.* lect. 8, nn. 1443–1459; *DV* 11.2, et ad 4; 4.6; *SCG* 1.29; *QDP* 5.1; *De malo* 1.3; *In Boet. De Trinitate* q. 1, a. 1, ad 4.

possess or have the power to actualize the whole form of what is generated, but only the power to actualize some part of it or a part of some part.[8] For Aquinas, the sun is a universal and equivocal cause of all living things on earth insofar as it contributes vital heat to the generation of all living things without contributing the substantial form in the eduction of substantial forms of plants or animals.[9]

Every instance of natural generation of a substance by the eduction of its substantial form from the potentialities of matter involves the concert manifestations of proximate particular and universal causes, along with proximate univocal and equivocal causes. God is always the Creator and primary universal cause of the secondary causal agents and patients of the cosmos, but there are also created universal causes like the active and passive elemental qualities of heat and cold (for Aquinas), or the four fundamental forces (weak and strong forces, electromagnetism, gravitation) of contemporary physics. Since proximate univocal causes are insufficient to generate substances on their own, universal causes contribute directly or indirectly as principal and instrumental causes to every case of generation and corruption, not as sources for the substantial forms educed from matter, but as equivocal causes indispensable to the eduction of substantial forms from matter.[10] Many of these universal equivocal causes are not only relevant to the individual instances of generation, but are also continuously co-manifesting or cooperating causal powers that are required to sustain the existence of these generated substances. This brings us to another piece of the puzzle.

All univocal changes, equivocal changes, and causal commerce within the cosmos occurs via a nexus of interacting hylomorphic substances. These substances interact as agents and patients that realize or exercise their passive and active causal powers in concert with each other. These powers are, of course, among the *propria* grounded by the essence of these hylomorphic substances; they enable and empower substances to engage in the various active and passive causal roles that comprise their causal interactions with each other. Aristotle's crucial insight is that the basic form of natural causation consists in a single, simultaneous event comprised of the actions and passions of co-manifesting causal power partners. This point, along with its attendant metaphysics of

---

8. *In VII Meta.* lect. 8, §1446: "Tertio modo quando ipsa tota forma generati non praecedit in generante, sed aliqua pars eius, aut aliqua pars partis; sicuti in medicina calida praecedit calor qui est pars sanitatis, aut aliquid ducens ad partem sanitatis. Et haec generatio nullo modo est univocal."

9. *CT* 1.198; *SCG* 3.69; *ST* 1.13.5; Brian Carl, "Thomas Aquinas on the Proportionate Causes of Living Species," *Scientia et Fides* 8, no. 2 (2020): 223–48.

10. *ST* 1.65.4 ad 2, ad 3; *ST* 1.71.1 ad 1.

mutually manifesting causal powers, had been lost in the aftermath of David Hume's skeptical argumentation that not only reduced causation to the temporal succession of categorically independent events, but also eliminated causation and powers from the world. Fortunately, the exigency for the Aristotelian picture of powers has made a comeback in recent decades, and there is a prospering program of research dedicated to defending the metaphysics of causal powers and disclosing their place in scientific discoveries. Anna Marmodoro nicely sums up how these Aristotelian powers work together.

> Causal partner-powers are mutually activated from potentiality to activity. All there is to their causal "interaction" is their mutual and simultaneous manifestation (e.g., heating and being heated). The power fulfilling the active causal role is activated, while the power fulfilling the passive causal role is activated, and, often, changes as well.[11]

Even though Thomists have always defended this Aristotelian picture of reciprocal causal powers and their mutual interactions or manifestations, they have nevertheless tended to paint a sort of "atomized hylomorphic" picture of reality. This is due to their failure to draw attention to the indispensable ways that hylomorphic substances are always dynamically nested within a complex matrix of co-manifesting active and passive powers with other hylomorphic substances. By focusing so much on individual hylomorphic substances, Thomists frequently omit these details pertaining to the ongoing and dynamic ontological, physical, chemical, biological, psychological, and social ways substances are interacting with each other as agents and patients via their active and passive powers for coupling and decoupling, activating and deactivating, and so forth. Many of these physical, chemical, and biological powers are always co-manifesting.

> Fundamental powers of elementary particles are continuously manifesting in their environment, given the presence of the ambient gravitational force in the universe, but also of the other fundamental forces. In complex objects, powers are continuously manifesting in the presence of other powers in the same object; for instance, the gravitational and electromagnetic powers of physical parts of a domino manifest in the presence of such powers of the other parts of the domino, etc. In the case of powers such as the power to topple, they presuppose structural constitutional complexity of the object that possesses them—size, shape,

---

11. Anna Marmodoro, "Aristotelian Powers at Work: Reciprocity Without Symmetry in Causation," in *Causal Powers*, ed. Jonathan D. Jacobs (Oxford: Oxford University Press, 2017), 70.

weight, hardness, etc. Many of these powers of a domino will be constantly activated, manifesting in the presence of the other powers of the domino, even if the power to topple is not. In short, there is a domino there to be toppled.[12]

Central to Thomism, therefore, is the often-overlooked understanding of the cosmos God has created as comprised of an ongoing, dynamically developing nexus of hylomorphic substances interacting through the co-manifestation of their causal power partners. This cosmic point just so happens to set up some further interconnected pieces crucial to eductive speciation.

Most complex interactive nexus of co-manifesting causal powers will exhibit both (i) natural or essential effects and outcomes and (ii) chance or incidental effects and outcomes. Powers are teleological; they are potencies that have definite tendencies to actively or passively manifest in limited ways by co-manifesting with certain power partners and not with other powers. A power for dissolving in water is not a power for combusting in water. The canonical ways active and passive causal powers co-manifest are the natural termini (or ends) that define their natural effects.[13] But these natural termini and effects cannot be understood and detailed apart from considering the complex and continuous ways teleological systems obtain among interacting substances in the cosmos. We fall into the void of "hylomorphic atomism" whenever we overlook and fail to explicate the reciprocal, manifesting causal power partners that comprise the objects or necessary conditions for the operations or manifestations of the powers of any substance's nature.[14] How should we characterize these natural, and even teleological, systems in the cosmos?

I cannot present here any detailed theory of hylomorphic systems, but it is worth pointing out that, from a Thomist point of view, one theory is waiting in the wings in another form of "staunch hylomorphism"; namely, that defended by pluriformists from Scotists to William Jaworski.[15] While Thomists

---

12. Marmodoro, "Aristotelian Powers at Work," 62

13. On the metaphysics of powers and their canonical manifestations, see Nancy Cartwright, *Nature, the Artful Modeler: Lectures on Laws, Science, How Nature Arranges the World and How We Can Arrange It Better* (Chicago: Open Court, 2019); Daniel De Haan, "The Power to Perform Experiments," in *Neo-Aristotelian Metaphysics and the Theology of Nature*, ed. William Simpson, Robert Koons, and James Orr (New York: Routledge, 2021), chapter 7, 191–219.

14. Aristotle, *De anima* 2.4; *ST* 1.77.3.

15. Staunch hylomorphism includes both uniformist and pluriformist understandings of substantial form. For discussion of these views, see Robert Koons, "Staunch vs. Faint-Hearted Hylomorphism: Toward an Aristotelian Account of Composition," *Res Philosophica* 91 (2014): 1–27; Daniel De Haan, "Staunch Hylomorphism and its Emergentist Credentials: A Comparison of Uniformism, Pluriformism, and Machretic Emergentism," in

have good reasons for rejecting the pluriformists' defense of the possibility of a plurality of substantial forms in a single substance insofar as it undermines the unity of a substance, Thomists should not toss their detailed explanatory frameworks into the rubbish. For what these pluriformists do provide, contrary to their own intentions, is the kind of detailed framework Thomists need to explain not individual substances, but the systems of interacting and co-manifesting powers of powerful particular substances. Contrary to the portrait of hylomorphic atomism, hylomorphic substances cannot be understood apart from the landscape perspective provided by "hylomorphic systems." Hylomorphic substances can only realize and exercise their powers within hylomorphic systems that are comprised of the ongoing dynamic commerce of co-manifesting active and passive powers of powerful particulars. It is within distinct systems that hylomorphic substances are enabled to actualize and have actualized their powers, which otherwise would not be so manifested outside the nexus of coupled powers afforded by these systems. But unlike hylomorphic substances, these hylomorphic systems (e.g., solar, planetary, atmospheric, and plate tectonic systems, rock and water cycles, aquatic and terrestrial ecosystems) are not substances, and so they neither substantially transform and assimilate their members nor provide them with their fundamental ontological identities.[16] The cosmos is the megasystem in which all hylomorphic substances and systems inhabit, but the cosmos itself—at least the present cosmos—is not a substance; that is, cosmic hylomorphic monism is false.[17] Because the cosmos is not a hylomorphic substance, the hylomorphic substances within this megasystem cannot be its integral or component parts *sensu stricto*; rather, hylomorphic substances are "members" of the cosmos.

The hylomorphic substances interacting in these systems of the cosmos exhibit the canonical, natural outcomes or effects of their co-manifesting powers, as well as a variety of chance effects and outcomes. As Aristotle establishes in *Physics* 2.4–6, chance effects, outcomes, and variations are rooted in the natural teleology of the powers of hylomorphic substances interacting within these systems.

The large number and variety of causes stem from the order of divine providence and control. But, granted this variety of causes, one of them

---

Rethinking Emergence (Oxford: Oxford University Press, forthcoming); William Jaworski, *Structure and the Metaphysics of Mind* (Oxford: Oxford University Press, 2016); and Thomas Ward, *John Duns Scotus on Parts, Wholes, and Hylomorphism* (Leiden: Brill, 2014).

16. See David Oderberg, "Teleology: Inorganic and Organic," in *Contemporary Perspectives on Natural Law*, ed. Ana Marta González (Aldershot: Ashgate), 259–79.

17. See Robert Koons, "Essential Thermochemical and Biological Powers" in Simpson, Koons, and Orr, *Neo-Aristotelian Metaphysics*, 66–93.

must at times run into another cause and be impeded, or assisted, by it in the production of its effect. Now, from the concurrence of two or more causes it is possible for some chance event to occur, and thus an unintended end comes about due to this causal concurrence. For example, the discovery of a debtor, by a man who has gone to market to sell something, happens because the debtor also went to market.[18]

The distinction between canonical outcomes and coincidental outcomes is needed to capture the fact that all natural co-manifesting powers are defeasible; their co-manifestations can be modulated or prevented. And sometimes the coincidental convergence of powerful particulars results in novel outcomes, since some powers only ever co-manifest due to such coincidental convergences.

These incidental effects and variations can exhibit more subtle, complex patterns of convergences and schemes of recurrence that are obscured by the summary description of "chance" events. Some chance variations and schemes of recurrence are more probable than others, and some among the more probable over time give rise to convergent manifestations that do not systematically diverge in their occurrences, even though they are coincidental effects that supervene upon the natural termini of co-manifesting powers of substances. The varieties of DNA mutations in germ and somatic cells by base substitutions, deletions, and insertions by errors in replication, recombination, and chemical and radiation damage to DNA serve as one among many probative examples of these coincidental convergent manifestations. Trillions upon quadrillions of occurrences of the natural processes of DNA replication and recombination, as well as RNA transcriptions and translations and protein foldings, over millions of years have coincidentally resulted in the accumulation of generative mutations and other events producing properties that have incidentally increased the fitness of the organisms they occur in.[19] Many of these initially coincidental attributes eventually become integrated into the natural tendencies of the powers, properties, and natures of organisms.

These recurring and convergent "coincidental manifestations" exhibit real difference-making patterns and regularities that serve as the basis for truth-tracking statistical regularities. Bernard Lonergan brilliantly details this phenomenon in *Insight* and demonstrates how such coincidental schemes of recurrence conspire with the abiding finality of the cosmos to enkindle the flashpoints of "emergent probability."

---

18. *SCG* 3.74.
19. Eva Jablonka and Marion Lamb, *Evolution in Four Dimensions: Genetic, Epigenetic, Behavioral, and Symbolic Variation in the History of Life* (Cambridge, MA: MIT Press, 2014).

It is emergent probability that supplies the initial coincidental manifolds of events in which the higher conjugate forms [i.e., attributes] emerge. It is emergent probability that provides the compound conditioned series of things and of schemes of recurrence such that the developing organism or psyche or intelligence will have an environment in which it can function successfully. It is with respect to this field of emergent probability that [any generative] sequence enjoys a twofold flexibility: a minor flexibility that reaches the same goal along different routes, and a major flexibility that shifts the goal in adaptation to environmental change. Not only do conjugate forms emerge in coincidental manifolds of lower events; not only do flexible circles of schemes of recurrence result from the conjugate forms; but also operations in accord with the schemes (1) are linked with occurrences outside the organism, the psyche, the intelligence, (2) effect the higher systematization of the lower chemical, neural, or psychic manifold, and (3) so transform the lower manifold as to evoke the emergence of the next conjugate forms that will yield new schemes that will enable the developing subject to function in its environment towards still further development.[20]

It takes a good chunk of Lonergan's magisterial tome *Insight* to explicate and defend everything summed up in this quote, but the gist of emergent probability relevant to evolution is this: God's cosmos comprehends not merely the natural outcomes from the natural interactions among substances, but also the ways in which the coincidental outcomes of these natural interactions collaborate with evolutionary processes. Both canonical and coincidental manifestations together contribute to the ratcheting up and accumulation of novel attributes, and ultimately the eduction of novel hylomorphic species from the latent potentialities of the hylomorphic substances within the hylomorphic systems that comprise the cosmos. On the Thomist conception of providence, little do they know, by playing their parts as agents and patients in the teleological interactions among systems of hylomorphic substances, they are thereby coincidentally playing parts within the orchestrated finality of the cosmos.[21] We need to keep in mind both the teleology of hylomorphic substances and the coincidental roles they fulfill with respect to the numinous finality of the cosmos.

---

20. Lonergan, *Insight*, 487.
21. For further discussion, see Bernard Lonergan, *Grace and Freedom: Operative Grace in the Thought of St Thomas Aquinas*, vol. 1 of *Collected Works of Bernard Lonergan*, ed. Frederick E. Crowe and Robert M. Doran, Collected Works of Lonergan 1 (Toronto: University of Toronto Press, 2000); Oliva Blanchette, *The Perfection of the Universe according to Aquinas* (State College: Pennsylvania State University Press, 1992); Simon Maria Kopf, "Teleology, Providence, and Powers," in Simpson, Koons, and Orr, *Neo-Aristotelian Metaphysics*, 383–407.

The finality of proximate potentialities and actualities makes possible numerous remote potentialities and actualities. Systems of substances within the cosmos can scale up to form galactic, stellar, and planetary systems that generate further novel substances. The finality of these systems of interacting hylomorphic substances can ratchet upwards, rendering latent remote potentialities and actualities into proximate potentialities and actualities for generating water within interstellar clouds containing hydrogen and oxygen, or for the generative eduction of gold and other heavy metals by rapid neutron capture in the aftermath of a neutron star merger. The finality of the cosmos is manifested in this recurring convergence of certain proximate potentialities and actualities that render remote possibilities into less remote ones, and more and more proximate probabilities to occur. Lonergan states, "But what is probable, sooner or later occurs. When it occurs, a probability of emergence is replaced by a probability of survival; and as long as the scheme survives, it is in its turn fulfilling conditions for the possibility of still later schemes in the series."[22]

2.2 Eductionism

With these preliminary pieces in place, we can now explore the central piece of eduction in more detail. Eduction is a constitutive feature of hylomorphic generation, for eduction is simply the actualization of a substantial form from the material potentialities of hylomorphic substances; that is, *materia secunda*. Eductionism and *dator-formarumism* are similar to the extent that prior to the generation of a substance, active causal agents curate the material potentialities of the total nexus of proximate causes disposing them toward corruption and generation. If a threshold is crossed, then substances corrupt and substantial forms are displaced by another substantial form, and another substance is generated. Eductionism and *dator-formarumism* fundamentally disagree about the source of the substantial form in this local system of corruption and generation.

> The Platonists together with Avicenna through denying the eduction of forms from matter were obliged to hold that natural agents merely dispose matter, and that the form is induced by a principle that is separate from matter. On the other hand if with Aristotle we hold substantial forms to be educed from the potentiality of matter, natural agents will dispose not only matter but also the substantial form, only, however, in regard to its eduction from the potentiality of matter into actual existence, as stated above [*QDP* 3.9 et 11]: so that they will be

22. Lonergan, *Insight*, 145.

principles of existence as considered in its inchoation but not as considered absolutely.[23]

Whereas *dator-formarumism* postulates an extrinsic cause beyond the cosmos for the source of the substantial form, eductionism maintains the substantial form is potentially present within the cosmos and that proximate univocal and equivocal agents of nature are sufficient, actualizing causes for educing the substantial form from the potencies of matter.

Eductive generation is instantaneous. This is because motion presupposes a substance that can be the subject of quantitative, qualitative, or local motion, but in generation and corruption there cannot be a subsisting subject without a substantial form; matter must be instantaneously transformed. Even though the displacement and eduction of substantial forms in corruption and generation is instantaneous, this does not exclude processes antecedent to the eductive generation. The corruption and generation of a substance is often sparked by a barrage of accidental changes, especially qualitative alterations, which dispose the material potentialities of a hylomorphic substance toward corruption and the generative eduction of a different substantial form.

> Thus the form of Fire is not produced in the Air so as gradually to advance from imperfection to perfection, since no substantial form is subject to increase and decrease, but *it is the matter alone that is changed by the previous alteration so as to be more or less disposed to receive the form*: and the form does not begin to be in the matter until the last instant of this alteration.[24]

In addition to these accidental changes, minor substantial changes to a substance's integral parts can catalyze corruption and generation as well. For instance, significant trauma, damage, or even the destruction of an animal's integral parts, including organs like its liver, heart, or respiratory system, often in combination with alterations, will precipitate the corruption of an animal substance. These alterations and minor substantial changes render the substance as a whole too unstable to continue subsisting and grounding these radical variations and transmutations in its attributes; eventually a threshold is traversed, and the substance corrupts: "Corruptible things cease to exist, in so far as their matter receives another form, with which its previous form was incompatible: wherefore their corruption requires the action of a certain agent, whereby the new form is educed from its potential state into actual existence."[25]

---

23. *QDP* 5.1 ad 5. See *QDP* 3.8; *SCG* 3.69–70; *De mixtione elementorum*.
24. *QDP* 3.9 ad 9. mod. Translation and emphasis my own.
25. *QDP* 5.3 ad 2.

While the substance is becoming too unstable to ground these changes, some of the transmuted attributes and other material potentialities of the substance actually increase the viability of other proximate potentialities to be actualized. This contributes to the displacement of the substance's substantial form and the eduction of a different substantial form. Some of the attributes introduced within the substance on its way to being corrupted will be appropriated or fused within the generated substance and will become present by power (*virtute*)—what is often called "virtual presence," but better conceived as "appropriated empowerments."[26]

One example of this kind of teleological system is Aquinas's theory of embryology, wherein numerous intermediate stages of corruption and generation occur that are ordered toward an end beyond the natural ends of the substances at each stage in the process.[27] A biological subject is substantially transformed into an incomplete organism with a vegetative soul, which is corrupted when an organism with a sensitive soul is generated (which is corrupted if the terminus is the generation of a human), all through the orchestration of the formative power of semen and other instrumental causes.[28] The active and passive elemental qualities, the vegetative powers of nutrition, growth, and reproduction, along with the integral parts of the incomplete vegetative organism's embryonic body, will all be substantially fused and assimilated into the substantial identity of the generated sensitive organism; some of them will become present by power (*virtute*). Similarly, when animals consume food, the substances that comprise its food will be corrupted by the animal's nutritive power and transmuted into the integral substantial parts of the animal, but not without transformationally appropriating certain attributes of the food. This is the nutritive point of assimilating food: food possesses properties that animals need.[29]

While its own corruption through the generation of another substance is coincidental to the intrinsic teleology and powers of hylomorphic substances, this is not incidental to the numinous finality of the cosmos. There are,

---

26. See Christopher A. Decaen, "Elemental Virtual Presence in St. Thomas," *The Thomist* 64 (2000): 271–300; W. Scott Cleveland and Brandon Dahm, "The Virtual Presence of Acquired Virtues in the Christian," *American Catholic Philosophical Quarterly* 93, no. 1 (2019): 75–100. On appropriated empowerments, see De Haan, "Staunch Hylomorphism and its Emergentist Credentials," in *Rethinking Emergence*.

27. Aquinas's embryology is problematic for both scientific and philosophical reasons. For a scientifically informed Thomist approach to contemporary embryology, see Samuel B. Condic and Maureen L. Condic, *Human Embryos, Human Beings: A Scientific and Philosophical Approach* (Washington, DC: The Catholic University of America Press, 2018).

28. *SCG* 2.86–89; *ST* 1.118.1 ad 4; *QDP* 5.1.

29. *QDP* 3.11 ad 7.

according to Aquinas's embryology, proximate potencies for generating a sensitive organism that the incomplete vegetative organism possesses, which the semen and menstrual blood do not possess. It is the semen's formative power that orchestrates the ongoing organic development of an incomplete vegetative organism, which increases the proximate potencies for generating a sensitive organism and renders it more corruptible as well.[30] These transmutations of the vegetative embryo's attributes, conducted by the formative power of semen, "push" toward an intension, remission, and configuration of various attributes that destabilize the vegetative substance and can only be stabilized by the eduction of a different substantial form. When a threshold is crossed, the vegetative substance corrupts, and a sensitive substance is generated that can assimilate and ground this accumulation of what had become the unstable, incompatible attributes of a vegetative substance.

The natural and coincidental transmutative introduction of novel attributes into hylomorphic substances and their destabilizing accumulation can also push toward generative novelty in the outcome of the total, proximate, and equivocal causal actualities and potentialities of a system of hylomorphic substances. It is precisely this convergence of natural and incidental factors that come together in Aquinas's explanation of the genesis of mules and the spontaneous generation of maggots. It is also what, according to Thomist naturalism, occurs in the nucleosynthesis of gold via rapid process neutron capture of iron nuclei in the wake of a binary neutron star collision and kilonova, as well as in evolutionary speciation events.

3. Thomist Naturalism Contra Thomist Supernaturalism

Thus far I have laid out the major pieces of the natural philosophy presupposed by Thomist naturalism's account of eductive speciation, which explains the evolutionary origins of novel ontological species. None of these major pieces of this natural philosophy should be objectionable to Thomist supernaturalism. The controversy concerns Thomist naturalism's contention that the total, proximate, and equivocal secondary causes—which actually educe a substantial form from the proximate potentialities of a nexus of interacting hylomorphic substances in the cosmos—are sufficient to educe a novel substantial form and so generate a novel hylomorphic substance. Thomist supernaturalism demurs, and points to a pair of problems for Thomist naturalism: where does both the potentiality and the actuality for the eduction of novel ontological species come from?

---

30. *QDP* 3.11 ad 7; 5.1.

3.1 Defending Thomist Naturalism

For Thomist naturalism, God created the remote potentialities and actualities for all wholly hylomorphic species by creating the beings that comprise the cosmos. The finality of the cosmos's systems of interacting hylomorphic substances are sufficient *qua* secondary causes to generatively educe new substances from the proximate potentialities and actualities of existing systems of hylomorphic substances. Furthermore, and contrary to Thomist supernaturalism, Aquinas goes out of his way to insist that the cosmos has the potentiality and actuality to educe all hylomorphic substances.

> The form pre-exists in matter imperfectly, not as though a part of it were actually there and another part not, but because it is wholly there in potentiality, and is afterwards educed wholly into actuality.[31]

The only exception—aside from miracles—belongs to the rational soul. There is however a probative principled explanation for why the rational soul cannot be educed from the potency of matter. It is immaterial *in se*, and the cosmos does not have material potentialities for immaterial substantial forms; immaterial forms must be created because they cannot be educed.[32] The souls and substantial forms of all other wholly hylomorphic substances can be educed from the potency of matter without the addition of anything extrinsic (*et hoc est educi formam de potentia materiae absque additione alicuius extrinseci*) like God or the *dator formarum*.[33]

It seems that the only *principled* argument available within the Thomist tradition for why nature cannot educe some substantial form is that there cannot be a material potentiality within the cosmos for an immaterial form. Since Thomist naturalism maintains that the novel substantial forms educed through evolutionary processes generate wholly hylomorphic species—that is, none of them have immaterial substantial forms—Thomist supernaturalism must look elsewhere for principled arguments against the central thesis of Thomist naturalism. Can Thomist supernaturalism demonstrate that God's created cosmos does not have either the potentiality or actuality for the eduction of novel ontological species?

If a created nature is truly hylomorphically natural, then the created cosmos has the latent remote potentiality for its actualization. The substantial forms for all inanimate and animate substances that have existed or can exist

---

31. *QDP* 3.8 ad 10. See *ST* 1.73.1 ad 3.
32. *QDP* 3.4 ad 7.
33. *QDSC* 2 ad 8.

within the cosmos—with the principled exception of immaterial rational souls—are wholly and truly hylomorphically natural. Hence, the *potential* for these substantial forms to be actually educed is latent within the material potentialities of the total system of interacting hylomorphic substances within the cosmos.[34] In terms of Lonergan's emergent probability, all natural substantial forms are possible. But are they probable? This brings us to the problem of actuality: What actuality is required to educe novel substantial forms?

There are three major ontological obstacles to Thomist naturalism's thesis that the cosmos possesses sufficient natural actuality to explain all novel eductive generations. Thomist naturalism needs to explain (1) how parents of a less perfect species can generate offspring with a different and more perfect species; (2) how less perfect living organisms can generate ontologically superior organisms of an entirely different genus, like the transition from vegetative organisms to sensitive organisms; and (3) how inanimate entities can generate living organisms. Thomist supernaturalism contends that in each of these purported cases of eductive speciation, there is more perfection in the effects than can be provided by the natural causes alone, and so the eductive speciation theory defended by Thomist naturalism violates the PPC. The only way to explain the origins of these new species without violating the PPC is by appealing to divine intervention, which can supply or supplement the actuality required to generate these novel species.

Thomist supernaturalism does draw attention to challenging issues, but its *dator-formarumism* is inconsistent with Aquinas's own natural philosophy, and it fails to raise insurmountable objections to Thomist naturalism's developments of his natural philosophy. Because Aquinas is committed to the natural potentiality and actuality for generating all wholly hylomorphic substances in the cosmos, he is also committed to uncovering naturalistic explanations of their generation.

Consider Aquinas's explanation of the generation of a new species via hybridization. Mules are generated from a male donkey and a female horse but neither parent acts as a univocal generator of its offspring. When humans beget humans and horses beget horses, "each natural thing produces something similar to itself in species, unless something beyond nature happens to result, as when a horse begets a mule. And this generation is beyond nature, because it is outside of the aim of a particular nature." For Aquinas, two natural causes can generate a *per se* effect (i.e., the generation of a living substance), even when this *per se* effect is an equivocal effect that is coincidental or "beyond" the ends of the natural causation of the generative powers of the parents.

---

34. Later I demonstrate the problems that arise from denying that this potentiality is in the cosmos God created.

For the formative power, which is in the sperm of the male, is designed by nature to produce something completely the same as that from which the sperm has been separated; but its secondary aim, when it cannot induce a perfect likeness, is to induce any kind of likeness that it can. And since in the generation of a mule the sperm of a horse cannot induce the form of a horse in the matter, because it is not adapted to receive the form of a horse, it therefore induces a related form. Hence in the generation of a mule the generator is similar in a way to the thing generated; for there is a proximate genus . . . common to horse and to ass; and mule is also contained under that genus. Hence in reference to that genus it can be said that like generates like.[35]

Against *dator-formarumism*'s explanation of the source of the educed substantial form of mules outside the cosmos, Aquinas turns to the latent potentialities of the cosmos and the way active equivocal causes can dispose matter toward the eduction of a different substantial form and the generation of a different substance. Equivocal generation by parents of different species occurs through the co-manifestation of generative powers, which are naturally directed toward different ends. But when the generative powers of a horse and donkey combine, they are disposed toward the eduction of a novel substantial form. It is precisely this convergence of natural and incidental factors that come together in Aquinas's explanation of the genesis of mules as well as in the spontaneous generation of maggots.

There is an important caveat here we cannot overlook. The eductive speciation of hybrids presents the easiest ontological obstacle for Thomist naturalism to overcome insofar as donkeys, horses, and mules share a common genus and none are obviously ontologically superior substances with respect to each other. Aquinas himself seems to acknowledge this in his claim that because donkeys and horses share a sufficiently common proximate genus, they can generate novel species within that genus. Hence, hybrids only provide an example of eductive speciation of a horizontal novelty. Does the eductive speciation of ontologically superior or vertically novel species confute Thomist naturalism by disclosing its violation of the PPC?

Aquinas's embryology illustrates his commitment to providing naturalistic explanations for how the cosmic finality of nature is sufficient for generating vertical novelty. The stages of corruptions and generations of embryos are teleologically directed toward educing ontologically superior substantial forms—a vegetative substance is curated for a telos beyond that of the vege-

---

35. *In VII Meta.* lect. 8, nn. 1432–33 (my emphasis). Note that the offspring of a male horse and female donkey is a "hinny" not a "mule."

tative "embryo" itself, and a sensitive substance can be fostered for a telos (the human embryo) beyond the sensitive embryo.

Advocates of Thomist supernaturalism might contend that Aquinas's embryology provides at best a rather murky illustration of eductive speciation, which achieves genuine vertical novelty. For even if Aquinas's empirically false embryology allows for cross-genus escalation, the entire train of ascending generations was initiated by animal substances whose generative powers empowered the now separately existing semen with these formative powers for cross-genus eductive speciation.

This brings us to abiogenesis, the ontological ascension and genus-crossing generation of animate substances from inanimate substances. Aquinas held that maggots can be spontaneously generated from inanimate putrefying flesh through the powers of celestial bodies cooperating with the active and passive qualities of corporeal matter. As with other forms of generation among living substances, the spontaneous generation of animate substances from inanimate ones is not miraculous; it is a form of natural generation.[36] Once again, Aquinas insists on providing a naturalistic explanation of purported empirical facts by articulating an account of spontaneous generation that rejects appeals to any factors that are extrinsic to secondary causation, like the *dator-formarum* hypotheses of Thomist supernaturalism. Aquinas does not think the cosmos requires primary causes to do the work of secondary causes. Creatures are fundamentally dependent upon God as the Creator—that is, *qua* primary cause of everything created—but creatures applied to their causal partners do not require an additional divine input to realize their creaturely manifestations *qua* secondary causes.[37]

In the face of these exegetical examples from Aquinas, Thomist supernaturalists might insist that even Aquinas's explanations of these phenomena are ad hoc and inconsistent with the principles of natural philosophy. The only reason Aquinas and Thomist naturalists make such arbitrary exceptions to these basic principles is because they uncritically take for granted purported empirical facts, which could be reinterpreted in other ways. Aquinas's and other Aristotelians' contorted efforts to explain evolution by employing what have since been shown to be empirically inadequate accounts of the generation of maggots in putrefying flesh and embryological development, provide illustrations of an important lesson for contemporary Thomists. Thomists should stick to the well-established principles of natural philosophy instead of violating basic ontological principles, like the PPC, to accommodate the pressures of pseudoscientific facts.

36. See *In II Sent.* d. 1, q. 1, a. 4; *SCG* 3.102; *ST* 1.73.1 ad 3.
37. On the Thomist theory of *applicare*, see Lonergan, *Grace and Freedom*, chapter 4; Kopf, "Teleology, Providence, and Powers."

What response can Thomist naturalism provide to the charge that these explanations are ad hoc and inconsistent with the principles of natural philosophy? Does Thomist naturalism violate the PPC? There are two rival construals of the PPC with respect to equivocal virtual causes; that is, causes (singularly or jointly) that do not possess the attributes or species they actualize in their effects. For Thomist supernaturalism, equivocal causes must be ontologically superior or more perfect than any attributes they cause. Call this the "ontologically superior" construal of the PPC. For Thomist naturalism, equivocal causes do not need to be ontologically superior to the attributes they actualize, they only need to possess sufficient power to actualize these effects. Call this the "sufficiently powerful" construal of the PPC.[38] Thomist naturalism contends that eductive speciation does not violate the sufficiently powerful PPC. This is because eductive speciation requires that the total, proximate, and distributed equivocal virtual causes have sufficient power to actually educe a novel substantial form from the proximate potentialities within a system of interacting hylomorphic substances.

What are the actualities of these distributed equivocal virtual causes? These causes can actually (1) introduce new attributes into patient substances, (2) alter the intrinsic attributes of patient substances, and (3) extrinsically reorganize these accumulated attributes or other agents, thereby disposing both (a) patient substances toward destabilization and corruption and (b) the proximate potentialities of the system of interacting substances toward a different stability and unity. If a critical threshold is surpassed, then an intrinsic unification and stabilization of attributes is achieved by the actual eduction of a novel substantial form from the proximate material potentialities. This generates a novel substance. In short, the distributed equivocal virtual causes can have sufficient actuality for eductive speciation if they can contribute similitudes of all the relevant attributes—which are themselves part of the total proximate potentiality—and can extrinsically organize and thereby incidentally dispose myriad attributes toward an intrinsic stabilizing unity. Thomist naturalism contends that this account of the potentialities and actualities for eductive speciation by distributed equivocal virtual causes does not violate the sufficiently powerful PPC.

---

38. See Norman Kretzmann, *The Metaphysics of Theism: Aquinas's Natural Theology in Summa Contra Gentiles I* (Oxford: Clarendon Press, 1997), 140–57; John Wippel, *Metaphysical Thought*, 572–75; John Wippel, "Thomas Aquinas on our Knowledge of God and the Axiom that Every Agent Produces Something Like Itself," *Metaphysical Themes in Thomas Aquinas II* (Washington, DC: The Catholic University of America Press, 2007), 152–71.

3.2 Arguments Against Thomist Supernaturalism

Which construal of the PPC should Thomists endorse? The simplest and least demanding construal of the PPC is that agents need to be sufficiently powerful to cause their effects. The burden of proof rests with the ontologically superior PPC to establish why the sufficiently powerful PPC fails, and why Thomists must endorse the ontologically superior PPC. Independent of any contentions concerning evolution, there are two major justifications for endorsing the sufficiently powerful PPC and rejecting Thomist supernaturalism's ontologically superior PPC. The first is that the cosmos is replete with examples of substances being generated by agents that are not ontologically superior to the substances they generate. In each of these putative cases of natural generation, exponents of the ontologically superior PPC will be forced to explain quotidian natural phenomena by appealing to some extra-cosmic supernatural *dator formarum*. A second, related justification is that the ontologically superior PPC leads Thomist supernaturalism into a problematic dilemma. Let us start with the first issue by considering embryogenesis.

Contemporary Aristotelians correctly recognize that gametes are neither substances that are lions or bears, nor are they substantial forms of lions or bears, nor do they possess the substantial forms of the substances they eductively generate. So, all sexually reproduced animate substances are generated from proximate generators that are ontologically inferior to the ontologically superior substances they generate. Gametes technically meet one of Aquinas's qualified notions of a univocal agent insofar as they fall under the same species of substance as the generator and the generated substances—albeit *secundum quid* and only by category reduction.[39] But even if we grant that gametes are qualified univocal agents, gametes still violate the ontologically superior construal of the PPC. This is because gametes neither actually exhibit the forms they cause (i.e., univocal cause criterion), nor are they ontologically superior to the substantial forms educed through their causal contributions (i.e., equivocal virtual cause criterion according to the ontologically superior PPC). Indeed, gametes are ontologically inferior. This obvious violation of the ontologically superior PPC has inspired many of its adherents to venture all sorts of implausible explanations of how ontologically inferior gametes, *qua* instrumental causes, can nevertheless achieve sufficient actuality to educe ontologically superior substantial forms by virtue of the reproductive powers of the parent substances, *qua* principal causes, that produced these gametes. Such proposals are not only far-fetched and recherché (especially in cases of semelparous and oviparous organisms), but they also still violate the ontologically superior PPC. More significantly for the pres-

---

39. See *In VII Meta*. lect. 8, nn. 1443–59; *SCG* 2.89.

ent dispute, these proposals often inconsistently require implicit appeals to the sufficiently powerful construal of the PPC, by insisting it is in virtue of the parent's powers that these independent, ontologically inferior seminal entities can achieve sufficient actuality to overcome the ontological gap as it is identified by the ontologically superior PPC. If these ad hoc sufficient actuality provisos can resolve the problems and inconsistencies that arise from endorsing the ontologically superior PPC, then the legitimacy of the sufficiently powerful PPC should be acknowledged in the first place.

Unlike the ontologically powerful PPC, the sufficiently powerful PPC provides a persuasive and straightforward explanation of the varieties of ordinary inanimate eductive generation and animate eductive generation. Consequently, and independently from the question of the evolution of novel species, there are probative arguments of natural philosophy for endorsing the sufficiently powerful construal of the PPC and rejecting the ontologically superior construal of the PPC. By endorsing the sufficiently powerful PPC, Thomist naturalism undercuts the charge that it violates the PPC, since the sufficiently powerful construal of the PPC is compatible with eductive speciation as a naturalistic explanation of the origins of novel inanimate and animate substantial forms.

Two cogent counterarguments are required for Thomist supernaturalism to relaunch a substantive case against Thomist naturalism. First, Thomist supernaturalism needs philosophical arguments both against the sufficiently powerful PPC and in support of the ontologically superior PPC. Second, it also needs a plausible alternative natural philosophy cum scientifically informed explanation of embryology, the genesis of elemental and other novel chemical substances, and the probative evidence for the evolutionary origins of biological species. This will require, among other things, demonstrating why *dator formarum* interventions that seem to be entailed by the ontologically superior PPC are not required for every case of sexual reproduction.[40]

---

40. To be clear, the embryology argument does not aim to explain how ontologically superior substances can be generated by ontologically inferior but sufficiently powerful causes. The main contention is to demonstrate that, despite the claims of advocates of the ontologically superior PPC to reject the sufficiently powerful PPC, they are nevertheless required to endorse it—at the very least—in every case of sexual reproduction. How might Thomist naturalism respond to a modified version of the ontologically superior PPC that acknowledges these exceptions? A revised version could maintain that sufficiently powerful entities (e.g., gametes) can only contribute to the generation of ontologically superior substances if they are the instrumental causes of already existing ontologically superior (or equivalent) substances. This revised position could then raise the counterobjection that no instrumental cause is sufficiently powerful to generate a substance that is ontologically superior to the substances that are the primary causes of any sufficiently powerful instrumental entities.

Or, if this profusion of *dator formarum* interventions is required, then why does this God-of-the-gaps explanation of natural reproduction not undermine the providential order of natural secondary causes in the cosmos, and also entail occasionalism, which Thomism rightly rejects? This brings us to a second justification for rejecting the ontologically superior PPC and endorsing the sufficiently powerful PPC.

The ontologically superior construal of the PPC entails two central tenets of Thomist supernaturalism. First, that no systems of interacting hylomorphic substances within the cosmos can eductively generate novel ontologically superior species, for no totality of distributed equivocal virtual causes can generate an ontologically superior substance. Second, God or some *dator formarum* outside the cosmos alone can be a causal source for ontologically superior novel species.[41] These commitments force exponents of Thomist supernaturalism to confront an insurmountable dilemma. Is God the causal source for both the potentiality and the actuality of all novel ontologically superior species? Or is God only the causal source for the actualization that educes a novel substantial form that was already a potentiality within the systems of hylomorphic substances in the created cosmos?

If Thomist supernaturalism takes the first horn of the dilemma by denying there is any potentiality for these novel substantial forms in the cosmos, then it faces three major problems. First, why would a providential God create a

---

My response to this revised position is threefold. First, it entails the unacceptable consequence that created substances can produce more powerful instrumental causes than God can. For the revised position must hold both (i) that (contrary to Thomist naturalism) God cannot create ontologically inferior instrumental causes that are collectively sufficiently powerful to generate ontologically superior substances, but (ii) that created substances can produce ontologically inferior instrumental causes that are sufficiently powerful to generate ontologically superior substances.

Second, this revised position still must explain and justify its stipulated exception against the original version of the ontologically superior PPC. How can some ontologically inferior entities, even if instruments, generate ontologically superior substances? Labeling gametes "instrumental causes" of ontologically superior (or equivalent) substances is not an explanation. At best, the label is a promissory note for an explanation that remains to be given. At worst, it is a question begging and ad hoc qualification.

Third, even if a justified explanation for this qualification can be made, this revised version of the ontologically superior PPC still faces the second justification's dilemma introduced below. I thank Austin Stevenson for drawing my attention to the possibility of this revised version of the ontologically superior PPC.

41. To simplify the variations of this position, I will presume Thomist supernaturalists identify God, not angels, as the proximate cause for novel ontologically superior species. If novel substantial forms are created, then God must be their source as angels cannot create. See *QDP* 3.4 ad 5; ad 14.

cosmos that lacked the natural potentialities and actualities for creatures that God will now need to specially create within the cosmos? The second problem is that novel wholly hylomorphic species are not eductively generated, since there is no potential for them in the cosmos. God must create—within an already created cosmos—the novel potentialities and actualities for these novel species. So, like immaterial rational souls, these novel substantial forms are directly created by God. But unlike rational souls, there is no principled explanation for why there cannot be a *potentiality* for these substantial forms within the systems of hylomorphic substances in the cosmos. The ontologically superior PPC only explains why the cosmos lacks the actuality for educing novel substantial forms; it does not explain why there cannot be a potentiality for them in the cosmos.

The third problem is that by contending the cosmos is not already created with potentialities for novel species, Thomist supernaturalism requires not only that God needs to create within the already created cosmos a new potentiality for every novel species, but also that God needs to recreate and modify all the relevant already existing substances. This is because, up to this point in the history of the cosmos, none of these existing substances possesses any potentialities relevant to novel substances. Prior to God's special creation of water, oxygen and hydrogen did not have the potentialities to be substantially assimilated or virtually present within water. Prior to God's special creation of living organisms, carbon, hydrogen, nitrogen, oxygen, phosphorus, and sulfur (CHNOPS), and all the "organic" molecules they comprise, like amino acids, did not already have the potentialities for being substantially integrated into any living substance. God needed to create within existing creation *both* living substances *and* create in existing inanimate substances and their attributes new potentialities for being substantially integrated into living substances. Prior to God's special creation of multicellular organisms and endothermic organisms, none of the organic molecules or relevant metabolic and developmental attributes of unicellular organisms and ectothermic organisms had the potential for being substantially assimilated into the substances of these evolutionarily later organisms. In each case, God must create new potentialities in existing creatures in addition to creating the specific potentialities and actualities for the novel substances and their attributes. Consequently, this first horn of the dilemma would entail endless absurdities like arbitrarily denying some potentialities for substances that are indistinguishable from potentialities the substances already possess. For example, prior to the special creation of water, oxygen in virtue of its electron orbitals will already possess the potential to bond, but not the potential to bond with two hydrogen atoms. Amino acids will have the potentiality to be components in proteins for all existent organisms but will not yet have the potentiality to be components in proteins of novel species until God creates both these novel species and a new intrinsic potentiality within existing amino acids. Clearly, the first horn of the dilemma leads to arbitrary and absurd results incompatible with Thomism.

If Thomist supernaturalism endorses the second horn of the dilemma, then it concedes that God created the cosmos with the potentiality for novel hylomorphic species. But God still needs to intervene directly within the cosmos to provide the actuality required to educe novel substantial forms, since God did not create secondary causes with sufficient actuality to educe these forms. The unique problem of this second horn of the dilemma is Thomist supernaturalism now seems committed to two basic but incompatible theses: That God, who is omniscient and providential, (1) created a cosmos with the secondary causal potentialities for naturally evolving novel species, but (2) did not create the cosmos with sufficient secondary causal efficacy to actually educe these novel species. Thomist supernaturalism must provide an explanation for why God would create a natural potency in the cosmos that will be actualized but deny the cosmos the natural agency required to actualize it. This explanation would need to be consistent with the principles of natural theology and natural philosophy; namely, that God does not create a cosmos with natures—including potential natures that will be actualized—in vain.

Finally, it is worth reiterating that even if Thomist supernaturalism can overcome this dilemma, it remains committed to the inherently problematic, ontologically superior PPC, which implies that no instance of sexual reproduction can naturally educe substantial forms for generation. All cases of sexual reproduction require God's special divine intervention to supply the actuality that no gametes can provide to educe the ontologically superior substantial forms of generated substances. The consequence of this *datorformarumism* is manifestly absurd for any position that claims to be committed to the principles of the Thomist tradition.

Conclusion

In this chapter, I started with a distinction between Thomist naturalist and Thomist supernaturalist explanations of the origin of species. In order to overcome the mistaken portrait of an atomized hylomorphism, I detailed why it is not each individual hylomorphic substance, taken on its own in isolation from all other hylomorphic substances, that has the potentiality and actuality for educing novel substantial forms. It is the cosmos's systems of hylomorphic substances that possess both the potentiality and actuality for the eduction of the substantial forms of all hylomorphic species. Thomist naturalism contends that God created the cosmos with the latent potentiality and actuality required for the eductive generation of all wholly hylomorphic species. Thomist supernaturalism rejects this thesis, arguing that it violates the PPC. I demonstrated that the account of eductive speciation defended by Thomist naturalism does not violate the sufficiently powerful construal of the PPC, and that the ontologically superior construal of the PPC is itself inherently problematic. I also showed that Thomist supernaturalism's endorsement of this problematic understanding of the PPC leads to an insurmountable dilemma and entails an unacceptable *dator-formarumism* account of how sexually reproduced substances are generated.

I have argued that Thomists should defend the reality of creaturely causes of natural phenomena like evolution. God's omnipotence and glory are not hampered but magnified by the reality of his created cosmos, which is populated by created substances with created natures that possess sufficient causal efficacy to realize and exercise the causal powers they were created to manifest. It would be contrary to God's providential purpose in creating natures if God was to create natures incapable of realizing their natural powers. Among these natural powers are those present within systems of interacting hylomorphic substances in the cosmos. These systems of interacting hylomorphic substances collaborate in the univocal and equivocal generation of substances of the same and even of ontologically superior hylomorphic species. Thus, Thomist naturalism presents a coherent account of how God created a cosmos endowed with the natural powers required to originate novel species.[42]

---

42. I am grateful to Fr. Nicanor Austriaco, OP, and everyone who participated in the meetings of the Thomistic Evolution Project. I am especially thankful to Brandon Dahm, Fr. Jeff Dole, Simon Kopf, William Simpson, Brian Carl, Austin Stevenson, Fr. Richard Conrad, OP, and Fr. Mariusz Tabaczek, OP, for detailed feedback on earlier versions of this chapter, and the Templeton World Charity Foundation's Conceptual Clarity Concerning Human Nature project for supporting my research.

CHAPTER FIVE

Is Thomistic Ethics Compatible with Evolutionary Biology?

RAYMOND HAIN

Thomistic ethics has not yet resolved its relationship to evolutionary biology.[1] Nevertheless, there are substantial resources at its disposal, not least of which is the ongoing uncertainty within the philosophy of biology about the theoretical implications of evolution for traditional natural kinds.[2] This chapter summarizes the history of conflict between ethics and evolutionary biology, outlines the specific problems raised for Thomistic ethics, and develops what I believe is the most fruitful account from the perspective of the Thomistic tradition of the relationship between ethics and evolutionary biology.

The claim that evolutionary biology has significant implications for philosophical ethics is an old one. Darwin himself devotes space to the evolution of our moral powers in *The Descent of Man* (published in 1871, twelve years after *On the Origin of Species*). "Of all the differences between man and the lower animals, the moral sense or conscience is by far the most important," he writes, though he nevertheless concludes that "the difference in mind between man and the higher animals, great as it is, certainly is one of degree and not of kind."[3] He argues that human ethical behavior is a result of our

---

1. See, for example, Travis Dumsday, "Is There Still Hope for a Scholastic Ontology of Biological Species?" *The Thomist* 76, no. 3 (2012): 372. Dumsday writes, "The lack of engagement between contemporary natural-law theory and contemporary philosophy of biology could end up being seriously detrimental to the former. Yet despite the importance of the issue there have been few exchanges between recent Scholastic thought and the anti-essentialist majority in analytic philosophy of biology. With the notable exception of David Oderberg, recent work in the Scholastic philosophy of nature tends to pass it by (e.g., the work of Leo Elders), while older studies by such well-known figures as Mortimer Adler, John Deely, and Etienne Gilson remain valuable but are in need of supplementation and further development in the face of new challenges."

2. See the chapter in this volume by Mariusz Tabaczek, OP, "Essentialist and Hylomorphic Notions of Species and Species Transformation."

3. Charles Darwin, *The Descent of Man and Selection in Relation to Sex* (London: John Murray, 1871), 70, 105.

moral sense, itself a development of our social and altruistic instincts that together promote survival.[4] In turn, opposition to any substantive relationship between evolutionary biology and philosophical ethics arose as soon as Darwin and others published their work. Henry Sidgwick, the most important English moral philosopher of the late nineteenth century, opens *The Methods of Ethics* (1874) with a quick dismissal of the relevance of evolutionary biology: "There is something under any given circumstances which it is right or reasonable to do, and . . . this may be known. If it be admitted that we now have the faculty of knowing this, it appears to me that the investigation of the historical antecedents of this cognition, and of its relation to other elements of the mind, no more properly belongs to Ethics than the corresponding questions as to the cognition of Space belong to Geometry."[5]

Darwin and Sidgwick, publishing only a few years apart, established what remains today the basic framework of the debate over evolutionary biology and moral philosophy. It seems eminently plausible that the genealogy of human moral reasoning and behavior has implications for theoretical ethics, and yet there seems to be no necessary logical connection between the two, for one can always reply that how we became moral animals and what our behavior consists of does not entail any particular conclusions about which moral rules are the right ones and why we should follow them. Descriptive explanations do not allow us to draw prescriptive conclusions. Indeed, a generation after Darwin and Sidgwick, the philosopher Theodore de Leguna states flatly that "it has been demonstrated again and again that the Darwinian theory will lie down peacefully with almost any variety of ethical faith."[6]

This fundamental dialectic persisted throughout the twentieth century.[7] Biologist E. O. Wilson establishes the terms of our own contemporary iteration in his influential and controversial *Sociobiology* (1975), boldly proclaiming in the final chapter that "scientists and humanists should consider together

---

4. Darwin, *The Descent of Man*, 165–66.

5. Henry Sidgwick, *The Methods of Ethics*, 7th ed. (London: Macmillan, 1907), v–vi. Sidgwick develops at greater length the reasons for this quick dismissal in an article published two years later: "The Theory of Evolution in its Application to Practice," *Mind* 1, no. 1 (January 1876): 52–67.

6. Theodore de Leguna, "Stages of the Discussion of Evolutionary Ethics," *The Philosophical Review* 14, no. 5 (1905): 583. De Leguna had the benefit of over thirty years of academic debate on which to draw as evidence, but Sidgwick had already arrived at the same conclusion in 1876: "When [evolution] is all admitted, I cannot see that any argument is gained for or against any particular ethical doctrine" ("The Theory of Evolution in its Application to Practice," 54).

7. For a historical summary and analysis, see Paul Lawrence Farber, *The Temptations of Evolutionary Ethics* (Berkeley: University of California Press, 1994).

the possibility that the time has come for ethics to be removed temporarily from the hands of the philosophers and biologicized."[8] More boldly still, Wilson claims that "ethical philosophers intuit the deontological canons of morality by consulting the emotive centers of their own hypothalamic-limbic system. . . . Only by interpreting the activity of emotive centers as a biological adaptation can the meaning of the canons be deciphered."[9] Wilson was particularly interested in the development of altruistic behavior, and he often speaks as if his primary task is to uncover the evolutionary origins of our moral capacities and their contribution to genetic success. In other words, he seems principally interested in a descriptive project, as Darwin was before him. But occasionally he flirts with prescriptive conclusions. For example, in *On Human Nature* (1978), he concludes his chapter on altruism with the claim that "human behavior—like the deepest capacities for emotional response which drive and guide it—is the circuitous technique by which genetic material has been and will be kept intact. Morality has no other demonstrable ultimate function."[10] For many scholars, the evolutionary development of moral behavior, and its connection to the propagation of our species, is an overwhelming temptation for prescriptive statements about morality.[11]

And yet a century after Darwin, Wilson met philosophical opposition just as quickly. Perhaps most notably, the English philosopher Mary Midgley engages with Wilson's *Sociobiology* extensively in *Beast and Man*, published three years later. "The traditional business of moral philosophy," she writes, "is attempting to understand, clarify, relate, and harmonize so far as possible the claims arising from the different sides of our nature."[12] The idea that

---

8. Edward O. Wilson, *Sociobiology: The New Synthesis* (Cambridge, MA: Harvard University Press, 1975), 562.

9. Wilson, *Sociobiology*, 563.

10. Edward O. Wilson, *On Human Nature* (Cambridge, MA: Harvard University Press, 1978), 167.

11. See, for example, John Mackie's "The Law of the Jungle: Moral Alternatives and Principles of Evolution," *Philosophy* 53, no. 206 (October 1978): 455–64. Instead of Wilson's *Sociobiology*, "The Law of the Jungle" appropriates Richard Dawkins's equally provocative *The Selfish Gene* (Oxford: Oxford University Press, 1976) and claims that "some moralists, including Socrates and Jesus, have recommended . . . turning the other cheek and repaying evil with good. . . . Now this, which in human life we characterize as a Christian spirit or perhaps as saintliness, is roughly equivalent to the strategy Dawkins has unkindly labelled 'Sucker'. . . . [It] allows cheats to prosper, and could make them multiply to the point where they would . . . ultimately bring about the extinction of the whole population. This seems to provide fresh support for Nietzsche's view of the deplorable influence of moralities of the Christian type" (Mackie, "The Law of the Jungle," 463–64).

12. Mary Midgley, *Beast and Man: The Roots of Human Nature*, rev. ed. (New York: Routledge, 1995), 169. Midgley also engages in extended debate with Dawkins on the

sociobiology could replace ethics is nothing but "romantic fancy." And like Sidgwick she supports her claim with an analogy to mathematics:

> Mathematics, too, is a branch of human thought, affecting conduct, for which no doubt certain specific parts of the brain are needed. . . . So these capacities have been subjected to natural selection. That much is true. But it cannot follow that the way to "explain" mathematics and mathematicians—the "fundamental" way—is to dissect the brain and watch the neurons. . . . Understanding mathematics involves being able, first, to do mathematics—to perform this sort of reasoning; second, to grasp the standards that govern it . . . ; and, third, to relate mathematical standards to other standards of thought, to work out the place of mathematics in life.[13]

As before, though moral philosophers can and should learn from evolutionary biology, ethics remains its own distinctive discipline, and even if we can learn from evolutionary history and sociobiology the origin and nature of human behavior, at the very least, ethics will still need to "harmonize so far as possible the claims arising from different sides of our nature."

Recent theorizing has not moved beyond the divide between the descriptive nature of evolutionary explanation and the normative content of moral philosophy. As William FitzPatrick argues, "The most that evolutionary biology can do is to point to some plausible causal influences in evolutionary history on some of our moral beliefs to some extent. It can't thereby rule out the philosophical possibility . . . that many of our moral beliefs are instead the result of *apprehending moral truths*, on the model of mathematical beliefs arrived at through understanding relevant reasons as such."[14] As with mathematics, the

---

implications of genetics for morality, beginning with her caustic reply to John Mackie's "The Law of the Jungle." See Midgley, "Gene-Juggling," *Philosophy* 54, no. 210 (October 1979): 439–58; Dawkins replies with "In Defense of Selfish Genes," *Philosophy* 56, no. 218 (October 1981): 556–73; and Midgley replies in turn with "Selfish Genes and Social Darwinism," *Philosophy* 58, no. 225 (July 1983): 365–77.

13. Midgley, *Beast and Man*, 170.

14. William FitzPatrick, "Evolutionary Theory and Morality: Why the Science Doesn't Settle the Philosophical Questions," *Philosophic Exchange* 44, no. 1 (2014): art. 2, p. 17 (emphasis in original), https://soar.suny.edu/handle/20.500.12648/3279.

This compressed essay draws on four other essays: "Morality and Evolutionary Biology," in *Stanford Encyclopedia of Philosophy*, ed. Edward N. Zalta, last modified December 23, 2020, http://plato.stanford.edu/entries/morality-biology/; "Biology, Evolution and Ethics," in *The Continuum Companion to Ethics*, ed. Christian Miller (London: Continuum, 2011), 275–89; "Why There is No Darwinian Dilemma For Ethical Realism," in *Challenges to Moral and Religious Belief: Disagreement and Evolution*, ed. Michael Bergmann and Patrick Kain (Oxford: Oxford University Press, 2014), 237–55; and "Debunking Evolutionary

evolutionary history of our moral capacities does not determine the content of morality itself or the metaphysical nature of moral truths. In turn, we should not be surprised by FitzPatrick's response to Philip Kitcher's *The Ethical Project*, which is perhaps the most ambitious recent attempt to base a normative ethics on a rich account of evolutionary biology and psychology. Kitcher, hoping to "reconcile ethics with a Darwinian picture of life," argues that ethics developed as a human practice in response to our limited capacities for altruism.[15] Ethics makes up for "altruism failures," and over time, ethics is itself a form of "social technology" whose functional purpose is to make possible the egalitarian flourishing of all. Ethical progress consists in more successful functional adaptation of ethical practices to increasingly complex social problems. FitzPatrick's criticisms are straightforward recapitulations of the dialectic that has developed over the last one hundred and fifty years:

> The remedying of altruism failures . . . has no more intrinsic (or noninstrumental) significance within this framework than the monopolization of mating privileges by a dominant male elephant seal has in the biological functional story of seal behavior: both have biological significance, but only as proximate effects that are instrumental to enhancing reproductive output, as we learn in the evolutionary accounts. So nothing in this functional story yet supports treating the remedying of altruism failures as a worthy goal in its own right for us as rational agents, demanding our attention and providing a standard of ethical progress for us.[16]

The story I have been telling so far suggests that evolutionary biology, while perhaps an important background for ethical theorizing, does not in itself settle any of the principle problems of moral philosophy (a conclusion supported by the continued confidence, in the face of evolution, of the major ethical traditions: Kantianism, consequentialism, contractarianism, and Aristotelian naturalism, as well as (perhaps less surprisingly) moral expressivism and moral skepticism.[17] Moral philosophy, though refined in various ways in

---

Debunking of Ethical Realism," *Philosophical Studies* 172, no. 4 (January 2014): 883–904. See also FitzPatrick's earlier *Teleology and the Norms of Nature* (New York: Garland Publishing, 2000), 323–70.

15. Philip Kitcher, *The Ethical Project* (Cambridge: Harvard University Press, 2011), 411.

16. William FitzPatrick, "Review of Philip Kitcher's The Ethical Project," *Ethics* 123, no. 1 (October 2012): 170.

17. For Kantianism, see Christine Korsgaard, "Morality and the Distinctiveness of Human Action," in *Primates and Philosophers: How Morality Evolved*, ed. Stephen Machedo and Josiah Ober (Princeton, NJ: Princeton University Press, 2006), 98–119. See also Korsgaard, *The Sources of Normativity* (Cambridge: Cambridge University Press, 1996),

response to scientific developments after Darwin, seems for the most part to be where it has always been.

And yet, Thomistic ethics seems particularly vulnerable to criticisms grounded in evolutionary biology. Although FitzPatrick convincingly shows that it is possible to construct a wide range of ethical views irrespective of developments in evolutionary biology, this is less comforting for Thomistic ethics, an approach that traditionally grounds moral philosophy in human nature. Here the analogy with mathematics is particularly troubling. Ethics, for Aristotle and Thomas, is precisely *not* like mathematics, for ethics is rooted in our material nature as rational animals, and flows from that nature. Whereas mathematics, we might suppose, is accessed differently by humans and angels, even though its content and metaphysical status are the same for both. But ethics as Thomas and Aristotle conceptualize it flows from our physical nature; therefore, fundamental changes in how we understand our development over time and the more or less universal nature we find ourselves with can be expected to have direct implications for morality.

The problems posed by evolutionary biology for a specifically Thomistic account of ethics are principally twofold. First, Thomistic ethics requires a stable human nature as the theoretical ground of an account of human flourishing that in turn provides the content and justification for the virtues and structures of natural law. The challenge posed by evolutionary biology is not that human beings evolved over time, but that the very processes of evolution entail that there is no such thing as a stable human nature. "Species," as traditionally understood, is nothing more than a convenient shorthand for grouping genetically related populations. This is the metaphysical challenge posed by evolutionary biology.

Second, Darwinian philosophers have argued that evolutionary biology does not determine the content or force of ethics because evolutionary biology tells us how things are and not how things ought to be. Evolutionary biology is descriptive, whereas ethics is normative; we cannot preclude an "ought" given an "is." In terms more familiar to Thomists, we might say that evolutionary biology is part of theoretical reason, whereas ethics is part of practical reason. But Thomists are well known for challenging the divide

---

157–60. For consequentialism, see Peter Singer, "Ethics and Intuitions," *The Journal of Ethics* 9 (2005): 331–52. For contractarianism, see Ken Binmore, *Natural Justice* (Oxford: Oxford University Press, 2005). For Aristotelian naturalism, see Philippa Foot, *Natural Goodness* (Oxford: Oxford University Press, 2001). For moral expressivism, see Philip Kitcher, "Biology and Ethics," in *The Oxford Handbook of Ethical Theory*, ed. David Copp (Oxford: Oxford University Press, 2007), 163–85. For moral skepticism, see Richard Joyce, *The Evolution of Morality* (Cambridge, MA: MIT Press, 2006).

between "is" and "ought," and one standard reading of Thomas concludes that we must begin with theoretical knowledge of human nature and then move to practical knowledge. But if this is the right way to conceive of Thomistic ethics, then Thomists not only cannot make use of the kinds of arguments developed by FitzPatrick and others, but indeed they are as vulnerable to them as the evolutionary biologists against whom they were first directed. How then should we conceive of the relationship between our knowledge of evolutionary biology (and the natural world more broadly) and our knowledge of the virtues and the natural law? This problem is broader than evolutionary biology, of course, but it is made particularly pointed by the arguments formulated by philosophers to protect the autonomy of ethics from recent developments in evolutionary theory. This is the epistemological challenge posed by evolutionary biology.

Although the metaphysical challenge is in some ways the deeper one, it is the epistemological challenge that has been worked over most carefully over the last half century of Thomistic scholarship, and it is there that I will begin.

The most helpful way to think through the epistemological challenge is by analyzing some elements of the debate between the so-called "new natural lawyers" and the traditional interpreters of Thomas.[18] John Finnis's *Natural Law and Natural Rights* represents the most sustained philosophical consideration of this problem from the perspective of the new natural lawyers, and Steven Jensen's *Knowing the Natural Law* represents the best recent restatement of the classical position. Finnis argues flatly that Thomistic ethics does not and cannot move from knowledge of human nature to ethical knowledge. According to Finnis,

> Aquinas asserts as plainly as possible that the first principles of natural law, which specify the basic forms of good and evil and which can be adequately grasped by anyone of the age of reason . . . are *per se nota* (self-evident) and indemonstrable. They are not inferred from speculative principles. They are not inferred from facts. They are not inferred from metaphysical propositions about human nature, or about the nature of good and evil, or about 'the function of a human being', nor

---

18. This tradition of natural law theorizing began with Germain Grisez's work in the 1960s challenging the traditional Thomistic interpretation of Aquinas on natural law. See especially Grisez's "The First Principle of Practical Reason: A Commentary on the Summa Theologiae, 1–2, Question 94, Article 2," *Natural Law Forum* 10 (1965): 168–201. John Finnis and Joseph Boyle were Grisez's most important collaborators, and many scholars have contributed to an extensive and ongoing literature considering the advantages and challenges of this approach. For a recent summary, see Patrick Lee, "The New Natural Law Theory," in *The Cambridge Companion to Natural Law Ethics*, ed. Tom Angier (Cambridge: Cambridge University Press, 2019), 73–91.

are they inferred from a teleological conception of nature or any other conception of nature.[19]

Instead, "by a simple act of non-inferential understanding one grasps that the object of the inclination which one experiences is an instance of a general form of good, for oneself (and others like one)."[20] Finnis's positive account reconstructs Thomistic ethics from a purely practical perspective (as a result of "experiencing one's nature, so to speak, from the inside"), and so is not vulnerable to criticisms derived from evolutionary biology.[21] For Finnis, Thomistic ethics is indeed based on human nature in a metaphysical sense, but it is the lived experience of practical rationality, the inner life of action and rational deliberation, that provides the material for ethical theory, and this inner life yields self-evident practical principles that are metaphysically independent of the story of human development. Of course, our nature must be such that we possess the practical inner life with its corresponding rational inclinations, but how and why we came to have that nature is irrelevant to ethics. Even more, we identify the content and implications of our rational inclinations for the basic human goods (such as knowledge, life, and friendship) not by looking to scientific considerations of our natural habitat or developmental history, but by recognizing them within our practically rational inner life. If this approach is successful, it would entail that evolutionary biology is simply irrelevant to Thomistic ethics (and, mutatis mutandis, Aristotelian ethics more generally[22]). And indeed, the new natural lawyers have almost nothing to say about the relationship between Thomistic ethics and evolution.

The most important criticism of this view is that it is not possible to separate practical reason from theoretical reason the way Finnis suggests, since our practical insights into basic human goods presuppose theoretical knowledge about our nature.[23] For example, consider the basic good of knowledge, the principal example identified and defended by Finnis. According to Finnis, all knowledge is noninstrumentally good in itself, meaning that "reference to

---

19. John Finnis, *Natural Law and Natural Rights* (Oxford: Clarendon Press, 1980; 2nd ed., 2011), 33–34. Citations refer to the first edition.

20. Finnis, *Natural Law and Natural Rights*, 34.

21. Finnis, *Natural Law and Natural Rights*, 34.

22. John Finnis's work parallels John McDowell's development of Aristotelian ethics. Like Finnis, McDowell accepts as fundamental a distinction between the description of our nature as it is and the normativity of ethics, and argues that Aristotle, properly interpreted, agrees. See especially his "Two Sorts of Naturalism," in *Virtues and Reasons: Philippa Foot and Moral Theory*, eds. Rosalind Hursthouse, Gavin Lawrence, and Warren Quinn (Oxford: Clarendon Press, 1995): 149–79.

23. See, for example, Russell Hittinger, *A Critique of the New Natural Law Theory* (Notre Dame: University of Notre Dame Press, 1989), 61–63.

the pursuit of knowledge makes intelligible (though not necessarily reasonable-all-things-considered) any particular instance of the human activity and commitment involved in such pursuit."[24] Although Finnis believes the principle that all knowledge is good is self-evident, he accepts that this truth is not innate, and indeed "the value of truth becomes obvious only to one who has experienced the urge to question, who has grasped the connection between question and answer, who understands that knowledge is constituted by correct answers to particular questions, and who is aware of the possibility of further questions and of other questioners who like himself could enjoy the advantage of attaining correct answers."[25] He continues, "awareness of certain 'factual' possibilities is a necessary condition for the reasonable judgment that truth is a value," even though "judgment itself is derived from no other judgment whatsoever."[26]

Given the necessity of background experience and factual knowledge, it is hard to see how we might conclude, in the purely practical sense that Finnis defends, that all knowledge is good. Suppose I experience—from my perspective as an acting person—an inclination toward knowing this or that particular truth, and I act on that inclination. According to Finnis, the truth in question—say, the number of blades of grass in a particular square inch of ground—itself makes intelligible my pursuit of that truth. But it is not easy to understand what this means. For example, if I am asked why I am counting the blades and I reply that I just want to know how many there are, this is not necessarily an intelligible reply. My behavior might be one form of insanity, precisely because observers will not be able to understand the point of what I am doing (especially if I continue to new squares of ground). It won't help to respond that the difficulty is caused by my single-minded focus, as if my actions would make sense if only I didn't have other important things to do. On the contrary, it is not clear why anyone would want to know how many blades of grass there are in that spot, and for this reason knowledge of the number of blades does not appear to rationalize my behavior. It is true that in certain contexts my actions will be perfectly intelligible; perhaps I am a scientist pursuing a unified body of knowledge to which this truth contributes. But then this truth appears at least partly, if not wholly, instrumentally valuable rather than valuable in itself, and my actions are made intelligible not by the truth in question but by the larger practice of which it is a part. There are an infinite number of truths like this that do not, in any obvious way, make intelligible the actions of those agents seeking to know them.

24. Finnis, *Natural Law and Natural Rights*, 62.
25. Finnis, *Natural Law and Natural Rights*, 65.
26. Finnis, *Natural Law and Natural Rights*, 73.

Because in many cases a particular truth does not seem to rationalize my pursuit of it, there is a fundamental difficulty in Finnis's move from particular truths as rationally explanatory to all knowledge as rationally explanatory. For example, consider Finnis's response to the skeptic: "The skeptical assertion that knowledge is not a good is operationally self-refuting. For one who makes such an assertion, intending it as a serious contribution to rational discussion, is implicitly committed to the proposition that he believes his assertion is worth making, and worth making *qua* true; he thus is committed to the proposition that he believes that truth is a good worth pursuing or knowing."[27] But the skeptic need only object to the claim that all truth, always and everywhere, is rationally explanatory and therefore good. The skeptic might accept that some truths are good, and good as true, including the truth that not all truths are good in themselves and therefore rationally explanatory. Finnis accepts that some truths are not, all things considered, good for particular persons (perhaps all persons always and everywhere?), but argues that nevertheless those truths are good in themselves and would make the actions of someone pursuing them rationally explicable. But Finnis does not give us sufficient reasons to conclude—from the explanatory power (and therefore goodness) of a wide range of truths—that all truths everywhere are good.[28]

The argument he does offer to support this move is suggestive:

> Knowledge is a state of affairs instantiated, centrally, when someone has grasped and correctly followed the reasons for judging a true proposition true, or a false proposition false. It is (so far forth) a leaving behind of ignorance and muddle, an avoiding of error, misinformation, and delusion. Indifference to its value makes one all too likely to remain the dupe of falsehood and delusion, to be myth-ridden, or simply benighted, ignorant. These are deficiencies, conditions of some indignity; to point to that indignity—to those deficiencies—is one way of explaining the value of knowledge, of the state of affairs (way of *being*) by which one (so far forth) escapes them.[29]

This is surely the right way to think about knowledge from a Thomistic perspective, and indeed for St. Thomas, knowing the number of blades of grass

---

27. Finnis, *Natural Law and Natural Rights*, 74–75.
28. For somewhat related arguments against knowledge as a basic good, see Joseph Raz, "Value: A Menu of Questions," in *Reason, Morality, and Law: The Philosophy of John Finnis*, ed. John Keown and Robert P. George (Oxford: Oxford University Press, 2013), 13–23.
29. John Finnis, "Reflections and Responses," in Keown and George, *Reason, Morality, and Law*, 460.

in each square of ground is indeed good and rationally explanatory, but only against a complex metaphysical background that identifies and defends a particular "way of being" that understands our rational nature in a particular way and likewise identifies God himself as omniscient and all good. It is this metaphysical background—which goes beyond "the awareness of certain factual possibilities" to include a metaphysical understanding of human nature, and not simply awareness of many particular good truths—that justifies the move from the intrinsic goodness of particular truths to the intrinsic goodness of all truths as such.

The traditional interpretation of St. Thomas, in opposition to Finnis, is that we must instead move from theoretical reason to practical reason, and so from a metaphysical philosophy of nature (especially human nature, and the results of empirical science) to moral philosophy. In recent scholarship, Steven Jensen has been the most careful and ambitious defender of this interpretation of St. Thomas and Thomistic ethics. In *Knowing the Natural Law*, Jensen argues that St. Thomas develops and defends a successful account of natural law ethics that moves slowly but confidently from purely speculative knowledge of human nature to fully practical knowledge informing our good (and bad) actions.[30] Jensen returns many times to a series of steps by means of which we move from speculative knowledge to practical knowledge: perception of (1) an event, (2) then agency, (3) then inclination, (4) then goodness, (5) and finally, obligation. Consider Jensen's initial, vivid example: we observe felled trees, and trace this back to the activity of beavers. We then recognize that beavers are inclined toward the felling of trees as an end, that felling trees is therefore good for beavers, and finally that beavers ought to fell trees. Though this is a nonhuman example, the general structure also applies to human nature and the human good. Jensen argues that the human intellect itself first knows being, is subsequently aware of its own act of knowing, then recognizes its own tendency toward being which is therefore a human good and a source of human obligation. This gives us the general structure for the future development of the overall human good; the goods of the moral life are goods discovered by attending to our inclinations toward truth, reproduction, eating and drinking, manual labor, and so on.

Finnis's response to this kind of argument is predictable: "Why should free human persons treat as foundationally directive for choice the natural goodness, or natural normativity, of the given-in-nature, even in 'human nature'? Why not strike out in new paths, and suppress or transform the immanent teleology,

---

30. Steven Jensen, *Knowing the Natural Law: From Precepts and Inclinations to Deriving Oughts* (Washington, DC: The Catholic University of America Press, 2015). The discussion that follows draws especially on pages 71 through 84.

in ways perhaps cautious or perhaps far-reaching?"[31] Natural philosophy (and likewise evolutionary biology) serves ethics by providing the minor (factual) premises of practical syllogisms, but cannot provide normative guidance.

But the deeper problem with Jensen's position is also a problem for Finnis. Suppose we see those felled trees, and then observe that this is caused by beavers. What allows us to suppose beavers are inclined toward the felling of trees? Perhaps all we have is a mere collection of interacting forces that happen to arrange themselves in certain ways, which we then happen to call "the felling of trees by beavers." Jensen needs us to recognize the nature of beavers *before* coming to an understanding of what is good for beavers, and this example is unpersuasive. After all, once we say that the felling of the trees is caused by beavers, we are already assuming that the felling is caused by an animate creature with certain ends, including the felling of trees.

Jensen draws on a suggestive passage from Aquinas to defend his general approach: "Final cause indicates three things. First, it is the terminus of motion, through which it is opposed to the principle of motion, which is the efficient cause. Second, it is the first thing in intention, for which reason it is said to be 'that for the sake of which [or the cause for which (*sic*)].' Third, it is desirable in itself, for which reason it is called good, for the good is that which all things desire."[32] Jensen reads this as structuring a temporal epistemological sequence: first, we recognize a terminus of motion and an efficient cause, then an inclination toward the terminus, and finally the terminus as good for the agent. But it seems more plausible that we understand all three aspects of a final cause all at once. Of course, we can use one or another aspect of final causality to shed light on another aspect, but no one aspect has epistemological priority. Recognizing that a "terminus of motion" is opposed to our understanding of somethings "good" does not force us to reconsider our understanding of the good in question; the contradiction could just as easily force us to reevaluate our understanding of the particular terminus of motion. The point is that we come to understand somethings nature and what makes it good at one and the same time—to recognize an animal as a beaver is already to recognize it as aiming toward a particular set of goods. If this is right, we cannot disentangle our speculative knowledge of human nature from our practical knowledge of the human good.

---

31. John Finnis, "Reflections and Responses," in Keown and George, *Reason, Morality, and Law*, 460. Finnis is replying to an earlier essay in the same volume by John Haldane who argues that Thomistic practical reason should not be completely independent of a speculative account of human nature.

32. Jensen, *Knowing the Natural Law*, 76. The quotation is from *In Meta.*, lib. 1, lect. 4, n. 71.

Consider again Jensen's example of the intellect. The intellect knows being, then knows it is inclined toward being, and finally, that understanding being is good for it. We are in the same situation here as we are with respect to the beaver. For there to be any recognition on our part that the intellect knows being, it must also be understood that an intellect is engaging in the act of knowing, which already implies recognition of the nature and good of the intellect itself. Just as we cannot pull apart in a series of temporally extended epistemological moments the felling, the inclining, and the perfecting of the beaver, so we cannot pull apart the knowing of being, the inclination toward the knowing, and the goodness of the knowing. Knowing what the intellect is doing cannot be epistemologically prior to knowing its nature, what is good for it, or what it ought to do; we can start with any of these four steps and arrive at any of the others.

The example of the intellect raises an additional problem. There are a great many inclinations that make up human nature, most of them nonrational and purely biological; for example, the immensely various cellular level inclinations. Why should we focus on such macroscopic inclinations as that of the intellect (or the entire reproductive system)? The obvious answer is that the intellect plays a special role in the overall human good. But how do we know this? As Jensen rightly notes, since we cannot simply read off what we are to do from the observation of our natural inclinations, how can we escape the conclusion that it is the joy resulting from our actions themselves that justifies the claim that the perfection of the intellect is a central element of fully human perfection? Jensen is attempting to show that we can use speculative knowledge as a foundation for practical knowledge. The new natural lawyers defend an autonomous practical rationality that is independent of speculative knowledge of human nature. The implication of the challenge I have been developing here is that, instead, neither speculative nor practical knowledge is epistemologically prior. Joyful satisfaction in the completion of an action might be evidence that my conception of human nature and its related natural inclinations should be revised, or it might just as easily be evidence that my understanding of the possibilities for human joy needs revision in light of my account of human nature.

In other words, Finnis and Jensen recapitulate the dialectic regarding the importance of an understanding of the natural world for moral philosophy. Finnis repeats the standard charge against biologically oriented philosophers: we cannot draw any normative conclusions from a description of human nature as it happens to be (or happens to have developed). Jensen repeats the standard charge against those philosophers who believe we can construct an account of ethics independent of an account of human nature: so-called "self-evident practical principles" depend—for their normative force—on hidden theoretical claims about human nature and its teleological structure. If what I argued above is right, then in a sense both positions are correct; neither foundational strategy works, simply because accounts of human nature and accounts of practical principles are mutually entangled in such a way that neither can be independently foundational for ethics. If we try to begin with speculative knowledge of human nature, we will find that the identification of a coherent and unified human nature, decisions regarding which parts of human nature are most important, and to what extent various inclinations are normative, already presuppose an understanding of the human good (and so also an understanding of human morality). Likewise, if we try to begin with the interior life of practical rationality, we will find that the identification and defense of self-evident practical principles, as well as the identification and resolution of potential conflicts between these principles, already presuppose a theoretical understanding of human nature.

The most helpful resource for the problems I am interested in here is the philosopher Michael Thompson, whose 2008 book *Life and Action* is a careful analysis of a range of concepts relevant to this discussion. Thompson's aim is a "logical treatment of the idea of life, and its near relatives, and their expression in language."[33] He begins by arguing that the language we use when talking about biological organisms has some striking features. According to a typical introductory biology textbook, living things are highly organized and homeostatic. In addition, they grow and develop, adapt, and take energy from the environment and change it from one form to another. They also respond to stimuli and reproduce themselves.[34] But what do we mean, for example, by claiming that living things, as opposed to nonliving things, "grow"? Merely "increasing in size" is insufficient, since crystals do that. We cannot fix the problem by saying instead that living things grow by "taking in new material and transforming it into themselves so as to increase their size." Lakes and rivers do the same every time it rains. We could, on the other hand, fix the problem by saying that living things grow by the processes of metabolization, but now we have a different problem. We have defined one living process in terms of another, and when it comes to defining what we mean by "metabolize" it will turn out that we are in the same situation we found ourselves in with respect to "growth." In short, attempts to define "growth" in a way appropriate to living things end up either unable to distinguish living growth

---

33. Michael Thompson, *Life and Action: Elementary Structures of Practice and Practical Thought* (Cambridge, MA: Harvard University Press, 2008), 27.

34. Thompson draws from Helena Curtis, *Biology*, 3rd ed. (New York: Worth, 1979), 20–21. He chooses Curtis for sentimental reasons but suggests any number of others might of course have been chosen.

from nonliving growth, or condemned to going round in a circle: living things are the ones that grow in the ways characteristic of living things. The language of living things is separate in important ways from the language of nonliving things, and we cannot talk about living things by means of more general concepts applicable to nonliving things. Thompson argues, "These concepts, the vital categories, together form a sort of solid block, and we run into a kind of circle in attempting to elucidate any of them."[35] There is something irreducible about the language of life.

Species concepts, critical for Thomistic ethics, represent a special subset of the words of this language. In order to develop a useful understanding of what a species is, Thompson analyzes sentences he calls "natural-historical judgments" or "Aristotelian categoricals." Consider the sentence "Black Angus cattle eat grass." This sentence is not quantifiable in any ordinary way. We do not mean to say that all Black Angus cattle eat grass. Many Black Angus are too young to eat grass or are fed other kinds of food, such as corn. And we do not mean that this or that particular Black Angus eats grass. In fact, it could easily be the case that no Black Angus is actually eating grass. It might even happen that Black Angus cattle become extinct, and yet the sentence will in an important sense still be true. This sentence and sentences like it are "categorical" since they do not allow for exceptions, even though this or that particular cow might not express the (surface) truth of the sentence. Rather, the universality implied by the sentence is of a different order. It is instead something like "all properly constituted and healthy Black Angus cows eat grass." There are many natural-historical judgments that we make:

> Horses have four legs.
> Acorns grow into oak trees.
> Adult humans have thirty-two teeth.
> The common lilac grows between eight and fifteen feet tall.

These statements are not straightforward claims about individuals. Instead, they say something about the particular lifeform in question. As a type of statement, they are about something that we might conveniently call a species. And like the conceptual vocabulary of life more generally, Aristotelian categoricals cannot be reduced to other kinds of sentences. Since these sentences do not say things about particulars, at least not in any straightforward way, we cannot turn "Horses have four legs" into "Each horse has four legs" or "If something is a horse, then it has four legs." It might seem more reasonable to translate this sentence into "Most horses have four legs." But this will not

---

35. Thompson, *Life and Action*, 47.

work either, and not only because we could maim all living horses and the sentence would still be true. As Thompson reminds us, although "the mayfly breeds shortly before dying" counts as an Aristotelian categorical, most mayflies die long before breeding. Aristotelian categoricals therefore have a special and irreducible logical form, and we use it to point toward a peculiar philosophical reality—a lifeform or species.

As the phrase "properly constituted and healthy" suggests, Aristotelian categoricals include normative content like "A Black Angus cow *should* eat grass" or "Horses *ought* to have four legs." Statements like these are (each in their own way) statements about health or illness or flourishing. These statements are normative judgments because they establish standards by which we judge individuals. Is a particular Black Angus healthy? We determine this by looking to the Aristotelian categoricals that apply to Black Angus cattle and evaluating this particular cow accordingly. Speaking generally about the relationship between Aristotelian categoricals and normativity, Thompson says, "What merely 'ought to be' in the individual we may say really 'is' in its form."[36] It is likewise possible to extend this to claims about human morality. Like claims about human health, claims about human morality are normative claims that are founded on the Aristotelian categoricals of the human form. "Humans have two eyes" provides a normative foundation for saying "I ought to have two eyes" and "Missing an eye is a defect in human beings." Likewise, "Humans are rational" provides a normative foundation for saying "I ought to be rational" and "Acting contrary to reason is a defect in human beings."[37] This does not make moral epistemology easy. Indeed, we still face two difficult tasks. First, we must identify those Aristotelian categoricals that are true of human beings. Is it an Aristotelian categorical, for example, that "Human beings tell the truth"? If so, then we have a normative foundation for the concept of the human species for statements like "Human beings should tell the truth." Second, although any Aristotelian categorical is a foundation for normative claims about human behavior, it is clear that in many instances we cannot satisfy the normative force of one categorical without contradicting the normative force of another. If "Humans beings tell the truth" and "Human beings are grateful" are both true Aristotelian categoricals, how

---

36. Thompson, *Life and Action*, 81.
37. Philippa Foot's *Natural Goodness* develops an account of Aristotelian ethics by drawing on an earlier version of Thompson's analysis of Aristotelian categoricals; see Michael Thompson, "The Representation of Life," in Hursthouse, Lawrence, and Quinn, *Virtues and Reasons*, 247–96. Thompson argues in *Life and Action* that Foot moves too quickly from the natural normativity of Aristotelian categoricals to ethics, but he is, generally speaking, supportive of this approach to ethics were the necessary conceptual philosophical analysis possible.

should one act when asked what one thinks of an ugly gift? Aristotelian categoricals show a conceptual link between practical and theoretical reflections, and so between the philosophy of nature (and empirical science) and Thomistic ethics. They provide an integrated framework for moral philosophy, but do not make the tasks of moral philosophy easier than we should expect them to be.

Jennifer Frey, following Thompson, argues that Thompson's account of our language about the human life-form allows us to "locate the ground of ethical judgments in human *nature*; in so doing, it supplies precisely that which is often lacking in contemporary natural law theories: viz. a clear enough and thick enough conception of 'nature' that can serve as the ground of normative ethical judgments."[38] Nevertheless, "the ethical naturalist's category of species or life form is most emphatically *not* the same as that employed by the evolutionary biologist, nor does it somehow stand in competition with it."[39] Instead, "A representation of something as alive is both logically and phenomenologically more primitive than the empirical concept of a biological species; after all, the evolutionary biologist would fail to have a topic of inquiry if she could not first merely represent something *as* a particular living being or life form."[40] We have reason to think that empirical science (including evolutionary biology) is an abstraction and depends implicitly on an Aristotelian understanding of life and the particular lifeforms under examination. Even the identification of a particular biological process as a "process," for example, and so as unified in particular ways, already suggests an entire range of concepts that depend on the form of judgment expressed by Aristotelian categoricals.[41]

---

38. Jennifer Frey, "Neo-Aristotelian Ethical Naturalism," in *The Cambridge Companion to Natural Law Ethics*, ed. Tom Angier (Cambridge: Cambridge University Press, 2019), 105.
39. Frey, "Neo-Aristotelian Ethical Naturalism," 97.
40. Frey, "Neo-Aristotelian Ethical Naturalism," 97.
41. Consider this passage from Thompson: "It is interesting that if the only categories we have to apply are those of chemistry and physics, there is an obvious sense in which *no such succession of goings-on will add up to a single process*. In a description of photosynthesis, for example, we read of one chemical process—one process-in-the-sense-of-chemistry, one 'reaction'—followed by another, and then another. Having read along a bit with mounting enthusiasm, we can ask: 'And what happens next?' If we are stuck with chemical and physical categories, the only answer will be: 'Well, it depends on whether an H-bomb goes off, or the temperature plummets toward absolute zero, or it all falls into a vat of sulfuric acid. . . .' That a certain enzyme will appear and split the latest chemical product into two is just one among many possibilities. Physics and chemistry, adequately developed, can tell you what happens in any of these circumstances—in *any* circumstance—but it seems that they cannot attach any sense to a question 'What happens next?' *sans*

Thus far, I have been working through the epistemological challenge to Thomistic ethics. The examples I have used are especially concerned with the structures of the natural law, but the same dialectic exists with respect to the virtues. Must our knowledge of ethical truths begin with theoretical (and perhaps scientific) knowledge of human nature? Or is this knowledge necessarily grounded on first-person practical experience alone? I believe Thompson's work shows that neither approach is fruitful. Given any particular attempt to ground ethics on preethical claims about human nature, or instead on purely practical knowledge that needs no speculative foundation, we will always be able to show ways in which particular nonethical claims, or particular truths of practical reason, depend conceptually on one another.

What implications might this have for the metaphysical challenge? Evolutionary biology, if its implicit presuppositions were spelled out with sufficient detail, would imply the deeper structures identified by Thompson, and so itself is part of a larger, intimate connection between nature and ethics. But do we have reason to think that our conceptual vocabulary represents actual realities out there in the world? This is of course one version of a very old problem in philosophy: what reason do we have for thinking that our first-person subjective perspective tells us anything objectively true about the external world? Given the framework of evolutionary biology, Aristotelian categoricals are all well and good, and perhaps species and lifeforms express an inescapable form of judgment, but are we justified in saying that species and lifeforms exist in the real world, and therefore that our morality has an objective foundation?

Here I wish to address only a particular form of this problem: given the inescapable conceptual framework of Aristotelian categoricals, does evolutionary biology give us reasons for or against the real existence of species? I take as an epistemological first principle—which I will not attempt to defend here—that our everyday beliefs about lifeforms, expressed in the natural-historical judgments Thompson describes, provide *prima facie* reason to believe these judgments correspond to metaphysical realities in the world around us. This puts the burden of proof on those who would deny such metaphysical realities.

At first glance, it seems that evolutionary biology clearly gives us reasons to deny the metaphysical reality of species. Evolutionary biology describes a temporally extended continuum of developing organisms, and any break in terms of species seems arbitrary and without a biological foundation. And yet

---

phrase. The biochemical treatise thus appears to make implicit play with a special determination of the abstract conception of a process, one distinct from any expressed in physics or in chemistry proper" (*Life and Action*, 41–42). See also Dumsday, "Is There Still Hope," 394–95.

the practices of evolutionary biology entail traditional breaks between organisms that are fittingly described as breaks between species. Consider, for example, the arguments of Michael Devitt. Devitt argues that "explanations in biology demand that there be essential intrinsic underlying properties."[42] Biological explanations are either historical or structural. A historical explanation will show the genealogical connections between this human being and other members of the species *Homo sapiens* to explain, for example, why a person has thirty-two teeth. This person has thirty-two teeth because she is a member of *Homo sapiens*, and she is a member of *Homo sapiens* because she is a descendant of members of *Homo sapiens*, whose members have (normally) thirty-two teeth. A structural explanation will instead point to genetic or other intrinsic properties of the species *Homo sapiens*. This person has thirty-two teeth because she is a member of *Homo sapiens*, and members of *Homo sapiens* possess a set of intrinsic properties that give rise (normally) to thirty-two teeth. Historical explanations explain by means of descent from a group, whereas structural explanations explain by means of the internal structural properties of a group.

Devitt's core claim is that meaningful biological explanation depends fundamentally on structural explanations. For this reason, if biology is to remain explanatory, it requires the existence of natural kinds that possess essential intrinsic properties. If we want to know why I am a member of *Homo sapiens*, we could offer a historical explanation and say that I am genealogically related to a particular grouping within evolutionary history. But purely genealogical explanations are problematic. Since historical explanations depend solely on genealogical connections, we have no way of knowing where breaks between species occur, since evolutionary theory entails that all living things are genealogically connected. If historical explanations depend on genealogical criteria alone, then it will turn out that there is only one species. If we supplement genealogical sameness with property differences, then we will have too many species, since every individual will turn out to be distinct from every other in terms of at least one property, and so every individual will constitute a unique species. Historical explanation alone results in either too much unity or too much difference.

Structural explanations look to the causal powers of shared characteristics as the foundation of biological explanation. This human being is a member

---

42. Michael Devitt, "Resurrecting Biological Essentialism," *Philosophy of Science* 75, no. 3 (2008): 349. See also his related papers "Defending Intrinsic Biological Essentialism," *Philosophy of Science* (forthcoming); "Historical Biological Essentialism," *Studies in History and Philosophy of Biology and Biomedical Science* 71 (2018): 1–7; and "Individual Essentialism in Biology," *Biology and Philosophy* 33, no. 39 (2018).

of *Homo sapiens* because he possesses genetic and other biological traits possessed by all members of *Homo sapiens*, and the concept *Homo sapiens* depends on structural explanations for its explanatory power. More broadly, while historical explanation is important in biology, it depends (at least in part) on structural explanation, and structural explanation itself is at the heart of biological practice. Why does this individual behave in these ways? Because he is a member of *Homo sapiens*, and as such is disposed to manifest these behaviors because of the structural features of *Homo sapiens*. Structural explanations reveal the shared causal powers possessed by a group of individuals, which in turn provides (at least part of) the basis for grouping them together as a single species. Species concepts are explanatorily useful only if grounded in shared intrinsic properties.

If this way of thinking about biological practice is correct, then we have reason to reject metaphysical skepticism about natural kinds. The practice of evolutionary biology itself depends on distinguishing between groups of individuals based on intrinsic properties, and the burden of proof is on the skeptic to explain our everyday practice in a way that preserves the explanatory power of empirical science while avoiding dependence on essential natural kinds.

Where does this leave Thomistic ethics? I believe there are three important conclusions to draw. First, neither theoretical reflection (be it natural philosophy, evolutionary biology, or other disciplines) nor practical reflection (i.e., the analysis of the first-person practical experience of human agents) provides foundational epistemological access to human morality. The compresence of normative and descriptive content in Aristotelian categoricals expresses the basic conceptually dependent relationship between human nature and human ethics—the content of each entails the content of the other, and neither is ultimately epistemologically prior to the other.

Second, although neither analysis of human nature nor analysis of first-person practical agency is epistemologically prior, both can provide content and correction to the other. For example, Finnis contends that all knowledge is intrinsically good. But while there are uncountably many examples of knowledge as rationally explanatory, this does not entail the conclusion that all truths are always in and of themselves rationally explanatory. What might justify confidence that any particular truth is such that under the right conditions it could be rationally explanatory? Though first-person analysis of the operation of practical reason does not entail that all knowledge is intrinsically good, theoretical reflection can give us reason to conclude that it is, and in two senses. In the first sense, theoretical reflection can provide a framework informed by the philosophical analysis of human nature (accompanied by evidence from empirical science, including sciences such as anthropology as well as evolutionary biology) that includes an architectonic place for reason in human life and human fulfillment, such that it would be reasonable to conclude that truth is always *prima facie* worth pursuing. This could be an account of "knowing" as a "way of being" and a source of ultimate fulfillment. Such a framework does not demonstrate that knowledge is a basic good— instead, it supports that claim by showing it is a plausible description of human nature as far as we can make sense of it, and therefore that we have reason to conclude from instances of truth as explanatory that truth as such is explanatory (and therefore good). Such a framework requires a stable and scientifically defensible account of human nature that includes a set of intrinsic causal powers. While evolutionary biology in some ways challenges the existence of a stable human nature, in other ways (if Devitt and others are right) it supports the existence of such a nature, even if we have no absolute guarantee that this nature came into existence during this or that phase of evolutionary history and might not change, or pass away, in a later phase of evolutionary history.

In a second sense, theoretical reflection can provide support for Finnis's claim about knowledge by confirming our own first-person practical analysis and by comparing our experience to that of countless other human experiences. Even if Finnis is right and it is in some deep sense self-evident that all knowledge is good, our grasp of self-evident truths is always vulnerable to the possibility of self-delusion (or, in the extreme, forms of insanity); no matter how certain I am that something is true, it might always be possible that I am self-deluded or in other ways mistaken. Theoretical reflection is—at least in part—the pooling of countless first-person practical perspectives, and therefore acts as a check on (or confirmation of) potentially misleading first-person practical experience. My approach here rejects epistemological foundationalism in ethics in favor of the epistemology of "traditions" developed by Alasdair MacIntyre, though I have not been using his vocabulary.[43]

Just as practical reflection depends on theoretical reflection for justification and confirmation, so theoretical reflection likewise depends on practical reflection. Jensen argues that the intellect is the (or at least a) primary human inclination. But there are many inclinations that make up human nature, including a diverse range of unconscious cellular level inclinations. So what justifies our focus on the intellect? First-person practical experiences of the sort described by Finnis show us that the pursuit and achievement of truth plays a special role, or even a dominant one, in our practical lives in a way far different from and superior to nonconscious inclinations. It is fundamentally important, for example, that intellectual frustration results in a special (and

---

43. See especially Alasdair MacIntyre, *Three Rival Traditions of Moral Enquiry: Encyclopedia, Genealogy, and Tradition* (Notre Dame, IN: University of Notre Dame Press, 1990), chapters 6, 8, and 9.

critical) form of human suffering (and likewise knowledge frequently yields a special form of human joy), whereas our cellular level inclinations do not result in a comparable practical experience. Our practical experience provides criteria by which we judge the relative importance of theoretical elements of human nature (and the natures of all other living things). Theoretical accounts of human nature are, at least in part, predictive models of what makes human beings flourish. If these models contradict our practical experience, we have reason to question our models, just as we likewise would have reason to question our practical experience if we could not find a plausible theoretical model of human nature that would fit that experience. This is one reason why a developmental account of altruistic behavior, like Philip Kitcher's, is unsatisfying as a model—it cannot give a plausible explanation of the first-person practical selflessness of our individual behavior.

The third and final conclusion that should be drawn is that evolutionary biology (at least in its current state) leaves Thomistic ethics for the most part where it has always been. Contemporary empirical science gives us new resources from which to draw for our reflections on human nature, human flourishing, the virtues, and natural law, but it does not force us to reject any of the core structuring elements of Thomistic ethics, or to revise (at least in any straightforward way) our conceptions of the virtues or the precepts of the natural law or the rich account of human life provided in the *secunda secundae*. Some versions of evolutionary biology might prompt substantial revisions or even wholesale rejection, but there is enough theoretical ambiguity and conflict within evolutionary biology—most importantly regarding the possibility of stable natural kinds—that the discipline as a whole is not in direct and decisive conflict with Thomistic ethics. But because Thomistic ethics requires theoretical confirmation and support in the ways outlined above, empirical science is integral to the defense and continued development of Thomistic ethics. Thomistic ethics is indeed compatible with evolutionary biology, but any confidence we might have that this will continue to be the case requires ongoing critical engagement with the methods, results, and implications of both.

CHAPTER SIX

The Teaching of the Catholic Church and the Evolution of Humanity

SIMON FRANCIS GAINE, OP

What does Christianity have to say about the evolution of the first human beings? This chapter investigates how Catholic teaching frames theological questions about the relationship between God's original creation of humanity and the scientific theory of evolution. In principle, Catholic theology pursues its characteristic inquiries in the light of divine revelation as it is transmitted in Scripture and tradition and in communion with the authoritative teaching of the pope and bishops. This means that, for a Catholic, undertaking any such investigation into human origins must involve awareness of how it is situated in relation to Church doctrine. In what follows, I shall clarify what the Church has to say about questions involving human evolution, taking into account the different recognized levels of its teaching authority. In this way, I hope to give an indication of what kind of theological approaches to evolution are possible within the context of fidelity not only to human scientific endeavor but also to Catholic doctrine.[1]

Any Catholic theologian rightly approaches questions of human origins in the light of both faith and reason. That one should have confidence not only as concerns faith but also about the power of human reason is characteristic of Catholic teaching, especially at a time when reason can be subjected to a postmodern relativism. The most significant articulation in recent times of the relationship between faith and reason proposed by the Catholic Church is surely Pope St. John Paul II's encyclical letter, *Fides et Ratio* (1998). Important expressions of this positive relationship can also be found in the nineteenth century in Pope Leo XIII's recommendation of the scholastic

---

1. For an earlier attempt at this task, see Ernest C. Messenger, *Evolution and Theology: The Problem of Man's Origin* (London: Burns, Oates & Washbourne, 1931), 1–3. A more recent contribution can be found in Nicholas E. Lombardo, OP, "Evolutionary Genetics and Theological Narratives of Human Origins," *The Heythrop Journal* 59 (2018): 523–33.

philosophy of St. Thomas Aquinas in *Aeterni Patris* (1879), and in the First Vatican Council's Dogmatic Constitution on the Catholic Faith, *Dei Filius* (1870). It is this confidence in both faith and reason—and the positive relationship between them—that explains why Catholics explore the issue of human origins not only by taking account of what is proposed by the word of God in the pages of Holy Scripture, but also by considering the contribution of human reason by way of the natural sciences.

The Catholic theologian, beginning from the perspective of faith, normally approaches questions of human origins with close attention to the early chapters of Genesis—read in the light the wider biblical canon, especially the New Testament—and to Christian Tradition. Genesis 1 brings the creation of living things of various kinds to a climax with the creation of humankind, male and female, in the image and likeness of God. Genesis 2 then presents the body of Adam—the first man—as formed by God from the dust of the earth, and Eve—the first woman—as formed by God from one of Adam's ribs. The Genesis narrative further presents this single couple as the beginning of the human race as a whole, where Eve is the "mother of all the living" (Gen 3:20). This couple enjoyed in the garden of Eden a certain intimacy with God and their surroundings, including access to the tree of life, which was denied them after they sinned and were expelled from Eden. In the New Testament, St. Paul interprets the Genesis narrative in terms of the origin and spread of sin and death throughout the human race as stemming from Adam's disobedience (Romans 5).[2] The chronology of the Old Testament positions these events as happening not many thousands of years ago.

What light Church teaching throws on these biblical texts is more pressing in the case of human origins because modern science appears to tell a different story. Modern science explains human origins in terms of the theory of evolution, where the biological species or subspecies to which we belong—*Homo sapiens*—takes its origin from a wider biological classing of human species or subspecies, of which *Homo sapiens* is the only living example today. This wider biological species or class of different humans is derived from a wider biological classing of hominids, and then from primates, and so on. Whether modern science considers *Homo sapiens* only, or humans more broadly, human beings have their origin from other living hominids by way of evolution.

Population genetics thinks of no single original couple in any of these cases of species or subspecies, but of a particular population that becomes relatively isolated on its own distinct evolutionary pathway.[3] Although there are

---

2. For discussion, see Fr. Isaac Morales, OP, chapter 9 in this volume.
3. For discussion of the evolutionary science behind the claims made in this paragraph, see Fr. Nicanor Austriaco, OP, chapter 10 in this volume.

ongoing debates about what precisely constitutes a biological species, it seems fair to say that over many generations, such a particular population emerges as a distinct species insofar as it can no longer breed successfully with those other populations to whom it is most closely related.[4] In terms of number, as far as *Homo sapiens* is concerned, we are speaking of a breeding population of some thousands. Moreover, there is no evidence from science of any kind of a primeval golden age in Eden, whether we date it at the origin of the first human species, at the origin of *Homo sapiens*, or of any other human species or subspecies. Neither is there in any of these cases evidence of anything other than human mortality. Finally, the emergence of *Homo sapiens* is dated some two hundred thousand to three hundred thousand years ago, and that of other closely related species far earlier.

It is not open to a Catholic theologian to suppose that, while divine revelation teaches the truth to faith, human reason—including scientific reason—can in principle deliver a truth of its own that conflicts with faith. While such approaches have appeared from time to time in Christian history, the Catholic Church takes the position that truth cannot contradict truth and that God is the source of both divine faith and human reason. When in 1513 the Church's Fifth Lateran Council condemned the philosophical opinions that there is one human soul common to all and that human souls are mortal, it made appeal to the fact that truth cannot contradict truth. The Christian teaching that the soul is individual and immortal and a philosophical theory in conflict with that teaching cannot both be true, and so the latter is false.[5] Vatican I reiterated this principle, stating that there "can never be any real discrepancy between faith and reason."[6] Hence, while it may be the case that a particular theory wrongly based on philosophical or scientific reason is false and incompatible with Christian faith, it is not the case that the relationship between faith and reason can be negotiated by regarding them as opposed in principle. Thus, while Catholics may be obliged by their faith to reject certain versions of the theory of evolution (such as atheistic or materialist interpretations), it is not open to them to reject a genuine delivery of scientific reason. But while the current *Catechism of the Catholic Church* repeats this positive view of the relation between science and faith, it makes no explicit mention of the theory

---

4. For discussion of the debate over the specification of a biological species, see Fr. Mariusz Tabaczek, OP, chapter 2 in this volume.

5. H. Denzinger, *Compendium of Creeds, Definitions, and Declarations on Matters of Faith and Morals*, 43rd ed., ed. Peter Hünermann, Robert Fastiggi, and Anne Englund Nash (San Francisco: Ignatius, 2012), 1441. References hereafter are given as "DH." Translations used in this chapter are either from DH or are modified versions.

6. DH, 3017.

of evolution per se.⁷ That is not to say that the theory of evolution as it regards human origins has escaped the notice of the Church teaching authority (or magisterium, as it is known).

Especially since the nineteenth century, theological reflection on the Church's teaching mission has led to clarification on the different levels of authority exercised by the Church's teaching authority. The document *On the Ecclesial Vocation of the Theologian*, issued by the Vatican's Congregation of the Doctrine of the Faith (today known as the Dicastery for the Doctrine of the Faith) in 1990, specifies these different levels (together with various distinctions) in relation to the work of a theologian.⁸ For example, it speaks of the "ordinary and universal magisterium"—which refers to the college of bishops, of which the pope is head—when the college teaches infallibly and therefore definitively, even when dispersed throughout the world. According to Catholic teaching, it is the gift of infallibility that enables the Church to reliably pass on what has been revealed by God to faith. When something is taught infallibly, it is taught definitively and so is not open to change. It may be further clarified and developed, and balanced by some other teaching, but it cannot be exchanged for some different teaching.

Through the ordinary and universal magisterium, this gift of infallibility is something at work continually in the day-to-day transmission of Catholic teaching. From the nature of the case, however, it is not so straightforward a matter to discern when something is infallibly taught by the college of bishops dispersed throughout the world. In lieu of an actual consultation of the bishops on some particular matter, theologians have their own ways of concluding what falls under the scope of the ordinary and universal magisterium, as we shall see in this chapter. It is in fact far easier to have clarity that something is taught infallibly when it is made the object of a solemn definition. This takes place through an extraordinary exercise of the Church's teaching authority by a pope, or the college of bishops gathered in an ecumenical council. An example of this "extraordinary magisterium" is the solemn definition in 1854 by Pope Bl. Pius IX that our Lady's Immaculate Conception is revealed by God such that it is to be firmly believed by all the faithful.⁹

This charism of infallibility is understood, however, not to be limited to truths revealed to faith, but to extend to certain propositions "intimately connected with them." Because of this strict connection, were such nonrevealed propositions not also affirmed, it would become impossible to expound and guard the truths of faith themselves. These nonrevealed truths then are taught

---

7. *Catechism of the Catholic Church*, rev. ed. (London: Bloomsbury, 1999), 159, 283.
8. DH, 4877. See also DH, 5071–72.
9. DH, 2803.

definitively by the Church and are sometimes known, in contrast to the primary truths of faith, as the "secondary object" of infallibility.[10] Such teachings might include philosophical questions about the nature of the human soul, which are not strictly revealed, but are closely connected to what God has revealed. An example would be the Council of Vienne's definition in 1312 that the soul immediately informs the body.[11] While the response of Catholics to what is divinely revealed is one of faith, the same cannot be said for matters that have not been so revealed. Given the definitive way in which these truths are taught, however, they need to be "firmly accepted and held." While they are not believed by faith, strictly speaking, they are nevertheless to be held definitively on the basis of faith.

While we need to ask to what extent questions of human origins fall under such infallible and definitive levels of teaching, we also need to take account of the fact that much of the Church's teaching falls outside the scope of the gift of infallibility. The mission of the Church can require there to be authoritative teaching in a multitude of areas, where the act of teaching will not be definitive or at least there will be no definitive act for the time being. The "ordinary magisterium" refers to popes, bishops, and local councils of bishops exercising such a noninfallible teaching ministry. The appropriate kind of assent across this broad category of nondefinitive teaching is called "religious obedience." It is understood to be not merely an exterior conformity but one that genuinely engages the intellect and will and is based ultimately on the obedience of faith. Since the matters included in this category are not taught definitively, *The Ecclesial Vocation of the Theologian* allows that this response of religious obedience can encompass serious difficulties and legitimate objections for theologians, and treats how theologians can best proceed for the good of the Church in such cases.[12]

In seeking to discern the level of authority attached to questions involving human origins, we have a resource not only in the distinctions between different levels of the Church's magisterium, but also in the related system of "theological notes" once widely employed by theologians. This systematic convention of assigning such qualifications to different theological propositions was used by modern scholastic manuals of theology well into the twentieth century. It offered a range of notes that covered both what was taught infallibly and what was not. While the precise designations have varied from theologian to theologian, they generally ranged from being *de fide* (of faith), to theologically certain, to being commonly taught by theologians, to probable

---

10. Avery Dulles, SJ, *Magisterium: Teacher and Guardian of the Faith* (Ave Maria, FL: Sapientia Press of Ave Maria University, 2007), 73–74.
11. DH, 902.
12. DH, 4878–85.

and more probable opinion, and even to tolerated opinion. The practice gave great clarity to theologians' understanding of what was nonnegotiable for Catholic theology, and what could be legitimately debated by them. Given that the work of theologians has been a standard resource for magisterial teaching, attention to this practice can help us in our assessment of how precisely the magisterium makes its approach to questions of human origins.

The magisterium is certainly able to draw on such theological methods in its presentation of doctrine without thereby employing any fresh act of definitive teaching. In that case, the proposition would retain the same theological note, and to that extent be essentially unaltered by the magisterium's authoritative use of it.[13] Not that the magisterium has set out to teach which propositions have which notes, or promulgate a definitive list of notes, in a systematic and comprehensive way. Its work tends to be more of a pastoral response to particular questions that arise. However, there are occasions where an act of the magisterium means that a theological note will have to change.[14] An example would be the solemn definition of the Immaculate Conception. Up to the time of the definition, theologians might give this teaching the note of theologically certain or proximate to faith, the latter indicating that, though it had not been defined, it was ready to be. After the definition, Catholic theology unanimously reclassified it as *de fide*.

Toward the upper end of the scale, then, after what is believed by faith and what is proximate to faith, comes theological certitude. That something might be held as strictly certain by a theologian, even when it is not explicitly confirmed by the Church as definitively taught, can be no surprise. While the explicitly definitive character of an act of magisterial teaching means that a Catholic can consciously receive that teaching definitively and be certain of its truth, the truth of any proposition is independent of whether it is explicitly taught in any particular way. There are cases where theologians, by their own methods, have attained certainty of the truth of some theological proposition and so concluded that it falls under the secondary object of the Church's infallibility. In its strict sense, such theological certitude was standardly established by theologians through the logical deduction of conclusions from premises, where the intimate connection of the resulting truths to the deposit of faith was clear. However, as we shall see, a distinct form of certainty was also proposed based on a general consent among theologians, but infallibility could not so easily be claimed for such common teachings.

---

13. See the explanatory note appended to *Lumen Gentium* in Austin Flannery, *Vatican Council II: The Conciliar and Post Conciliar Documents*, vol. 1, rev. ed. (Leominster: Gracewing, 1992), 423–24.

14. DH, 5071.

Going lower on the scale of theological notes, we come to positions that have not attracted theological unanimity, where theologians diverged among themselves. Here theologians spoke of probable or more probable opinions. Falling within the bounds of ecclesial orthodoxy, such positions are recognized as having strong arguments in their favor to one degree or another. Hence, conflicting theses could be advanced by theologians on debated points, which the magisterium may or may not eventually determine. In the famous case of the controversies between Dominicans and Jesuits on the relationship between divine grace and human freedom from the sixteenth century onward, the popes consistently refused to settle the debate, and the magisterium explicitly allowed a diversity of more or less probable positions on these issues. Pope Paul V had said the matter would be decided, but it never was, and in that respect he brought the controversy to an end.[15] Where the Church's teaching authority refuses to decide—or at least has not decided—between probable opinions, all such opinions may be said to be positively permitted by the magisterium.

At the lower end of the scale of theological notes is tolerated opinion. Propositions falling in this category are typically supposed to have the weakest theological foundation.[16] Despite not receiving the endorsement of the Church—not even the kind of permission positively extended to probable arguments—they are nevertheless tolerated, either explicitly or implicitly. Though the magisterium can hardly be said to teach such theological propositions, these propositions do have a relation to the Church's teaching authority insofar as they are tolerated by that authority. I suggest that sometimes these propositions can be tolerated by the Church's magisterium even as the ordinary magisterium teaches something quite different.

It seems to me that Dominican opposition to the Immaculate Conception during at least part of the seventeenth century is an example of an object of such toleration. Of course, once the doctrine of the Immaculate Conception had been defined by the extraordinary magisterium in 1854, its denial could no longer be viewed as anything else but heretical. Prior to its solemn definition, though, the Immaculate Conception had been the ordinary teaching of the Church for some time and was widely celebrated in the liturgy.[17] Moreover, up to the seventeenth century, the doctrine was still actively opposed

---

15. DH, 1997.
16. For example, Ludwig Ott, *Fundamentals of Catholic Dogma*, 2nd ed. (Cork: The Mercier Press, Limited, 1957), 10.
17. See René Laurentin, "The Role of the Papal Magisterium in the Development of the Dogma of the Immaculate Conception," in *The Dogma of the Immaculate Conception: History and Significance*, ed. Edward Dennis O'Connor, CSC (Notre Dame, IN: University of Notre Dame Press, 1958), 271–324.

from within the Dominican Order. Aquinas had not been unusual in his time by rejecting it, and if one were to retrospectively assign a theological note to the "maculist" position in the thirteenth century, it would definitely be common teaching. But with the appearance of Bl. Duns Scotus's solution to the difficulties that had been raised about the Immaculate Conception by Aquinas and others, from the fourteenth century onward maculism and immaculism became more or less probable opinions, as the maculist position ceased to be common teaching. The magisterium permitted both opinions, much as it would later permit both Jesuit and Dominican theories on grace and freedom. When in 1482 Pope Sixtus IV responded to claims by a Dominican that immaculism was heretical, he declared that neither immaculism nor maculism could be censured as heresy, and this decision was extended to the whole Church the following year.[18] The pope's intervention proved to be the beginning of increasing magisterial commitment toward the doctrine of the Immaculate Conception. He had acted to protect a doctrine already celebrated liturgically, while maculism was protected from censure simply because the Church had not yet determined the doctrinal question.

The discipline introduced by Sixtus IV was confirmed by his successors, and was in place more or less until 1617. Then, ten years after he ended the controversy on grace and freedom, Paul V declared that until this other matter had been determined, no one was to affirm maculism "in public acts of whatever sort."[19] While immaculists were not to attack maculism, they were nevertheless allowed to affirm immaculism publicly. This change in discipline clearly tipped the balance in favor of the Immaculate Conception. Although the pope made clear that he was not condemning maculism, and so we may conclude that from that point of view it was still technically a probable opinion, it was forbidden to express it in public. The next pope, Gregory XV, took matters even further in May 1622 when—again without condemning maculism—he extended its prohibition from public to private acts, whether oral or written. By July, the Dominicans were able to achieve no more than obtain the pope's "concession" that they could discuss the question freely among themselves, but not with anyone else.

In my view, this put maculism under such restrictions that what had once been common teaching and then probable opinion was now effectively only tolerated. As the theological note of immaculism had risen, so the note of maculism had fallen. Moreover, in 1661, Pope Alexander VII, despite his own unwillingness to move to a solemn definition, indicated that the discipline in operation in papal prohibitions from Sixtus IV onward presupposed a doctrinal commit-

---

18. DH, 1425–56.
19. On these bulls, see Laurentin, "The Role of the Papal Magisterium," 301–2.

ment of the magisterium in favor of the Immaculate Conception.[20] This means that, at least from 1622 to 1661, maculism was no more than a tolerated opinion, while the ordinary magisterium taught something quite different—namely, the truth of our Lady's Immaculate Conception. It appears that this example can throw some light on the case of magisterial teaching about human origins.

Having explained and illustrated something about both the Church's teaching authority and the theological system of notes, I now turn directly to questions of human origins by asking what the magisterium at its various levels has to say about these questions, beginning with its highest level of teaching. As I have already indicated, discerning that something is taught infallibly by the ordinary and universal magisterium is not so easy, and I shall refer to the work of theologians in this respect below. Concerning solemn definitions, all I can see with direct relevance to questions about human origins is from the Council of Trent, which responded to the Protestant Reformers in the sixteenth century. Part of what was at issue were the doctrines of grace and original sin. Trent's decree on original sin was promulgated in 1546. The council took great care to avoid all the details of what it regarded as legitimate debate on original sin among Catholic theologians and restricted its decree to where it felt it had to put clear water between Catholic teaching and heresy. The council also took care to clarify that it was not their intention to include the "Blessed and Immaculate Virgin Mary" in what it had to say about original sin.[21]

In approaching original sin, Trent used the traditional approach of condemning or anathematizing the position considered contrary to the faith in canons. It also integrated into its own teaching canons passed by local councils from the early Church against the heresy of Pelagianism in its different forms, thus distinguishing Catholic teaching from both Pelagianism and Protestantism. And so we have the following anti-Pelagian canon: "If anyone does not profess that Adam, the first human being, by transgressing God's commandment in paradise, at once lost the holiness and justice in which he had been constituted; and that, offending God by his sin, he drew upon himself . . . death . . . and that 'the whole Adam, body and soul, was changed for the worse through the offense of his sin,' let him be anathema."[22] What does this anathema mean for the extraordinary magisterium's teaching on human origins? It seems to me that the council defined that prior to the fall, human beings were constituted in holiness and justice and that these human beings experienced no death, and a better state in body and soul than that which came later through sin. It seems to me that a Catholic theologian is thus committed to a

---

20. DH, 2015–17.
21. DH, 1516.
22. DH, 1511.

real state of original justice or righteousness at the beginning of human history, which was then lost through sin. But if this is the case, what potential is there for this position to be contradicted by the findings of natural science?

None at all, given that original righteousness, with its gift of immortality, is not something that in principle falls within the scope of natural science. I suggest that this is because the magisterium also teaches that original righteousness is overall a state higher than nature, and so is one to which natural science has no direct access. That original righteousness transcends the natural order can be derived from the condemnation of the views of Michael Baius made by Pope St. Pius V in his bull of 1567, *Ex omnibus afflictionibus*. Baius was a Flemish theologian at the University of Louvain, who was present at Trent from 1563 to represent his university. Concerning grace, Baius taught that "the raising up of human nature and its elevation to participation in the divine nature was owed to the integrity of man in his first state, and is, therefore, to be called natural, not supernatural."[23] The implication that grace was owed to human nature and not a gratuitous gift to humanity would cause trouble for Baius. In the same vein, he also taught that the state of original righteousness "was not a gratuitous exaltation of human nature but its natural condition."[24] The implication is that the immortality enjoyed initially by humanity came to it by way of nature, rather than from some gift exalting humanity above its natural limits.

It is not immediately clear which of the seventy-six propositions in total Pius V intended to condemn as heretical or even as erroneous, since he intended to condemn only some as heretical or erroneous, with others condemned as suspect, rash, or offensive to pious ears.[25] Such a range of condemnations is of course reflected in the modern scholastic habit of assigning theological notes. But without clarity as to the grade of condemnation, it is not so easy to assert that the pope's rejection of original righteousness as merely natural was an exercise of extraordinary magisterium. By condemning Baius's views, however, Pius V nevertheless taught—at least by his ordinary magisterium—that original righteousness was in these respects a state that elevated humanity beyond the limits of human nature, affirming that immortality (and so on) was supernatural rather than natural.[26]

23. DH, 1921.
24. DH, 1978.
25. DH, 1980.
26. Immortality is sometimes characterized more precisely as "preternatural," which signifies a theological subdivision of the supernatural. Immortality cannot be identified as supernatural, absolutely speaking, because it is natural to some creatures; namely, the angels. Nevertheless, immortality is supernatural, relatively speaking, to human nature, and so is termed preternatural.

The distinction between natural and supernatural—previously employed in the medieval theology of grace and later used to exclude the views of Baius—becomes relevant in a new way when we consider the potential for conflict between faith and science concerning human origins. Given that original righteousness overall (including the gift of immortality) is something supernatural, it is not as such open to investigation by the natural sciences. That a human being has enjoyed such a gift is not something that is going to show up in the archaeological or genetic record. That I or anyone else received the supernatural grace of baptism is not going to be found directly in the examination of any human body as such, dead or alive. And the same goes for any supernatural gift of immortality once lost—it is not going to show up in the archaeological or genetic record. And in any case, no theologian has ever supposed that the state of original righteousness lasted long enough to produce artifacts indicative of some golden age that would survive today. But if there is no potential for conflict between the natural sciences and faith in the area of the supernatural, at the same time, this identifies the natural as the site of any possible conflict.

Moving on to consider the natural, I return to the extraordinary magisterium of Trent. If there is nothing infallibly defined by the council regarding the supernatural that will give us theological cause for concern, what about the natural? For example, what, if anything, did Trent define about the historical existence of Adam, whom Trent's canon on original righteousness referred to as the first human being, in line with the canons of earlier local councils? I argue that nothing was infallibly taught by Trent about the historical existence of the first human being, or about the size of the original human population from which all subsequent human beings are descended. Discerning what is solemnly defined or undefined in some formula is a matter of careful interpretation. In defining the Immaculate Conception, Pius IX made use of much supporting material in reference to what was defined, but it is not supposed that such material is itself the object of definition. When Lateran V supported its condemnation of certain views about the soul with an appeal to the fact that truth cannot contradict truth, it did not thereby necessarily define that truth cannot contradict truth.

We have already seen how theologians interpret magisterial statements with the aid of historical context. Similarly, to determine precisely what is condemned in an anathema, it is standard practice for theologians to begin by asking against what or whom the anathema was aimed. When we look into the Pelagianism and Protestantism against which Trent took its aim, we can find no one who denied the historical existence of Adam, the descent of the human race from a first couple, or something similar. Hence, we can conclude that Trent's anathema was not intended to exclude any such position, and that Trent defined nothing as such about the first human beings beyond the content of the canons on the state of original righteousness. In other words, nothing was defined by the council about how many first human beings there were, or about their natural origin. This conclusion is supported by the fact that the theologians who prepared the original documents for Vatican I (1869–70) put into their first draft of a document on the Catholic faith what seems to have been intended as an infallible definition on the common descent of the whole human race from Adam and Eve. After a brief survey of Scripture it concludes, "Whence under anathema we condemn the error by which this unity and common origin of the whole human race is denied."[27] A later draft likewise condemned those who denied that the whole human race was descended from a single first parent.[28] Had the theologians who drafted this schema thought that Trent had already defined the matter, they would not have proposed defining it here, but would have simply invoked Trent's anathema. But they did not. Since the content of the final document promulgated was in general much reduced, the proposal was not in the end put forward for approval. To me, it seems that the very fact of the proposal supports the conclusion that Trent did not solemnly define the matters at issue.

I turn now to the Church's ordinary magisterium. Here the most significant document is Pope Pius XII's encyclical letter of 1950, *Humani Generis*, which was the first time the question of evolution was explicitly addressed by the papal magisterium. Back in 1941, when he had given a speech to the Pontifical Academy of Sciences, the pope had mentioned that there were ongoing investigations about human origins in paleontology, biology, and morphology, by which he meant the study of species. He said that he would leave the question raised here for a future date, when science would be guided and illumined by the content of divine revelation.[29] Pius XII's own contribution to this question then came in *Humani Generis*. According to its title, the encyclical was largely concerned with "some false opinions threatening to undermine the foundations of Catholic doctrine," some of which had involved the general notion of evolution. The biological evolution of humanity itself, however, was an issue that only entered the drafting process at a relatively late stage.[30] The

---

27. Ioannes Dominicus Mansi, *Sacrorum Conciliorum nova et amplissima collectio*, vol. 50 (Arnhem & Leipzig: Société Nouvelle d'Édition de la Collection Mansi [H. Welter], 1924), col. 70.
28. Mansi, *Sacrorum Conciliorum nova et amplissima collectio*, vol. 53 (1927), col. 175.
29. *Acta Apostolicae Sedis* 33 (1941), 506.
30. Material regarding the drafting of the encyclical can be found in the Archives of the Dicastery for the Doctrine of the Faith under *Dubia Varia*, 1950, no. 3.2–3 (293/1946). For more detail and analysis, see Kenneth Kemp, "*Humani Generis* & Evolution: A Report from the Archives," *Scientia et Fides* 11, no. 1 (2023): 9–27.

commission responsible for the draft seems not to have found the evolution of the human species particularly difficult to deal with, and the encyclical proved, when viewed in its historical context, to be positive, if cautious, in its attitude toward evolution. When he turned to questions pertaining to the "positive sciences," which are "more or less connected" with the truths of faith, the pope wrote as follows:

> In fact, not a few insistently demand that the Catholic religion take these sciences into account as much as possible. This certainly would be praiseworthy in the case of clearly proved facts; but caution must be used when there is rather a question of hypotheses, having some sort of scientific foundation, in which the doctrine contained in Sacred Scripture or in Tradition is involved. If such conjectural opinions are directly or indirectly opposed to the doctrine revealed by God, then the demand that they be recognized can in no way be admitted. For these reasons the Church's magisterium does not forbid that, in conformity with the present state of human sciences and sacred theology, research and discussions, on the part of people experienced in both fields, take place with regard to the doctrine of evolution, insofar as it enquires into the origin of the human body as coming from pre-existent and living matter - for the Catholic faith obliges us to hold that souls are immediately created by God. However, this must be done in such a way that the reasons for both opinions, that is, those favorable and those unfavorable to evolution, be weighed and judged with the necessary seriousness, moderation and measure, and provided that all are prepared to submit to the judgment of the Church, to whom Christ has given the mission of authoritatively interpreting the Sacred Scriptures and of defending the dogmas of faith. Some, however, rashly transgress this liberty of discussion, when they act as if the origin of the human body from pre-existing and living matter were already completely certain and proved by the facts which have been discovered up to now and by reasoning on those facts, and as if there were nothing in the sources of divine revelation which demands the greatest moderation and caution in this question.[31]

While implicitly allowing for different views among Catholic theologians on the precise relationship between soul and body, Pius XII treats each distinctly.[32] One unsurprising point maintained by him was that the human

---

31. DH, 3895–96.
32. For example, the Thomistic teaching that the soul is the single substantial form of the body is not required of theologians by the magisterium, although it was formerly listed among the twenty-four approved theses of Thomistic philosophy (DH, 3616), which were proposed by the Sacred Congregation of Studies in *Acta Apostolicae Sedis* 8 (1916), 157, as "safe directive norms."

soul could not be explained in evolutionary terms. In his speech of 1941, he had already remarked that it was the spiritual soul that made humanity the highest creature in the animal kingdom. In the encyclical, he alludes to the teaching that the human soul is immediately created out of nothing in all cases by God; that is, not out of any preexisting matter. In other words, the existence of our souls as such is brought about by God alone out of nothing, and not by our parents.

It should be noted that when Pius XII said the Catholic faith requires us to "hold" this, he did not imply that the immediate creation of the human soul is a revealed matter of faith. Drafts of the encyclical had previously said—more ambiguously, one could argue—that the immediate creation of souls must be "held by faith," leaving it unclear as to whether this was to be believed as a matter of faith or simply held on the basis of faith as a matter closely connected with it.[33] This was understandable in view of the fact that theologians had been assigning to the thesis a variety of notes, including ones that were theologically certain, proximate to faith, and *de fide*. One of the commission's theological consultants, Édouard Dhanis, SJ, pointed out that a higher note was sometimes given if it was specifically the soul of the first human being that was at issue. He himself expressed a preference for the encyclical to follow what he called "approved authors," and said that only the immediate creation of souls "pertained to Catholic doctrine," a yet more general classification.[34] His suggestion was not taken up, but the expression of the final text was clearer that Catholics are not obliged to go so far as to believe by faith that human souls are immediately created. Rather, based on what they do believe by faith, Catholics must further "hold" that human souls are created immediately by God. Though various things concerning the soul have been defined by the extraordinary magisterium, such as at Vienne and Lateran V, the nature of the soul's origin has never been solemnly defined, even as a matter closely bound up with faith.[35] But the level of certainty implied in the way the pope speaks surely suggests that the soul's immediate creation falls under the ordinary and universal magisterium, according to the secondary object of infallibility.

Catholic teaching seems to have approached certainty about the issue as alternative explanations of the origin of the soul were ruled out. The idea that human souls existed before their bodies had been current in the time of the early Church among Origen and his disciples but fell out of favor among Cath-

---

33. For the fourth draft (May 1950), see *Dubia Varia*, 1950, no. 3.1.14, fol. 159, p. 12, and for the fifth (June 1950), see no. 3.1.16, fol. 192, p. 13.

34. His observation of May 25, 1950, can be found at *Dubia Varia*, 1950, no. 3.1.16, fol. 211, p. 8.

35. DH, 902, 1440–41.

olics. The preexistence of souls, together with the idea that souls originated out of God's substance, was condemned; for example, it was among the errors of the Priscillianist heresy condemned by the local Council of Braga in 561.[36] It was a long time, however, before there emerged a consensus as to whether one's soul was immediately created by God or was derived from the souls of one's parents. By the time of the theologian Peter Lombard in the twelfth century, the question was effectively decided in favor of immediate creation.[37] For Aquinas and others, reconciling the essential immateriality of the immortal soul with its simple production by a material process would be out of the question. Immediate creation was the last theory standing. And so, it came to be accepted as theologically certain and entered the Church's ordinary magisterium. For example, when speaking of the Immaculate Conception in the seventeenth century, Alexander VII spoke of the "creation" of Mary's soul.[38] What Pius XII did was confirm the same conclusion about the origin of the human race for every instance of human reproduction: just as the spiritual soul cannot be the product of the physical act of reproduction by human parents, so it cannot be the product of any material process of evolution.

In contrast, what Pius XII did not rule out was liberty for experts, with all due caution, to discuss the origin of the human body in terms of evolution.[39] While he did not oblige theologians to use the theory of evolution in their explanations of human origins, he declared that they were "not forbidden" to discuss it. The latter expression was his own choice. While the draft acknowledged that discussion was left by the magisterium to scientists and theologians, the Latinist (and the Secretary of Briefs to Princes and of Latin Letters) Antonio Bacci, who was engaged to polish the final draft for style, rewrote the text to say that the magisterium "permits" such discussion.[40] Pius XII amended the text again to say that discussion among experts was "not forbidden."[41] It seems to me that this was again a change in style, and no alteration of substantial content is found in any of these amendments. Rather,

---

36. DH, 455–56.
37. *Sentences* II, d. 31, c. 3.
38. DH, 2017.
39. On Catholic reactions in general to evolution, see Stefaan Blancke, "Catholic Responses to Evolution, 1859 to 2009: Local Influences and Mid-Scale Patterns," *Journal of Religious History* 37 (2013): 353–68.
40. For the fourth draft, see *Dubia Varia*, 1950, no. 3.1.14, fol. 159, pp. 12–13; and for the fifth, see no. 3.1.16, fol. 192, p. 13. For Bacci's rewriting of the text, see *Dubia Varia*, 1950, no. 3.1, fol. 505, p. 18; fol. 509, p. 18.
41. This amendment is reported in the letter dated August 15, 1950, from Bacci to Mario Crovini, a deputy notary at the Holy Office, which is archived at *Dubia Varia*, 1950, no. 3.1, fol. 289.

the pope was choosing to speak in such a way that expressed a note of caution. In other words, discussions were allowed, but they should proceed with due care for the issues involved. One implication for theology was that the very fact that these discussions were allowed presupposed that bodily evolution, as a hypothesis having some scientific basis, might not be contrary to what was found in "the sources of divine revelation." So we can deduce that, in accordance with this situation, theologians were permitted, as one probable opinion for which arguments could be given, the view that evolution could have had a role in the original formation of the human body.

This exercise of the ordinary magisterium by the pope might appear to be at variance in some way with what had come before. After all, even though some early modern theologians had speculated about the possibility that God could have employed angels as instrumental causes in the formation of the first human body, in the period just before the theory of evolution came on the scene, it was commonly held by theologians that the bodies of Adam and Eve had been "immediately formed" by God.[42] The immediacy of this divine action did not imply that either body had been created out of nothing, as was held for souls, even though this action was sometimes referred to as creation. Rather, while the soul was created out of nothing, the body was formed from preexisting matter, as was taken to be suggested by the formation of Adam's body from the dust of the earth and the formation of Eve's body from Adam in the narrative of Genesis 2. What was indicated by the idea of immediate formation was that, just as God made no use of secondary causes in the creation of the human soul out of nothing, so he also made no use of secondary causes in the formation of Adam's body from preexisting, nonliving matter or the formation of Eve's body from Adam's. But what authority did this thesis have regarding the Church's magisterium?

In 1860, a local provincial council of bishops in Cologne had taught by their own ordinary magisterium that "[t]he first parents were made immediately by God. Therefore, we declare as contrary to Sacred Scripture and to the faith the opinion of those who are not ashamed to assert that man, insofar as his body is concerned, came to be by a spontaneous change from imperfect nature to the most perfect and in a continuous process finally became human."[43] Evolution, or at least some account of it, was judged to be incompatible with immediate formation. The fact that Pius IX gave recognition to

---

42. For a balanced critique of some of his contemporaries, see Francisco Suárez, *De opere sex dierum*, lib. 3, cap. 1, n. 6 (*Opera Omnia*, vol. 3, Paris: apud Ludovicum Vivès, 1856, 172–73).

43. Mansi, *Sacrorum Conciliorum nova et amplissima collectio*, vol. 48 (Graz: Akademische Durck-u. Verlagsanstalt, 1961), col. 91.

the council did not raise this local condemnation to an infallible definition, because in canon law such recognition did not mean an approbation of individual teachings but a general recognition that the whole process of the council had been carried out lawfully. This principle is clearly found in the canon law textbooks of the time.[44] Thus, this condemnation, while being part of the local magisterium in Cologne, did not enter into the pope's own magisterium. It is also notable that other local councils that followed in the run-up to Vatican I decided to say nothing about the issue.

Just as one cannot draw any conclusions about the papal magisterium from this local council, it is also not straightforward to draw any conclusions of enduring value from the actions of those Roman dicasteries, which assisted the popes in their ministry. The Holy Office—the forerunner of today's Dicastery for the Doctrine of the Faith—made no declarations. Certainly, some writings concerned with evolution had been placed on the Index of Forbidden Books. The placing of a book on the Index, however, did not necessarily have any doctrinal implications. The Index did not give theologians or anyone else specific reasons why Catholics were forbidden to read any book—it might not have been for doctrinal reasons at all. But when a Jesuit journalist wrote in 1902 in the antievolution *La Civiltà Cattolica* that the Holy Office had intervened in some cases of books on evolution, the impression was left that the special formation of Adam's body was part of the ordinary magisterium of the Church.[45] Until the relevant archives were opened in 1998, it was generally unknown that in fact the Holy Office did not decide these cases, only the Index did.[46]

Human origins were, however, addressed by the Pontifical Biblical Commission in the first decade of the twentieth century through some disciplinary measures promulgated for teachers of Scripture. In 1905, the commission had allowed that where there were strong arguments for a particular case, one could say that the biblical author of a historical book might not have been writing history properly so-called at some point in his text but writing in the form of history.[47] But in 1909, it also declared that there was no solid foundation for those theories, which had proposed such an interpretation for the first three chapters of Genesis. The declaration continued, saying that it could not be taught that these chapters did not contain stories of events that really

---

44. Mariano Artigas, Thomas F. Glick, and Rafael A. Martínez, *Negotiating Darwin: The Vatican Confronts Evolution, 1877–1902* (Baltimore: John Hopkins University Press, 2006), 21–23.

45. Salvatore M. Brandi, SJ, "Evoluzione e Domma: Erronee informazioni di un inglese," *La Civiltà Cattolica*, 18th ser., no. 6 (1902), 76. For an English translation, see Artigas, Glick, and Martínez, *Negotiating Darwin*, 234–35.

46. Artigas, Glick, and Martínez, *Negotiating Darwin*, 24, 29, 279.

47. DH, 3373.

happened. Also, it could not be taught that they were fables devoid of a basis in objective reality, which instead set forth philosophical or religious truths under the guise of history. Furthermore, a teacher must not call into question the literal and historical sense of, among other things, the "special creation of the human being" and the "formation" of Eve from Adam.[48] These disciplinary measures were not promulgated as doctrinal declarations, although the then pope, St. Pius X, clarified that they required the same assent as was owed to declarations of those congregations concerned with doctrine.[49]

Since it was understood that the 1909 decree of the Pontifical Biblical Commission required the physical formation of Eve's body from Adam to be accepted as historical fact, during the first half of the twentieth century the question of how humanity evolved was discussed in relation to Adam. But while the special creation of Adam's soul did not fall below theological certitude among Catholic theologians, the theological notes about his body were more varied.[50] While some older theologians had even treated the thesis as *de fide* through its being taught definitively by the ordinary and universal magisterium, most theologians now counted the immediate formation of his body as certain; however, the teaching was sometimes said to be "certain enough" or "certain and common" or "more common" or something of the sort. In fact, the certainty at issue as regards Adam's body was not quite the same as the certainty regarding the soul's creation. As discussed earlier, the only explanation that could make possible the appearance of the immaterial soul was its immediate creation by God, which meant that it definitely could not be explained by evolution. However, despite some concerns about a cause having an effect superior to itself, it did not seem so easy to prove it impossible that God was able to use evolution to cause a human body to be united to a human soul.[51] The question was whether he had actually done so. Thus, while it was necessary to declare it impossible that the immaterial soul is the product of material evolution, it was difficult to suppose it altogether impossible that the material body could be the product of such evolution.

What made theologians certain that Adam's body had in fact been immediately formed was a common reading of Scripture going back to antiquity,

---

48. DH, 3512–14.

49. *Praestantia Scripturae Sacrae*, in *Enchiridion Biblicum: Documenta Ecclesiastica Sacram Scripturam Spectantia auctoritate Pontificiae Commisionis de Re Biblica edita*, 2nd ed. (Rome: Arnodo, 1954), 97.

50. See Thomas Motherway, SJ, "Current Theology: Theological Opinion on the Evolution of Man," *Theological Studies* 5, no. 2 (1944): 198–221.

51. For further discussion, see the chapters in this volume by Brian Carl, "Thomas Aquinas on the Proportionate Causes of Living Species"; and Daniel D. De Haan, "*Nihil dat quod non habet*: Thomist Naturalism Contra Supernaturalism on the Origin of Species."

which took the formation of Adam's body as described in Genesis 2 to be historical fact. However, as theologians looked over at scientists, they saw a kind of mirror image of themselves. While scientists did not appear to have established incontrovertible certainty of the evolution of the first human being—in the way theologians did not have quite the same certainty about the body as they had about the soul—they nevertheless had common consent about the evolution of the body, just as theologians had common consent on the special formation of Adam's body. While some theologians continued to see immediate formation as excluding evolution altogether, others speculated that Adam's body could have been formed in some respects by evolution and in others by God operating without secondary causes.[52]

As with the issue of the human soul and evolution, the commission preparing *Humani Generis* seemed to have no special difficulties in drafting the wider section that discussed the evolution of Adam's body—it recognized that theological debate had already been taking place. The statement in the draft that the words of Genesis 2, if read in their obvious sense, were unfavorable to evolution was deleted as "inopportune."[53] Pius XII's intervention allowed theologians to continue balanced speculation about the possibility of a place for evolution in God's plan. And because it made no mention of immediate formation, the encyclical also seemed to allow theologians the space to experiment with the idea that, granted the formative role of the soul, the production of the human body by God might be explained simply by reference to his working through the secondary causes of evolution. In addition, the fact that the pope did not speak exclusively of Adam suggested the possibility that Eve's body might also be legitimately explained by evolution.

The pope's cautious opening to the evolution of the human body should not lead us to suppose that he was endorsing evolution or ruling out the older theory of immediate formation. Although not stated in exactly these terms, immediate formation, evolution, and combinations of the two all seem to enjoy the note of more or less probable opinions permitted to theologians by the magisterium. To that extent, there was something similar to the magisterium's permission of different probable positions on grace and freedom, and the relatively even situation regarding maculism and immaculism during the sixteenth century. Something different is found, however, when we arrive at John Paul II's words to the Pontifical Academy of Sciences in 1996. In contrast to Pius XII's cautious words, he spoke to the academy about "new knowledge that leads us toward the recognition of evolution as more than a

---

52. See Motherway, "Current Theology."
53. See the note made by Sebastian Tromp, SJ, a member of the commission, on the fifth draft at *Dubia Varia*, 1950, no. 3.1.16, fol. 192, p. 14, n. 13.

hypothesis."[54] What can we take John Paul II to mean here, and what are the theological implications for human origins? I take his words to mean that there was now no remaining competition within science to explain what evolution sets out to explain, and that as regards natural science on this point, theology was now dealing with evolution alone. In other words, insofar as the theology of creation draws from reason as well as from faith, it must admit the truth of the evolution of the human body.

However, while this might seem to imply that immediate formation of the body, inasmuch as it excludes evolution, can no longer be held by theologians, there seems to have been no move by the magisterium to declare this to be the case exactly. Despite John Paul II's words, the *Catechism of the Catholic Church*, which was officially promulgated the following year, had nothing explicit to say on the subject. Nevertheless, I suggest that, as regards the magisterium, the older version of immediate formation of the body, which excluded evolution, was now in a position similar to that occupied by the denial of the Immaculate Conception. While denial of the Immaculate Conception had been the common position in the thirteenth century, after Duns Scotus's argument in favor of our Lady's privilege, maculism became more of a probable opinion. As we saw above, a position once common—then reduced to a probable opinion—eventually became merely tolerated as the Church's ordinary magisterium embraced the Immaculate Conception. Similarly, I suggest that the older version of immediate formation of Adam's body has over time given way to formation by evolution. Though the body's evolution is proposed by scientific reason and not by faith or theology as such, it has offered a development comparable to Duns Scotus's argument for the Immaculate Conception. With the hindsight of evolutionary theory, we can see the weakness of immediate formation, at least insofar as it excluded evolution. Thus, I suggest that a position once commonly held, but effectively reduced by Pius XII to the status of a probable opinion, is merely tolerated by the magisterium from the time of John Paul II. Not that we can expect that evolution will ever be infallibly defined by the extraordinary magisterium. Unlike the Immaculate Conception, the positive truth of evolution ultimately falls under the competence of science, not of faith.

54. John Paul II, "Address to the Pontifical Academy of Sciences (October 22, 1996)," in *Papal Addresses to the Pontifical Academy of Sciences 1917–2002* (Vatican: Pontifical Academy of Sciences, 2003), 372. An erroneous English translation of the French original of this sentence ("new knowledge has led to the recognition of more than one hypothesis in the theory of evolution") initially appeared in *Osservatore Romano*, and a correction was subsequently announced by the editor. See Artigas, Glick, and Martínez, *Negotiating Darwin*, 287n2.

However, any such reevaluation of the status of immediate formation of Adam's body must go hand in hand with a reassessment of how the biblical text is to be read, since theologians' former certainty had been based on the standard reading of Genesis 2 as literal history. Some movement on the interpretation of the early chapters of Genesis had already been taking place prior to *Humani Generis*. In a 1943 encyclical, *Divino Afflante Spiritu*, Pius XII emphasized the importance of continuing biblical research and the challenge of identifying and interpreting ancient texts according to their genre.[55] In answer to a letter from Cardinal Suhard of Paris in 1947, the Secretary of the Biblical Commission replied that the historicity of the early chapters of Genesis could not be affirmed or denied en bloc without unjustifiably applying to them the rules of some literary genre in which they could not in fact be classified.[56] Nevertheless, he denied that history was not present in some sense of the word. Fundamental truths presupposed to the economy of salvation were presented in figurative language, together with a popular description of humanity's origins. *Humani Generis* commented that the cardinal's letter clearly indicated that these chapters, "although properly speaking not conforming to the historical method used by the best Greek and Latin writers or by competent authors of our time, do nevertheless pertain to history in a true sense, which however must be further studied and determined by exegetes."[57] In 1954, in presentations of the Pontifical Biblical Commission's new *Enchiridion* by its secretary and undersecretary, it was stated that its earlier disciplinary decrees were only in force so far as they touched on questions of faith rather than literary ones, on which exegetes now enjoyed full liberty in their research.[58] In view of *Humani Generis*'s reduction of immediate formation to a probable opinion, the theory's reading of Genesis 2 could now hardly be required.

In line with these developments, along with John Paul II's words to the Pontifical Academy of Sciences, today's ordinary magisterium speaks of the use of figurative language in the early chapters of Genesis. This principle seems to more or less favor a figurative interpretation of the formation of Adam's and Eve's bodies. It is also consonant with regarding early biblical chronology in a similar way, such that nothing is proposed about the precise dating of the creation of human beings, however many thousands of years ago that may be taken to be. Nevertheless, it should be noted that this does not mean that there is nothing historical in these chapters, nor that their figurative language speaks

---

55. DH, 3829–31.
56. DH, 3862–64.
57. DH, 3898.
58. For a contemporary assessment, see E. F. Siegman, "The Decrees of the Pontifical Biblical Commission: A Recent Clarification," *Catholic Biblical Quarterly* 18 (1956): 23–29.

simply about human reality and its condition in a general kind of way without reference to events that lie at the origins of human history. Rather, the *Catechism* speaks more precisely about the use of figurative language in affirming a primeval event; namely, the fall.[59] Likewise, it is said that the Church authoritatively interprets the symbolic language of Genesis 2 to teach that humanity was first constituted in a state of original righteousness.[60] As we have already seen, the holiness and justice of the prelapsarian condition and the fact of the reality of original sin were infallibly defined by the Council of Trent. Thus, Scripture proposes something genuinely historical about original righteousness and the fall through genuinely figurative language rather than literal historical description. This leads us to the further question of how many first human beings there were. What exactly do Adam and Eve symbolize here?

In addition to the question of the body's evolution, *Humani Generis* broached a further question that, in contrast to that of the body's evolution, had been on the commission's agenda since its inception. This was the thorny issue of polygenism and monogenism. In the nineteenth century, "polygenism" meant the independent evolution of the human race in different parts of the world, which is today referred to as the "multiregional hypothesis."[61] By the twentieth century, the term had been extended in theology to encompass the idea of the evolution of the human race in a single population of many individuals, a hypothesis which has been more or less confirmed by genetic research since the 1980s.[62] Some had already attempted to incorporate polygenism into Catholic thinking.[63] Pius XII's intervention, however, was aimed against anything but the descent of the human race (or at least all true human beings after the fall) from a single couple. In other words, what had come to be known by the term "monogenism" was the teaching of the ordinary magisterium.

Having affirmed the liberty of experts to explore the possibility of the evolution of the human body, the pope continued:

> When, however, there is the question of another conjectural opinion, namely polygenism, the children of the Church by no means enjoy such liberty. For the faithful cannot embrace that opinion which maintains

---

59. *Catechism of the Catholic Church*, 390.
60. *Catechism of the Catholic Church*, 375.
61. See James R. Hofmann, "Catholicism and Evolution: Polygenism and Original Sin," *Scientia et Fides* 8, no. 2 (2020): 95–138.
62. For the origin of the more recent use of the terminology of polygenism and monogenism, see Robert de Sinéty, "Transformisme," in *Dictionnaire Apologétique de la Foi Catholique* 4 (Paris: Gabriel Beauchesne, 1922), cols. 1793–848.
63. See Jean and Amédée Bouyssonie, "Polygénisme," in *Dictionnaire de théologie catholique* 12.2 (Paris: Letouzy et Ané, 1935), col. 2536.

that either after Adam there existed on this earth true human beings who did not take their origin through natural generation from him as from the first parent of all, or that Adam represents a certain number of first parents. Now it is in no way evident how such an opinion can be reconciled with that which the sources of revealed truth and the documents of the Church's magisterium propose with regard to original sin, which proceeds from a sin actually committed by an individual Adam and which, through generation, is passed on to all and is in everyone as his own.[64]

While a certain theological probability attaching to the formation of Adam's body in connection with evolution allowed for certain scholarly discussions, it seems that no comparable discussion could be allowed for Catholics in the case of polygenism because no comparable probability could be claimed for that theory. It is interesting to note that the pope did not directly base his claim here on a reading of Scripture, as proponents of the immediate formation of Adam's body had done. Consonant with his implicit reduction of immediate formation to a probable opinion, Pius XII did not argue that the Genesis narrative itself simply solved the question of monogenism and polygenism. Rather the nub of the question was whether polygenism could be reconciled with Catholic teaching on original sin, which itself of course arises from an authoritative reading of "the sources of revealed truth."

Thus, in terms of what kind of certainty was involved in this case, the question bore more relation to the way the immediate creation of the soul was handled rather than to the former approach to immediate formation of the body. It was a question of polygenism implying that there were true human beings who appeared after Adam who had not inherited original sin from him by descent, or that Adam in the doctrine of original sin (and thereby in at least some respect in the Genesis narrative) represented a larger original population from within which all subsequent true human beings inherited original sin.[65] Neither implication seemed compatible with the doctrine of original sin. This fits with the fact that theologians in the period before the encyclical had gone so far as to judge monogenism not only as "certain," but even as "proximate to faith" or *de fide* by way of the ordinary and universal magisterium. Nevertheless, despite such confidence on the part of those theologians, there is no evidence that a solemn definition of monogenism was ever intended at any stage in the drafting of *Humani Generis*. Moreover, while

---

64. DH, 3897.

65. The text technically allows for the possibility of an older view that there had been human beings prior to Adam ("pre-Adamites") to whom the transmission of original sin from Adam was not relevant.

drafts articulated the "Catholic dogma" of the transmission of original sin in explicitly monogenist terms by reference to "one Adam, an individual human being,"[66] Dhanis pointed out that many very good theological authorities did not exactly say that monogenism was a dogma. Here he cites Réginald Garrigou-Lagrange, OP, a prominent theologian who had judged it only proximate to faith.[67] The text was amended in such a way that it was clearly no longer implied that monogenism had the highest theological note.

Such restraint is also reflected in the fact that the pope said that it was "in no way apparent" how polygenism could be reconciled with original sin, rather than assert that they were incompatible, simply speaking. While some interpreters treated the pope's statement as not excluding the possibility that such a reconciliation might be made apparent at some point, others treated the statement as equivalent to an assertion of absolute incompatibility.[68] While the latter would imply theological certainty at the very least for monogenism, the former would seem to allow for the opening up of a possibility of a lower grade of note. More recent research in the Archives of the Dicastery for the Doctrine of the Faith reveals that the pope himself made a choice between two texts: one from the commission that made the two strictly irreconcilable, and another from Dhanis, which said that it was "not apparent" how they could be reconciled.[69] The pope chose Dhanis's formula, though strengthening it to say "it is in no way apparent."[70] A few years after publication, an attempt by former members of the commission to have this clarified as an absolute incompatibility was refused by the pope.[71]

At the time of the encyclical, it was still largely unclear to theologians (and to the pope himself) that monogenism, as it was then generally understood, had been or would be fully discounted by science. Shortly after the

---

66. See the fourth draft in *Dubia Varia*, 1950, n. 3.1.14, fol. 159, p. 13, and the fifth at 3.1.16, fol. 192, p. 14.

67. Dhanis's observation can be found at *Dubia Varia*, 1950, n. 3.1.16, fol. 211, p. 9. See Réginald Garrigou-Lagrange, OP, "Le Monogénisme n'est-il nullement révélé, pas même implicitement?" *Doctor Communis* 2 (1948): 191–202.

68. See Charles Boyer, "Les leçons de l'Encyclique 'Humani Generis,'" *Gregorianum* 31, no. 4 (1950): 526–39.

69. See the fourth draft at *Dubia Varia*, 1950, n. 3.1.14, fol. 159, p. 13; and the fifth draft at 3.1.16, fol. 192, p. 14. Dhanis's proposed revision can be found at *Dubia Varia*, 1950, n. 3.1, fol. 511.

70. The pope's decision is documented in Bacci's correspondence of August 3 and 4, 1950, in the Vatican Apostolic Archive, *Epistolae ad principes, Positiones et minutae* 179, fasc. 44. See Kemp, "*Humani Generis* & Evolution," 23.

71. This is documented in a *Relazione* of June 1, 1955, preserved in the Archives of the Dicastery for the Doctrine of the Faith, *Dubia Varia*, 1950, n. 3.4 (221/1955), fols. 64–65, together with details of the papal audience held on July 4 in fols. 70–72.

encyclical, however, it was proposed by Camille Muller that the eventual descent of all human beings from one couple was compatible with their being part of a wider breeding population of true human beings.[72] This approach regarded Adam and Eve as marked off from the wider breeding population through their elevation to the supernatural state of original righteousness, from which they then fell. After a period of some generations, the entire population would have been descended from this couple, and the inheritance of original sin would by then be universal. In this way, Muller's theory appears monogenist in a limited sense, but it was otherwise polygenist because it allowed for a wider breeding population whose members were truly human because of their natural possession of immortal souls, and for the inheritance of original sin from the wider original population, at least during the generations immediately after the fall.

Muller's proposal did not attract a great deal of attention, although a reprint of his article was placed on the Index in 1953.[73] His general approach of placing Adam and Eve within a wider breeding population was again taken up in 1964 by Andrew Alexander in *The Clergy Review*, and a variation on Alexander's view from Kenneth Kemp appeared in 2011 in the *American Catholic Philosophical Quarterly*.[74] In each of these two cases, however, we have a more strictly monogenistic understanding of human origins. The first couple, from whom all true human beings descend, is indeed marked off from the wider breeding population by their state of supernatural grace. But in terms of species, they are distinguished from the rest of the population by their natural possession of immortal, immaterial souls. In this view, the children of the first couple can produce offspring within the wider breeding population, whereas those who are descended from parents where only one parent has a truly human soul also have such a soul themselves. Hence all true human beings after the first couple are their descendants. It should be noted that while this position is monogenistic, the element of true human beings interbreeding with a wider population brings its own challenges for theology.

Just as an infallible definition was originally prepared for Vatican I, a preparatory draft for Vatican II (1962–65) had restated *Humani Generis*'s teach-

---

72. Camille Muller, "L'Encyclique 'Humani Generis,'" *Synthèses: Revue mensuelle international* 5, no. 57 (1951): 296–312.

73. On Muller and other responses to *Humani Generis*, see James R. Hofmann, "Catholicism and Evolution: Polygenism and Original Sin (Part II)," *Scientia et Fides* 9, no. 1 (2021): 63–129.

74. Andrew Alexander, "Human Origins and Genetics," *The Clergy Review* 49 (1964): 344–53. Kemp, "Science, Theology, and Monogenesis," *American Catholic Philosophical Quarterly* 85, no. 2 (2011): 217–36. Kemp differs from Alexander in not requiring a genetic change in the first human beings.

ing on polygenism as a condemnation, but the proposal did not reach the final documents.[75] Taking account of *Humani Generis*'s precise language of "apparent," some theologians were already indicating an openness to thinking in terms of a single-population polygenism—including Joseph Ratzinger, the future Pope Benedict XVI.[76] This appeared to lessen the theological certainty that could be attributed to monogenism. It was urged that, should it be made apparent how original sin and polygenism could be compatible after all, polygenism in some form would thereby become a legitimate view for Catholic theologians, who were themselves now becoming better appraised of the scientific basis for polygenism. Pope St. Paul VI issued a warning against this trend, telling a theological symposium on original sin held in Rome in 1966 that it would be evident to the participants that some recent explanations of original sin, which started from the "unproven" presupposition of polygenism, seemed incompatible with genuine Catholic teaching.[77] However, the contributors at the symposium included Karl Rahner, who was already inclined to polygenism.[78] Germain Grisez is a prominent example of a theologian who subsequently entertained polygenist theories of original sin in the first volume of his work on moral theology in 1983.[79] Then, in a catechetical address on original sin delivered during a papal audience in 1986, John Paul II quoted the words of Paul VI, affirming their validity and presenting them as a stimulus for further research.[80]

No mention, however, was made of the question of monogenism versus polygenism by John Paul II in his more significant address to the Pontifical Academy of Sciences ten years later. Moreover, while it is true that the *Catechism* says that the human race forms a unity, citing Acts 17:26 to the effect that God made all nations "from one," it contains no explicit endorsement of monogenism over polygenism.[81] Though the English translation of the

---

75. See *Acta et Documenta Concilio Oecumenico Vaticano II Apparando*, ser. 2 (Praeparatoria), vol. 2, part 2 (Vatican: Typis Polyglottis Vaticanis, 1967), 370–93; Commissio Theologica Concilio Oecumenico Vaticano II Apparando, *Constitutio de deposito fidei pure custodiendo* (Vatican: Typis Polyglottis Vaticanis, 1961), 37.

76. Matthew J. Ramage, *From the Dust of the Earth: Benedict XVI, the Bible, and the Theory of Evolution* (Washington, DC: The Catholic University of America Press, 2022), 189, refers to Ratzinger's unpublished 1964 Münster lecture notes, Joseph Ratzinger, "Schöpfungslehre" (unpublished manuscript), 190–93.

77. *Acta Apostolicae Sedis* 58 (1966), 654.

78. See Karl Rahner, "Evolution and Original Sin," *Concilium* 26 (1967): 61–73.

79. Germain Grisez, *Christian Moral Principles*, vol. 1 of *The Way of the Lord Jesus* (Chicago: Franciscan Herald Press, 1983), 339–41, 342–44.

80. *Insegnamenti di Giovanni Paolo II*, vol. 9.2 (Vatican: Libreria Editrice Vaticana, 1986), 760–61.

81. *Catechism of the Catholic Church*, 360.

Catechism, employing the New Revised Standard Version, renders this "from one ancestor," not all translations do so. The Latin, following the original Greek of Scripture, simply has "from one," and the text itself could as easily be rendered "from one blood" or "from one stock." Equally, the whole question of monogenism and polygenism has not figured in the papal magisterium of either Benedict XVI or Francis.

This raises the question of where the magisterium stands now as regards the inclination to polygenism among many theologians: Has the Church's teaching authority now withdrawn its support for monogenism? On the one hand, were the magisterium to have fully reversed its support for monogenism based on scientific evidence, one would suppose that some version of polygenism was now at least a probable opinion in theology, and monogenism no more than tolerated at most. On the other hand, were the magisterium to have withdrawn its support for monogenism in order to take up a more neutral position, one would have to count both polygenism and monogenism more or less probable in principle, given that monogenism can also be construed in a way that is compatible with scientific evidence, as I indicated above. Indeed, should both positions be considered compatible with science, the choice between them would fall more to theological discussion than to simply mirroring the conclusions of scientists.

I propose that we should not jump to the conclusion that the ordinary magisterium has withdrawn its support for monogenism. Christ's earthly beatific vision is one example of something taught by the ordinary magisterium under Pius XII but not explicitly mentioned again until it was referred to by the Congregation of the Doctrine of the Faith in 2006 under Benedict XVI.[82] Likewise, I suggest that the ordinary magisterium may have not given up monogenism at all; instead, it has effectively tolerated the use of polygenism (or at least of some versions of it) by Catholic theologians, not just since the 1980s but going back to the late 1960s.[83] In other words, like the immediate formation of Adam's body to the exclusion of evolution, polygenism is now a tolerated opinion. However, there is a significant difference between the magisterium's toleration of either. Each is tolerated, I suggest, for a quite different reason. As with the denial of the Immaculate Conception in the seventeenth century, immediate formation, though no longer regarded as theologically probable, is treated with a measure of respect in view of a venerable theological

---

82. DH, 3812, 5107. See Simon Francis Gaine, OP, *Did the Saviour See the Father? Christ, Salvation and the Vision of God* (London: Bloomsbury T&T Clark, 2015), 7–13.

83. Cf. Karl Rahner, SJ, "The Sin of Adam," in *Confrontations 1*, vol. 11 of *Theological Investigations* (London: Darton, Longman & Todd; New York: Seabury, 1974), 252. This lecture was originally delivered in 1968.

past when it was commonly held. Polygenism, however, has no such venerable past, but at least some form of it is tolerated for the sake of theological progress in light of and out of respect for advances in scientific reason.

It is in this way that we can make sense of the possible suggestion of polygenism in a document issued in 2004 by the International Theological Commission—whose task is to advise the magisterium—though the text could also be interpreted in terms of monogenism in the context of a wider breeding population.[84] In any case, theological progress may eventually mature either way, with a choice ultimately made in favor of monogenism or polygenism. So, for the present, the ordinary magisterium continues to teach monogenism but at the same time tolerates at least certain forms of polygenism, one way or another, to benefit the advance of our understanding of the Catholic faith and the teaching of the Church. As maculism was once tolerated among the Dominicans while the ordinary magisterium taught our Lady's Immaculate Conception, so polygenism is now tolerated while the ordinary magisterium continues its commitment to monogenism.

Evolution as such falls within the competence of science rather than of faith. Nevertheless, since the Church affirms that reason, like faith, comes from God, Catholics are encouraged to learn from science as well as from faith and the teaching of the Church. In light of this, and that of current science, it is not feasible for Catholic theology to deny evolution in its reflections on the theology of creation and providence. While the spiritual soul cannot be the product of the material process of evolution, theology is bound to explore the positive role of evolution in God's formation of the human body. While Catholics firmly believe that the first human beings were constituted in a state of original righteousness from which they fell, theologians continue, under the guidance of the Church's magisterium, to seek deeper understanding of the question of human origins.

---

84. International Theological Commission, "Communion and Stewardship: Human Persons Created in the Image of God," in *International Theological Commission: Texts and Documents 1986–2007*, ed. Michael Sharkey and Thomas Weinandy (San Francisco: Ignatius Press, 2009), 339–43. The question is hardly touched by the Pontifical Biblical Commission's document of 2019; see *What Is Man? A Journey through Biblical Anthropology*, trans. Fearghus O'Fearghail and Adrian Graffy (London: Darton, Longman and Todd Ltd, 2021), 240.

CHAPTER SEVEN

What if "Adam" Had Not Sinned?
Explorations on How Human Vulnerabilities Might Have Been Overcome in the First Human Beings and Their Descendants

RICHARD CONRAD, OP

This chapter addresses an apparent conflict between the traditional Christian picture of humanity's original condition and the recognition of our evolutionary origins. It does not follow from evolution that there are no clear boundaries between species.[1] Nevertheless, our descent from prehuman hominins underlines the *continuities* between the first true humans and their ancestors: both inhabited the same geographical area, with its dangers as well as its affordances; and both were vulnerable to similar kinds of injury and disease-causing factors. In addition, the social structures of the two species conferred analogous benefits and risks. In the traditional Christian picture, the first human beings lived in a more-than-natural harmony with God, with each other, and with the natural world, to the extent that they enjoyed immortality and invulnerability. If "Adam" had not sinned, their descendants would have continued to enjoy these gifts.

Many recent and contemporary theologians dismiss elements of this picture. Some accept an original supernatural harmony with God, while holding that the first humans experienced death and even (in some cases) the psychological factors that we experience as a propensity to sin, though they experienced neither of these as we do now.[2] Others deny there ever was a

---

1. See, for example, Mariusz Tabaczek, OP, chapter 2 in this volume, section 4.4.
2. Siegfried Wiedenhofer surveyed interpretations that focus on aspects of the human condition, rather than on a primeval event that has rendered us vulnerable to, say, "structural sin." See Siegfried Wiedenhofer, "The Main Forms of Contemporary Theology of Original Sin," *Communio* 18, no. 4 (1991): 514–29. Edward Yarnold judged that such an exclusive focus on "the sin of the world" did not do justice to tradition. He held that, "before sin entered the world, man was in a state of grace"; but suggested that, "as a consequence of this union with God, concupiscence [in its sense of a range of psychological factors] . . . was simply part of man's make-up, which man turned to good." Likewise, "Man always was . . . mortal . . . it is sin that makes death seem an evil . . . The same can

pre-fall interval of time.³ In this chapter, I propose we need not reject, as a "myth of a lost Golden Age," the concept of an original state of complete integrity. It is not implausible that natural vulnerabilities were overcome in the first humans, born as they were from prehuman hominins, nor that subsequent generations could have enjoyed similar privileges in the kind of world in which *Homo Sapiens* evolved and spread.

Aquinas assists this project in two ways. First, he recognized that our belonging to the animal kingdom explains many of our physical, psychological and sociological vulnerabilities. He did not know that we evolved; but his accounts of human and animal psychology are hospitable to seeing elements of our dependence on, and vulnerability to, each other as due to our having evolved from other primates. Our current vulnerabilities are straightforwardly consequent on our nature; in the original state, *super*natural gifts overcame natural limitations. Second, Aquinas's account of "the state of innocence" is determinedly nonmythical. In particular, his hints of what humanity might have been like if Adam had not sinned imply that an unfallen race would have enjoyed a *relative* immortality, a *relative* immunity from suffering, and a *relative* absence of personal and social sin. Thus, elements in Aquinas's account of the primeval human condition can come into fruitful conversation with the growing body of research on human origins.

After setting out concepts and theses that contextualize my discussion, I identify theological principles for thinking about the unfallen state and the natural neediness God's gifts overcame. I then explore how the first human beings and their offspring might have known God, and what effects grace might have had on their moral-psychological development, and on their human relationships, so as to remedy our vulnerability to factors that can damage our relationships with God and each other, thereby ensuring that social structures remained relatively unmarked by sin.⁴ Finally, and more

---

be said about pain." See Edward Yarnold, *The Theology of Original Sin* (Cork: Mercier Press, 1971), 78–90.

3. Michael Schmaus proposed the first humans were never in a state of integrity, but at the same moment as they became able to reflect upon God, also rejected him as their measure, and so "lost" the grace they would have had. See Michael Schmaus, *Dogma*, vol. 2 (London: Sheed and Ward, 1972), 170–71. Karl Rahner argued against an *empirically temporal* gap between the beginning of human history as set up by the Creator, and the "beginning" of this history as established by a culpable free act. See Karl Rahner, "Brief Theological Observations on the 'state of Fallen Nature'," *Theological Investigations*, vol. 19 (New York: Crossroad, 1983), 50–51.

4. "Grace" often refers to *gratia gratum faciens*, usually translated as "sanctifying grace." This transforming gift makes us "sharers of the divine nature" (2 Pet 1:4) and, so to speak, deploys itself in the form of virtues, especially charity. The term "grace" can also

tentatively in view of the "quirks of human anatomy" that result from our evolutionary origins, I consider how physical vulnerabilities might have been remedied in an unfallen world to confer a *relative* immunity from sickness and death.[5]

1. Some Contextualizing Concepts and Theses

1.1. The Human Being's Immortal Soul and Complex Life and Language

Aquinas saw bodies as composed of *materia prima* and substantial form. It might be better to translate *materia prima* as "materiality" rather than as "prime matter"; it is not any kind of "stuff," but the "principle" that locates things in space and embeds them in a history of change.[6] Substantial form is not mere structure, but a pervasive pattern of being that locates something in a species of which we can form a universal concept.[7] The forms of living things are souls—forms-of-life—that, rather than inhabiting bodies, express themselves as intricate living bodies which rise above the limitations of mere materiality: plants draw in nourishment and reproduce for the future, and animals sense what is distant, interpret their environments, react in complex ways, and pursue goals.[8]

Aquinas insisted that, as in the case of other souls, the human soul is by nature the form of the body.[9] But, as a rational soul, it rises higher than other

---

refer to God's special love, to God's indwelling the graced soul, and to a range of gifts and inspirations that help us journey to glory. See *ST* I-II q. 110; Daria E. Spezzano, *The Glory of God's Grace: Deification According to St. Thomas Aquinas* (Ave Maria, FL: Sapientia Press, 2015).

5. The phrase "quirks of human anatomy" comes from Lewis I. Held, Jr., *Quirks of Human Anatomy: An Evo-Devo Look at the Human Body* (Cambridge: Cambridge University Press, 2009).

6. See, for example, *ST* I q. 66, a. 1.

7. See, for example, Jeffrey E. Brower, *Aquinas's Ontology of the Material World: Change, Hylomorphism, and Material Objects* (Oxford: Oxford University Press, 2014), chapter 1 and parts III and IV.

8. *ST* I q. 78; q. 80, a. 1. See also Daniel D. De Haan, "Approaching Other Animals with Caution: Exploring Insights from Aquinas's Psychology," *New Blackfriars* 100, no. 1090 (2019): 715–37.

9. *ST* I q. 76, aa. 1, 4, 6 and 7. Aquinas's position was vindicated by the Council of Vienne in 1312. See H. Denzinger, *Compendium of Creeds, Definitions, and Declarations on Matters of Faith and Morals*, 43rd ed., ed. Peter Hünermann, Robert Fastiggi, and Anne Englund Nash (San Francisco: Ignatius, 2012), no. 902. References hereafter are given as "Denz."

animal souls—in acquiring universal concepts, it transcends the material conditions of space and time.[10] Hence, Aquinas argued, its being is not intrinsically dependent on matter. God directly creates each rational soul, though this "infusion" of the soul meshes intimately with the biological process of procreation. In creating it, God gives the human soul an existence which it shares with its body and retains after death. Hence the human soul is immortal, though to exist without the body is not natural to it—it is more than, but not less than, the body's substantial form.[11]

Our souls do not come into being endowed with concepts. We acquire concepts by working on sense-data, and deploy them in thinking processes that involve the imagination and other interior senses, which Aquinas located in the brain.[12] Our senses are accompanied by *passiones animae*—patterns of attraction and aversion by which an animal reacts.[13] Intellect is accompanied by will—a rational appetite attracted by the good the mind perceives.[14] There is a coherence to human life in addition to its immense complexity: our animal faculties are transformed in communion with our intellectual faculties, and vice versa, so that we are less instinctive and more imaginative than other animals, and have distinctively human emotions.[15] Our uniquely sensitive body is basically well-proportioned to the rational soul.[16] Modern Thomists have seen a parallel proportion in the way human language, with its unique, hierarchical character, is apt to express and organize universal concepts.[17]

1.2. Meanings of "Matter"

1.2.1. Proportionate Matter

Thomists use "matter" in analogous ways. *Materia prima* is not any kind of stuff but is made by substantial form into some kind of stuff. By contrast,

---

10. *ST* I q. 79, aa. 2 and 3; q. 84, a. 6; q. 85, a. 1.

11. *ST* I q. 75, aa. 2, 4 and 6; q. 76, a. 1 ad 5 and ad 6; q. 77, a. 8; q. 89, aa. 1 and 3; q. 90, a. 2; q. 118, a. 2.

12. *ST* I q. 78, a. 4; q. 84, aa. 3, 6 and 7; q. 85, a. 1; q. 91, a. 3 ad 1; q. 101, a. 1. On the interior senses, see Herbert McCabe, *On Aquinas* (London: Continuum, 2008), chapters 12 and 13.

13. *ST* I q. 81; I-II qq. 22, 23 and 25; McCabe, *On Aquinas*, chapter 8. I often employ the Latin term, since neither "passion" nor "emotion" maps perfectly onto Aquinas's concept of *passio*.

14. *ST* I qq. 80 and 82; I-II qq. 9 and 10.

15. Candace Vogler, "The Intellectual Animal," *New Blackfriars* 100, no. 1090 (2019): 663–76; *ST* I-II q. 9, a. 2; q. 17, a. 7.

16. *ST* I q. 76, a. 5; q. 91, a. 3.

17. For example, Nicanor Austriaco, chapter 10 in this volume, pp. 226, 228–234, especially pp. 231-232; McCabe, *On Aquinas*: Chapters 4 through 7.

we say that alabaster, for example, which is a kind of stuff, is "proportionate," that is, suitable, matter for a delicate statue. In a related way, the kind of stuff a plant or animal body is, is proportioned to functioning as that kind of living thing. The difference is that, while a block of alabaster can be carved into a statue, a living body is, strictly speaking, only such as already formed by the soul.[18]

1.2.2. Proximate Matter

We use "proximate matter" to capture an aspect of how one material being changes into another. A thing of a particular kind cannot resolve into formless *materia prima*; its existing structures and elemental composition make it apt for certain changes and not others.[19] Flour and water can be baked into bread, but not into a pane of glass. In an analogous way, the first true humans were born of hominins, not of species similar to the current species of apes.

1.3. Evolutionary Scenarios

It is widely held that the human race is descended from a single, relatively small group, though this is contested, as is the precise way human intelligence evolved.[20] Unless (or until) we can be scientifically certain about human origins, our philosophical-theological discussions must bring various evolutionary scenarios into conversation with the Thomist and Catholic doctrine concerning the direct creation of the rational soul, which implies a metaphysical saltation, but need not imply a *dramatic* anatomical saltation.[21] Here I briefly discuss a few possibilities for when and how the first truly rational human beings emerged.

---

18. For example, *ST* I q. 76, aa. 4 and 6. Karl Rahner points out: "in Thomist metaphysics . . . man consists of *materia prima*, and of *anima* as *unica forma* and *actualitas* of this *materia prima*, so that 'body' already implies the informing actuality of the 'soul'." See Rahner, *Theological Investigations* Volume IV (Baltimore: Helicon Press, 1966), 340–41n16.

19. Daniel D. De Haan, chapter 4 in this volume, section 2.2.

20. For example, Michael D. Petraglia and Huw S. Groucutt, "Out of Africa: The Evolution and History of Human Populations in the Southern Dispersal Zone," in *Rethinking Human Evolution*, ed. Jeffrey H. Schwartz (Cambridge, MA: MIT Press, 2018), 129–38. See also Cecilia Padilla-Iglesias, "Did Humanity Really Arise in One Place?" *Sapiens*, February 1, 2023, https://www.sapiens.org/archaeology/human-evolution-east-africa/. Regarding the way human intelligence evolved, Held presents a number of opinions, though without a conversation between neurophysiology and philosophy. See *Quirks of Human Anatomy*, chapter 7.

21. For one doctrinal statement of the rational soul's direct creation, see Pius XII, Encyclical Letter *Humani Generis* (August 12, 1950) (Denz., 3896).

1.3.1. Cranial Morphology (Scenario i)

Ian Tattersall and Jeffrey Schwartz recognize a distinctive *Homo sapiens* cranial morphology.[22] Tattersall associates this morphology with both the neural structure that made the brain "language-ready," and "the highly-derived vocal tract necessary for . . . modern articulate language."[23] If the possession of a rational soul went with this morphology, and assuming infants were born with this morphology as a result of a final mutation, then the soul could have been infused at their conception.[24] In this case, the first truly human infants would have been morphologically distinct from their parents, and would have been born about two hundred thousand years ago.

1.3.2 Behavioral Innovation (Scenario ii)

Tattersall points to the "virtually instantaneous cognitive transformation" that took place between one hundred thousand and seventy-five thousand years ago, when truly symbolic behavior appeared. He argues that a behavioral stimulus, which relied on an already-present underwriting biology, "provoke[d] this established species into behaving in an entirely new and unprecedented way." He also suggests "a small subset of individuals . . . began to attach meanings to specific spoken sounds, starting a self-reinforcing feedback in their brains between those spoken symbols and their mental representations, as they combined and recombined them to produce the beginnings of what we now experience as thought."[25] If the transition to rationality took place in this way, then rationality was at first passed on by imitation of the new behavior by peers and offspring; it was not associated with any mutation. It would have led to subtle changes in neural pathways, but it is not immediately clear how human infants came to be born hard-wired for language-acquisition.

---

22. Ian Tattersall and Jeffrey H. Schwartz, "The Morphological Distinctiveness of *Homo sapiens* and Its Recognition in the Fossil Record: Clarifying the Problem," *Evolutionary Anthropology* 17, no. 1 (2008): 49–54. They conclude (p. 53): "Living *Homo sapiens* is a highly distinctive morphological entity that is readily diagnosable when compared with its closest living relatives and all, or almost all, of its extinct ones."

23. Ian Tattersall, "Brain Size and the Emergence of Modern Human Cognition," in Schwartz, *Rethinking Human Evolution*, 329.

24. Tattersall, "Brain Size": ". . . it most likely involved a structurally minor alteration in gene regulation" (329).

25. Tattersall, "Brain Size," 327–29.

1.3.3. The Infusion of the Rational Soul into Some Members of the Species (Scenario iii)

While it is beyond Tattersall's remit to associate the behavioral change he envisages with the infusion of a rational soul, Kenneth Kemp proposes that God infused a rational soul into two humans (and their descendants) who did not differ *biologically* from their relatives.[26] This preserves Adam's (and Eve's) unique role; it requires (as Kemp recognizes) that rational and non-rational humans interbred, to ensure our descent from a group numbering a few thousand. Interbreeding with people unable to make the rational commitment of marriage would have been required had there been no fall. An answer to that difficulty lies in Kemp's distinction among the biological, philosophical and theological species,[27] of which the second and third possessed rational souls; the third alone were destined to eternal life. If God infused rational souls into some biological humans without calling them to eternal life (which raises its own difficulties), then Adam's descendants could have married truly rational human beings not descended from him.

1.3.4. A Final Dominant Mutation (Scenario iv)

As formulated, Kemp's proposal gives an impression of dualism, in that the rational soul's presence seems independent of any (neuro)physiological alteration. From a Thomistic perspective, it seems more *conveniens* that, as in the case of subsequent human beings, the first true human beings possessed rational souls from conception because the biological process of procreation rendered the conceptus of each apt for the infusion of a rational soul.[28] Thus in chapter 10 in this volume, Nicanor Austriaco offers the model of a mutation in a single individual yielding "a language-enabled brain"—a change in neural structure too subtle to leave a trace in the fossil record, and not yielding a new biological species. Adam would have been able to mate, and all who inherited the mutation would have possessed rational souls. This allows for a unique Adam and for our descent from a population of some thousands. It also requires that, for some generations—even if Adam had not sinned—rational human beings mated with pre-rational human beings.

---

26. Kenneth Kemp, "Science, Theology, and Monogenesis," *American Catholic Philosophical Quarterly* 85, no. 2 (2011): 230–32.

27. Kemp, "Science," 230.

28. When exploring the wisdom of God's ways, Aquinas frequently explores the *convenientia* ("fittingness") of what he actually has done and is doing, while allowing that he could have acted otherwise. For the conceptus being apt for the infusion of a rational soul, see Daria Spezzano, chapter 11 in this volume, section 1.1.

1.3.5. A Final Recessive Mutation (Scenario v)

If, however, the mutation yielding a language-enabled brain were recessive, it could have spread in the population without being expressed, until, over a number of generations, offspring were conceived with two copies of the mutated gene such that the conceptus of each was apt for the infusion of a rational soul. As the offspring matured, they could have recognized each other; hence it would not have been necessary for them to mate with pre-rational hominids, even if this in fact happened. There is also no need to posit rational human beings not called to eternal life. This scenario makes it less easy to envisage a single Adam—maybe he was the first to receive a rational soul, and thus, in a sense, he established rational human nature. In addition, or alternatively, he may have emerged as the natural leader of an initial group.

In scenario (ii) the first rational humans did not, as infants, differ from their parents in any way; only in scenario (i) did they differ in terms of large-scale anatomy. Their psychological abilities differed in scenarios (iii), (iv) and (v). In scenarios (iv) and (v) they differed genetically, and their neurophysiology developed in a subtly but profoundly different way during their fetal period, so that at birth they were hard-wired for the acquisition of human language. Most of these scenarios therefore require us to consider the situation of rational infants born of prerational parents, as we shall do below. A more extended discussion would consider further evolutionary scenarios.

1.4. Evolution's Imperfections

Some of our natural vulnerabilities derive from the fact that evolution is not an inexorable march towards flawless design. Because no mechanism is available for going back to the drawing board, much DNA, and many biochemical pathways and bodily structures, are conserved and adapted to serve new purposes. In some ways, organisms may resemble software or machines that have been elaborated in many stages, with much tinkering to iron out problems that have arisen, rather than something designed *de novo* as a coherent whole. Some features are left as evolutionary hangovers, and some are "spandrels"—not purposeful, but offshoots of developments that have been selected for.[29] If a new organism fits its environment well enough to reproduce successfully, problems that could be evolved out may well remain. There is no evolutionary pressure to resolve problems that occur rarely or manifest after reproductive age. Our continuity with other life-forms is closer-knit than Aquinas knew; some vulnerabilities are due to our bodies' not being designed *de novo* in the way he supposed.

---

29. Held, *Quirks of Human Anatomy*, 68. See also pp. 90 and 132.

1.5. Limitations of the Proportionate and Proximate Matter

In *De malo* (q. 5, a. 5), and *Summa theologiae* (I-II, q. 85, a. 6 and II-II, q. 164, a. 1), Aquinas asks whether defects such as mortality are natural to humanity. His answer is yes and no. When we make things, we accept the limitations that come with the proportionate matter—a saw, made of iron so that it will cut wood, eventually rusts; we compensate by polishing. Analogously, since our exterior and interior senses nourish an intellect, our immortal soul must be the form of an organic, hence corruptible, body. It must be more complex, and (at least overall) more sensitive, than other animal bodies; our skin's sensitivity must not be lessened by protective fur or scales. Hence we feel pain acutely, and are vulnerable. The deftness with which we make clothing and other means of protection partly compensates for this vulnerability.[30]

Our sensitivity also leads to moral-psychological liabilities. Some *passiones animae* are concupiscible—everyday patterns of attraction and repulsion. Challenging situations provoke irascible passions, which may overrule the concupiscible for the sake of fight or flight;[31] hence there is a natural possibility of tension among the passions. On occasion, reason must overrule the passions for the overall good (e.g. to agree to an uncomfortable medical procedure); the passions may resist reason, owing to their natural dynamics, which in a sense is unnatural, since they are meant to enhance our moral life.[32] Furthermore, the complexity of our psyche goes with complex social interactions, which enable fulfilling relationships, but result in vulnerability to each other and an increased risk of moral error. It is as if the hominin has evolved "beyond its comfort zone" into a complexity that is uniquely liable to tensions.

These limitations are the flip side of a rationality that requires a sensitive body as proportionate matter. Some vulnerabilities are the flip side of providence employing, as proximate matter for humanity, not a body designed from scratch, but the *hominin* body of our ancestors, with its neurophysiological complexity. In *Wickedness*, Mary Midgley explores how dynamics inherited from primate ancestors lead to bad, even monstrous, behavior, when more subtle dynamics fail to balance them, or more humane considerations to

---

30. *ST* I q. 91, a. 3, corpus and ad 2.
31. *ST* I q. 81, a. 2; I-II q. 23.
32. See *ST* I q. 81, a. 3 for the basic cooperation of the *passiones* with reason; q. 95, a. 2 on how their obedience is imperfect after the fall. On this imperfection, and the complexities of the interactions, see *ST* I-II q. 6, a. 7; q. 9, a. 2; q. 10, a. 3; q. 17, a. 7; q. 23, a. 1; q. 24; q. 85, a. 3. Difficulties caused by the *passiones* appear in I-II q. 37, a. 1; q. 77. On the need for virtues to harmonize the *passiones* with reason, see I-II q. 56, a. 4; q. 59; q. 60, aa. 4 and 5.

control them.[33] We will qualify this in section 3.2, but Midgley's insight chimes with Aquinas's recognition of how demanding a task it is to integrate *passiones* with reason. If to his list of *passiones* we add inherited complex primate patterns of interaction, we can see how hard it is for reason to monitor—and, as necessary, rise above—our psychological drives, for the socialization of infants to proceed perfectly, and for adults to cooperate smoothly. The inherited components of our psyche may well have resisted flawless integration into the human form of life.

2. Theological Principles for Envisaging the Unfallen State

2.1. Pilgrim Humanity's Need for Supernatural and Preternatural Gifts

Rationality implies a capacity for communion with God.[34] As open to unlimited truth, the intellect can be "enlarged" so as to receive the self-gift of God who is Truth.[35] As open to the-good-in-general, the will can be enlarged so as to receive the self-gift of God who is Goodness.[36] Human beings, as images of the Triune God, are called to reach perfection when each divine Person gives himself to them to be known, loved, possessed and enjoyed.[37]

Aquinas held it *conveniens* that rational creatures *journey* to bliss through acts of will, thereby having the dignity of personal involvement in laying hold on God's self-gift.[38] It is also *conveniens* that there are angels who would make the journey by one intense act of love, and creatures like us who make the journey by repeated acts of love.[39] This means we must live in a world of space and time, and as a family of rational animals so that the love of God that empowers our journey may overflow into sharing God's friendship for our fellow-pilgrims.[40]

---

33. Mary Midgley, *Wickedness: A Philosophical Essay* (London: Routledge and Kegan Paul, 1984).

34. *ST* I-II, q. 113, a. 10; *De veritate*, q. 22, a. 2 ad 5.

35. Psalm 119(118):32 says, "You have enlarged my heart"; in biblical terminology, "heart" can mean "mind" or "understanding." For God as Truth, see *ST* I q. 16, a. 5; for receiving God's self-gift, I-II q. 3, a. 8; q. 5, a. 1.

36. *ST* I q. 6, aa. 1–3; I-II q. 2, a. 8; q. 5, a. 1.

37. Richard Conrad, "Humanity Created for Communion with the Trinity in Aquinas," in *A Transforming Vision: Knowing and Loving the Triune God*, ed. George Westhaver (London: SCM, 2018), 121–34. This draws especially on *ST* I qq. 43 and 93, and q. 12, aa. 1–10.

38. *ST* I-II q. 5, a. 7.

39. *ST* I q. 62, aa. 1–5; q. 77, a. 2.

40. *ST* II-II q. 25, aa. 1, 4, 6, 8 and 12.

Since it is unnatural for our soul to be without the body, a truly human destiny must include bodily glory. Thus Aquinas saw the earth as our temporary home—we were always intended to transition to a higher state in which our share in divine bliss overflowed into bodily radiance.[41] The need to journey into bliss was not caused by the fall; rather, the journey's nature was altered, so that it now involves passing through death in solidarity with Jesus, to a resurrection, pledged—and caused—by his own resurrection.[42]

Aquinas insisted that a journey to so divine a goal requires *super*natural resources. These comprise (a) the theological virtues (divine strengths) of faith, hope and charity by which we recognize God's offer, have the energy to seize it, and love God as Friend and Goal; (b) the gifts of the Holy Spirit that attune us to the Spirit's guidance; and (c) the infused moral virtues that configure the faculties required for our complex life in view of a divine Goal.[43] All these are habits that elevate what we can do; they flow from the share in God's own life that we call grace, which molds what we are.[44] The core element of our natural neediness consists in our dependence on God for these resources; Aquinas saw it as part of our dignity to be open to a divine joy that natural resources cannot attain.[45] These virtues and gifts can be present in a latent way ("habitually"), shaping our behavior even when we do not advert to them, in the way that concepts and priorities we are not actively conscious of can shape our thinking and behavior.[46] It is important for our subsequent discussion that they can be present habitually even before the age of reason, as happens now in infant baptism.

Aquinas affirmed the tradition that, when the first human beings were created, they already possessed grace and the supernatural virtues that flow from it; to remedy other elements of human neediness and vulnerability, they enjoyed further gifts beyond what strictly belongs to human nature.[47] Later

---

41. Aquinas saw the empyrean heaven as suited to the glorified body and hence as our destined home (*ST* I q. 46, a. 3; q. 66, a. 3; q. 102, a. 4). Modern cosmology requires us to translate this into other terms—tentatively, since the New Testament does not provide a clear picture of what, as Paul says (1 Cor 2:9), we cannot imagine. Perhaps Christ's risen Body established a space suited to it, one not continuous with the space of this cosmos. Maybe, at the end of history, Christ will take the saints' risen bodies to *that* space; maybe he will transform this space into a fitting shrine for them.
42. *ST* I-II q. 4, a. 6; III q. 56, a. 1.
43. *ST* I-II qq. 62, 68, and 63, aa. 3 and 4.
44. *ST* I-II q. 110. Note that in this context "habits" does not mean compulsions that take us over, but enabling, settled dispositions analogous to a life skill.
45. *ST* I-II q. 5, a. 5 ad 1 and ad 2. See also *ST* I q. 77, a. 2; q. 95, a. 4 ad 1.
46. Cf. *ST* I-II q. 112, a. 5, on conjecturing we have grace on the basis of signs it gives.
47. *ST* I q. 95, aa. 1 and 3.

theologians called these further gifts "*preter*natural."[48] Four such gifts are sometimes listed as:

- Moral-psychological integrity, in which our reason and various affective powers are in perfect harmony.
- Impassibility—a freedom from pain, suffering and distress.
- Immortality.
- Infused knowledge—a God-given knowledge the first human beings could not have acquired by themselves.[49]

Moral-psychological integrity is of particular relevance, since it rendered the journey into God smooth. Aquinas's holistic ethics affirmed the basic goodness of the *passiones animae*. If they are integrated with reason, we *savor* good acts, so that, in those who love God, the *passiones* contribute to a wholehearted love of the Highest Good, with the result that our animality contributes to our pilgrimage.[50] If the *passiones* are not so integrated, they can impede good decisions, and even lead to serious sins that destroy charity and thus thwart our journey.[51] We may speak of the possibility of sin and our liability to temptations to sin as vulnerabilities. The preternatural gift of integrity freed the first humans from temptations due to the *passiones* resisting reason, though not from the possibility of the sins of pride and envy.[52]

The other preternatural gifts are not so intrinsically connected with the journey to God, so that it is possible to maintain a deep charity while suffering, and Christians see passing through death as part of journeying in and with Christ to glory.

---

48. While Aquinas did not use the term "preternatural," the distinction is implicit in *ST* I-II q. 109, where he asks what would be possible in a state of integrity that did not include supernatural grace.

49. The entry "Preternatural" in *The New Catholic Encyclopedia* focuses on "integrity" and "immortality." George Smith gives a text-book account of bodily immortality, immunity from pain and sickness, and moral-psychological integrity, in *The Teaching of the Catholic Church: A Summary of Catholic Doctrine Arranged and Edited by Canon George D. Smith* (London: Burns, Oates & Washbourne, 1948), 48, 239, 322–27. The Father John A. Hardon, S.J. Archives includes infused knowledge, attributed (as by Aquinas) to Adam alone. See https://www.therealpresence.org/archives/God/God_013.htm (accessed October 2, 2024).

50. *ST* I-II qq. 24 (on the goodness of the *passiones*), 55 (virtue) and 59 (moral virtues ordering the *passiones*).

51. *ST* II-II q. 24, a. 12.

52. *ST* II-II q. 163, a. 1. See also I q. 63, a. 2.

2.2. God Governs Suaviter

Aquinas accorded great weight to Wisdom 8:1, which teaches that God orders all things both *fortiter* (powerfully), and *suaviter*—sweetly, gently, even courteously and tactfully.[53] God does not render natures and causal powers redundant, but causes them to be what they are, and to perform their proper actions.[54] Since he gives other animals the natural resources they need if they are to flourish, it was *conveniens* for him to endow the first human beings with the resources for reaching their proper Goal; namely the supernatural gifts mentioned above.

Aquinas saw the union of the rational soul with the proportionate matter of the human body as making a unique contribution to the beauty of the cosmos.[55] We now know God chose to create a cosmos in which life *evolves*, rather than one with a different form of beauty; as Daria Spezzano explains, our evolutionary connection with the whole of life on earth enables us to exercise a priestly role as we render thanks to God on behalf of all life.[56] In this light, God's governing *suaviter* made it *conveniens* for him to work with the dynamics of evolution to bring humanity into being, despite the limitations of the proportionate matter. It also made it fitting for him to bestow the preternatural gift of integrity in intimate connection with supernatural grace, so that the first humans' moral well-being was not ensured by a stream of corrective impulses that could look like fixing earlier mistakes, but by grace gently permeating their natural condition to work a life-enhancing integrity.

It is beyond the scope of this chapter to explore how, in a fallen world, grace—restored through Christ—still operates *suaviter*, except to note that it typically engages our inbuilt openness to God, perfects nature rather than bypassing it, and, through the theological and infused virtues, restores some moral-psychological integrity.[57] Also, insofar as it includes effort and suffering, the journey to God involves solidarity with Christ's own victory.[58]

---

53. Aquinas quotes or alludes to this text ten times in *Summa theologiae*. See especially *ST* I-II q. 110, a. 2; II-II q. 23, a. 2; q. 165, a. 1.
54. *ST* I q. 105, a. 5.
55. See, for example, *ST* I q. 91, a. 1, on the human being as microcosm.
56. Chapter 11 in this volume, section 1.3.
57. For grace perfecting nature, see, for example, *ST* I q. 1, a. 8 ad 2; II-II q. 165, a. 1.
58. Daria Spezzano, chapter 11 in this volume, section 2.1, especially pp. 256–s257.

2.3. Revelation and Authority

Augustine saw sufferings such as those of pregnancy, childbirth and infancy as incompatible with the paradisal state.[59] Chesterton pointed out evidence for a doctrine of universal sinfulness.[60] This exemplifies a tendency to suppose that "something must have gone wrong." Perhaps surprisingly, Pius V's *Ex omnibus afflictionibus* implies God could have created the human race more-or-less in the condition we find it in now.[61] Since the fact of an historical fall from a higher state needed to be revealed, we must consider briefly what has been revealed, and how to appropriate it faithfully.

2.3.1. Scripture and Its Interpretation

Aquinas saw Scripture as the privileged channel of revelation.[62] It employs several genres; to take metaphors in a literalistic way, or parables as history, is to mistake the *literal* meaning.[63] Scripture records some historical facts that unaided reason cannot discover; but it cannot falsify, or be falsified by, truths discovered by reason.[64] As Newman later wrote, ". . . if anything seems to be proved by an astronomer, or geologist, or chronologist . . . in contradiction to the dogmas of faith, that point will eventually turn out, first *not* to be proved, or secondly, not *contradictory*, or thirdly, not contradictory to anything *really revealed*, but to something which has been confused with *revelation*."[65]

Aquinas recognized that biblical events often have symbolic meanings.[66] However, since Genesis looks like an historical narrative, Aquinas took it to be primarily such and held that all human beings descend from one couple who were created as adults.[67] To revise this judgment would not be unfaithful

---

59. *Contra Julianum* III iv, 10; III v, 11–12 and vi, 13; *Opus Imperfectum contra Julianum* III, cliv.

60. *Orthodoxy*, chapter 2.

61. Oct. 1, 1567; Denz., 1901–80. Against Baius, who held that God was *obliged* to endow the first humans with all that remedied their natural neediness, the bull condemned the proposition, "God could not have created man from the beginning in the state in which he is now born" (Denz., 1955).

62. *ST* I q. 1, aa. 1 and 8.

63. *ST* I q. 1, aa. 9 and 10; q. 13, a. 6.

64. For example, it needed to be revealed that the world was created at a definite time in the past (*ST* I q. 46, a. 2)—the black-body radiation left by the Big Bang was unknown until the 1960s. For preserving the truth of Scripture and its compatibility with what reason is certain of, see *ST* I q. 68, a. 1.

65. John Henry Newman, *The Idea of a University* (London: Longmans, Green and Co., 1902), 466–67 (p. 342 in the 1947 edition).

66. *ST* I q. 1, a. 10; and, for example, *ST* I q. 74, a. 2; q. 102, a. 1.

67. *ST* I q. 91, a. 2; q. 94, a. 3; q. 102, aa. 1 and 4.

to Aquinas's actual practice. For example, a literalistic reading of Genesis 1 implies the earth is flat, but Aquinas knew it is spherical, and meshed the details of Genesis with the best cosmology available.[68] One key principle in his interpretation of the Scriptural doctrine of the fall runs:

- Nature and natures were not changed by Adam's fall.[69]

Hence the primordial vegetarianism of Genesis 1:30 applied to only some animals. *The Catechism of the Catholic Church* (nos. 375 and 390) sees Genesis 2–3 as a figurative story about humanity's origins, which does indicate an historical fall from a higher state. Hence we may seek to discern the meaning of Genesis (a) with sensitivity to its genre, (b) in the light of the whole of Scripture and tradition, and (c) in dialogue with scientific discoveries and theories—not by reading it literalistically.

Aquinas affirmed the goodness of nature and of natural causal powers.[70] This, combined with his reliance on a revelation that does not contradict truths proved by reason, leads to the following principle for considering the unfallen state:

- Avoid unnecessary myth. If Scripture does not tell us that, by some gift or provision of God, something was different before the fall from the way it is now, we should assume it was not different.[71]

2.3.2. The Council of Trent

Aquinas saw the Church's doctors as trustworthy—not infallible—guides to the interpretation of Scripture.[72] He also relied on Church councils and papal decrees. For our reflection, the most important dogmatic text remains the Council of Trent's *Decree on Original Sin*.[73] This requires us to acknowledge that:

- By his transgression the first man lost the holiness and justice in which he had been constituted, incurring God's wrath, the death with which he had been threatened, and captivity to the devil; he was changed for the worse in body and soul.[74]

---

68. *ST* I q. 1, a. 1 ad 2; q. 68.
69. *ST* I q. 96, a. 1 ad 2.
70. *ST* I q. 22, a. 3; q. 103, aa. 4 and 6.
71. *ST* I q. 99, a. 1; q. 101, a. 1.
72. *ST* I q. 1, a. 8 ad 2.
73. Session V, June 17, 1546 (Denz., 1510–16).
74. Note that, unlike love, wrath is attributed to God only metaphorically (*ST* I q. 3, a. 2 ad 2).

- Adam's sin lost holiness and justice for his descendants too: defiled by his sin, he handed on to them not only death and bodily *poenas*, but also "sin" which is "the death of the soul."[75]

We may summarize the points most relevant for the present chapter thus:

- The first human being(s) enjoyed holiness and justice.
- The original human state also involved a physical, moral and spiritual invulnerability, including an immunity from death.
- If the first human being(s) had not fallen, they would have transmitted this God-given condition to their descendants, who would have inherited holiness and justice, immunity from death and other bodily vulnerabilities, and an ability to resist the devil.

It is generally agreed that "sin" is used *analogically* (i.e., with related but distinct meanings) in the terms "original sin," "mortal sin," and "venial sin." Unlike the second and third of these, the first is not personally deliberate on the part of one conceived in the state of original sin.[76]

2.3.3. Rethinking Adam and Eden

If humanity's descent from one man were mentioned only at the beginning of Genesis, we might take it simply as a symbolic story. However, the New Testament repeatedly contrasts Christ—the Second Adam—with the first.[77] As Simon Gaine explains, this must be taken seriously, even though Trent was not concerned with defining humanity's descent from one man, but with ruling out errors such as the denial that we all need Christ's grace for the removal of original sin.[78] The genetic evidence, however, is against seeing all humans as descended from only one man (or one couple). Hence some theologians take the biblical Adam to stand for the first human group. For the purposes of this chapter, we need only suggest that, (1) owing to exceptional gifts, one man could have emerged as natural leader of the initial group, or (2) the first recipient of a rational soul functioned as "prototype"

---

75. *Poena* can mean "punishment," "penalty," or "suffering," "pain." As Isaac Morales shows (chapter 9 in this volume), in Romans Paul focuses on "the death of the soul." Nevertheless, Trent envisaged (human) physical death also as a consequence of Adam's sin.

76. Rahner, "Brief Theological Observations," 52.

77. Explicitly: Romans 5:12–21; 1 Corinthians 15:21–22, 45–49. Implicitly: Mark 1:13; John 18:1, 19:41; Philippians 2:5–11.

78. Chapter 6 in this volume, pp. 123, 125–126.

or exemplar for subsequent human beings. Of course, the first recipient of a rational soul could also have become the leader.

Aquinas read Genesis 2 historically and thus defended the *convenientia* of God creating Adam as an adult on the grounds that "in the natural order the perfect precedes the imperfect," which seems contrary to an evolutionary scenario.[79] However, Aquinas means that if God did create Adam as an adult, this fits with one of the patterns observed in nature; namely, when an existing species propagates, adult organisms generate immature offspring. Aquinas does not impose this principle outside its proper context; when needed, he argues that works attributed to God fit with a different pattern; namely, the way in which, in the order of generation, the imperfect precedes the perfect.[80] As Brian Carl and Daniel De Haan explain in chapters 3 and 4 in this volume, Aquinas's metaphysical principles do not rule out the appearance of new species that are higher than the matter from which they are generated, provided sufficiently powerful proximate causes exist. Hence Thomistic principles do not rule out an evolutionary process that issued in the conception of embryos that were higher than their parents, embryos into which God appropriately infused rational souls. Thomists are free to explore the *convenientia* of God creating humanity through such a process.

Aquinas held Eden to be an inaccessible geographical place, blessed with a temperate climate and free from deleterious environmental factors such as dangerous animals.[81] He seems to have thought that, if Adam had not fallen, each of his descendants would have dwelt in Eden until he or she transitioned to heaven.[82] No such geographical region exists; the human race, evolving in Africa, always inhabited a world that contained dangerous species and was subject to natural disasters. The biblical Eden must be reinterpreted, perhaps as a symbol of an original harmony where humans were wise stewards of nature.

2.3.4. Original Justice

Owing to its policy of leaving room for all legitimate theological opinions, the Council of Trent did not define the original justice Adam lost, or specify its relationship to the holiness granted him. Aquinas accepted Augustine's picture of a state of "holistic harmony" in which:

79. *ST* I q. 94, a. 3.
80. E.g., *ST* I q. 66, a. 1, on the Creator bringing relatively unformed matter into existence, then gradually forming it. Cf. *ST* I q. 99, a. 1 sc; q. 101, a. 2 sc; II-II q. 1, a. 7 ad 3.
81. *ST* I q. 102, aa. 1 and 2.
82. *ST* I q. 102, a. 4, end of corpus.

(i) the soul's higher powers (intellect and will) were subject in obedience and love to God;
(ii) the soul's lower powers (especially the *passiones animae*) were subject to the higher ones; and
(iii) the body was subject to the soul.[83]

Although supernatural gifts can (and in our present state do) exist without preternatural gifts (and vice versa), in historical fact, as Aquinas saw it, the possession of the latter was bound up with the retention of the former. Grace was given to human nature at its origin, in such a way that anyone inheriting human nature would have inherited that gift, and the preternatural gifts along with it.[84] This made humanity vulnerable in the sense that if Adam did lose grace, all humans would inherit human nature shorn of both the supernatural and the preternatural gifts.[85]

3. Knowledge of God, Growth in Virtue, and the Effects of Grace, in the Unfallen State

Since it is chiefly the moral-psychological wounds due to the fall that impede our journey to God, I enquire in this section how our vulnerability to such wounds might have been overcome in the state of original justice, in which grace would have caused a preternatural, life-enhancing moral-psychological integrity.[86] A crucial difference between the unfallen and the fallen states is that, in the former, grace would have been bestowed at conception, whereas in the latter it comes later, typically at baptism. I explore how, in the unfallen state, integrity, caused by a grace-given knowledge and love of God, could plausibly have continued. First, I ask what knowledge and experience of God the earliest

---

83. *ST* I q. 95, aa. 1 and 2.
84. *ST* I q. 100, a. 1.
85. It is beyond my current remit to explore the *convenientia* of this vulnerability and of God's permitting the fall. However, in "The Sin of Adam" (*Theological Investigations*, vol. 11 [New York: Seabury Press, 1974], 247–62), Karl Rahner proposes that our derivation from and union with the single human race *was meant to be* the medium and basis of God's self-gift, which can no longer be the case because of the guilt of those who constituted the origin of our race. Hence God's offer and gift of himself to all human beings is made only in virtue of their relation to Christ, not through the medium of human descent. This prioritizes God's positive and basically unchanged plan to grace us; what changed is the human condition in which grace takes flesh. Owing to the primeval sin, inheriting human nature ceased to be fit for purpose as the medium of grace; it became *conveniens* for God to bestow grace on the basis and through the medium of solidarity with Christ the Redeemer—which of course involves a distinctive glorious victory.
86. *ST* I q. 95, a. 1.

humans might have had. I then examine what grace would have worked in, with, and on. Finally I look at what its moral effects might have been.

3.1. Natural and Revealed Knowledge of God

Since unfallen human beings were intended to journey to God by grace, in faith, rather as we do, Aquinas denied that Adam enjoyed the beatific vision.[87] Fallen human beings achieve a philosophical knowledge of God's existence with difficulty.[88] By contrast, Aquinas held, Adam had an ease in "penetrating to God's intellectual effects"—he was struck by the wonder of the very being of the things around him, pointing him to the One who truly possesses being, and was aware of his own mind, whose intellectuality pointed to God.[89] It does not follow that he articulated all this in terms of scholastic metaphysics and psychology.

Truths beyond the reach of unaided reason, notably the Triune God's invitation to share his bliss, intrinsically need to be revealed.[90] Although Jesus, the Incarnate Word, is our great Teacher, Aquinas also discussed how God spoke through prophets.[91] By exceptions to the general pattern whereby we learn through the senses, God "infused" images into their imaginations, along with the ability to learn from them, or infused concepts directly into their intellects. Something similar happened in Adam's case, as Aquinas saw it: to fit his unique role as *principium* of all human beings "not only by bodily generation, but also by teaching and governing," he enjoyed a high degree of infused knowledge, including knowledge of the Triune God's friendship.[92]

If the first humans began life as infants, born of parents who did not speak truly human language and could not have spoken to them rationally about the Creator, we must ask what natural or infused knowledge of God they could plausibly have had. God does give some children, such as Catherine of Siena and Therese of Lisieux, a profound sense of his presence, providing resources for later lives of holiness. Maybe some such experience of God's presence was given to the first human beings.[93] This would have engaged their natural sense of wonder to provide a sense of a world "charged with the

---

87. *ST* I q. 94, a. 1; II-II q. 5, a. 1.
88. *ST* I q. 1, a. 1.
89. *ST* I q. 94, aa. 1 and 2.
90. For example, *ST* I q. 32, a. 1; I-II q. 62, a. 1.
91. *ST* II-II qq. 171–75.
92. *ST* I q. 94, aa. 1 and 3; q. 101, a. 1 ad 1.
93. Aquinas held that charity typically brings a spiritual joy (*ST* II-II q. 28), and that experiences of "sweetness" are granted (I-II q. 112, a. 5; II-II q. 97, a. 2 ad 2). The image of God walking in the garden (Gen. 3:8) suggests such an experience.

grandeur of God."[94] Since prophetic knowledge has been given, and revelations made, to people who have not been highly educated, including children such as Bernadette Soubirous, we must allow that some or all of the first human beings could have had truly prophetic knowledge, or at least an intuitive awareness of God's friendship, or even an inchoate sense of the Holy Trinity. God-given faith and insight, present habitually from conception, could have enhanced the first humans' receptivity to these gifts.[95]

In an unfallen world, subsequent generations would have possessed faith and insight, habitually, from conception. They need not as a rule have possessed prophetic or infused knowledge; instead, they would have been taught about God by their parents, receiving a tradition passed down from Adam.[96] A graced experience of God's presence, however, would presumably have remained ubiquitous.

Aquinas distinguished between faith, on the one hand, and theological articulacy, on the other, for supernatural grace is not proportioned to natural abilities. Thus the Apostles, who were neither trained scholars, nor prolific writers, possessed a greater faith than later saints.[97] More significantly still, the same faith has been held since the beginnings of our race—all the truths of faith were implicit in the two components Hebrews 11:6 mentions: God's existence and his rewarding of those who seek him.[98] To attribute a real faith to the first human beings, as infants, and to attribute prophetic insights to many of them, or at least to their leader, does not imply they used technical theological language. After all, the powerful stories by which Scripture articulates faith, and the deceptively simple imagery by which it expresses profound truths, have priority over the technical language of the theology which depends on Scripture. Thus a graced experience of God's presence could have grounded a real friendship with God while human language was developing. Over maybe only a few generations, parents would have become able to speak about God to their offspring, whose habits of faith and insight would have primed them to learn more of the Creator, and in due course to judge for themselves that the Creator exists.

---

94. For example, Catherine L'Ecuyer, "The Wonder Approach to Learning," *Frontiers in Human Neuroscience* 8 (Oct. 2014), art. 764. The quotation is from Gerard Manley Hopkins' poem "God's Grandeur."

95. For faith and the gift of insight, see *ST* II-II qq. 1–8. For habitual presence, see section 2.1 above.

96. *ST* I q. 101, a. 1.

97. *ST* II-II q. 1, a. 7 ad 4.

98. *ST* II-II q. 1, a. 7.

3.2. What Did Grace—and Training—Work In, With and On?

Aquinas discussed *gratia* in *Prima secundae*, the part of the *Summa* where he described the psyche in which grace, so to speak, takes flesh to have moral effects.[99] Much goes on in that psyche pre-consciously. Rarely do we need to force ourselves to process sense-data or abstract concepts from it. Even in fallen humanity, the *passiones animae* and will incline toward the good and away from the noxious.[100] Thus Aquinas recognized "roots of virtue" on which training and practice can build a life-enhancing harmony.[101] He also recognized individual propensities toward certain virtues, attributing such differences to the influence of climate and the heavenly bodies.[102] We would now invoke genetic and epigenetic factors to explain some people's greater aptitude toward emotional intelligence and other moral skills. Because of such natural variations in character, the material on which moral education, then personal maturation, worked, would—even in the unfallen state—have been to some extent given rather than chosen.[103]

Aquinas ruled out propensities to vice from the unfallen state. This does not rule out the natural possibility of tension among our appetites mentioned above, since, as Rahner pointed out, spontaneous, pre-reflective desire that takes shape in our psyche on the basis of natural dynamisms is necessary if free choice is to proceed.[104] It can naturally take time—even effort—for reason to reach a decision; Christ's prayer in the garden exemplifies this.[105] It is in fallen humanity that spontaneous desire can precede free decision *and resist it*, giving rise to the experience of an impersonal power that we cannot fully absorb into what we want ourselves to be; this is traditionally called "concupiscence." Humanity's now lost immunity to this difficulty was a preternatural gift that, however, did not make redundant the need to grow to maturity, including moral maturity, by coming to understand moral truth and personally to own and savor moral goodness.

Even in an unfallen state, the intellect would naturally begin as a blank slate, and children would acquire the use of reason only after some years.[106] However,

---

99. See especially I-II qq. 109–114.
100. *ST* I-II q. 5, a. 8; q. 8, a. 1; q. 23, a. 2.
101. *ST* I-II q. 63, a. 1.
102. *ST* I q. 96, a. 3. This considers innate bodily differences; but, according to *ST* I q. 85, a. 7, these have psychological effects.
103. *ST* I q. 96, a. 3.
104. Karl Rahner, "The Theological Concept of Concupiscentia," *Theological Investigations*, vol. 1 (Baltimore: Helicon Press, 1961), 347–82.
105. *ST* III q. 18, aa. 2, 3, 5, and 6.
106. *ST* I q. 101, a. 1 sc; a. 2.

the infant psyche is not a blank slate, but hard-wired for interaction and learning, which may explain why human infants engage with the world in a more open ended, less instinctive way than other mammalian infants. Early experience and training help lay down or fine-tune neural pathways, so that infants are subject to a bottom-up influence of inherited brain physiology, and a top-down causal influence of their human environment. This environment is at first the family, then the wider society of which they gradually become aware. As personal responsibility develops, often aided by grace, it must work with and on the deliveries of nurture as well as of nature, to develop or deepen virtues. Some of these mold intellect and will to promote a healthy top-down causal influence, others enrich the harmony between moral reasoning and the *passiones animae*.

As mentioned in section 1.5, the material on which moral education, self-control, and grace, work includes dynamics inherited from our prehuman ancestors. This material may be difficult for humane, rational considerations to control. As Robert Barry notes, some theorists emphasize "the adaptive advantages of selfishness."[107] Others, however, explore the adaptive advantages of cooperation (among species as well as within species) and altruism.[108] Since Midgley wrote *Wickedness*, we have learned more about the neural structures that underlie psychological dynamics, and about how human sexuality, childhood, means of bonding, and so on differ from those of other primates. Moreover, the social patterns of our immediate ancestors would not have been those currently found among apes, but distinct *hominin* patterns; current research on Neanderthals suggests what they may have been like. If evolution gave us a distinctive set of hominin dynamics to promote social cohesion, one that is more fundamentally a resource largely suited to our needs rather than an unqualified difficulty, this would chime with the *convenientia* of our evolutionary connection with other forms of life. It would also chime with Aquinas's recognition of the roots of virtue, and his theory of natural law. The *Secunda pars* of the *Summa* begins with our inbuilt drive toward *beatitudo* ("flourishing," "bliss"); our natural inclinations toward self-preservation, the propagation of the species, the good of our society—and knowledge of God—ground Natural-Law thinking.[109] Any difficulties with integrating our hominin inheritance into human life and society are the flip side of our need to be lifted above our natural level. In the unfallen state,

---

107. See Barry, chapter 8 of this volume, section 3.

108. For example, Andrew Davison, "Christian Doctrine and Biological Mutualism: Some Explorations in Systematic and Philosophical Theology," *Theology and Science* 18 (2020): 258–78. Samir Okasha discusses biological altruism philosophically in *Stanford Encyclopedia of Philosophy*, ed. Edward N. Zalta, https://plato.stanford.edu/entries/altruism-biological/ (accessed July 22, 2022).

109. *ST* I-II q. 94, a. 2.

grace and charity enlarged the human heart, working *suaviter* to pervade and affirm our complex psyche as well as impart a divine dignity and preternatural harmony. In a fallen humanity lacking preternatural moral integrity, it may have been the growing size and complexity of human societies that showed up the limitations of our hominin dynamics, to the extent—as Aquinas saw it—that corrupt customs and the accumulation of sins obscured the natural law, making revelation necessary to show us what is truly fulfilling.[110]

A difficulty attends the likelihood that the first humans, hard-wired for interaction and learning, were born to *pre*human parents, for it is not clear how their parents could have guided them to mature in *truly human virtue*. In fact, their infant needs might not have differed from those of other infants in an immediately striking way: they would have needed suckling, affection, help with learning to walk, introduction to their environment and its affordances. Their parents would have had complex social structures, and would have socialized *all* their infants. There would have been nurture on which the first human children could build as they explored their world, developed practical wisdom concerning its use, and came to recognize and socialize with each other. We might suggest that the relationship between these children and their parents was somewhat analogous to that between a human couple and a child who turns out to be precociously intelligent and talented.

3.3. The Moral-Psychological Effects of Grace

In this subsection I offer suggestions as to how grace, present from conception in the first humans and in any children born in the unfallen state, could have caused moral-psychological integrity.[111] While the conscious, deliberate use of the theological and infused virtues would have awaited the age of reason, their *habitual* presence from conception might have had a benign effect on the developing psyche, subtly working on developing neural pathways—the hard-wiring—by a top-down causation to enhance the roots of virtue.[112] This

---

110. *ST* I-II q. 98, a. 6; q. 99, a. 2 ad 2; III q. 70, a. 2 ad 1.
111. As implied by *ST* I q. 100, a. 1 c and ad 2.
112. Studies on fetal and neo-natal consciousness range from those that judge the level of consciousness is quite low to those which emphasize its complexity and significance. For the former, see, for example, Hugo Lagercrantz and Jean-Pierre Changeux, "The Emergence of Human Consciousness: From Fetal to Neonatal Life," *Pediatric Research* 65 (2009): 255–60. For the latter, see, for example, Alessandra Piontelli, *From Fetus to Child: An Observational and Psychoanalytic Study* (London: Routledge, 1992); Alessandra Piontelli, Luisa Bocconi, Chiara Boschetto, Alessandra Kustermann and Umberto Nicolini, "Differences and Similarities in the Intra-Uterine Behaviour of Monozygotic and Dizygotic Twins," *Twin Research and Human Genetics* 2 (1999): 264–73. The different judgments are partly due to the criteria used.

would be analogous to the way the later acquisition of virtues has a top-down influence—a firmly-held set of values filters down into our ways of perceiving and reacting to the world, and the priorities we implicitly hold influence how we behave. Basically, a top-down causation could have tipped the balance towards a smoother harmony among the relevant faculties and inherited dynamics (which are naturally transformed within the distinctive human psyche) to promote their co-operation and to relieve the tensions and resistance that a complex primate psyche risks. Perhaps more significantly, rather as a healthy human environment benefits infants' developing psyche, so a graced experience of God—an intuition that God is our "environment"—could have promoted balance, security and strength starting before birth, so that education in virtue would not have had to contend with passions as unruly as can happen now. These factors would have promoted freedom from concupiscence (in its bad sense), the freedom that Rahner calls "habitual self-domination." Spontaneous desires would have arisen pre-reflectively, but would have been more characterized by attitudes already shaped by charity, and in due course personally owned.[113] Thus spontaneous desires, and inherited (but transformed) hominin dynamics, could in due course readily be integrated into reasoned decision-making.

Aquinas envisaged a fairly seamless cooperation between the infused and the acquired virtues. In our fallen world, one kind of virtue often compensates for deficiencies in the other.[114] Had there been no fall, the infused virtues, present from before birth, would have promoted the development of acquired virtues as children grew.

In the special case of the first generation of humans, born to prehuman parents, the environment in which they were reared would have included hominin parental care and social structures. It would have been relatively simple; presumably a hunter-gatherer life without the moral demands of even modest cities, so that the instincts of the natural law would have sufficed for day-to-day life without the need for a developed, detailed ethics. We may propose that, along with supernatural grace, God bestowed an exceptional degree of preternatural moral wisdom to make up for the lack of truly human parenting, analogous to the infused knowledge Aquinas attributed to Adam, but more instinctive, and tailored to their infant condition. The first human

---

113. Towards the end of a discussion of the state of integrity ("The Theological Concept of Concupiscentia," 367–74), Rahner suggests that the loss of integrity providentially made repentance possible.

114. Richard Conrad, "Human Practice and God's Making-Good in Aquinas's Virtue Ethics," in *Varieties of Virtue Ethics*, ed. David Carr, James Arthur and Kristján Kristjánsson (London: Palgrave Macmillan, 2017), 163–79.

beings and their immediate descendants need not have been moral philosophers in the league of Aristotle, for Aquinas distinguishes between those who possess virtues by connaturality and those who have theoretical knowledge about them but might not practice them.[115] The first human generation belonged to the former group, as would subsequent generations had there been no fall.

In the case of subsequent generations, a problem is posed by Aquinas's conviction that, had there been no fall, it would have been possible for members of subsequent generations to sin—how widespread sin would have become is unknowable.[116] While in the next section we shall ask how society as such might have remained relatively sinless, here we must ask how the presence of grace could have mitigated children's vulnerability to any poor parenting they received, to bad example set by others, and to damaging social structures—for we now know what lasting damage can result from neglect and abuse, and take special care to guard against it. Even now, however, some children who are subject to bad parenting prove resilient. The presence of grace from conception, and an experience of God's presence, could have promoted both resilience, and strength to persist in virtue regardless of bad example. Catholics have a test case in the Virgin Mary, who was conceived in a state of grace; the universal tradition holds that, by grace, she remained free from all actual sin.[117] God-given, habitual charity shaped her psyche such that there was no inclination to sin.[118] Although her parents are venerated as saints, the society into which she was born was deeply flawed, owing, for example, to unjust and oppressive governments—yet she remained sinless.

4. Language, Learning, Leadership and Law

Leadership structures are found in primate communities; hominin parental nurturing went on within social groups. Human societies have developed languages in which to communicate growing bodies of theoretical and practical knowledge. We must ask what this might have looked like in a race not subject to original sin, and in particular how humans born of prehuman

---

115. For example, *ST* II-II q 45, a. 2.
116. *ST* I q. 100, a. 2. Any sins of Adam's descendants would not have affected *their* offspring: *ST* I-II q. 81, a. 2.
117. The Bull of Pius IX *Ineffabilis Deus* (December 8, 1854) (Denz., 2803) explicitly defines Mary's freedom from original sin; the natural implication of this is the presence of sanctifying grace. The tradition of her freedom from all actual sin is mentioned by Aquinas in *ST* I q. 100, a. 2; III q. 27, a. 4.
118. Cf. *ST* III q. 27, a. 3.

parents might have developed human language, and learned of the world by exploring, not paradise, but an area of Africa.

4.1. Language

Our hominin ancestors would have employed complex forms of communication, which, however, did not embody true rationality. If the infusion of the rational soul coincided with the development of the human larynx's distinctive anatomy, it went with the availability of a wider range of sounds. If it coincided with evolution's "great leap forward," the full range of sounds was already available; what was new was the ability to associate them with *universal* concepts.

God has reportedly given some saints, such as Vincent Ferrer and Francis Xavier, the charismatic gift of tongues so that they could preach to people whose language they had not learned. He could have given the first human infants a ready-made language in a similar way, but we need not suppose that he did so, for human infants are to some extent hard-wired for language.[119] Indeed, Nicaraguan Sign Language has indicated children's ability to invent a language. It would fit God's governing *suaviter* if the preternatural gifts bestowed on the first human infants *gently* enhanced the natural propensity to communicate humanly, so that besides their affectionate communication with their parents they gradually developed a truly hierarchical vocal language in peer-group cooperation. However, since children are sometimes born with prodigious skills in, say, music or mathematics, providence may have granted precocious gifts of communication to the first human children to meet their uniquely needy situation, or to at least some of them to enable them to help their peers.

4.2. Acquired Knowledge of the World

The human psyche is more open ended and less instinctive than that of other primates. This goes with the dignity of being able to investigate the world and learn how to employ its resources, along with the interpersonal fulfilment that comes from teaching and learning. Being less instinctive than infants of other species, human infants are more vulnerable to their environment and need extra care and guidance. If the first humans began life as infants, they would have been physically vulnerable; as not yet possessing the use of reason, they would have needed a lot of guidance, especially if they did not possess

---

119. For example, Ghislaine Dehaene-Lambertz, Ana Fló, and Marcela Peña, "Infants' Early Competence for Language and Symbols," in *The Social Brain: A Developmental Perspective*, ed. Jean Decety (Cambridge, MA: MIT Press, 2020), 127–41.

the body of infused knowledge that Aquinas envisaged in Adam's case.[120] (He did not attribute omniscience to Adam, or the cultural advances made over the course of history; on a need-to-know basis Adam possessed the truths he had to teach his offspring, who would, in a natural way, have learned from him.[121]) However, the social group into which they were born would have known the affordances of their environment, and would have had ways to pass on advice about places of safety and danger, healthy foodstuffs, and so on. In addition, preternatural gifts may have contributed helpful instincts about the natural world; the Holy Spirit could have directed the first humans' natural curiosity as they began to explore their world.

There is no need to suppose the first humans had advanced scientific knowledge; *prudentia* ("practical wisdom" about living well), *ars* ("practical know-how") and *scientia* (ordered bodies of "abstract" knowledge) are not so interlinked that the possession of one entails the possession of the others.[122] The archaeological remains that indicate a great leap forward show that our race's cultural infancy was never crude. Had there been no fall, grace need not have short-circuited the progress of scientific discovery—or of technology, poetry, music, philosophy, and so on—but gently promoted it, making it, on balance, more successful than it has been, and less marred by rivalry and the mistakes that have led to environmental damage.

4.3. Ethical Training of Children

Besides imparting knowledge about the world, parents and other caregivers socialize infants and, ideally, give good ethical advice, teach them moral principles, and encourage practices that build up acquired virtues in the hope that their practice will become more personally owned. In our fallen condition, this constitutes a real, if limited, natural ability to remedy potential moral defects; grace can enhance this ability. Infants are hardwired to bond with their caregivers; in an unfallen world, the habitual presence of charity and infused moral virtues could have ensured infants bonded well with their caregivers and were receptive to good mores that were passed on.

---

120. *ST* I q. 99, a. 1; q. 101.
121. *ST* I q. 94, a. 3. Since Adam named the animals, Aquinas thought he knew the natures of all species (*ST* I q. 94, a. 3, sc, quoting Gen. 2:19f). This was not detailed biological knowledge, but the ability to recognize the basic ways in which, say, lions differ from leopards, and would not have seemed unrealistic to one who supposed his teacher Albert the Great knew perhaps a third of all existing species! On unfallen children's ease of learning, see *ST* I q. 101, a. 1.
122. On these virtues, see *ST* I-II q. 57, aa. 2–5.

In the case of human infants born to prehuman parents, I invoked above the gift of a preternatural moral wisdom to supplement the natural forms of socialization present in the prehuman community. The relative simplicity of the earliest human communities may have lessened the risk of distorted mores being imparted.

For human family life goes on within societies that can become large and complex, and whose ethos (like that of a family or local community) can to some extent perpetuate itself, for ill as well as for good. We must go on to explore how, in an unfallen world, this feature of our nature could have constituted a force for good rather than a problematic natural vulnerability.

4.4. Social Structures and Law

Aquinas held that government is natural, hence in an unfallen race people would have been governed, but only as free citizens, both for their own good and (inseparably) for the common good; no one would have been used as a slave.[123] Given natural biological and psychological variations, some people, building on innate or charismatic gifts, would have excelled in knowledge or justice to become especially suited to leading others.[124] We should add—what Aquinas had no occasion to add—that the instinct for leadership to emerge and social structures to form builds upon inherited hominin instincts; under grace, these would have been integrated in a morally healthy way. We may add, too, that parents who made better progress in justice or knowledge could have helped their children make better progress and become more apt to lead. Human dependence on wise and good leaders, and on worthy customs, goes with the good of cooperation, and with the vibrancy of societies in which people put varying talents into enriching tasks. The flip side is our vulnerability to bad leadership and corrupt customs. As Aquinas maintained, actual sin would have been possible in a history not marked by original sin, hence pride, envy, and greed for power could still have arisen; someone could have misused personal charisma to seize leadership then exploit others. To mitigate this risk, grace, building on the tendency of a society's ethos to perpetuate itself, could have tipped the balance in favor of the survival of a morally healthy ethos and of humane and just social structures. Good laws could have been put in place to guard against the corruption of social structures.

---

123. *ST* I q. 92, a. 1 ad 2; q. 96, a. 4.
124. *ST* I q. 96, a. 3. As suggested in section 2.3.3, among the first generation of humans, one may have stood out as leader in such a way as to be the "Adam" whose fault Christ redeemed.

For one task of leaders is to make laws.[125] The basic principles of the natural law are built into everyone; in an unfallen world, they would have been obvious to all.[126] Aquinas held that in humanity's actual history, knowledge of the natural law weakened as sin's hold grew stronger, while God's revelation remedied this gradual worsening.[127] If grace, present from conception, had reinforced natural instincts in all infants, awareness of the natural law would not have weakened. However, the wise would still have needed to formulate detailed natural law precepts. In particular, legislators would have had to determine the details of how increasingly complex societies should live, as humanity's expansion required the application of ethical principles to varying social, geographical and economic conditions.[128] They would have had to revise laws and policies as circumstances changed, and in light of experience. The prevalence of grace and an ethos of virtue could have led to these being wiser and more just than many laws and policies have in fact been.

Since actual sin remained possible, law would also have needed to inhibit wrong-doing, but the penal elements of legal systems would presumably have loomed less large than they do now, for besides sanctions, healthy customs would have done their part to exert pressure on people inclined to commit crimes. People who did sin could have been pressured by good laws and a morally healthy social ethos to raise their children in accord with mores better than their own.

5. Liability to Death, Injury and Sickness?

It is logically possible that the first humans were endowed with supernatural grace but were not physically invulnerable, for many human beings are now in such a state. But Scripture, tradition, and Catholic dogma all imply that humanity's fall involved the loss not only of grace, but also of (preternatural) gifts that overcame physical vulnerabilities. Aquinas helps us see such gifts as not implausible, because he held that unfallen human beings' invulnerabilities were not of a mythical, "Kryptonian" kind, since nature and natures were not altered by the fall. He also leads us to expect that vulnerabilities intrinsic to an evolved rational animal were overcome *suaviter*, not by a kind of magic,

---

125. A substantial part of Aquinas's discussion of law in *ST* I-II qq. 90–97, 100, and 104–5 would be relevant in an unfallen world. See also Richard Conrad, "Aquinas on the Unfolding of Law," *Law and Justice: The Christian Law Review* no. 183 (Trinity/Michaelmas 2019): 118–33.

126. *ST* I q. 101, a. 1 ad 3.

127. *ST* I-II q. 98, a. 6

128. For "legislative prudence" and its nobility, see *ST* II-II q. 50, a. 1.

or by something like the transhumanism envisaged by researchers today, but in a way that courteously refined all that is natural.

The sensitive skin humans need could not have been impervious to sharp instruments or animals' teeth.[129] Good sense and the education of children in the safe use of tools could have ensured a degree of protection from accidental injury. Aquinas envisaged that savage beasts did not inhabit Eden.[130] Since in fact humanity evolved where they were present, we may propose a preternatural ability to overawe animals akin to the natural power some people presently have to tame, bond with, or control certain animals.[131] Since sin remained possible, we cannot rule out from unfallen humanity the risk of murder; this risk could have been lessened by sin's relative infrequency and by more effective legal protections. Initially, the risk of poisoning could have been reduced—for the first human infants as well as for subsequent generations—by parental care and teaching, for our immediate hominin ancestors would have taught their offspring to avoid eating certain things. Since human infants exhibit a relative lack of instincts in comparison with many mammalian infants, the ongoing danger of curiosity and indiscriminate tasting might have been met by wise care and unfallen infants' enhanced receptivity to parental instruction. The taught ability to read the environment, supplemented by cautious investigation of the world, could have led human beings to avoid areas of particular danger, mitigating the vulnerability to natural disasters.

All of this amounts to a relative invulnerability to violence from the outside. Aquinas attributed to unfallen humanity a relative immunity from disease and death, too. Freedom from premature death would have been due in part to a preternatural power given the soul to enable it to preserve the body—not the mastery the soul will have over the risen body, but something closer to current anecdotes of people clinging to life long enough to say goodbye to a loved one.[132] Aquinas also supposed the tree of life of Genesis 2:9 and 3:22 had a limited power to stave off natural decline; we might replace it with the first humans' being attuned, by instinct and training, to which foods are especially healthy.[133]

Aquinas seems not to have ruled out vulnerability to disease-causing factors from the unfallen state, since he took pains to argue that Eden was

---

129. *ST* I q. 97, a. 2 ad 4.
130. *ST* I q. 102, a. 2 ad 2.
131. Cf. *ST* I q. 96, a. 1 ad 4.
132. *ST* I q. 97, a. 1; q. 102, a. 2.
133. *ST* I q. 97, a. 4. On the need of unfallen human beings to take food as a remedy against natural loss, see *ST* I q. 97, a. 3 and q. 102, a. 2.

free from "corrupt air."[134] We may propose that vulnerability to pathogens could have been mitigated by a more robust immune system—even by providential care over the chance evolution of bacteria, if we see the biblical Eden as a symbol of God's providential care.[135]

Aquinas ruled out birth defects from the unfallen state.[136] A preternatural strengthening of natural repair mechanisms might have reduced the risk of birth defects, but it is difficult to give a fully satisfying account of how birth defects could have been completely excluded without invoking a providential care over the elements of chance involved in reproduction. Aquinas also suggested that childbirth, which is dangerous owing to the large size of human babies' heads, would have been painless because mothers would have been better able to relax their birth canal.[137] Given the range of women's experiences of childbirth, and the factors that tend to increase and decrease labor pains, we might invoke a preternatural enhancement of factors that decrease pain and of the mechanisms that work against delayed as well as premature birth. However, it is difficult to envisage how childbirth could have been completely pain- and problem-free. Indeed, it is not easy to see how there could have been complete immunity from all the physiological problems that cause suffering or threaten health and life, some of which are due to our evolutionary inheritance.[138] These include:

- The danger of choking is due to how, after babyhood, the larynx develops to allow the range of sounds human language requires, risking malfunctioning of the epiglottis. If separate tubes for breathing and eating had developed a long way back in evolutionary history, the danger would have been averted.
- The frequent crowding of teeth is traceable to the evolutionary shortening of the human jaw, and we cannot suppose the first human beings had modern techniques of dental surgery.
- The branches of the abdominal aorta leading to the legs overlap with those of the inferior vena cava. This can lead to May-Thurner Syndrome—blood clots in the left leg. A slight difference in the development of the vascular system during evolution might have averted this danger.

---

134. *ST* I q. 102, a. 2. He did not, of course, know about microbes.
135. Cf. *ST* I q. 97, a. 2 ad 4 on providential care over unfallen humanity.
136. *ST* I q. 96, a. 3.
137. *ST* I q. 98, a. 2 ad 4. On the relatively large size of human infants' heads, see *ST* I q. 99, a. 1. Held (*Quirks of Human Anatomy*, 123–25) explains that the problem is more complex.
138. Held, *Quirks of Human Anatomy*, 105–28.

- The danger of ectopic pregnancy is due to the length of the oviduct, which conceivably could have been shorter if evolution had taken a different path.

The danger of choking might have been mitigated by an ingrained greater care with breathing and talking while eating. But it is not immediately obvious how unfallen human beings could have been totally immune to the remainder of these problems, unless we invoke a providential control over each human being's life, which often took the form of miracles. In this area especially further reflection is called for. A relative impassibility may be adequate to satisfy dogmatic data.

Certainly a relative immortality satisfies dogmatic data, for human beings were always meant to transition to a state of permanent glory and immortality.[139] In the case of fallen human beings, it is Christ's resurrection that secures a transition through death to eternal life.[140] Had the fall not occurred, the transition to glory would presumably have occurred at a suitable time in the life of each human being.[141] This transition would have been similar to the bodily assumption of the Blessed Virgin Mary into heaven, in which Catholics and Orthodox believe. There are two traditions concerning Mary's assumption; Pius XII did not decide between them.[142] The older tradition (as depicted in many Eastern icons and Western paintings) held that she "fell asleep," and her body was raised from the tomb on the third day, which provides a model for how unfallen human beings might have passed through something like death but without the wrench that is now experienced, as some scholars suggest.[143] The more recent opinion that Mary was assumed without going through any process analogous to death fits better with the biblical and traditional doctrine that (human) death is due to (original) sin. This need not exclude death by

---

139. *ST* I q. 97, a. 4.

140. *ST* III q. 56, a. 1.

141. Since human beings not subject to original sin could still have committed sin, and we have no *right* to the grace of repentance, Aquinas might have supposed that members of an unfallen race could still have chosen hell instead of glory, and been allowed to persist in that choice.

142. Apostolic Constitution *Munificentissimus Deus* (November 1, 1950) (Denz., 3900–3903).

143. Besides Yarnold (see note 2 of this chapter) see Alexandre Ganoczy: "the grace of the original state would" not "have prevented termination of earthly life; rather, this termination . . . would have occurred as an unbroken transitional return of the person into the hands of a merciful God." Alexandre Ganoczy, "Original State," in *Handbook of Catholic Theology*, ed. Wolfgang Beinert and Francis Schüssler Fiorenza (New York: Crossroad, 1995), 516–18.

murder in an hypothetical unfallen state; presumably, anyone murdered would have been raised soon after.

Conclusion

Reflections such as the above are necessary in order to bring into conversation with evolutionary science (a) the Christian hope for eternal communion with God and bodily glory, (b) the doctrine of the fall, and (c) the radical distinction between the rational soul and the souls of other animals. At first glance, Aquinas's account of the first man as *principium* of all human beings seems unpromising, since it contradicts any evolutionary scenario. If, however, we interpret "Adam" as the first recipient of a rational soul, or as leader of the first truly human generation, or as both, elements in Aquinas's thought prove helpful. God governs *suaviter*; his providence does not short-circuit the processes of evolution. While there is a radical metaphysical distinction between those hominins with, and those without, rational souls (which need not imply a huge difference in physical morphology), the human psyche incorporates—but in a subtly transformed way—the psychology of our ancestors. We need not attribute to the first truly human generation a mythical degree of knowledge or culture, for neither faith nor the experience of God depend on these.

Because of the complexity of the human psyche and of the body that supports it, tensions and vulnerabilities are intrinsic to a human nature that is basically coherent and good. Likewise we may see our physical, psychological and social evolutionary inheritance as something grace does not typically need to bypass or suppress. In our present condition, grace must of course overcome vulnerabilities and tensions due to this inheritance; if "the state of innocence" had continued, grace would have overcome them more fully. The presence of grace from conception, and a sense of God's presence even before birth, might have molded the developing psyche so as to promote spiritual strength and moral health. These would not have ensured no one ever sinned, but could have tipped the balance to make the human community and its developing social structures and laws relatively sinless when compared with our fallen world.

In the unique case of the first true humans, born of prehuman parents, their situation and role as the human race's ancestors called for special preternatural gifts. These need not have been spectacular or mythical; we can envisage them working *suaviter* to grant a precocious yet not magical infancy and childhood while the first true humans were cared for within their ancestral hominin society.

It is more difficult to envisage how unfallen human beings could have enjoyed freedom from suffering and death in the geographical area in which we evolved. Aquinas's account of the relative immortality and freedom from injury enjoyed in the state of innocence takes us some way toward a plausible picture, for he does not accord unfallen human beings a mythical degree of invulnerability and immortality. Their natural physical vulnerabilities would not have been totally overcome until they enjoyed something equivalent to the resurrection Christ has established for us. Further reflection is needed on how, and to what extent, preternaturally strengthened natural repair mechanisms, along with similar resources, might have worked in unfallen humanity.

In sum, Aquinas's nuanced accounts of human nature and of the state of innocence can fruitfully come into conversation with the growing bodies of research in many areas, such as fetal and infant psychology, and the psychology of virtue, as well as with evolutionary science.

CHAPTER EIGHT

The Transmission of Original Sin in Light of Evolution

ROBERT BARRY

The depiction of all humanity descending from Adam and Eve—a single human couple—is impossible to square with today's genetic evidence. The traditional reading of Genesis 2 as a historical monogenetic account of human origins requires all humanity to have descended from a single breeding couple and *only* from that one breeding couple. Present-day scientific models accounting for human biological origins range from positing our origins in a small population of hominins (of about ten to twenty thousand) residing relatively recently in Africa to accounts of modern humans emerging in multiple regions over many millennia.[1] Even genetic evidence that might indicate all present-day humans as sharing one common male ancestor (a "genetic Adam") or one common female ancestor (a "mitochondrial Eve") cannot confirm in a straightforward way the monogenetic reading of Genesis 2 as historical. That same genetic evidence indicates that we did not descend only from those individuals, and that those individuals were not a single contemporary breeding pair but rather individuals from generations separated by millennia.[2]

This chapter intends to clarify how a Catholic theologian might rightly conceive of the transmission of original sin in light of the conclusions about human origins generated by evolutionary theory as summarized above. The theological problem may be put as follows: How could we have emerged from many ancestors—whether from a single group or many groups—yet be subject to a sin common to our nature that has arisen from the act of only one indi-

---

1. A recent summary of the developing range of scientific positions on this question may be found in Chris Stringer, "The Development of Ideas about a Recent African Origin for Homo Sapiens," *Journal of Anthropological Sciences* 100 (2022): 5–18. For a discussion of the diverse positions as they pertain to theological questions considered in this chapter, I would recommend Daniel W. Houck, *Aquinas, Original Sin, and the Challenge of Evolution* (Cambridge: Cambridge University Press, 2020), 189–97.

2. A concise presentation of the conundrum of genetic Adam and mitochondrial Eve can be found in Scot McKnight and Dennis R. Venema, *Adam and the Genome: Reading Scripture after Genetic Science* (Grand Rapids, MI: Brazos Press, 2017), 45–66.

vidual (or couple)? At first glance, this seems to pose a sharp dichotomy: Catholic theologians must reject the Church or reject science. If the former, then they would reject as untenable Pope Pius XII's teaching in *Humani Generis* that the Catholic faith requires affirming monogenesis, the claim that all human beings today are descended from an original couple.[3] The latter requires that theologians reject the scientific evidence outright, or otherwise to interpret it in such a way that divine power or intervention brings humanity into existence from a single couple and *only* from that single couple, contrary to what is known through current biological theory.

I will not contest or modify the findings of the biological sciences in order to resolve this question. For the purposes of this chapter, I intend to propose an account of the transmission of original sin that is as general as possible and apply it equally to each of the possible scientific models of human origins. I will suggest that there is no contradiction between the doctrine of original sin as inherited from Adam and the evolutionary account of human origins. The perception of such an opposition between the two is grounded in a misunderstanding of what it means to speak of an "inheritance" of original sin. To clarify what it would mean to "inherit" original sin, I turn to Thomas Aquinas for a more coherent account of evil and sin in general and original sin in particular. Through those clarifications, I will show that this dichotomy turns out to be merely apparent.[4]

1. Evil as Privation

Thomas Aquinas builds upon the thought of Augustine in giving a consistent account of evil in its metaphysical dimensions. Following Augustine, Thomas

---

3. Pope Pius XII, Encyclical Letter *Humani Generis* (August 12, 1950), §37: "When, however, there is question of another conjectural opinion, namely polygenism, the children of the Church by no means enjoy such liberty. For the faithful cannot embrace that opinion which maintains that either after Adam there existed on this earth true men who did not take their origin through natural generation from him as from the first parent of all, or that Adam represents a certain number of first parents. Now it is in no way apparent how such an opinion can be reconciled with that which the sources of revealed truth and the documents of the Teaching Authority of the Church propose with regard to original sin, which proceeds from a sin actually committed by an individual Adam and which, through generation, is passed on to all and is in everyone as his own."

4. I take great pleasure in noting that since I began this project, an excellent and detailed account of this same topic has been published by Daniel W. Houck in his book *Aquinas, Original Sin, and the Challenge of Evolution*, referenced above. In this chapter I also draw upon and summarize a more extensive argument I made on these matters in my article "Original Sin and Pure Nature: What's the Difference, and What Difference Does It Make?" *Josephinum Journal of Theology* 25, no. 1–2 (2018): 1–28.

understands evil—and sin as moral evil—to be the privation of a due good rather than any substance in itself. Each theologian will account original sin to be, then, not a positive trait added to human nature but rather a more specific type of privation of a due good; namely, the privation of the good of original justice and thus the privation of all the good consequent to it. On this point, Augustine possesses and presents insights that Thomas later sharpens with the aid of Aristotle's philosophy.

As Augustine learned from the Neoplatonists, evil is not itself a thing but a privation in an otherwise good thing—an absence of some particular good. A privation is unlike a mere negation, for it is not simply the absence of a good but rather the absence of a good that is due and proper to a particular subject. Thus "flightless" is the absence of the power of flight—in a man, it is a mere negation to note that he lacks the ability to fly; but in a mature eagle, such an absence is a privation of a good that ought to be found in a creature of that nature. Augustine likens evil to darkness (as an absence of a light that ought to be there) and silence (as an absence of a sound that ought to be heard). This understanding of evil as privation avoids the dualistic tendency to identify certain kinds of things (material ones, usually) as evil and makes possible the affirmation that all existing things, inasmuch as they exist, are the creations of a good God.

Employing the further precision afforded by Aristotle's metaphysics, Thomas extends this definition in two particular ways. First, he employs a metaphysically richer account of the being that is subject to privation. It becomes difficult grammatically to speak of an existing subject at all if every privation is taken as a privation of the goodness of that subject's very being itself. If evil is a "nothingness," then how can you speak about evil doing anything or being anywhere?[5] Thomas's employment of Aristotle's metaphysical distinctions allows us to consider a subject's goodness to be found not only in that subject's existence simply, or in the perfect completion of an action, but also in that subject simply existing in potency to some further good action.

---

5. Augustine adverts to this difficulty in his *City of God*, bk. 12, ch. 7: "For of course when we know things not by perception but by its absence, we know them, in a sense, by not-knowing, so that they are not-known by being known—if that is a possible or intelligible statement!" And Jacques Maritain puts the difficulty as such when speaking of privation of action: "We should say, in trying to express this initiative of non-being, this initiative of absence on which I have placed so much emphasis,—we should say that the will nihilates, that it noughts; it has an initiative, yet we can only translate that initiative by words which express action. But, it is an initiative of non-action; we must therefore necessarily have recourse to a paradoxical language and say that created will then 'does nothingness,' 'makes non-being.'" See Maritain, *St. Thomas and the Problem of Evil*, The Aquinas Lecture, 1942 (Milwaukee: Marquette University Press, 1942), 33–34.

We can then speak of a true but imperfect goodness that consists of the perfection of a subject's ability. This perfection of that ability underlies the further perfection of that subject acting according to said ability. Thus, we can designate a person as a good archer, even if that person does not happen to be currently firing an arrow. Should that person be called upon to fire an arrow but fail to do so or fire but miss the target and instead hit a nearby tree, they do not diminish in being or cease to exist. The privation is found in the exercise of the powers of archery with nothing taken from the subject itself. Such privation does not involve a change in the substance of the subject but rather in the capacities or the actions of that subject. In fact, in what is called a sin of omission, the privation that constitutes that sin consists precisely in there being no change in that subject, a subject who becomes culpable for remaining merely in potency to a due act, or for failing to act.

A second refinement in Thomas's account of evil as privation can be seen in his consideration of the privation of contrariety. In such a case, the good that is due and proper to a subject is not merely absent but is actually replaced by another, contrary good. This complicates the restitution of the subject to the fullness of its proper goodness, for this involves more than attaining the requisite good that one lacks. In place of that requisite good stands a different good that one has attained instead.[6] This undue good that one attains is not merely different than one's proper good, but in one way or another actively inhibits the attainment of the proper good, or purports to take the place of that proper good altogether. This obstruction is not a privation of a power but the disordering of the exercise of rational powers, and as such is capable of piling up more and more obstacles to proper human action:

> Now a subject becomes less in potency to a form not indeed by the mere subtraction of some part of that subject, nor by the subtraction of some part of its potency, but by the fact that the potency is hindered by a contrary act from reaching to the act of the form. Thus, according as heat is the more increased in a subject, the less is that subject potentially cold.

---

6. We might be inclined to label such a good a merely "apparent" good, for goods are labeled "apparent" by Thomas on account of how they function. Contrary goods are frequently genuine goods that might be the kind capable of being ordered and directed to the proper, highest human good; their evil does not necessarily lie in their kind, but in whether they are or are not chosen as directed to one's proper good. So, acting to preserve one's family is a natural and genuine good, for that kind of good can be directed toward beatitude. Serving that good of one's family but *not* ordering it toward one's love of God makes that genuine good of one's family a contrary good; choosing it in that way is what makes it merely an "apparent" good, and the choice of that good stands as deficient in relation to the attainment of one's proper good.

Therefore, good is diminished by evil more by the addition of its contrary than by the subtraction of good.[7]

One cannot attain that requisite good until that contrary good has been removed. A contrary good is particularly difficult to displace, however, when it is a genuine though only partial good. A rational subject's capacity for attaining a due good still seems to be perfected somewhat in that choice of a merely apparent good. The recognition of the partiality of the good that one has attained may be obscured by the genuineness rightly perceived in that partial good. Such a condition of contrariety is apparent when we choose something that appears obviously good at the time, but which precludes us from attaining a further and more perfect good.

A trivial example may suffice to illustrate this dynamic. I have at home the ability to watch any of the half-dozen college football games airing during a single time slot on any given Saturday; I fulfill my capacity for being entertained by watching the Georgia Tech game instead of any of the other five games airing at the same time. I only later discover to my dismay that I missed watching my alma mater, Boston College, dominating Florida State in an unexpected victory. I would have found this game, which was airing at the same time, much more satisfying to watch. And of course, watching either game stands as contrary to some more important activity I ought to choose, such as grading student papers. Yet, at the time, I regarded the choice to watch the Georgia Tech game as a genuine good, and perhaps an eminently entertaining one at that. To attain any other due good would have required me to abandon the first course of action, not merely recognize and choose another good as greater, as more properly due. So, my action is not best conceived as a simple privation, but primarily as an attainment of some genuine good, which stands as contrary when considered in light of some further good.

This understanding of evil as privation in these various senses gives rise to a useful grammatical rule: when speaking of evil, we can designate either the privation itself or the subject of the privation. So, we can speak of flightlessness, or of the eagle who lacks the power of flight that it ought to have. We can speak of an arrow missing its target, or of an arrow hitting a nearby tree. We can speak of the negligence of the professor who has failed to grade his student's papers, or of a professor frittering away a Saturday afternoon watching an entertaining college football game. While evil and sin may remain mysterious at the macro level, at the particular level of this particular evil, its explanation can involve two components. First, we can speak of the privation or contrariety that belongs to the subject. Or we speak of the subject of that

---

7. *Summa contra gentiles* bk. 3, ch. 12.

privation, in itself or as a subject attaining some due but contrary good. This second component can even be understood without ever adverting to or even noticing that it lacks some further due good. This second way of speaking of evil will be useful for our consideration of the transmission of a human nature subject to original sin.

2. Original Sin as Privation

Now when we speak of the particular evil of original sin, it is not an evil in an equivocal or analogical sense but rather in a true sense as defined above. Original sin is a privation that produces a contrariety in the human capacity to attain the genuine and full human good. In accordance with the practice proposed above, when speaking of original sin, we can speak of the privation that is original sin, or we can speak of the subject of that privation. The subject of that privation is the human nature of the person who lacks the grace by which she is united with God and, in turn, the deficiencies that result from that lack of grace. It will be this kind of subject that I will employ in an explanation of the transmission of original sin that is congruent with the evidence evolution provides. The transmission of original sin is not best understood as passing on a privation as though it were some genetic trait but rather as the passing on of a human nature that will necessarily be a subject of a privation. A human existing by that nature indeed attains some good, but that attained good obstructs the attainment of the further genuine due good to which it is contrary.

But first, a brief clarification of this account of original sin, again drawing on Thomas Aquinas's explanation. Here "sin" refers to the privation of a particular good and "original" refers to a privation that arises from one's origin (*peccatum originale originatum*). This is in contrast to privations of good in one's particular actions, which is counted as actual sin. This sin from origin is distinct from the first or primal sin (*peccatum originale originans*), that actual sin of Adam and Eve from which the state of original sin follows as a punishment. The subject of original sin is human nature itself, and the good of which human nature is deprived is original justice and all that follows from it. The latter refers to a state of man where sanctifying grace makes his soul subject to God, and the body subject to the soul.[8] This condition of original justice is taken to characterize the life of the first couple prior to the primal sin; the just punishment for that primal sin is the deprivation of original justice, thereby leaving humanity to its own nature, which necessarily falls under the domination of original sin in the absence of sanctifying grace.

---

8. *ST* I q. 95, a. 1, corp.

It is precisely at this point that most accounts of original sin introduce what is taken to be the fly in the ointment: How is this privation of the good of human nature transmitted to all of humanity, especially if all humans are not the progeny of only that first couple who committed the sin that deformed humanity's very nature? Let us first turn to the subject of that privation—human nature itself, as Thomas Aquinas understands it—and then to the good of original justice of which original sin is the deprivation.

Thomas holds humans to be composites: of body and soul; of a number of rational and sensitive powers that are appetitive, apprehending, and vital; and of elements of contrary qualities. The nature of such composites are marked by the various abilities to act in manifold and contrary ways: we can feel hot and cold, we can walk forward or backward, and we can subordinate our passions to our reason or enslave our reason in the service of the passions. In considering these different components of our nature, Thomas asks whether this or that fact—such as death, immortality, concupiscence, and virtue—are "natural" to humanity. Readers familiar with Thomas's approach will not be surprised to find that his answer to each of these is "No" and "Yes"—just not in the same sense at the same time. In this nature of us as composite creatures, Thomas can point to a particular element that gives rise to each of these things and another part of us that gives rise to (or makes appropriate) its contrary.[9]

Thus death is "natural" in that it follows from the corruptibility that follows from our being composed from contrary elements. "Eternal life," however, follows from the suitability of an immortal soul being restored to its bodily existence.[10] Concupiscence follows upon the powers by which humans find particular things to be desirable or detestable, while virtue follows upon the right balancing and ordering of those powers to the genuinely human good as perceived through reason.[11] Though these contrary possibilities and operations follow from the elements of which humans are constituted according to their nature, the right ordering of those elements and the direction of them to the proper ultimate end of human nature—namely, beatitude—does not follow from that nature itself. To put in terms that readers of Thomas will recognize, the state of integrity necessary for the perfection of a creature of this nature is not itself a proper accident of that nature.[12]

---

9. Thomas's most full and direct treatment of this subject may be found in his *Disputed Questions on the Soul*, q. 8.
10. *ST* I-II q. 85, a. 6.
11. *ST* I-II, q. 30, a. 3. *Disputed Question on Virtue in General*, a. 8, corp.
12. *ST* I q. 95, a. 1.

Theologians like Thomas will therefore propose a state of original justice, thereby describing that integrity of human nature in itself, in its causes, and in its concomitant adjuncts. First, in itself, the state of original justice is the right ordering of the diverse powers of the human soul, such that the soul is subject to God, the lower powers of the soul are subject to the higher powers, and the body is subject to the soul.[13] The cause of this state is the sanctifying grace that the first couple had from the beginning of their creation. Concomitant with this supernatural grace are the preternatural gifts, which are ordered to humanity's natural good but are supernaturally caused. They constitute the divine help that humanity needs to remedy the faults of mortality, ignorance, and concupiscence.

It is often forgotten now, but the relationship between sanctifying grace and original justice served as a topic of vigorous debate in the first half of the twentieth century. The consensus arising from that debate is that sanctifying grace produced the state of original justice, and the loss of that grace constituted the privation of original justice in the first couple.[14] With this loss comes the loss of the preternatural gifts, resulting in the wounds of original sin: weakness, ignorance, malice, concupiscence, and death.[15] Thus the loss of that grace results in the privation of man's inclination toward and capacity for attaining the supernatural end of beatitude, as well as the loss of the human ability even to attain the good proportionate to the highest elements of human nature.

3. The Transmission of Nature as the Transmission of Original Sin

In such a state of original sin, the moral scope of human action is limited by a profound moral nearsightedness. Humanity does not lose its inclination to the good; but the goods that it does pursue are the most immediate, particular, and obvious goods that benefit the individual or the group. Further, ulti-

---

13. *ST* I q. 95, a. 1.

14. See Houck, *Aquinas, Original Sin*, 57–59 for a recap of the argument; for a fuller contemporary treatment of the debate, see William A. Van Roo, *Grace and Original Justice According to St. Thomas*, Analecta Gregoriana, Series Facultatis Theologicae, sec. a, v. 75, n. 13 (Romae: Apud Aedes Universitatis Gregorianae, 1955). Houck will in fact propose in his book an alternative to Thomas's claim that sanctifying grace is the cause of original justice; an engagement of that issue is beyond the scope of this chapter. For the purposes of this chapter, I will take original justice as the concomitant right ordering of the powers of the soul that follows from and accompanies the sanctifying grace that makes beatitude possible.

15. *ST* I-II q. 85, a. 3. Death is more than a wound, but nonetheless is a natural consequence following from the principles of human nature in the absence of external helps. See *ST* I q. 97, aa. 1 and 4.

mate or eternal goods are only seen obscurely, if they are seen at all; and when they are seen, they are very rarely chosen in preference to the goods that benefit oneself or the most immediate group with whom one identifies. In this way, those goods that benefit the individual or group function as contraries to those higher goods—they serve as the rationale behind the moral actions that are directed toward inner-worldly benefits and advantages. This ordering of human action to those inner-worldly goods displaces an ordering toward the eternal good that is the proper aim of all spiritual creatures like humans, for it appears not just as a good but as the highest rational good.[16]

This description of human nature apart from original justice turns out to be congruent with accounts of the development of human nature through the processes of evolution. Daryl Domning has proposed to explain in depth how the kind of short-sighted moral perspective I am describing as the condition of original sin is the natural product of adaptive advantages of selfishness: "The primate behaviors that are homologous with our human sins are no more than particular (albeit dramatic) instances of the 'selfishness' that, in its broadest, evolutionary sense, is the common heritage of *all* life."[17] From this observation, Domning draws the conclusion that original sin, like selfishness, does not therefore originate with a sin of some first couple but instead predates the emergence of humanity by being present in their immediate evolutionary predecessors.

On the other hand, competing accounts of the emergence of human nature through evolutionary dynamics posit cooperation and a degree of altruism as adaptive traits that would be present in those evolutionary predecessors.[18] The continuation of those traits of cooperation and altruism in an emerging humanity may seem to contradict the claim that humans bear a mark of universal sinfulness. And yet:

> This explanation widens the circle of concern, but even it does not get us to full-blown neighbor love in Jesus's sense. If one sacrifices for a limited group, even one including persons unrelated to you, this is tribalism, not altruism.[19]

16. *ST* I-II q. 109, a. 2.
17. Daryl P. Domning and Monika Hellwig, *Original Selfishness: Original Sin and Evil in the Light of Evolution* (Hampshire: Ashgate, 2006), 107.
18. This account is presented and developed through the chapters in M. A. Nowak and Sarah Coakley, eds, *Evolution, Games, and God: The Principle of Cooperation* (Cambridge, MA: Harvard University Press, 2013).
19. Timothy P. Jackson, "The Christian Love Ethic and Evolutionary 'Cooperation': The Lessons and Limits of Eudaimonism and Game Theory," in Nowak and Coakley, *Evolution, Games, and God*, 317.

Thus the type of action that sanctifying grace makes possible—via original justice—is not mere altruism but rather a deeper kind of agapic love, which involves the willingness to offer up one's own life even for the sake of one's enemy. The cooperation and altruism explainable by evolution, on the other hand, falls short of agape and instead into the realm of tribalism, as explained by Domning in the preceding quotation.

Tribalism is an instance of the selfishness of the group rather than the individual; in both cases, the reference point for the good sought is some created good that falls short of divine beatitude as the proper end of the individual and the whole of humanity. And in fact, humans (both individually and collectively) pursue such proximate goods not as ordered toward but as contraries in place of the higher and eternal goods that would rightly be the final end of human action in a world where original justice still reigned. Whichever trait (or set of traits) constitutes the evolutionary inheritance of the first emerging humans—whether it be individual or group selfishness—this chapter argues that this is precisely the dynamic that constitutes original sin. Original sin is hereby understood to be, then, the inheritance and continuation of such "natural" tendencies in an emergent humanity in the absence of the grace of original justice that would serve to temper such tendencies.[20]

To transmit original sin, then, is nothing more than the transmission of such a nature that lacks the grace of original justice. Though original sin directly designates the privation of a due good—namely, original justice—it substantively designates human nature under a certain condition, which is characterized by traits traditionally counted as the "wounds of sin": weakness, ignorance, malice, pain, and death. Such wounds are transmitted because, without the grace of original justice, the human nature that is transmitted will inevitably give rise to such wounds. The hominin transmission of natures with such traits happened prior to and up to the evolution of *Homo sapiens*; that it did and does continue through today is perhaps the one element of the doctrine of original sin clearly in congruence with any and every model of human origins generated by a scientific theory of evolution in a way that needs no further explanation.

This account of the kind of human behavior that proceeds from those powers and tendencies accords with a much-neglected point in Thomas—his ascription of the "Law of the Fomes" as an operative principle of man's actions in the state of original sin.[21] This law designates the manner in which humans

---

20. This consequence of evolution generating such traits in man has also been recognized by Jerry D. Korsmeyer, *Evolution and Eden: Balancing Original Sin and Contemporary Science* (Mahwah, NJ: Paulist Press, 1998), 120–23.

21. Mark Johnson, "St Thomas and the 'Law of Sin,'" *Recherches de théologie et philosophie médiévales* 67, no. 1 (2000): 80–95.

act according to the principles they share with other animals when those principles are not directed by reason toward the highest good of friendship with God, as they ought to be in humans:

> Accordingly under the Divine Lawgiver various creatures have various natural inclinations, so that what is, as it were, a law for one, is against the law for another: thus I might say that fierceness is, in a way, the law of a dog, but against the law of a sheep or another meek animal. And so the law of man, which, by the Divine ordinance, is allotted to him, according to his proper natural condition, is that he should act in accordance with reason: and this law was so effective in the primitive state, that nothing either beside or against reason could take man unawares. But when man turned his back on God, he fell under the influence of his sensual impulses: in fact this happens to each one individually, the more he deviates from the path of reason, so that, after a fashion, he is likened to the beasts that are led by the impulse of sensuality, according to Ps. 48:21: *Man, when he was in honor, did not understand: he hath been compared to senseless beasts, and made like to them.*[22]

This selfishness is characteristic of human actions according to the nature they receive from their ancestors. Thomas recognizes that this selfishness not only serves the preservation of individuals but is the means by which entire species are preserved: "If the inclination of sensuality be considered as it is in other animals, thus it is ordained to the common good, namely, to the preservation of nature in the species or in the individual."[23] Thus the concupiscible power is present in both nonrational and rational animals, by which animals seek the particular good of their individual existence or the species as a whole through an individual selfishness or an altruism limited to members of one's immediate group. To Thomas's claim, Domning adds the details of how those concupiscible powers are present and operative in the very same evolutionary process by which distinct biological species emerge, *Homo sapiens* included. Both Thomas and Domning regard the persistence of the dominance of those powers to be characteristic of humanity functioning according to the natural principles from which that humanity originates and proceeds.[24] For humans to exist, live, and operate by doing what is ordered to the survival of the individual or the group (just like all other animals but lacking the right order of reason) constitutes the very state of original sin. For these other animals, such behavior is merely natural; for humans, however, to act according to those

---

22. *ST* I-II q. 91, a. 6, corp.
23. *ST* I-II q. 91, a. 6, ad 3.
24. Domning and Hellwig, *Original Selfishness*, 120.

powers that are "merely" natural is to act precisely from within that state of original sin.

Thomas presents an illuminating image of how we ought to consider the deficiency of our actions when they follow only from those same principles of nature that we share with other animals:

> Such help [of original justice] was not conferred on other animals, nor did they previously lose anything through moral fault, from which such ills would result, as in the case of human beings. And so the reasoning is not the same. Just so, in the case of those who stumble along because of the blindness with which they have been born, their stumbling walk has the character of natural defect, not of a punishment relating to human justice. But in the case of those who have been blinded because of their crimes, their stumbling walk has the character of punishment.[25]

In both states—the man born blind and the man blinded as punishment—the same condition is to be found: the identical set of principles for operation (namely, the lack of sight), and an identical kind of operation according to those principles (namely, stumbling). The difference lies only in the character of the negation: what in the case of animals is merely an absent good—namely, the absence of powers by which nonrational animals might order their actions to eternal life—is in the case of humans a privation. The capacity necessary for humans to order their actions toward the enjoyment of eternal life was once present and due as a matter of divine gift; on account of the sin of the first parent that sanctifying grace has now been removed as punishment. In both cases, the subject is the same: creatures living and procreating through the powers they have from their natures alone. But what is simply absent in the case of animals is in the case of humanity a deprivation, which is the result of divine punishment.

Theologians, philosophers, and anthropologists will continue to argue about what human nature is. Whatever it might be, human nature can be considered something common to a population group that differs substantially in capacities and activities from other hominins. Those capacities and activities distinctive of human nature are grounded in the distinct genetic information shared by that population group. According to genetic evidence, modern humans perhaps evolved from a relatively small group of hominins in which the biological substrate necessary for a distinctly rational capacity emerged. While no single individual might have constituted modern human nature in a sharp break from all immediate ancestors, over a span of time the distinct biological substrate necessary for rational thought emerged and propagated through the entire population group, distinguishing it from other groups in that capacity.

---

25. *De malo* q. 5, a. 4, ad 2.

For our purposes, that is sufficient to count as the emergence of human nature common to all in that population group and all who descend from that group—even if this does not involve a strict biological monogenesis of all descending only through a single individual or couple at some point in time.

The concern of this chapter, however, is not the transmission of that nature but the transmission of original sin. I have argued above that original sin is best considered like all sin as a privation, here though of something neither inherent to nor produced by that nature (i.e., original justice). Original justice and its corresponding preternatural gifts are accidental qualities of the soul gratuitously produced in man by God. They are neither additional genetic traits inherent in human nature nor proper accidents emerging from the very traits of human nature itself. In principle, then we can distinguish the question of the origin and transmission of the nature from the origin and transmission of the privation found in that nature of something that is neither inherent in nor generated by that nature.[26] We can account for the origin of that nature with its distinctive aptitudes and tendencies through evolutionary biology. It is a different matter to account for how human nature, with those characteristic aptitudes and tendencies, is to be counted as fallen.

This brings us to the proper concern of *Humani Generis*: moral monogenesis. This concerns not the common origin of the nature shared by all humans but rather the common *peccatum* of original sin as suffered by all. Under this consideration, the condition of moral nearsightedness is not just a trait common and concomitant to a hominin nature. Rather, the condition of original sin is counted as a punishment that deprives all rational hominins of the grace necessary for beatitude, as this follows upon our descent from a single individual who is the root of this deprivation.[27]

Thus, the human nature that emerges in some original population group in a given environment arises like all other distinct animal species do: out of

---

26. Johnson ("St. Thomas and the 'Law of Sin,'" 88) designates original justice as a "proper accident" of humanity after God gifted it to Adam; Thomas does not designate it as such, but just calls it an accident of the nature, not generated by those natural principles themselves (which is what I would take to be a proper accident), but rightly due to that nature as the fulfillment of the promise of a gratuitous gift by which "man is made right." Original justice would not follow "naturally" in the sense of from the principles of that nature, the usual way Thomas understands proper accidents. See Thomas's *Commentary on Aristotle's Metaphysics*, bk. 4, lect. 2 (#559).

27. The same distinction between the origin of humanity and the origin of moral responsibility has been proposed using the terms "theological species" or "philosophical species" to distinguish the origin of morally culpable fault from the origin of humanity as a biological species. See Kenneth Kemp, "Science, Theology, and Monogenesis," *American Catholic Philosophical Quarterly* 85, no. 2 (2011): 230–32.

genetic variation that introduces traits and the suitability of those traits for operation in that environment. Since the traits of hominins who enjoy an evolutionary advantage include individual and group selfishness and the other qualities of the condition of original sin, there is nothing mysterious about the transmission of original sin—it is merely the transmission of human nature itself. To that bare fact of the transmission of human nature itself, the theologian adds the consideration that would not be obvious to a scientific or philosophical investigation: the state of that transmitted nature is to be considered as one suffering a privation. The grace of original justice that would have been duly given to all who were born of that human nature had Adam not sinned is now absent. Thomas articulates this concisely as such:

> [O]riginal justice, as stated above [ST I, Q,100, A1] was a gift of grace, conferred by God on all human nature in our first parent. This gift the first man lost by his first sin. Wherefore as that original justice together with the nature was to have been transmitted to his posterity, so also was its disorder.[28]

The explanation of the transmission of that nature is sufficient explanation of the transmission of the effects that are consequent (or concomitant) to a being existing through that nature—again, without the aid of the sanctifying grace productive of original justice.

Further, the "wounds" of a human nature deprived of grace can be understood as transmitted with original sin for they are, in a sense, self-inflicted. Thomas counts these wounds as emerging from the composite character of each human being when those different powers are not rightly ordered through grace.[29] Ignorance, weakness, malice, concupiscence, the stain (*macula*) of sin, and death all follow from the principles of a human nature unaided by divine grace. The suffering of such wounds was staunched in the first man by God's granting of the preternatural gifts that accompany original justice. But deprived of grace, human nature inevitably suffers those wounds.

For Thomas—and all theologians who follow him in ascribing the ills of our present state to a deprivation of grace alone rather than to a subtraction of the principles of human nature—the transmission of original sin is sufficiently explained solely by the transmission of human nature. On this point, there is great congruence between the claims of evolutionary biology and a Christian theological anthropology. That is, once you explain the transmission of human nature through ordinary human generation, you have thereby explained the transmission of humanity in the state of original sin.

28. *ST* I-II q. 81, a. 2, corp.
29. *ST* I-II q. 85, a. 3, corp.

4. Complication One: The Question of the Infusion of the Immaterial Soul

The argument I have presented thus far might seem to be complicated by the Catholic teaching that the rational soul of the human being is something infused directly by God, rather than something emerging through the power of the human nature itself operating in the biological substrate. This idea of the infusion of the rational soul was formulated in medieval thought and remains fundamental to Catholic teaching about human origins.[30] If one holds the Catholic teaching of the infusion of the rational soul, humanity would not have evolved into existence simply when the biological substrate of human nature achieved the power to generate the rational soul from itself. According to this teaching, material stuff generating a spiritual soul is impossible. Rather, evolution is understood as that biological substrate developing to the point where it is capable of fittingly receiving the infusion of a rational soul directly by God. And indeed, I have cast the explanation of the condition of original sin in just such terms: one who receives a rational soul from God, but who does not immediately receive the gift of original justice from God upon that infusion of the rational soul, is someone subject to the state of original sin.

If one is to hold the traditional account of a rational soul requiring divine infusion, then evolution provides an explanation of the emergence of the biological substrate fitting for the operation of the rational soul. That rational soul would only be infused by God in those hominins who descend from the individual, or individuals, in whom those traits emerge. Thus, God would have infused the rational soul, along with the grace of original justice, in the first human (i.e., Adam). Due to the primordial turning away of that first man, the nature that had been elevated by original justice devolves to a merely natural state, bringing the consequent deprivations and failings counted as punishments of the first couple in Genesis and lamented in the Psalms and Wisdom writings. The "wound" to the nature is simply the condition of that humanity left to itself—a condition that would pertain to the descendants of the first human, who was biologically complex enough to be fittingly animated by a rational soul. This condition would already pertain, however, to any other hominins in whom such complexity develops and in whom God has consequently infused the rational soul. All humans who do not enjoy the benefit of the original justice offered through Adam will suffer that same condition, even if they were not descended from Adam. Whether those consequences that follow from the absence of original justice are to be counted as a "stain" on that nature will be addressed in the following section.

---

30. *Catechism of the Catholic Church*, 366.

While I am not intending to challenge the ordinarily accepted Catholic teaching of the necessity of the direct infusion of the rational soul, the argument I present in this chapter for understanding the transmission of original sin is indifferent to whatever theory of the acquisition of the rational soul one might hold. One may argue that rational souls are not infused but rather are generated from the sufficiently complex biological substrate itself, emerging in certain hominins, at once or at different times, in one place or many places. Consider the most extreme case of polygenesis, where hominins of discrete lineages exist in widely separated areas, and each separately evolve a biological complexity capable of generating from itself a rational soul. When such souls emerge, they will bear the same mark of that selfishness or group-centeredness that characterizes the hominin traits of successful development and adaptation. The account of original sin as humans left to their own nature, deprived of the grace of original justice, as an element of a theological understanding of the transmission of original sin, turns out to be the same. In this case, the human nature passed on through ordinary generation would carry with it the condition of original sin, wherever and however that nature and the rational soul characteristic of it emerges.

This account does not solve all questions connected to the claims about the infusion of the rational soul. There remains the further question of whether God could or should create a rational soul—or permit such a soul to emerge—without concomitantly infusing the gift of original justice. A related question would be whether the condition of such a creature lacking the benefits of such grace should be counted as a punishment or rather as simply the byproduct of an unfortunate finite condition. We will address both questions in the next section. But the origin of a gift of grace attached to human nature, and the justice of the giving or withholding of such grace, are distinctly theological questions. The suggestion here is that the condition of humanity in the state of original sin—understood as the state of a rational creature deprived of original justice—is the same as the condition of humanity generated by the processes of evolution. Thomas's account of original sin and evolutionary accounts of human nature agree on this point. This agreement between the theological and scientific claims holds true no matter which avenue leads to humans possessing a rational soul.

5. Complication Two: The Transmission of the Stain (*Macula*) of Sin

From his theological tradition, Thomas receives and continues to use the language of there being a stain (*macula*) of original sin that seems also to be inherited by all humanity from the first parents. He doesn't seem to speak of this stain in terms of a privation but rather as an accidental quality of the soul, which attaches to an individual and transmits to their offspring. Even if original sin is counted as a privation, it seems that the *macula* of sin would originate in Adam and be inherited only by his genetic descendants. Clarity on this question requires us to first unravel something of Thomas's account of the peculiar "mechanics" of the transmission of humanity—sullied or unsullied—from one generation to the next.[31]

Thomas draws on the Aristotelian account of children being the combined product of principles provided by each parent: the mother providing the "matter" and the father providing the "active principle" of generation. This active principle functions instrumentally to transmute the matter from the mother into a separate organism with its own principle of generation and movement. That active principle from the father is the "sensitive soul" of that child begotten of those parents.[32] The rational soul—the proper unitive principle of an individual human as a single rational substance—is not further generated by that organism existing and operating through that sensitive soul. Rather, in accord with Thomas's account of the unity and immateriality of the human soul, the human fetus becomes a full human person by God directly infusing the rational soul into the fetus, thereby replacing that sensitive soul as the principle of unity and operation.[33]

This account of human generation complicates the issue of the transmission of original sin as human nature, for it would seem that human nature is generated afresh in each individual with each infusion of the rational soul by God, as the substantial form for that individual substance of a rational nature. As such, it would seem that anything attached to that individual as a property

---

31. This question is distinct from how we might understand this same matter today in light of modern biological and genetic accounts of human reproduction. The account I have given in this chapter of the transmission of original sin as a privation is not tied, however, to a specific process of generation, for what is at stake is *whether* a human nature prone to the predominance of the concupiscible power is transmitted, not specifically *how*. Yet this focus on the particulars of Thomas's account of procreation remains instructive, for the issue is not the particular mechanics of the transmission of human nature itself, but how we can understand unmediated grace to "belong" to a human nature as such. We will follow Thomas and take as an uncontroversial given that individuals might be redeemed and transformed by a mediated grace.

32. See *ST* I q. 98, a. 2 corp. for the general account as well as *ST* I q. 118, a. 2, ad 4 and q. 119, a. 2, ad 2 for the nitty-gritty details of Thomas's account of the succession of substantial forms in the child's development, which differs from the dominant account of his day that posited the addition of substantial forms. For a recent, concise overview of this matter, see Melissa Rovig Vanden Bout, "Thomas Aquinas and the Generation of the Embryo: Being Human before the Rational Soul" (PhD diss., Boston College, 2013).

33. *ST* I q. 118, a. 2, corp.

or "accident" is not transmitted from the parents, but rather given by God at that time of the infusion of the rational soul. Original justice is not a proper accident generated by the principles of that subject.[34] As an effect of grace, one might expect original justice to also be given afresh by God along with the creation of the rational soul for each individual human being. This would seem to apply then to the privation of original justice as well: upon the infusion of the rational soul, God would refrain from infusing that gift of sanctifying grace productive of original justice. The problem then can be stated: Why would God not give to the descendants of Adam the grace of original justice at the time he infused human nature in those descendants with the infusion of the rational soul?

This is where Thomas's characterization of original sin as a "sin of a nature" comes into play. Unlike personal sins or anything else pertaining to the individual, Thomas repeatedly states that original sin is said to pertain to human nature itself. But human nature is not first found in a subject of human generation only with the infusion of the rational soul: Thomas insists that the active principle of the sperm is the principle of the human nature of the creature composed out of that principle and the matter from the mother's womb, and that it is this active principle of the sperm that lacks original justice. As detailed above, the process of human generation initiated and propelled by the vital power of the father that is instrumentally at work in the sperm is a principle of human generation, or more precisely the principle of generation of an individual subject of human nature. In that respect, the sperm from the father and the matter from the mother combine to produce a subject who is specifically human in potency, and thus a being of human nature, one who is to be born (*natus*) a human, even prior to the infusion of the rational soul. One's individual nature is from one's father, even though one's rational soul is directly produced by God.[35]

Thomas understood that if Adam had not fallen, original justice would have been given to Adam's descendants through a corresponding process. The gift of original justice produced by sanctifying grace was given both to Adam's person and to his nature.[36] The effects of this gift on that nature were not limited to the elevation of the soul:

34. See my comment on Mark Johnson's characterization of it as such in note 26 above.

35. The various senses of *natura*, including this sense, are laid out most clearly by Joseph Bobik in his discussion of Thomas's *De principiis naturae* in Bobik's *Aquinas on Matter and Form and the Elements: A Translation and Interpretation of the De Principiis Naturae and the De Mixtione Elementorum of St. Thomas Aquinas* (Notre Dame, IN: University of Notre Dame Press, 1998), 11–14.

36. *ST* I q. 100, a. 1, corp.

It also diffused to the lower parts of the soul, which the power of the aforementioned gift kept completely subject to reason, and even diffused to the body, in which nothing contrary to the gift's presence in the soul could happen as long as the gift remained. And so this gift would have been transmitted to Adam's posterity . . . because it reaches even to the body, which is transmitted by generation.[37]

If Adam had not sinned, the nature he communicated to his descendants through the ordinary processes of reproduction would have—through the natural principles of generation that operated bodily—also conveyed a suitability to the full reception of sanctifying grace. There would be no darkness or tendency in those natural principles conveyed through that received nature to thwart the perfection of the higher parts of the soul of that offspring through a fresh gift of sanctifying grace. This sanctifying grace was a gift to that human nature. It was given to Adam for him to be the concrete starting point for a humanity descended from him and was meant to be transmitted through the ordinary means of reproduction:

> If children were born in original righteousness, they would also have been born in grace; thus we have said above that the first man was created in grace [ST I, Q. 95, A. 1]. This grace, however, would not have been natural, for it would not have been transfused by virtue of the semen; but would have been conferred on man immediately on his receiving a rational soul. In the same way the rational soul, which is not transmitted by the parent, is infused by God as soon as the human body is apt to receive it.[38]

To summarize: generation through a flesh not merely uninfected by original sin but also retaining the effects of the grace of original justice that operated in Adam would produce a man suited to an immediate reception of sanctifying grace upon the infusion of the rational soul. The loss of that grace in Adam—as the principle of that process of transmission—results in a flesh darkened by the effects of sin, unsuited to the immediate reception of that sanctifying grace. This more detailed consideration of the transmission of original sin raises a number of questions worth taking up in turn.

First, we must consider whether it is proper to speak of a nature being the subject of an accident like sanctifying grace. It would seem that such an accident can only be properly predicated of individual substances. If so, what does it mean to attribute some accident, or a privation of such an accident, to

---

37. *De malo* q. 4, a. 8, corp.
38. *ST* I q. 100, a. 1, ad 2

a nature? This is not a problem when speaking of proper accidents, which follow from the principles of a nature itself. In that case, wherever there is a subject that exists through that nature, a proper accident will emerge in that subject as an effect following its principles.[39] A subject existing by that nature will come to possess that accident with no further principles added. But what of accidents that follow from principles extrinsic to the nature, such as supernatural gifts like the sanctifying grace productive of original justice? In that case, it seems that Thomas regards the "dueness" or fittingness of receiving that gift as a quality present in the first instance with Adam. This dueness is a characteristic attached to that concrete nature possessed by Adam and transmitted by the ordinary processes of bodily generation from Adam onward.[40] So if Adam had persevered in that state of sanctifying grace when he transmitted that human nature to his offspring (in the ordinary course of generation through sexual intercourse), then all recipients of that nature would have rightly received and possessed that same sanctifying grace. The dueness or fittingness of the immediate reception of that sanctifying grace upon the infusion of the rational soul would have been present in any subject existing through that human nature derived, by way of origin, from Adam.

The attribution of dueness raises the further question of the extent to which this quality is then attributed to human nature. If grace were something due to human nature absolutely speaking, then we would have a problem finding any human nature at work in the cosmos beyond that derived from Adam, which would give rise to individuals subject to the privation of original sin. This is frequently presented as the root of the problem posed by a polygenetic model of human origins, and as the reason *Humani Generis* rejects that model of human origins. In other words, how would humans born from a genetic line other than Adam's be subject to an original sin only traceable to that one man's actions? The reasoning behind this argument is formulated by Kenneth Kemp as follows:

> [T]he teaching of the Church was clearly articulated at the Council of Trent (1545–1563)—the guilt of this sin is inherited by us all. The

---

39. See note 26 above, and Thomas's *Commentary on Aristotle's Metaphysics*, bk. 4, lect. 2 (#559).

40. *ST* I q. 100, a. 1, corp.: "Man naturally begets a specific likeness to himself. Hence whatever accidental qualities result from the nature of the species, must be alike in parent and child, unless nature fails in its operation, which would not have occurred in the state of innocence. But individual accidents do not necessarily exist alike in parent and child. Now original righteousness, in which the first man was created, was an accident pertaining to the nature of the species, not as caused by the principles of the species, but as a gift conferred by God on the entire human nature."

Council went on to say: the sin of Adam is in its origin one, and being transfused into all by propagation, not by imitation, is in all men and proper to each. This gives us what we need to see the force of Pius's argument. If

    (P4) "One by origin" means "committed as one act;" and
    (P5) "By propagation" means "through biological descent"; and
    (P6) Man's origins were polygenetic (or polyphyletic);

it would follow that

    (P7) Adam's contemporaries (and perhaps some of their descendants) would have been men free from original sin.

Since the denial of P7 is clearly intended by the Council of Trent, and P4 and P5 always seemed to be reasonable interpretations of what the Tridentine Fathers intended, Pope Pius rejected P6 as incompatible with the doctrine of original sin.

Theological Conclusion. This Catholic account of original sin, then, if not the text of Genesis 2–4, has seemed to many to require a monogenetic account of the origins of the human race.[41]

Premise 7 (P7) in Kemp's argument seems to imply that if Adam's contemporaries are true humans born apart from Adam's lineage and thus not subject to the stain of original sin, such humans would be "immaculate," and therefore not in need of salvation by Christ. But if the condition of humanity as darkened and wounded in the state of original sin is due to the dynamics of the principles of human nature operating without the help of sanctifying grace, then such a condition will also be found in those humans born apart from Adam's lineage—on account of the same dynamics of the same principles. Those humans born outside of the lineage of Adam would be immaculate then, but not in the sense that they are free from original sin. Rather, they would suffer those defects concomitant to human nature that we have identified with the condition of original sin, but without ever having had any gift to remedy them. Such grace would merely not be present; a simple absence, rather than a privation of a grace that had once been given but then lost. In that second case, the suffering of these defects would not be the same as bearing a stain that follows from the privation of the grace of original justice, as it was for the nature derived from Adam that had once been illuminated by glory. The condition of humans in both lineages would be identical, to the extent that their natures are composed of the contrary principles described earlier. What is a mere absence for those born apart from Adam's lineage would be counted as a punishment for the descendants of Adam, a privation

---

41. This is formulated by Kenneth W. Kemp as the fundamental premise in "Science, Theology, and Monogenesis."

of the good of sanctifying grace and all concomitant ordering of a soul and its powers ordered toward friendship with God.

As a punishment for the first sin of Adam, the concrete human nature by which Adam exists is deprived of that sanctifying grace and concomitantly of original justice. Thomas clarifies that it is not human nature as such that is subjected to the deprivation of original justice but only the human nature in Adam that is transmitted to his progeny: "Original sin does not belong to human nature absolutely, but to that [human nature] derived seminally from Adam, as I have said."[42] The personal fault of Adam results in the punishment of Adam as a concrete subject—a punishment both to his person and to his nature. In this punishment of Adam in his nature, he is in a way "all men" who follow from him by way of generation, of which he is the concrete individual originating principle of an entire human nature. Thomas clearly states this in his discussion of original sin in the *Summa theologiae*, when he considers whether a human formed afresh from human flesh would inherit original sin:

> Now there is no movement to generation except by the active power of generation: so that those alone contract original sin, who are descended from Adam through the active power of generation originally derived from Adam, i.e., who are descended from him through seminal power; for the seminal power is nothing else than the active power of generation. But if anyone were to be formed by God out of human flesh, it is evident that the active power would not be derived from Adam. Consequently he would not contract original sin: even as a hand would have no part in a human sin, if it were moved, not by the man's will, but by some external power.[43]

The conclusion most readers will draw incorrectly from this explanation is that anyone born from any lineage other than Adam's would be free from original sin and its defects. In consequence, it is assumed such a person would be free of the stain of sin, would be able to live a life without any disordered concupiscence (and never sin), would be capable of raising their mind to God, and therefore would not need to be redeemed by Christ. This is the concern that *Humani Generis* expresses about the implications of evolution's challenge to monogenism, which Kemp implies in Premise 7 of his argument.

In light of the above consideration of original sin as simply the condition of humanity left on its own when deprived of original justice, the alternative to being born in original sin is not being born in a humanity living through

---

42. *De malo* q. 4, a. 7, ad 3. This is my translation of "Ad tertium dicendum, quod peccatum originale non pertinet ad naturam humanam absolute, sed secundum quod derivatur ab Adam per viam seminalem, ut dictum est."

43. *ST* I-II q. 81, a. 4, corp.

a human nature purified from sin. Rather it is being born with a human nature subject to all the flaws, limits, and disorders of the condition of original sin, and *never* having had the benefit of the grace of original justice. Those who are born without original sin would still be born of a nature that suffers a darkness—just without it being counted as a stain.

Daniel Houck deftly points out the universality of this diminished state of human nature devoid of grace by directing his reader's attention to Thomas's fuller discussion of the prospect of a humanity formed apart from Adam. In his earlier *Commentary on the Sentences*, Thomas states that if someone were to be generated from a principle of human nature other than Adam's and not given a gift of grace productive of original justice, that person would exist in a condition identical to the condition of original sin. The only difference is that the condition would be a punishment (*poena*) in one born from Adam's lineage who is deprived of that gift, whereas in the second case the condition would merely follow from something being absent that was never given in the first place:

> If, by divine power, someone were formed from a finger, she would not have original sin. Nevertheless, *she would have all the defects of those born in original sin*, without the character of guilt. This is clear from the following. When God created humanity in the beginning, he could have formed a different human being from the mud of the earth—left to the condition of her nature, mortal and passible, feeling concupiscence rage against her reason. In this state nothing would be subtracted from human nature, because these defects follow the principles of human nature. Still, as this defect would not be caused through [human] will, it would not have had the character of guilt or penalty.[44]

All humans who exist with only their natural principles of acting are subject to the same ills, weaknesses, and darknesses. For those born apart from Adam, a remedy would never have been due to them in the first place, so the absence of that remedy cannot be considered a privation. Those born from the humanity of Adam come from a lineage that once enjoyed an immediate remedy to that condition that is no longer given to them. What is a mere lack in the former, then, is counted as a punishment in the latter—as a deprivation of a capacity that humanity once possessed.[45]

---

44. *In II Sent.* d. 31, q. 1, a. 2, ad 3, as cited by Houck, *Aquinas, Original Sin*, 93.

45. Thomas sets the groundwork of this more fundamental notion of punishment as a privation of a capacity for right action in his *De malo* q. 1, a. 4, corp.: "And intellectual creatures also suffer evil when they are deprived of forms or dispositions or anything else potentially necessary for good activity, whether the things belong to the soul or the body or external things. And such evil, in the judgment of the Catholic faith, needs to be called punishment."

This would seem to be the import of Thomas's account of the stain (*macula*) of original sin—as something that inheres in the human nature derived from Adam, rather than as something inhering in human nature simply—whether derived from Adam (which Thomas considers to be the actual case for all humans) or not (as in Thomas's hypothetical case of one formed from a finger). Thomas speaks of the *macula* as a shadow or a darkness that follows from sin. This is not a positive quality added to the human soul or to human nature as an additional trait to be passed on to descendants. If it were, the question of how this stain could be found in humans not born from the lineage of a historical Adam would indeed be a problem. As a type of privation, this stain is solely an absence of the illumination that would come from such grace as the grace of original justice:

> And so the stain in itself does not include of its essence anything but the privation of grace, but it includes as its cause the obstacle of sin, which obstructs the reception of grace. And because of this the stain is also called "darkness" by reason of the likeness mentioned.[46]

In the case of original sin, concupiscence—otherwise restrained by the reason rightly ordered to God through the grace of original justice—is allowed to dominate in human actions. This disposition of being dominated by a love for lower things is what stains the person, or makes him unclean:

> But it should be known that man through sin first incurred uncleanness: *you are stained in your iniquity* (Jer 2:22); second, defilement: *their face is now made blacker than coals* (Lam 4:8). And he hopes that these two things will be removed from him, namely, uncleanness and spiritual defilement. Uncleanness results when a man's inclination cleaves to temporal things, which renders him like them, just as if something is added to something base, like gold to lead, it is made base: *they are become abominable, as those things which they loved* (Hos 9:10).[47]

So what Adam confers on his descendants, through his semen as an instrumental active principle, is a nature that is stained through not being suited to the immediate reception of that grace of original justice, as it would have been

---

46. *In IV Sent.* d. 18, a. 2, ad q.a 1, corp.
47. In Psalm 50, n. 4 "Sciendum est autem, quod homo per peccatum primo incurrit immunditiam: Jer. 2: maculata es in iniquitate tua. Secundo incurrit turpitudinem: unde Thr. 4: denigrata est super carbones facies eorum. Et haec duo sperat a se removeri: immunditiam scilicet et turpitudinem spiritualem. Immunditia contingit ex hoc, quod affectus hominis inhaeret rebus temporalibus quibus similis efficitur; unde si adjungatur vilioribus, ut aurum plumbo, vilis efficitur: Oseae 9: facti sunt abominabiles, sicut ea quae dilexerunt."

if Adam had not sinned.[48] What is in this case a darkness that falls on a human nature that was at one time luminous and unstained is, in the case of a humanity outside of Adam, a mere darkness concomitant with a human nature that was never illuminated by grace. In either condition, such darkness functions in the same way: one's mind does not join itself to the divine good as its end, and one's actions decline from the attainment of that highest good to the attainment of some lower good in its place.

The common character of the human condition arising from a human nature unelevated by grace allows us to clarify what is meant by the stain of sin that once seemed to be an additional trait derived from Adam on account of his fall. Rather than being something peculiar to Adam's descendants, such a darkness would be a quality concomitant with any human nature not perfected by sanctifying grace. In the framework of Thomas's account of original sin as privation, a *macula* is likewise a privation, a shadow or darkness attached to human nature as something following from its principles. It is not an additional inherited quality but an outcome of human nature being passed on from one generation to the next without the immediate accompaniment of sanctifying grace.

6. Application to the Diverse Models of Human Evolution

Here we can begin to make sense of how one could conceive of the transmission of original sin in light of the questions raised by evolution and by the multitude of speculative scenarios that might account for human origins. To start with the scenario closest to traditional Christian belief and the narrative of Genesis: if all humans do descend from one progenitor—or one couple to whom grace had been given but who then subsequently lost that grace—the humanity passed on from that one ancestor is said to be darkened since it had at one point been illuminated by grace. There is no humanity other than that derived from one ancestor—Adam—and thus all humanity conceived from that line is not only dark but darkened.[49]

If human nature can be understood to have emerged not from that one individual but perhaps among many in a group in the same time frame, then those first humans without grace would have a humanity that was dark to begin with—having never been illuminated—and thus indistinguishable from the humanity counted as darkened because of the loss of grace. An account congruent with a traditional Christian account of original sin would have one individual (or pair) infused with the gift of sanctifying grace, which would

---

48. See *ST* I q. 100, a. 1 for Thomas's account.
49. With the exception of one conceived immaculately as proving the rule.

have elevated their souls with capacities that differentiated them from others in that group sharing their nature. They would have loved God above all things; and thus, would have rightly ordered love toward themselves, their neighbor, and the world around them. But when they sinned, they would have rejected that gift of sanctifying grace, and thereby suffered the concomitant effects of being left to live according to the principles of their own nature and nothing more. In the aftermath—among all of humanity, emerging by any development whatsoever—the difference would not be whether there is a darkness, but rather whether it is considered as a mere darkness in their humanity, or as a once-luminous humanity that has been darkened by having lost what once was given. Eventually, through interbreeding across a number of generations, the proneness to concupiscence typical of the whole population would be countable in each descendant as a matter of stain rather than a simple absence of grace.

Karl Rahner's article "Evolution and Original Sin" outlines a multitude of such possibilities to address *Humani Generis*'s concerns about polygenesis. Among the solutions he considers is humanity as a "biological-historical unity" as to its origin, its population, its common biological and social history, and—more theologically important—its destiny as subject to redemption by Christ.[50] In that case, the subject of the stain of sin is the prior condition of a humanity united in all those above ways:

> If man is inextricably both personal *and* communal and both these aspects *presuppose* each other; if the original group (monogenetic or polygenetic) is in any case a biological and historical unit and this group in any case determined in many ways as a unit the further development of mankind in its existential situation, then there is no reason why the decision of one individual *within* this unit could not influence the grace-communicating function of this group. If one asks how one can know this without just imagining it, we may simply answer that we know that we receive grace *only* through Christ as source and as the one who transmits and, on the other hand, that such a transmission had to exist from the origin of mankind. One can insist on this second point. But we know this from revelation which clearly implies that all grace comes from Christ.[51]

Rahner's speculative proposal works backward from what is known as a theological premise: all are saved by Christ because all are in need of that salvation, even apart from and prior to any personal sin one might commit. In whatever way humanity concretely originated, Rahner posits that the consequence is

---

50. Karl Rahner, "Evolution and Original Sin," *Concilium* 26 (1967): 30–35.
51. Rahner, "Evolution and Original Sin," 33–34.

the same: humanity has lost the capacity to be a transmitter of grace. Whatever humanity is transmitted is stained and thus in need of cleansing by Christ's redemptive work.

This entire set of speculative possibilities concerning the origin and transmission of human nature as stained raises several distinctively theological questions: Is God justified in making the grace due to descendants dependent upon a single ancestor remaining morally and spiritually upright? Would God be just in creating, through evolutionary means, biological humans without infusing a rational soul in each? Would God be just in infusing rational souls into separately evolving biological humans without immediately infusing the accompanying grace that would justify them? These questions properly concern only the theological matter of the origin and status of original sin and its stain. This chapter has aimed to address the problem resulting from the overlap of the scientific explanation of the origin and propagation of the human species and the theological understanding of the transmission of a human nature that is said to bear a stain of original sin. In Thomas, we find that the transmission of that stain—like the transmission of original sin—follows simply from the transmission of human nature itself. Here we have a congruence between theological and evolutionary claims, as far as each can go on the matter. Further, though this conclusion follows from the theology of Thomas Aquinas in particular, it can be generalized to apply to any theology that takes original sin to be a privation in the senses described above, so as to engage any of the various possibilities for the origin and descent of the first human beings.

Conclusion

This account of the transmission of original sin is meant to resolve one major theological question prompted by evolutionary theory. It does not presume to address all related questions. For example, I assume the distinguishability of biological monogenesis from moral monogenesis, and that the primary concern of *Humani Generis* with the former is to establish the latter. This is not an uncontested interpretive claim, so it bears further consideration. Further, this account prescinds from the question of whether it is just of God to deprive descendants—on account of their ancestor's moral fault—of receiving the unmediated grace necessary for their moral and spiritual integrity. Such a long-running theological argument should continue fruitfully.

My central point has been more restricted: to explain the transmission of original sin. We are misled when we speak of original sin as something transmitted in a manner akin to a biological trait of human nature. If instead, we speak not of the transmission of the privation but of the transmission of the subject of that privation, the question looks very different. Scientifically, it is impossible to distinguish a human nature shorn of the grace of original justice from a human nature that never received that grace at all. Whether that nature is fit to receive a particular grace is not a biological property, but a moral property accounted for by divine justice and divine punishment. But those are matters of theological discussion and investigation, which are not subject to biological explanation, verification, or rejection.

CHAPTER NINE

What Kind of Death?
Romans 5 and Modern Science

ISAAC AUGUSTINE MORALES, OP

Does Darwin's theory of evolution—and the results of modern science more generally—require a radical break with the tradition rooted in the writings of the apostle Paul and the theology of St. Augustine? Many modern thinkers have suggested as much. In a 2013 essay considering the origin of death from both a theological and a scientific perspective, Izak J. J. Spangenberg concludes, "Theologians should be bold enough to abandon the ideas of Paul and Augustine on sin and death and formulate new concepts of death that are in accordance with our current knowledge."[1] Spangenberg is neither novel nor unique in this assertion. At least since the early to mid-twentieth century, some theologians have suggested that the doctrine of original sin stands in need of a moratorium. Paul Tillich, for example, suggested that no one use the phrase "original sin" for at least thirty years "until the term regained some meaning."[2]

Although other modern thinkers have offered very different assessments—John Henry Newman considered the doctrine "almost as certain as that the world exists" and G. K. Chesterton famously called it "the only part of Christian theology which can really be proved"—it is not hard to see why many people find the doctrine unappealing, to put it mildly.[3] This discomfort with the notion of original sin is rooted in at least two ideas. First, many understand the doctrine in an Augustinian sense, according to which human beings inherit the guilt of Adam; the idea of being punished for the sin of another sounds like an injustice. Second, the apparent connection between the sin of Adam and the introduction of death into the world (Rom 5:12)

---

1. Izak J. J. Spangenberg, "On the Origin of Death: Paul and Augustine Meet Charles Darwin," *HTS Teologiese Studies/Theological Studies* 69, no. 1 (2013): 7, art. 1992.
2. D. Mackenzie Brown, *Ultimate Concern: Tillich in Dialogue* (New York: Harper and Row, 1965), 89.
3. John Henry Newman, *Apologia pro Vita Sua: Being a History of his Religious Positions* (New York: Penguin, 2004), 242–43; G. K. Chesterton, *Orthodoxy* (London: The Bodley Head, 1908), 11.

seems to fly in the face of the scientific evidence that this planet has sustained life (and death) for billions of years.

Although many texts have contributed to the Christian doctrine of original sin and its relation to death, at the heart of the question has been Romans 5:12–21.[4] On its surface, this text seems fraught with the difficulties regarding original sin just mentioned. The goal of this chapter is to show that a proper understanding of the text can avoid at least some of these difficulties. The death of which Paul speaks in this passage applies only to human beings, not to the natural world at large.[5] Even in the case of human beings, this death does not refer to the cessation of biological life, but rather to alienation from God and the consequences that follow from that alienation.

In order to make the case that the text of Romans 5:12–21 refers not to biological death but to alienation from God, the chapter will proceed in four steps. First, I will consider the exact nature of the doctrine of original sin as dogmatically defined by the Catholic Church. Despite the common misconception that original sin necessarily entails the passing on of guilt from one generation to the next, I will show that the actual teaching understands guilt only in an analogous sense. Second, I will explore what Paul means by "death" in the Letter to the Romans. As others have shown, Paul uses the term in various ways throughout Romans 5–8.[6] It is necessary to survey the range of meanings in order to determine how he uses the term in Romans 5:12–21. Third, I will offer a similar, though briefer, analysis of the word "sin" in Romans. Finally, I will consider Romans 5:12–21 as a whole, showing that for Paul, Adam's sin had consequences for the whole human race; these consequences map well onto the later Christian formulation of the doctrine of original sin. In this section I will also discuss the meaning of the phrase ἐφ' ᾧ, the (mis)translation of which played a significant role in the development of Augustine's understanding of original sin.[7]

---

4. For a discussion of other biblical texts relating to original sin, see André-Marie Dubarle, *The Biblical Doctrine of Original Sin*, trans. E. M. Stewart (London: Chapman, 1964); more recently from a Lutheran perspective, see Charles Gieschen, "Original Sin in the New Testament," *Concordia Journal* 31 (2005): 359–75.

5. This is not to say that the death spoken of in Romans 5 has no consequences for the natural world. Paul seems to suggest as much in Romans 8:20. Nevertheless, the effect he speaks of there is "futility" (ματαιότητι), not death. I am grateful to Thomas Stegman for raising this question.

6. For two studies on this question from different perspectives, see Thomas Barrosse, "Death and Sin in Saint Paul's Epistle to the Romans," *Catholic Biblical Quarterly* 15 (1953): 438–59; C. Clifton Black, "Pauline Perspectives on Death in Romans 5–8," *Journal of Biblical Literature* 103 (1984): 413–33.

7. The possibilities for translating this phrase into English are vast. For a full exploration of the question, see Joseph A. Fitzmyer, "The Consecutive Meaning of ΕΦ' Ω in

1. Original Sin: What Exactly Is It?

In the relationship between theology and exegesis, one always runs the risk of allowing later theological ideas to exercise undue influence on the interpretation of biblical texts. For that reason, it might seem safer to begin with the text of Romans and only then move on to the doctrine of original sin. There is good reason, however, to reverse the order in this case. Although the phrase "original sin" is widely known even in a largely post-Christian culture, the actual nature of the doctrine is less well known, and many people reject it based on misconception and misunderstanding. One of the biggest stumbling blocks in this regard is the fact that all the sins we personally encounter involve the agency of the sinner and their consequent culpability. To say that human beings are born in or with sin seems counterintuitive. How can a person be held responsible for an act they did not commit?

The notion of inherited guilt, though not official Catholic doctrine, goes back at least to the time of St. Augustine and perhaps even earlier. Augustine's understanding of original sin famously relied in part on a common Latin translation of the Greek phrase ἐφ' ᾧ in Romans 5:12. As is widely known, Augustine's translation rendered this phrase by the Latin *in quo*. He was not the first to read the text this way. The commentary on Romans by an unknown author commonly called Ambrosiaster follows the same reading and seems to have influenced Augustine.[8] Augustine took the phrase to mean that in some sense all human beings actually sinned in Adam by way of origin. Adam's sin is not his alone but rather belongs to all human beings, who thereby inherit guilt for the act.[9]

Influential though Augustine has been in countless areas of theology, the Church did not adopt his explication of original sin wholesale. Even before the controversies of the Protestant Reformation that led the Council of Trent to define the doctrine more precisely, medieval theologians already were modifying Augustine's interpretation by making it less pessimistic.[10] St. Thomas Aquinas, for example, maintains Augustine's idea that Adam's descendants inherit the guilt of that first sin. Nevertheless, he does so in a way that at the same time acknowledges the distinction between a person's actual sin and that

---

Romans 5.12," *New Testament Studies* 39 (1993): 321–39; Fitzmyer, *Romans: A New Translation with Introduction and Commentary* (AB 33; New York: Doubleday, 1993), 413–17.

8. David Weaver, "From Paul to Augustine: Romans 5:12 in Early Christian Exegesis," *St. Vladimir's Quarterly* 27, no. 3 (1983): 200.

9. See, for example, Augustine, *Against Julian* 6.75.

10. A point fairly noted by Weaver, "From Paul to Augustine," 205.

which is inherited from Adam. Like Augustine, Aquinas sees all human beings as forming one man in Adam because of their shared human nature. Indeed, he goes on to suggest that all human beings are, by analogy, members of one body. Because of this unity, the actions of a part of that body redound to the whole body. In committing a crime, only certain parts of the body are actually engaged in the act. Nevertheless, the guilt for the crime is not ascribed merely to the body parts involved but rather to the whole person. In a similar way, the sin of Adam, committed as the head of the body of the human race, is attributed to the whole race. Despite this solidarity, however, Aquinas acknowledges that original sin does not constitute a personal sin on the part of each human being. Rather, the sin of Adam affects the nature that each person receives from the first human parents.[11]

The Canons of the Council of Trent affirm that original sin is passed on by generation without endorsing any particular explanation of how that transmission takes place.[12] However Adam's sin is passed on, Trent maintains the longstanding tradition that all human beings, in solidarity with their first parents, suffer the consequences of their trespass. In making this affirmation, the council fathers appeal to Romans 5:12. Moreover, the council implicitly defines original sin as a death of the soul:

> "If anyone asserts that Adam's sin harmed only him and not his descendants" and that the holiness and justice received from God that he lost was lost only for him and not for us also; or that, stained by the sin of disobedience, he transmitted to all mankind "only death" and the sufferings "of the body but not sin as well, *which is the death of the soul*," let him be anathema.[13]

The canon thus suggests multiple punishments (both physical and spiritual) stemming from Adam's sin, which include both physical and spiritual consequences. When defining the sin that Adam passed on to his descendants, however, the council fathers define it only as the death of the soul.[14] Such an interpretation of Scripture is no innovation. In fact, one can find a similar assessment in Augustine, who describes the punishment of Adam due to his

---

11. *ST* I–II q. 81.

12. The *Catechism of the Catholic Church* follows Trent's lead and makes this even more explicit, noting, "the transmission of original sin is a mystery that we cannot fully understand" (*CCC*, 404).

13. Denz, 1512, emphasis added. H. Denzinger, *Compendium of Creeds, Definitions, and Declarations on Matters of Faith and Morals*, 43rd ed., ed. Peter Hünermann, Robert Fastiggi, and Anne Englund Nash (San Francisco: Ignatius, 2012).

14. I owe this point to Scott W. Hahn and Curtis J. Mitch, "The Diffusion of Death: Romans 5:12 and Original Sin," *Letter and Spirit* 12 (2018): 33.

transgression as "total death"; that is, a death involving both the death of the soul and the (eventual) death of the body.[15] In his commentary on Romans, Aquinas closely links alienation from God (that is, the loss of original justice) with the physical death that humans then had to suffer, with the former being the cause of the latter: "Thus, therefore, after man's mind was turned from God through sin, he lost the strength to control the lower powers as well as the body and external things. Consequently, he became subject to death from intrinsic sources and to violence from external sources."[16] For Aquinas, the human body is perishable by nature, since it is composed of matter. Nevertheless, in the state of original justice, the body was perfectly subject to the soul, and so was to remain incorruptible by virtue of this union.[17]

Much more could be said about the theological tradition regarding original sin and death, but space precludes it. The question to consider now is whether this tradition finds a legitimate basis in Romans 5. In order to address this question, we turn first to the nature of death in the Letter to the Romans.

2. What Kind of Death?

Few ideas dominate Romans 5–8 like the themes of sin and death. The noun form ἁμαρτία (sin) occurs forty-two times in these chapters alone, more than half the total number of occurrences of *all* sin-related expressions (sinner, to sin, sinful) in the undisputed letters of Paul (eighty-one times total).[18] Death also plays a central role in this section of the letter. As C. Clifton Black notes, more than half the occurrences of the word θάνατος (death) in the undisputed letters appear in Romans (forty-nine out of ninety-five), and the vast majority of these occur in Romans 5–8.[19] Even a cursory glance at the many ways Paul discusses the term shows that it has a wide range of meanings. In order to determine the relationship between sin and death, it is necessary to ascertain what Paul means by the punishment of death in Rom 5:12–21. To that end,

---

15. See Augustine of Hippo, *The City of God*, trans. Henry Bettenson (New York, NY: Penguin Books, 1972), 13.12–15. In 13.12, Augustine writes with respect to God's threat in Genesis 2, "Was it the death of the soul? Or of the body? Or of the whole person? Or was it what is called the second death? Our reply to the question is, 'All of these deaths.' For the first death consists of two; total death consists of all of them."

16. *In Rom.* c. 5, lect. 3 (416).

17. For an excellent discussion of this aspect of Thomas's thought with respect to Romans 5, see J. A. Di Noia, "Christ Brings Freedom from Sin and Death: The Commentary of St. Thomas Aquinas on Romans 5:12–21," *The Thomist* 73 (2009): 381–98, esp. 387–89.

18. Beverly Roberts Gaventa, "The Cosmic Power of Sin in Paul's Letter to the Romans: Toward a Widescreen Edition," *Interpretation* 58, no. 3 (2004): 229–30.

19. Black, "Pauline Perspectives on Death," 413n2.

let us first consider the various ways Paul describes death in Romans 5–8 outside of 5:12–21 in order to establish the range of meanings for the word. Once we have surveyed Paul's usages in this section, we will return to the question in Romans 5:12–21, and particularly to the connection between sin and death.[20]

The language of death in Romans 5:1–11, which includes both the verbal form of dying and the noun form of death, focuses on Christ's gift of self. In this context, the death spoken of clearly refers to the cessation of biological life, a death that has important consequences for others. In Romans 5:6 Paul writes, "For while we were still weak, at the right time, Christ died (ἀπέθανεν) for the godless." Three more times in the following two verses, Paul speaks of the act of dying, referring to the kinds of persons or causes for which a person might die. Summing up his argument, he concludes, "For if while we were enemies we were reconciled to God through the death of his son, how much more being reconciled will we be saved by his life" (Rom 5:11). Christ's act of handing over his life brings about reconciliation with God and instills in Paul a deep confidence that by his life (most likely a reference to the resurrection) Christ will complete the act of salvation for those who belong to him.

Skipping ahead to Romans 6, while the actual death of Christ on the cross still plays a central role, its significance for the Christian life takes on new shades of meaning. In this chapter, Paul moves to correct a possible misunderstanding of his statement toward the end of Romans 5: "Where sin increased, grace increased even more" (Rom 5:20b). Responding to a possible false conclusion (Rom 6:1), Paul appeals to the meaning and effect of baptism. He reminds his audience that in baptism, the baptized died to sin (ἀπεθάνομεν τῇ ἁμαρτίᾳ). Here the death in question clearly does not refer to the cessation of biological life, though it is related to Christ's own death. Paul describes the rite as a baptism into the death of Christ (Rom 6:3). Through this ritual the baptized are "buried with Christ" and as a result of this burial they are called to a new life (Rom 6:4). Moreover, this baptismal burial with Christ provides the basis for hope in the future resurrection (Rom 6:8–10).[21] In the present, the baptized are to consider themselves "dead to sin but alive to God in Christ Jesus" (Rom 6:11).

---

20. This survey is in no way intended to be an exhaustive analysis. My approach will in some ways reflect that of Black, though without an extensive discussion of the Second Temple Jewish and Greco-Roman background to Paul's thought. The reason for this choice is not because this context is unimportant, but simply for lack of space.

21. For a fuller discussion of Romans 6:1–11, see Isaac Augustine Morales, "Baptism, Holiness, and Resurrection Hope in Romans 6," *Catholic Biblical Quarterly* 83 (2021): 466–81.

In this baptismal context, then, the death of the baptized does not refer to the end of their biological life on earth. Rather, death language must be taken metaphorically or spiritually. Given the negative connotations of death that so frequently appear in Scripture, it is perhaps somewhat surprising that in this case, metaphorical death appears to be something positive. Death to sin is the prelude to and the anticipation of the fullness of life in the resurrection. The source of this hope is Christ's actual, biological death, which features prominently throughout (Rom 6:4, 10).

In the second half of Romans 6, death takes on a more characteristically negative connotation. Continuing to address the question of whether the baptized should sin because of their freedom from the law (Rom 6:15), Paul shifts to the imagery of enslavement: "Don't you know that if you present yourselves to someone as slaves for obedience, you will be slaves to the one you obey, either to sin [leading] to death or to obedience [leading] to righteousness?" (Rom 6:16). Slavery to sin, Paul suggests, leads to death—but what kind of death? It seems unlikely that Paul simply means natural death, which comes for everyone. Rather, Paul seems to be speaking of a spiritual death, as he does in the first half of Romans 6—only in this case, the spiritual death is negative. A little later in the passage, speaking of the shameful deeds his audience performed when they were (formerly) enslaved to sin, he notes, "the end of those things is death" (Rom 6:21). Once again, the death spoken of here cannot be biological death; rather, Paul has in mind once again a spiritual death, which he now proceeds to contrast with holiness and eternal life (Rom 6:22).[22] Interpreted in this context, the famous closing verse of this chapter must refer not to biological death but rather to some kind of spiritual death, perhaps what is sometimes referred to as the "second death": "For the wages of sin is death, but the gift of God is eternal life in Christ Jesus our Lord" (Rom 6:23).

This spiritual understanding of death continues into Romans 7.[23] Once again describing life "in the flesh" (another common Pauline phrase for life under slavery to sin), Paul writes, "For when we were in the flesh, the desires

---

22. This is not to deny that there is a connection between spiritual death and biological death. As noted in the section below, in 1 Corinthians 15, Paul seems to connect Adam's sin with biological death. Romans seems to suggest that biological death follows from the spiritual death that was the primary effect of Adam's sin.

23. Black ("Pauline Perspectives on Death," 426n36) prefers the adjective "existential" to "spiritual," not because it is any less anachronistic, but rather because it "captures more fully in modern parlance the death, in life, of the whole person." Moreover, he notes that the only thing Paul describes as "spiritual" is the law in Romans 7:14. This latter point, however, speaks in favor of referring to spiritual death rather than against it. Paul describes the problem as one of being too "fleshly" and not spiritual, a point that is captured more clearly with the phrase "spiritual death."

of our sins through the law were at work in our bodily parts, in order to bear fruit unto death" (Rom 7:5). Throughout the rest of the chapter, Paul repeatedly draws on the imagery of death and its relationship to sin in such a way that, once again, death cannot be characterized as the cessation of biological life. When sin "came to life," Paul writes, "I died and the commandment which was [meant to be] life for me was found to be death for me" (Rom 7:9b–10). Using this commandment, sin "deceived" Paul and "killed" him (Rom 7:11). For the purposes of this chapter, we need not answer the controverted question of how to interpret the first-person singular pronouns in this section. Regardless of whether Paul is speaking of himself or in the person of Adam, the death resulting from sin seems to be something other than biological death. Indeed, in some verses, death seems to be an ongoing effect of sin in the midst of life.[24] So, for example, in Romans 7:13 Paul writes, in part, "Sin, in order that it might be seen as sin, worked death in me through the good thing [i.e., the law, Rom 7:12]."

Although the word "death" does not reappear in Romans 7 until verse 24, the chapter seems to be an explication of the "death" that sin works in a person, and once again, that death is not the cessation of biological life. Rather, Paul speaks of the struggle against sin (that is, the disorder of not being able to do the good that one wants but instead falling into the evil that one wants to avoid).[25] Paul speaks of this inability twice: "For I do not do the thing that I want, but the thing I hate I do. . . . For I do not do the good that I want, but the evil that I do not want I do" (Rom 7:15b, 19). In light of this emphasis on the effects of sin with respect to action, it seems likely that in speaking of "this body of death" in Romans 7:24, Paul has in mind the spiritual malady that sin introduces into the life of a person.[26]

In Romans 8, death takes on several shades of meaning, but the connotation of hostility toward God remains, especially in the first eleven verses. Toward the beginning of the chapter Paul writes, "For the law of the Spirit

---

24. Black, "Pauline Perspectives on Death," 425–26. Dubarle, *The Biblical Doctrine of Original Sin*, 151. A little later (154–55) Dubarle notes a helpful parallel with Ephesians 2:1–3, which uses death in a similar way.

25. At the risk of anachronism, the disorder described in Romans 7 sounds remarkably like some of the wounds of original sin as described in later Christian tradition, especially weakness and concupiscence.

26. In this respect, I am largely in agreement with Black ("Pauline Perspectives on Death," 426), who writes, "In my estimation, the primary sense in which death is to be understood in this textual unit [Rom 7:7–25] is as the existential estrangement from God which derives from sin." As Black himself notes, this need not rule out other connotations of death in the passage; it simply means that alienation is the primary understanding of death in this case. See also Dubarle, *The Biblical Doctrine of Original Sin*, 174–75.

of life in Christ Jesus has set you free from the law of sin and death" (Rom 8:2). The death Paul speaks of here is a present reality (or, perhaps more accurately, a reality that was present to the Romans until the Spirit liberated them). The Spirit moves people from the realm of the flesh to the realm of the Spirit, thus reconciling them with God. A few verses later Paul writes, "The mind of the flesh is death, but the mind of the Spirit is life and peace" (Rom 8:6). What kind of death does the mind of the flesh bring about? Paul explains in the following verse, "Because the mind of the flesh is hostility toward God, for it is not subject to the law of God, for it cannot [be subject]" (Rom 8:7). In other words, the death that sin brings about is not biological; it is the same alienation from God that Paul describes in Romans 7.

This is not to say that there is no relation between death as alienation from God and death as the cessation of life. In fact, Paul brings the two together toward the end of this passage:

> But you are not in the flesh but in the Spirit, since the Spirit of God dwells in you. Now if anyone does not have the Spirit of Christ, that one is not his. But if Christ is in you, the body is dead because of sin but the Spirit is life because of righteousness. And if the Spirit of the one who raised Jesus from the dead dwells in you, the one who raised Christ from the dead will give life to your mortal bodies through his Spirit dwelling in you. (Rom 8:9–11)

In light of the repeated emphasis on the connection between sin and spiritual death in Romans 7 and the opening verses of Romans 8, the death Paul ascribes to the body in verse 10 most likely refers to a spiritual reality—the death effected by baptism (Rom 6:6).[27] As the argument develops in verse 11, however, Paul shifts into an eschatological mode, speaking of a future gift of life analogous to Christ's own resurrection from the dead. The gift of the Spirit, then, has both a present effect of bringing about life and peace (Rom 8:6) and a future effect of bodily resurrection.

In the following verse, Paul again uses the imagery of death in a spiritual sense, once negatively and once positively. First Paul writes, "For if you live according to the flesh, you are destined to die" (Rom 8:13a). The death involved here cannot refer to biological death; by such logic, those who live according to the Spirit would never have to face biological death, which is clearly absurd.[28] Rather, Paul seems to have in mind some kind of

---

27. See Black, "Pauline Perspectives on Death," 427.
28. See Dubarle, *The Biblical Doctrine of Original Sin*, 175. Black ("Pauline Perspectives on Death," 427–28) refers to an "ethical component" in this reference to death. While there certainly is an ethical component, insofar as living "according to the flesh"

spiritual death. Given the eschatological connotation of the preceding verses, he is most likely speaking of a punishment beyond the present spiritual death caused by sin. This verse also contains a positive reference to death, recalling the imagery of death used in Romans 6: "But if by the Spirit you put to death the deeds of the body, you will live" (Rom 8:13b). As with the dying in the earlier part of the verse, it seems unlikely that the life mentioned in this verse ("you will live") refers to mere biological life, either as it is presently experienced or simply extended over time. Rather, in light of Romans 8:11, the life the Spirit will bestow on those who put to death the deeds of the body must be eschatological life, patterned on Christ's own resurrection.

The last few references to death in Romans 8 more naturally refer to biological death. Toward the beginning of the final paragraph of the chapter, Paul describes Christ as the one who died and (more importantly) who was also raised (Rom 8:34). Finally, in the stirring conclusion to Paul's argument, as he answers his own question: "Who can separate us from the love of Christ?" (Rom 8:35). By excluding anything as capable of bringing about this separation, he concludes: "For I am persuaded that neither death nor life nor angels nor rulers . . . nor any other created thing can separate us from the love of God which is in Christ Jesus our Lord" (Rom 8:38–39). In this context "death" and "life" must refer to biological realities. The kind of death Paul describes in Romans 7 and the earlier sections of Romans 8—to say nothing of the death that serves as the subject of Romans 5:12–21, to which we will return shortly—clearly does have the capacity to separate people from the love of God, if only by allowing them to reject it.

Having surveyed the references to death in Romans 5–8, we can categorize Paul's use of this term into at least four groups.[29] On some occasions, death denotes the cessation of biological life, either in general (e.g., Rom 8:38) or with respect to Christ's death on the cross (e.g., Rom 5:10). In other

---

has ethical connotations for Paul, the death of which Paul speaks seems to refer to a further punishment, rather than the death that leads to the situation described in Romans 7, discussed above.

29. For a far more detailed account of the meaning of death, not just in Paul but also in Second Temple Jewish texts and Paul's Greco-Roman context, see Black, "Pauline Perspectives on Death," 414–19, with a convenient summary on 418–19. For a concise discussion of the effects of Adam's sin or Eve's sin as seen in various Second Temple Jewish texts, see Joel B. Green, "'Adam, What Have You Done?' New Testament Voices on the Origins of Sin," in *Evolution and the Fall*, ed. William T. Cavanaugh and James K. A. Smith (Grand Rapids, MI: Eerdmans, 2017): 71–81, esp. 71–74; and earlier, Thomas H. Tobin, "The Jewish Context of Rom 5:12–14," *Studia Philonica Annual* 13 (2001): 159–75, esp. 165–70.

cases, death refers to a spiritual reality in a negative sense—a death that consists of alienation from God. This seems to be the meaning throughout much of Romans 7 and the early verses of Romans 8. In some verses, Paul speaks of death as a spiritual reality with a positive dimension. This is most obviously the case in his discussion of baptism, where he describes the rite as bringing about a kind of union between the baptized and Christ's own death (Rom 6:3–4). Related to baptism, Paul also exhorts his audience to "put to death" sinful actions so that they might live to God (Rom 8:13b). Finally, on at least one occasion, death seems to refer to a punishment after this life is over (Rom 8:13a; perhaps also Rom 6:16). Before we move on to the next section of this chapter, it is worth noting that although Paul's description of death as a spiritual reality is not identical with the language of Trent, the council's account of death is nevertheless quite compatible with Paul's thought in at least some instances. This is especially true in Romans 7 and the early verses of Romans 8, where Paul speaks of the death resulting from sin both as a hostility toward God and as an inability to perform the good.

The question that remains to be answered is this: What kind of death does Paul see as the punishment for sin in Romans 5:12–21? Before we can address this question, though, it is necessary to consider the various meanings of the term "sin" in Romans.

3. Sin and Sins

As noted above, words related to "sin" appear with an even higher proportionate frequency in Romans than do words related to "death."[30] An exhaustive study of the various meanings of sin in the letter is far beyond the scope of this chapter. Rather, in this section I would like to focus on three aspects of sin. First, we will briefly consider its universality. Second, we will take up the question of whether sin (or "Sin" with a capital "S," as some like to translate the word) should be seen as an apocalyptic or cosmic power. Finally, we will consider the relationship between individual acts of sin and Sin (whether one sees it as a cosmic power or as something else).

Despite recent revisionist readings of the opening chapters of Romans, it is hard to avoid the conclusion that one of Paul's main goals in Romans

---

30. See Gaventa, "The Cosmic Power of Sin," 229–30.
31. For one such revisionist reading, see Stanley K. Stowers, *A Rereading of Romans: Justice, Jews, and Gentiles* (New Haven, CT: Yale University Press, 1994). See also the helpful discussion in Gaventa, "The Cosmic Power of Sin," 232–34. Green ("'Adam, What Have You Done?'" 75) puts it well: "[Paul's] is a universalistic presentation, an analysis of the human situation understood corporately, as God hands the human family over to experience the consequences of the sin they choose (Rom. 1:18, 24, 26, 28)."

1–3 is to establish the universality of sin.[31] Although the words ἁμαρτία and ἁμαρτάνω appear much less frequently in the first section of the letter (four and three times, respectively, in Romans 1–4) than they do in Romans 5–8, they nevertheless appear at important points in the argument and underscore the effects of sin on all human beings, both Jews and gentiles. Moreover, while using words related to sin sparingly, these chapters nevertheless give countless examples of acts that a first-century Jew like Paul would have considered sins, especially in Romans 1:18–3:20. Romans 1:18–32 details numerous sins that first-century Jews commonly associated with gentiles.

At some point in Romans 2, Paul shifts his attention from gentile sins to Jewish sins, though interpreters disagree about where this shift takes place—either at Romans 2:1 or 2:17. For our purposes the answer to this question does not matter. More important is Paul's brief statement toward the middle of the chapter regarding the sins of both Jews and gentiles: "For as many as have sinned without the law will also perish without the law, and as many as have sinned with the law will be judged through the law" (Rom 2:12). Here Paul acknowledges that sin is a problem that afflicts Jews and gentiles alike. The phrasing of Paul's statement might lead one to conclude that only some Jews and gentiles sin ("as many as have sinned"). Nevertheless, as the argument proceeds, it becomes clear that for Paul all human beings, both Jew and gentile, are in some way implicated in sin.

The noun form of sin (ἁμαρτία) first appears in Romans 3, and it anticipates the way Paul will use the term later in the letter, while at the same time serving as a kind of summary of his argument to this point. At the end of a brief consideration of whether the Jews are any better off than the gentiles, Paul concludes, "What then? Are we [Jews] better off? Not at all. For I have already charged that Jews and Greeks are all under sin [ὑφ' ἁμαρτίαν]" (Rom 3:9). Paul follows this statement with a catena of biblical citations cataloging some of the sins found commonly among both groups. In the verses that follow, Paul shifts from the language of being "under sin" in Romans 3:9 to speaking of offenses committed by "all": "For all have sinned and are deprived of the glory of God" (Rom 3:23).

In these early chapters of the letter, then, we see at least two different meanings of the language of sin. On the one hand, Paul speaks of human beings actually committing sins (Rom 2:12; 3:23). On the other hand, he also describes sin as something in some sense "over" human beings (Rom 3:9—"all are under sin"). With respect to both connotations of sin, Paul insists that it is universal; that is, it affects both Jews and "Greeks." But what exactly does he mean by "sin"?

For some time now, interpreters have pointed out that in Romans 5–8, "sin" (ἁμαρτία) frequently serves as the subject of verbs.[32] Paul speaks of sin performing acts like "reigning" (Rom 5:21; 6:12), "producing desire" (Rom 7:7), and "deceiving" and "killing" (Rom 7:11).[33] Among New Testament scholars, there have been a number of ways of interpreting this material, but the two most prominent are associated with Rudolf Bultmann on the one hand and his student Ernst Käsemann on the other.[34] For Bultmann and those who follow him, the ascription of certain actions to sin is an instance of metaphorical language. As Thomas Tobin puts it, "For the sake of vividness [Paul] is using one form of the rhetorical figure of personification, the personification of concepts."[35] In the case of Bultmann, one motivating factor is his overall project of demythologizing. Another motivation behind Bultmann's reading, however, might be to maintain the responsibility of human beings for their actions.[36]

Scholars who have followed Käsemann interpret Paul's language not as personification but as something more substantial. Rather than serving simply as a rhetorical device, these interpreters argue that Paul sees Sin (always with a capital "S") as a cosmic power in opposition to God that actually reigns over human beings.[37] The apparently metaphorical imagery points to something deeper—Sin as an "anti-God power" that (or who?) holds sway over human beings, forcing them to do things they would rather not do (see, e.g., Romans 7).[38] Using particularly vivid imagery, Gaventa describes Paul's depiction of Sin as "*the portrait of a cosmic terrorist.*"[39] A little later in the same paragraph,

---

32. For an informative recent discussion of this phenomenon, see Gaventa, "The Cosmic Power of Sin." For an intriguing recent proposal of how to interpret this idea in light of the notion of emergence and emergent properties, see Matthew Croasmun, *The Emergence of Sin: The Cosmic Tyrant in Romans* (Oxford: Oxford University Press, 2017). Unfortunately, the scope of this chapter does not permit a close engagement with Croasmun's argument.

33. For a similar list, see Gaventa, "The Cosmic Power of Sin," 230.

34. For an insightful discussion of these approaches, as well as Liberationist interpretations of the phenomenon, see Croasmun, *The Emergence of Sin*, 3–21.

35. Tobin, "The Jewish Context of Rom 5:12–14," 171. In the footnote, Tobin points to both modern and classical examples of this kind of personification. See also Brendan Byrne, *Romans*, Sacra Pagina 6 (Collegeville, MN: Liturgical, 1996), 175.

36. See Croasmun, *The Emergence of Sin*, 7–8.

37. One of the most prominent proponents of this interpretation is the late J. Louis Martyn. See especially J. Louis Martyn, *Galatians: A New Translation with Introduction and Commentary*, Anchor Bible 33A (New York: Doubleday, 1997). For a concise explication of this approach, see again Gaventa, "The Cosmic Power of Sin"; Green, "'Adam, What Have You Done?'" 74–75.

38. On "anti-God powers," see Martyn, *Galatians*, 370–73.

39. Gaventa, "The Cosmic Power of Sin," 235, emphasis in the original.

she goes on, "Sin cannot be avoided or passed over, it can only either be served or defeated."[40]

One can see the advantages and disadvantages in both of these main interpretations of sin. The metaphorical interpretation of the language safeguards human accountability. On the other hand, this account might fail to take the gravity of the problem that sin poses for the human race seriously enough. The Sin-as-power interpretation, by contrast, recognizes the gravity of the situation but runs the risk of minimizing human responsibility.

More recently, the theologian Paul Allen offered a helpful analogy that can account for the aspects of both slavery and responsibility.[41] Analyzing Romans from the angle of evolutionary psychology, Allen suggests that the condition of sin might be compared to addiction. Addiction can compromise free will, but it does not do away with it altogether. Nevertheless, addicts frequently experience their condition as a kind of slavery. And, like the condition of sin, addiction begins as the result of an act freely committed, whether it be the free act of the addict themselves or the act of a progenitor.[42]

This serves as a natural transition to the question of the relationship between acts of sin and the condition of sin in Romans, in which we see a similar dynamic. In both the opening chapter of Romans and in Romans 5:12–21, an act (or acts) of sin precedes the condition of sin. In Romans 1, the refusal to give God glory and thanks (Rom 1:21) results in the condition of slavery to the (disordered) desires of the heart (Rom 1:24–32).[43] The same is true of Romans 5:12–21, to which we now turn.

---

40. Gaventa, "The Cosmic Power of Sin," 235.

41. Paul Allen, "Evolutionary Psychology and Romans 5–7: The 'Slavery to Sin' in Human Nature," *Ex Auditu* 32 (2016): 50–64.

42. Allen, "Evolutionary Psychology and Romans 5–7," 61–63. See also Daniel D. De Haan, "Thomistic Hylomorphism, Self-Determination, Neuroplasticity, and Grace: The Case of Addiction," *Proceedings of the American Catholic Philosophical Association* 85 (2012): 99–120. Although Allen does not make this point, addiction has another helpful analogy with original sin. Often—and sadly—babies born to mothers with a drug addiction inherit that addiction themselves. They do so through no fault of their own, yet they must suffer the consequences of their mother's actions. Byrne (*Romans*, 175) offers another helpful image: "In personifying sin, Paul in no way wishes to suggest that human beings become helpless tools of a power somehow separate from themselves. Sin for Paul represents a kind of deadly virus in human life, a fundamental revolt against the Creator that places self and the perceived needs of self in the position that should only be occupied by the sovereignty of God." Again, for an account of s/Sin in Romans that draws on the notions of emergence and emergent properties, see Croasmun, *The Emergence of Sin*, esp. 102–39.

43. Gaventa ("The Cosmic Power of Sin," 233) rightly recognizes this: "The beginning point of this grand depiction of Sin is certainly humanity's willful choice to deny God, even to create its own gods. Paul's depiction of humankind opens with an action taken by humanity itself rather than by another power."

4. Sin, Death, and Life

As many have rightly noted, the primary theme of Romans 5:12–21 is not some theory about the introduction of sin into the world, but rather the abundant gift of salvation brought about by Christ's act of obedience.[44] While this is no doubt true, the passage nevertheless interprets Christ's act of redemption in light of the condition from which he redeems human beings. Two questions in particular merit our consideration. First, how are we to understand the consequences of Adam's transgression vis-à-vis the human race? Second, to what kind of death does Paul refer when he speaks of death as the punishment for sin?

With respect to the first question, the history of interpretation on both sides has focused too much on Romans 5:12, especially the translation of the last phrase of the verse into Latin. Before considering this verse, it is worth focusing on the bigger picture of the passage. In contrasting the effects of Adam's transgression and Christ's act of righteousness and obedience, Paul repeatedly emphasizes the effects of Adam's act on his descendants. In Romans 5:15b he writes, "For if by the transgression of the one the many died, much more will the grace of God and the gift by the grace of the one human being Jesus Christ abound to the many." We will return to the question of what Paul means by "died" here. The important point for now is that Adam's transgression affected his descendants. We see the same thing a few verses later: "For if by the transgression of the one death reigned through the one, much more will those who have received the abundance of grace and of the gift of righteousness reign in life through the one Jesus Christ" (Rom 5:17). Once again, Adam's offense brings about death. Paul continues this contrast with different language in the subsequent two verses: "So then as the transgression of the one [Adam] led to condemnation for all human beings, so also the righteous act of the one [Christ] led to the justification of life for all human beings. For just as through the disobedience of the one human being the many were constituted sinners, so also through the obedience of the one the many were constituted righteous" (Rom 5:18–19). Here Paul shifts to language of condemnation and sin (rather than death), but the basic structure remains the same: Adam's offense had consequences for all his descendants, and so likewise Christ's act of obedience had consequences for all those who receive his grace.

---

44. Karl Kertelge, "The Sin of Adam in Light of Christ's Redemptive Act according to Romans 5:12–21," *Communio* 18, no. 4 (1991): 505–6; Douglas J. Moo, "'The Type of the One to Come': Adam in Paul's Theology," *Trinity Journal* 40 (2019): 151; Thomas R. Schreiner, "Original Sin and Original Death: Romans 5:12–19," in *Adam, the Fall, and Original Sin: Theological, Biblical, and Scientific Perspectives*, ed. Hans Madueme and Michael Reeves (Grand Rapids, MI: Baker Academic, 2014), 271.

Paul's emphasis on death—which begins in Romans 5:12—once again raises the question of what kind of death serves as the punishment for sin. Our earlier survey of the language and imagery of death in Romans 5–8 turned up at least four different ways of interpreting the term in this section of the letter: biological death, spiritual death in a positive sense, spiritual death in a negative sense, and eternal death. Several factors suggest that the primary meaning of the word in Romans 5:12–21 is spiritual death in a negative sense.

Consider the connection between sin and death in Romans 7 and the early verses of Romans 8. As noted above, when Paul says that sin "killed me through [the commandment]" (Rom 7:11b), he cannot mean the cessation of biological life, because he describes the ongoing effects of sin in the experience of the first-person speaker. For the same reason, he cannot be referring to the ultimate punishment for unrepented sin either. The context clearly rules out the positive connotation of spiritual death, which leaves the negative sense of spiritual death. This is, in fact, what Paul goes on to describe throughout the rest of the chapter. Moreover, in the following chapter, Paul equates the "mind of the flesh [τὸ φρόνημα τῆς σαρκός]"—which is closely allied with sin (Rom 7:14: "For we know that the law is spiritual, but I am carnal [σάρκινος], sold under sin")—with hostility toward God (Rom 8:7), a hostility that is also equivalent to death (Rom 8:6).[45]

In addition to the connection between sin and spiritual death, it is worth noting again the different ways that Paul lays out the parallels between Adam and Christ. Here, a chart may be helpful.

By the transgression of one, the many died (Rom 5:15a)	The grace of God . . . will abound for the many (Rom 5:15b)
Death reigned (Rom 5:17a)	Those who received . . . the abundance of grace . . . will reign in life (Rom 5:17b)
The transgression of one leads to condemnation (Rom 5:18a)	The righteous act of one leads to the justification of life (Rom 5:18b)
Many were constituted sinners (Rom 5:19a)	Many were constituted righteous (Rom 5:19b)

Paul speaks twice of death (in different ways), then once of condemnation, and finally once of the sinfulness of Adam's descendants. While it would be

---

45. In his commentary on Romans, Aquinas sees the death of Romans 5:14 as referring both to spiritual death and to bodily death, with the latter serving as a sign of the presence of sin. See *In Rom.* c. 5 lect. 4 (424–25).

unwise to suggest that all four of these terms are identical, there seems to be a close relationship between them.

The closing verse of the passage also seems to support such a reading. Paul writes, "So that just as sin reigned in death, so also grace would reign through righteousness unto eternal life through Jesus Christ our Lord" (Rom 5:21). The contrast between sin and grace is significant: sin reigns in death, whereas grace reigns through righteousness. In the following chapter, Paul speaks again of the reign of sin in "mortal bodies"—a reign manifested in obedience to the desires of the body (Rom 6:12). Again and again, the primary sphere in which sin and death cooperate is in the present life of the believer. This is not to say that sin will not result in an ultimate death (see Rom 8:13) or that there is no connection between the spiritual death of sin and physical death (a connection seen more clearly in 1 Corinthians 15 than in Romans). Nevertheless, in the context of Romans 5, the death Paul has in mind seems to be spiritual death—that is, alienation from God.[46]

What, then, are we to make of Romans 5:12, the verse on which so much of the debate regarding original sin has focused? Most modern interpreters agree that Augustine relied on a mistranslation. The Greek phrase ἐφ' ᾧ simply does not mean "in whom" or "in which," as Augustine's Latin translation rendered it. Beyond this almost universally acknowledged point, however, there is no consensus on how to render the phrase, although the most common interpretation takes the phrase in a causal sense ("because all sinned").[47] As space precludes a full discussion of the question, a few brief remarks will have to suffice.

The first point to make concerns the introduction of sin and death into the world. The passage taken as a whole makes it clear that for Paul, sin entered the world as a result of Adam's transgression, and "through sin death."[48] In

---

46. This seems to be the interpretation of N. T. Wright, "The Letter to the Romans: Introduction, Commentary, and Reflections," in *The New Interpreter's Bible* (Nashville: Abingdon, 2002), 10:526; Stanley E. Porter, "The Pauline Concept of Original Sin, In Light of Rabbinic Background," *Tyndale Bulletin* 41 (1990): 28. See also Moo ("'The Type of the One to Come,'" 153): "Moreover, in vv. 16 and 18, Paul uses 'condemnation' in the same way that he uses death here. These points suggest that Paul may refer here to 'spiritual' death: the estrangement from God that is a result of sin and that, if not healed through Christ, will lead to 'eternal' death." Byrne (*Romans*, 176) argues that Paul means physical death in continuity with the account of Genesis 3. This reading, however, misconstrues both Genesis 3 and Paul. On Genesis, see Scullion, "What of Original Sin?" 25–30.

47. Some version of "because" or "for" (in a causal sense) is found in the following English translations: ASV, ESV, ISV, KJV, NASB, NIV, and every edition of the NRSV, as well as the RSV.

48. Fitzmyer (*Romans*, 417) puts it well: "The universal causality of Adam's sin is presupposed in 5:15a, 16a, 17a, 18, 19a. It would then be false to the thrust of the

light of the discussion of the relationship between sin and death throughout Romans 5–8, Romans 5:12 must mean what the rest of the verses in this passage mean: Adam's sin brought about a kind of spiritual death for the whole human race. As Romans 7 makes clear, the primary malady afflicting human beings as a result of Adam's sin is a disorder in the soul that prevents them from doing the good they want. As already noted, Paul can also describe this disorder as enmity or hostility with God (Rom 8:6–7).

Another question Romans 5:12 raises is this: Do human beings experience this death because of their own sins or because of Adam's sin? In other words, is there a dual causality behind the experience of death? This tension is particularly acute if one accepts the common translation of the phrase ἐφ' ᾧ as "because." On this reading, death seems to have two causes: Adam's introduction of sin into the world and the personal sins of each human being. Some argue that these two can be reconciled by seeing Adam's sin as the primary cause and the sins of individuals as secondary causes.[49]

But there is another way of interpreting the phrase ἐφ' ᾧ, as proposed by Joseph Fitzmyer.[50] Having canvassed a wide array of biblical and nonbiblical Greek sources, Fitzmyer argues that the phrase actually means "with the result that" or "so that." On this reading, Paul says in Romans 5:12b: "And in this way death spread to all human beings, with the result that all sinned." Fitzmyer himself still sees in this verse a dual causality behind the death of human beings, stemming from both Adam and each individual.[51] But one can take his translation a different way. What Paul is saying is not that each human being dies—even in part—because of his own sin. This would contradict what he says later in the same passage, that by Adam's transgression "the many" died (Rom 5:15a). Rather, he is saying that the death that Adam's sin introduced has resulted in the spread of sin throughout the human race. Schreiner rejects this explanation, arguing that the point of Romans 5:12–21, indeed

---

whole paragraph to interpret 5:12 as though it implied that the human condition before Christ's coming were due solely to individual personal sins." See also Juan Luis Caballero, "Rm 5,12 y el pecado original en la exégesis católica reciente," *Scripta Theologica* 46 (2014): 133.

49. Schreiner, "Original Sin and Original Death," 280. It remains unclear to me how Schreiner reconciles the suggestion that people die because of their individual sins with his statement later in the same essay (282–83) that "human beings enter the world spiritually dead (and physical death will follow in due course) because of Adam's sin. Human beings do not enter into the world in a neutral state. They are 'dead upon arrival' because of Adam's sin!" If human beings are dead upon arrival, it is hard to see how their sins contribute to their death.

50. Fitzmyer, "The Consecutive Meaning of ΕΦ' Ω."

51. Fitzmyer, *Romans*, 413.

of Romans 5–6, is that death is the consequence of sin, not the other way around.[52] As we have seen in Romans 7, however, the relationship between sin and death is more nuanced. Sin "kills" the speaker of Romans 7:11 with the result that he commits further sins; he is no longer able to do the good that he wants to do and moves to do the evil that he does not want to do (Rom 7:13ff.). For Paul, the death of the soul—that is, the alienation human beings experience as a result of Adam's sin—leads to the human proclivity to commit sins.

5. A Note on Death in 1 Corinthians 15

Romans 5 is not the only passage in Paul's writings that talks about Adam and death. In the famous resurrection chapter, 1 Corinthians 15, Paul again links Adam with death. In the course of an exposition of the way that the general resurrection follows from Christ's own resurrection, the apostle speaks of Adam as the one through whom death came: "For since death [is] through a human being [δι' ἀνθρώπου], so also the resurrection of the dead is through a human being [δι' ἀνθρώπου]" (1 Cor 15:21). The following verse explicitly names Adam and the fate that all his descendants share: "For just as in Adam all die, so also in Christ all will be made alive" (1 Cor 15:22). The context of these verses suggests that Paul is talking about biological death, which he contrasts with the bodily resurrection of Christ. These verses might seem to call into question my interpretation of Romans 5:12 as speaking of spiritual death. Two points can be made in response.

First, although the reference to death coming through Adam is compressed, nevertheless it can be reconciled with my interpretation of Romans as follows. The brief phrase δι' ἀνθρώπου θάνατος seems to imply that Adam in some way caused death.[53] But it would not make sense to speak of Adam introducing death if Paul is speaking of the natural phenomenon of corruptible bodies falling apart. One would not say of frogs that "death is through a frog" (whatever we might name the Ur-frog). The death of frogs simply is. If Paul is implying that Adam introduced death, then it must be something more than just natural death, even if the focus of the passage is on biological death. It must be something akin to the spiritual death that, as I have argued, Paul has in mind in Romans 5.

---

52. Schreiner, "Original Sin and Original Death," 274; Schreiner also cites Wright in agreement on this point. See Wright, "The Letter to the Romans," 527.
53. It is worth noting that the phrase resembles that of Romans 5:12, where Paul says that sin, and consequently death, entered the world "through one human being [δι' ἑνὸς ἀνθρώπου]."

Second, as I suggested above, in the case of humans, spiritual death is not unrelated to the cessation of biological life. As Aquinas argues, although the body is by nature corruptible because it is a composite, the gift of original justice allowed the first human beings to preserve their bodies incorruptible.[54] It was only after our first parents rebelled against God that, with the loss of original justice, the corruptibility of the body took hold. Admittedly, Aquinas's argument moves well beyond what Paul actually says in Romans 5 and 1 Corinthians 15. Nevertheless, his extrapolation helps to make sense of the data by explaining both how the first human being could be the source of death and why, especially in Romans 5, the emphasis seems to fall on spiritual death, even as that spiritual death also had biological consequences for the human race.

Conclusion: Sin and Death

The goal of this chapter has been relatively modest, focusing primarily on whether Paul's discussion of sin and death contradicts modern science. As I hope to have shown, on at least two points, there is no inherent conflict between Paul's account and that of modern science. First, when Paul writes that death entered the world through the sin of Adam, he does not mean the death of plants and animals in general. He is concerned with the redeeming act of Christ as the remedy for the condition that Adam introduced into the human race, not with explaining why plants and animals have a limited lifespan. Second, because the reality he speaks of is a spiritual one—that of alienation between human beings and God—it can be neither proven nor disproven by science and therefore cannot contradict any scientific account of human origins. Needless to say, many questions beyond the scope of this chapter remain to be resolved. How, for example, does one reconcile Paul's focus on one individual with modern accounts of human origins? How (and why) is the disorder that Paul describes passed on? These are questions for further research and debate. On the narrower question of whether the billions of years of life and death on this planet require a radical break with the tradition stemming from Paul and Augustine, however, the answer is unequivocally "No."

---

54. *In Rom.* c. 5, lect. 3 (416). It is worth noting that in 1 Corinthians 15:47 Paul writes, "The first human being was from the earth, made of dust [ἐκ γῆς χοϊκός]." For a helpful discussion of the possible connection between this earthy nature and death, see Ernest C. Lucas et al., "The Bible, Science, and Human Origins," *Science and Christian Belief* 28 (2016): 74–99.

CHAPTER TEN

Defending a Historical Adam and Eve after Darwin

NICANOR PIER GIORGIO AUSTRIACO, OP

For many contemporary Christian theologians, both Catholic and Protestant, Adam and Eve have ceased to be historical figures. In his book, *Christianity in Evolution: An Exploration*, Jesuit theologian Jack Mahoney, SJ, proposes that the truths of evolutionary biology have made the Catholic Church's traditional teachings on human origins obsolete: "I argue that with the acceptance of the evolutionary origin of humanity there is no longer a need or a place in Christian beliefs for the traditional doctrines of original sin, the Fall, and human concupiscence resulting from that sin."[1] Evangelical scholars, too, have been engaged in an ongoing dispute regarding the historicity of Adam and Eve.[2] When he was asked whether or not all humans descended from Adam and Eve, Dennis Venema, a professor of biology at Trinity Western University, responded: "That would be against all the genomic evidence that we've assembled over the last 20 years, so not likely at all."[3]

In contrast, the *Catechism of the Catholic Church* appears to accept as a given the historicity of our first parents. The *Catechism* teaches that their fall is a historical event that is described in the opening pages of the Bible using figurative language:

> The account of the fall in Genesis 3 uses figurative language, but affirms a primeval event, a deed that took place at the beginning of the history

---

1. Jack Mahoney, *Christianity in Evolution: An Exploration* (Washington, DC: Georgetown University Press, 2011), 71.
2. For details, see R. Albert Mohler, Jr., "False Start? The Controversy Over Adam and Eve Heats Up," Albert Mohler, August 22, 2011, https://albertmohler.com/2011/08/22/false-start-the-controversy-over-adam-and-eve-heats-up. See also, Hans Madueme, "Adam and Eve: An Evangelical Impasse?" *Christian Scholar's Review* 45, no. 2 (2016): 165–83.
3. Barbara Bradley Hagerty, "Evangelicals Question the Existence of Adam And Eve," National Public Radio, August 9, 2011, https://www.npr.org/2011/08/09/138957812/evangelicals-question-the-existence-of-adam-and-eve.

of man. Revelation gives us the certainty of faith that the whole of human history is marked by the original fault freely committed by our first parents.[4]

Elsewhere, this magisterial text discusses the Church's teaching on original sin, again in the context of a historical Adam:

> Following St. Paul, the Church has always taught that the overwhelming misery which oppresses men and their inclination towards evil and death cannot be understood apart from their connection with Adam's sin and the fact that he has transmitted to us a sin with which we are all born afflicted, a sin which is the "death of the soul."[5]

How do we reconcile these theological and historical claims of the *Catechism* with the findings of evolutionary science? Can they be reconciled?[6]

Over the past several years, I have published a handful of essays that have defended the historicity of Adam in light of the most recent discoveries of contemporary evolutionary biology.[7] In this chapter, I synthesize the insights laid out in these essays into a single account. I also address a significant objection raised against my account, and then explore the fittingness of a historical Eve. I begin with a brief scientific narrative of the origins of our biological species, *Homo sapiens*, as biologists understand it today. To weave a theological narrative of our origins, I then make a crucial distinction between our biological species and our natural kind by proposing that the first member of our natural kind was the first member of the biological species, *Homo sapiens*, who had the capacity for language. This human being—to whom divine revelation gives the name Adam—was the first rational animal. All of us are descended from this individual because all of us are born with the capacity for language, which we have inherited from him. Finally, I turn to Eve and propose that a fittingness

---

4. *Catechism of the Catholic Church*, 390.
5. *Catechism of the Catholic Church*, 403.
6. There have been Catholic critics who have opined that it is regrettable that the *Catechism* continues "to treat the Genesis accounts in a Tridentine fundamentalist light." See Joan Acker, "Creationism and the Catechism," *America Magazine*, December 16, 2000, https://www.americamagazine.org/issue/392/article/creationism-and-catechism.
7. See the following essays: Nicanor Pier Giorgio Austriaco, "Defending Darwin After Darwin: On the Origins of *Sapiens* as a Natural Kind," *American Catholic Philosophical Quarterly* 92, no. 2 (2018): 337–52; "Thomistic Thoughts About Thought and Talk," *American Catholic Philosophical Quarterly* 95, no. 1 (2021): 117–29; and "On the Limits of Abstraction: A Response to Professor Marie George," *American Catholic Philosophical Quarterly* 95, no. 1 (2021): 145–48. The current chapter is heavily indebted to these previous publications.

argument can be made for her existence. She is the mate of the first speaking primate; she was able to speak and therefore was able to know and love God.

1. Defending Adam After Darwin

A scientific narrative for *Homo sapiens* would go something like this.[8] Around two hundred thousand years ago, anatomically modern humans—defined by a light-built skeleton, large brain, reduced face, and prominent chin—first evolved in East Africa from a more ancient African hominin population.[9] Significantly, the ancestral population of humans never shrank below a number of approximately ten thousand individuals.[10] These modern humans eventually spread first across Africa, and then out of Africa and into Eurasia around eighty thousand to sixty thousand years ago, replacing Neanderthals in Europe and western Asia as well as other more ancient human-like species (i.e., archaic humans) in eastern Asia and Oceania. This replacement was accompanied by interbreeding among these human-like species such that all non-African populations today inherited roughly 2 percent of their genomes from their Neanderthal ancestors, and all Melanesians today inherited between 3 and 5 percent of their genome from another extinct species of archaic humans called Denisovans. Clearly, our history as a biological species is shaped by migration, interbreeding, and unrelenting adaptation that has generated much diversity within the human population.

How can we reconcile this scientific narrative with the claim in the *Catechism* quoted earlier that "the whole of human history is marked by the original fault freely committed by our first parents"? Most importantly, in my view, we need to make the distinction between our biological species, *Homo sapiens*, and our natural kind, which I will call *Sapiens*.

For the most part, contemporary anthropologists define *Homo sapiens* using a historical analysis of archaeological data that begins in the past and

---

8. For a recent and comprehensive review, see Anders Bergström, Chris Stringer, Mateja Hajdinjak, Eleanor M. L. Scerri, and Pontus Skoglund, "Origins of Modern Human Ancestry," *Nature* 590 (2021): 229–37.

9. For citations to the scientific literature for the narrative given here, see the following reviews: Bastien Llamas et al., "Human Evolution: A Tale from Ancient Genomes," *Philosophical Transactions of the Royal Society B: Biological Sciences* 372 (2017): 20150484; Christ Stringer, "The Origin and Evolution of *Homo sapiens*," *Philosophical Transactions of the Royal Society B: Biological Sciences* 371 (2016): 20150237; and Marta Mirazon Lahr, "The Shaping of Human Diversity: Filters, Boundaries and Transitions," *Philosophical Transactions of the Royal Society B: Biological Sciences* 371 (2016): 20150241.

10. H. L. Kim et al., "Divergence, Demography, and Gene Loss Along the Human Lineage," *Philosophical Transactions of the Royal Society B: Biological Sciences* 365, no. 1552 (2010): 2451–57.

moves forward to the present. By examining the fossil record, they have identified a set of anatomical characteristics, especially a light-built skeleton, large brain, reduced face, and prominent chin, which uniquely sets us apart from our hominin ancestors.[11] Presumably, these anatomical characteristics are linked to a still unknown set of genetic traits that specify our anatomical form. Presumably, these individuals would also be able to interbreed to generate viable progeny. This is an account of who we are as a biological species.

In contrast to this archeological approach, I contend that it is also reasonable to characterize human beings by beginning in the present and moving backward into the past since we know more about ourselves than our now-extinct ancestors. Notably, contemporary anthropologists acknowledge that the *Homo sapiens* living today—that is, us—are anatomically modern humans that have an additional suite of behavioral and cognitive traits that sets us apart from our recent human ancestors, also members of *Homo sapiens*, who lived about one hundred thousand years ago. These traits have been linked to symbolic behavior, and their revolutionary emergence in recent human history has been called the great leap forward.[12] This suggests that there are actually two populations of individuals in the biological species *Homo sapiens*—those who did not think symbolically, and those that do. Thus, if we were able to identify a single biological trait that is shared by all extant human beings today that would distinguish us from these nonsymbolic human ancestors and from all the other animals around us, then we would be able to specify ourselves as a distinct population of living things. This would be an account of who we are as a natural kind.

Can we identify such a distinguishing characteristic? I propose that human beings can be specified by our capacity for language. This language faculty meets the three criteria one would expect for a specific difference that would define our natural kind.

First, the capacity for language is rooted in our biology.[13] As Robert Berwick and Noam Chomsky, two of the world's foremost linguists, explain: "From the biolinguistic perspective, we can think of language as, in essence,

11. For references, see note 9.
12. Ian Tattersall, "The Great Leap Forward," *Weber: The Contemporary West* 28 (2011): 40–47. Also see Tattersall, "Human Evolution and Cognition," *Theory in Biosciences* 129 (2010): 193–201. For an opposing minority perspective, see Sally McBrearty and Alison S. Brooks, "The Revolution That Wasn't: A New Interpretation of the Origin of Modern Human Behavior," *Journal of Human Evolution* 39 (2000): 453–563.
13. For recent discussion, see Koji Fujita and Cedric Boeckx, *Advances in Biolinguistics: The Human Language Faculty and its Biological Basis* (Oxford: Routledge, 2016).

an 'organ of the body,' more or less on a par with the visual or digestive immune systems. . . . In this case, it is a cognitive organ."[14] Supporting evidence for the claim that there is an innate biological faculty of language includes the "instinctive" ability of infants to learn the complex rules of their native language(s), and the shared architectural principles and parameters that structure the world's seven thousand or so languages.[15] It is striking that newborn babies already know something of the language of their mother on the day of their birth, where the newborns of English-speaking mothers can distinguish the melodic structure of English from that of French, and vice versa.[16] Note that this biological basis for the human capacity for language clearly does not rule out environmental effects, since the specific language(s) an infant learns as his native tongue, whether it is English or French or Filipino, is determined not by his nature but by his nurture.

Second, the capacity for language, understood correctly, is unique to our kind. Other animals have vocalizations, but human beings uniquely have language. As Berwick and Chomsky put it: "We are therefore concerned with a curious biological object, *language*, which appeared on earth quite recently. It is a species property of humans, a common endowment with no significant variation apart from serious pathology, unlike anything else known in the organic world in its essentials, and surely central to human life since its emergence."[17] In support of this claim, they present evidence demonstrating that human language is radically different from other forms of animal communication because it has three distinctive properties: (1) human language syntax is hierarchical, and is blind to considerations of linear order, with linear ordering constraints reserved for externalization; (2) the particular hierarchical structures associated with

---

14. Robert C. Berwick and Noam Chomsky, *Why Only Us: Language and Evolution* (Cambridge: MIT Press, 2016), 56. For a recent response to their critics, see Robert Berwick and Noam Chomsky, "The Siege of Paris," *Inference* 4, no. 3 (March 1, 2019), https://doi.org/10.37282/991819.19.1.

15. For discussion, see John H. McWhorter, *The Power of Babel: A Natural History of Language* (New York: Harper Collins, 2001); and Mark C. Baker, *The Atoms of Language* (New York: Basic Books, 2001). Recently, Tom Wolfe has challenged the claim that there is an innate capacity for language. Instead, he proposes that language is not a result of evolution but essentially a memory aid, a mnemonic, to store away information. I did not find his arguments persuasive because they simply do not explain how infants learn these mnemonics without explicit instruction and why the diversity of human languages is restricted to a few structural variants. See Tom Wolfe, *The Kingdom of Speech* (New York: Little, Brown, and Company, 2016).

16. Jacques Mehler et al., "A Precursor of Language Acquisition in Young Infants," *Cognition* 29, no. 2 (1988): 143–78.

17. Berwick and Chomsky, *Why Only Us*, 55.

sentences affects their interpretation; and (3) there is no upper bound on the depth of relevant hierarchical structure.[18]

To illustrate these distinctive properties of human language, consider the sentence: "Matt is too angry to eat." Because of the hierarchical structure of human language, this sentence actually has two meanings. First, it could mean that Matt is so angry that he cannot eat. This would be the favored reading. However, it could also mean that Matt is too angry and therefore I cannot eat him. (Compare this meaning to that of the sentence, "The soup is too hot to eat.") Both of these meanings are possible only because human language does not simply use a left-to-right ordering of words. Berwick and Chomsky explain this hierarchical structure of human language by positing the existence of a basic linguistic operation that they call "Merge." Merge is the operation that takes the units *the* and *phone* to form {*the, phone*}. Further operations of Merge can lead to more complex linguistic structures like {*answer*, {*the, phone*}} and so on. According to Berwick and Chomsky, Merge is necessary and sufficient to yield the grammatical structure for all human languages.

In contrast, nonhuman primate vocalizations and all other known animal communication systems are restricted to linear sequencing of sounds to convey meaning. For example, apes can recognize a series of sounds such as "eat ... banana ... outside." However, their capacity for vocal communication is limited because it becomes increasingly difficult for them to keep track of longer and longer linear strings of sounds and they do not acquire the capacity to combine and manipulate these sounds.[19]

Though it is difficult to empirically prove at this time, it is also noteworthy that Ian Tattersall, a distinguished anthropologist, has proposed that the human capacity for language is what distinguishes behaviorally modern humans from their anatomically modern ancestors.[20] For Tattersall and his collaborators, the evolution of the language capacity would explain the recent revolutionary appearance of culture (i.e., the great leap forward), which occurred in the past one hundred thousand years. In a review of Berwick and Chomsky's book, *Why Only Us*, Tattersall writes: "The clear implication [of the archaeological evidence that shows an abrupt appearance of symbolic behavior] is that something had abruptly changed the way in which humans

---

18. Berwick and Chomsky, *Why Only Us*, 8.

19. As one example, Charles Yang has shown that a chimp named Nim who was trained from birth on American Sign Language simply memorized two- and three-sound combinations and was not able to exercise the combinatorial capacity that is the hallmark of human language. See Charles Yang, "Ontogeny and Phylogeny of Language," *Proceedings of the National Academy of Sciences (USA)* 110, no. 16 (2013): 6324–27.

20. Ian Tattersall, "An Evolutionary Context for the Emergence of Language," *Language Sciences* 46B (2014): 199–206.

handled information. . . . Most plausibly, that stimulus was the spontaneous invention of language."[21]

Third, the capacity for language is intimately linked, in my view, with our rational capacity for abstract thought, which Aristotle and Aquinas had identified as the specific difference of our species. Recently, Berwick and Chomsky have proposed controversially (but convincingly, in my opinion) that language evolved not for communication but for thought.[22] Their supporting evidence for the claim that language evolved for thought rather than explicitly for speech includes the hierarchical and nonlinear structure of human language, the similarities between spoken and signed languages both in their structures and in how they are acquired, and the recent discoveries of genetic mutations that appear to specifically affect only the externalization process of human language. After listing several intriguing design properties of human language, they conclude: "These facts at once suggest that language evolved as an instrument of internal thought, with externalization as a secondary process."[23] To me, this suggests that we are rational animals because we are speaking primates.

But why language? One could object that there is no reason to believe that language should uniquely serve as a benchmark for abstract thought, and as such, as the specific difference for that which makes us rational animals. In fact, there have been many counterproposals for proxies for the appearance of human cognition in the archaeological record, including the controlled use of fire, the crafting of jewelry, and the invention of specific tool-types.[24]

In response (and as I have argued elsewhere), I believe that the capacity for language is inextricably linked with the capacity for abstract thought.[25] As

---

21. Ian Tattersall, "At the Birth of Language," *The New York Review*, August 18, 2016, https://www.nybooks.com/articles/2016/08/18/noam-chomsky-robert-berwick-birth-of-language.

22. For a counterproposal that human language evolved primarily for a social function, especially for communication, rather than for an individual function, see Szabolcs Számadó and Eörs Szathmáry, "Selective Scenarios for the Emergence of Natural Language," *Trends in Ecology and Evolution* 21, no. 10 (2006): 555–61.

23. Számadó and Szathmáry, "Selective Scenarios," 74.

24. For examples of these counterproposals, see April Nowell and Iain Davidson, eds., *Stone Tools and the Evolution of Human Cognition* (Boulder: University of Colorado Press, 2010); Marlize Lombard and Miriam Noël Haidle, "Thinking a Bow-and-Arrow Set: Cognitive Implications of Middle Stone Age Bow and Stone-Tipped Arrow Technology," *Cambridge Archaeological Journal* 22 (2012): 237–64; and C. M. Duarte, "Red Ochre and Shells: Clues to Human Evolution," *Trends in Ecology and Evolution* 29 (2014): 560–65. See also Frederick L. Coolidge and Karenleigh A. Overmann, "Numerosity, Abstraction, and the Emergence of Symbolic Thinking," *Current Anthropology* 53 (2012): 204–25.

25. For discussion, see my "Thomistic Thoughts About Thought and Talk," *American Catholic Philosophical Quarterly* 95, no.1 (2021): 117–29; and "On the Limits of

such, the appearance of the latter could not have predated the appearance of the former. Briefly, I have proposed that to perfectly actualize his agent intellect to form and to perfect an abstract concept, the rational creature needs to speak with himself, not only to distinguish the essential qualities of an object of the intellect from those that are accidental to it, but also to label and sort the numerous universals that are instantiated in every intelligible species. Thus, the formation and perfection of an abstract concept presupposes language. I have also argued that the speaking primate needs to abstract and distinguish the many meanings that can be instantiated in a single sentence in order to converse with himself and with others. Therefore, language presupposes abstraction. Both capacities of the soul are inextricably linked with each other.

How did this shift from vocal communication to language occur? I have proposed that because brute animals already use vocal sounds to enhance their survival, words could have easily replaced vocal sounds once the capacity for language and the capacity for abstraction appeared in evolutionary history with the infusion of the first rational soul.

Though we cannot know the cognitive capacities of our immediate prelinguistic hominin ancestors, I think that it is reasonable to believe that they would have had some vocal communication system that linked phantasms to vocal sounds. For example, Vervet monkeys use different alarm calls for different predators.[26] Recordings of the alarms played back when predators were absent caused the monkeys to run into trees (for leopard alarms), look up (for eagle alarms), and look down (for snake alarms). Our prelinguistic hominin ancestors probably had a similar system of vocal communication. In the same way that vocal sounds enhance survival, words would have done the same.

I therefore believe that it is reasonable to think that the emergence of a rational creature endowed simultaneously with both the capacity for abstraction and the capacity for language could transform a vocal communication system into a language. Here, the phantasms would be replaced with concepts, and the vocal sounds would be replaced with words. In fact, the vocal sounds would have become words in that the same particular sounds that were once linked to particular phantasms would now be able to signify the concepts abstracted from those same phantasms.

In sum, for these three reasons, I propose that the human language faculty defines extant human beings as a natural kind, the natural kind I will call

---

Abstraction: A Response to Professor Marie George," *American Catholic Philosophical Quarterly* 95, no.1 (2021): 145–48.

26. R. M. Seyfarth, D. L. Cheney, and P. Marler, "Monkey Responses to Three Different Alarm Calls: Evidence of Predator Classification and Semantic Communication," *Science* 210, no. 4471 (1980): 801–3.

Sapiens, within the population of individuals that evolutionary biologists have called the biological species *Homo sapiens*.

Finally, I propose that if human beings are specified as a natural kind by our capacity for language, then the origins of our natural kind should be linked to the evolutionary appearance of this linguistic capacity. Though much work remains to uncover the mystery of language evolution—and I want to emphasize that there are many other plausible models for how this could have occurred—it is still intriguing that Chomsky has proposed that this capacity arose in a *single* human individual, who was living among our ancestral population of anatomically modern humans in East Africa:

> It looks as if—given the time involved—there was a sudden "great leap forward." Some small genetic modification somehow that rewired the brain slightly [and] made this human capacity [for language] available. . . . Mutations take place in a person, not in a group. We know, incidentally, that this was a very small breeding group—some little group of hominids in some corner of Africa, apparently. Somewhere in that group, some small mutation took place, leading to the great leap forward. It had to have happened in a single person.[27]

This mutation in the single individual could have altered the wiring structure to link language-related areas of the brain that are connected in human beings but remain isolated in chimpanzees and other nonhuman primates.[28] This would be a language-enabled brain capable of Merge that would have allowed the speaking primate to speak to himself.

Though Chomsky's model remains only one of many plausible accounts for how specific changes in the genome and in the brain could lead to the appearance of human language, I think that it highlights one significant point that is relevant for the Christian theologian considering the origins of human beings as a natural kind. Given the species-universality of human language, the striking architectural similarities among human languages, and the recent provenance of human language, it is very likely that the capacity for human language appeared only *once* in evolutionary history. There simply is not enough historical time in the past one hundred thousand years for us to posit

---

27. For discussion of the plausible models of language evolution, compare Johan J. Bolhuis, Ian Tattersall, Noam Chomsky et al., "How Could Language Have Evolved?" *PLoS Biology* 12 (2014): e1001934; and Marc D. Hauser, Charles Yang, Robert C. Berwick et al., "The Mystery of Language Evolution," *Frontiers in Psychology* 5 (2014): 401. Noam Chomsky, *The Science of Language: Interviews with James McGilvray* (Cambridge: Cambridge University Press, 2012), 12.

28. Berwick and Chomsky, *Why Only Us*, 157–64.

two independent events that gave rise to a linguistic capacity so shared among all extant human beings that we can expect newborns from Timbuktu, Mali, to easily learn American English in Darien, Connecticut. This makes it more likely than not that the biological change that heralded the appearance of human language—defined by Berwick and Chomsky as the appearance of Merge—occurred in only one historical individual. This is the nature of biological mutation.

Therefore, regardless of the precise evolutionary and biological process that actually occurred, I claim that it is still reasonable to trace the origin of our kind to an original individual. He would have been the first anatomically modern human to have evolved this capacity for hierarchical and nonlinear language that allowed him to think abstractly and to thus construct an internal map of his world. He would have been the first individual person belonging to *Sapiens* as a natural kind, living among a population of nonlinguistic individuals belonging to *Homo sapiens*, the biological species. Since we are all born with the capacity for language, all of us are descended from him because each of us has inherited from him the genetic change that produces a language-enabled brain. Divine revelation has named this first speaking primate, this first rational animal—Adam.

2. Responding to a Significant Objection

There has been one significant objection raised against the account that we are descended from an original speaking primate. It is the objection foisted against Berwick and Chomsky's single mutation hypothesis by Martins and Boeckx, who argue that Merge could have evolved in several steps.[29] Recall that Merge is the operation that takes the units *the* and *phone* to form {*the, phone*}. Further operations of Merge can lead to more complex linguistic structures like {*answer*, {*the, phone*}} and so on. According to Berwick and Chomsky, Merge is necessary and sufficient to yield the grammatical structures for all human languages. Prior to Merge, there would have been no human language. After Merge, every human language became a possibility.

In their paper, Martins and Boeckx proposed both that Merge could have evolved in a stepwise fashion involving subroutines called "Internal Merge" and "External Merge," and that computer modeling of evolving hominin populations favors an account where language gradually appeared in a population. Thus, in their view, there would be no one single individual who was first able to speak. There were numerous individuals with Internal Merge, and others

---

29. Pedro Tiago Martins and Cedric Boeckx, "Language Evolution and Complexity Considerations: The No Half-Merge Fallacy," *PLoS Biology* 17, no. 11 (2019): e3000389.

with External Merge. As Berwick and Chomsky retort, however, even a series of mutations requires a final mutation that triggers the development of a language-enabled brain that has the combinatorial properties that come with the capacity for language.[30] This final mutation would be the mutation that brings Internal Merge and External Merge together in a single individual for the first time. It would have transformed a vocal communication system into a language. This would be the mutation that makes the speaking primate. Thus, even a stepwise account for the evolution of language does not preclude a historical Adam.

3. Defending the Fittingness of a Historical Eve

As we discussed above, there are robust scientific reasons to think that the capacity for language emerged in a single historical individual. However, science cannot specify whether that original individual was male or female. I have proposed that this first speaking primate was male only because divine revelation gives him a name—Adam. But what about Eve? Was there a historical Eve? There are two possible scenarios to account for the spread of language among the ancestral human population. These two scenarios cannot be resolved by contemporary scientific analysis; however, I will propose that the second of the two narratives is more fitting. As Joseph Wawrykow observes, for Aquinas, arguing from fittingness involves understanding why an end is attained better and more conveniently with the choice of a particular means rather than another.[31]

In the first scenario, there would have been no historical Eve. Rather, the first speaking primate, Adam, mated with a nonspeaking female *Homo sapiens*, who would not have been a rational creature. Recall that both Adam and his mate would have belonged to the same biological species even though they would have differed in philosophical kind. As such they could have mated, and their offspring would have also belonged to the biological species *Homo sapiens*. Some of the offspring would have been speaking primates—they

---

30. Robert C. Berwick and Noam Chomsky, "All or Nothing: No Half-Merge and the Evolution of Syntax," *PLoS Biology* 17, no. 11 (2019): e3000539.

31. Joseph Wawrykow, *The Westminster Handbook to Thomas Aquinas* (Louisville: Westminster John Knox Press, 2005), 58. In his magisterial examination of theological fittingness and beauty, the Dominican scholar Gilbert Narcisse describes fittingness arguments this way: "Theological fittingness displays the significance of the chosen means among the alternative possibilities, and the best reasons for which God in his wisdom effectively realized and revealed, freely and through his love, the mystery of salvation and the glorification of mankind." See Gilbert Narcisse, *Les Raisons de Dieu* (Fribourg: Editions Universitaires Fribourg Suisse, 1997), 572 (my translation from the French).

would have been humans like us—while others would not have been. It is likely that the speaking offspring would have preferentially mated with each other given their shared linguistic capacities, thus giving rise to children who were also speaking primates. Over time, the speaking *Homo sapiens* would have come to dominate the population. All of us are descendants of this population of speaking primates.

In the second scenario, there would have been a historical Eve who herself was a speaking primate. I must acknowledge that, probabilistically speaking, it is very unlikely for a rare mutation like the one that gave us the capacity for Merge to arise in two distinct individuals living in the same population. It is not impossible, however. Thus, one could propose that it would have been fitting for God to cause the appearance of two contemporary speaking primates, one male and one female, who would become our first parents. It would have been fitting because this divine act would have revealed the equality and complementarity of the two sexes, both of whom are made in the image and likeness of God.

Conclusion: Modeling Our Historical Origins

To end, I want to emphasize once again that the historical narrative described above remains a theological model for the plausible origins of our kind as speaking primates. It is the fruit of an exercise of faith and reason that seeks to explain how the facts of divine revelation can be brought into conversation with the discoveries of contemporary science. By their very nature, however, theological models (like their scientific counterparts) remain provisional explanations that are open to revision in light of new discoveries and insights. For this reason, I have been told that these models are useless because truth by its very nature does not change. I disagree with this view. Theological modeling helps bring clarity to disputed questions. For instance, theological modeling of the hypostatic union during the first centuries of the Church's history helped her to clarify the nature of the incarnation. In the same way, theological modeling of our human origins can illuminate the possible ways that God could have created us through evolution.

CHAPTER ELEVEN

"You Prepared a Body for Me" (Heb 10:5)
The Eschatological End of Evolution

DARIA SPEZZANO

A common objection to the idea of human evolution by those who reject it for religious reasons is that it seems too materialistic, reducing human beings to the status of animals descended from other animals by chance and so undermining the teaching that humans are purposefully made to the image of God, capable of reaching with God's help a glorious destiny for soul and body in eternal life. On the other hand, many who accept that humans have evolved from primate ancestors assume that any divine explanation for the origin of the human species, along with any claim that this species has a particular "destiny" other than further evolution or extinction, are thereby excluded. One similarity between these two viewpoints is that by opposing natural and divine causality as mutually exclusive, they do not accept the possibility of a noncontradictory distinction between proximate natural causes and ultimate divine causes when considering both the "how" and the "why" of human evolution.[1] Theologians and scientists who seek to embrace both terms of this distinction might not only consider how God creates through evolution by the governance of natural processes and how this can be understood in light of revelation, but also why God has created anatomi-

---

1. The notion of proximate and ultimate causes is not foreign to evolutionary anthropology, of course, but is confined to the natural realm. In 1961, Ernst Mayr made this classic and much-debated distinction in his widely influential paper, "Cause and Effect in Biology," *Science* 134 (1961): 1501–6. Mayr distinguishes between the proximate causes of evolution (the "how?") studied by functional biology, and the ultimate causes (the "why?" in the sense of "how come?") that are the concerns of evolutionary biology. Ultimately, evolutionary biology seeks to explain why particular forms have developed within particular historical frameworks. At the same time, Mayr sets aside any teleological claims of "plan and design" in evolutionary processes, which would seek to answer the question "why," in the sense of "what for?" (1502, 1506). From the evolutionary record alone, such truly ultimate questions cannot be answered.

cally modern humans with our proportionately large brains as well as our unique capacity for symbolic thought with the linguistic capacity to express it, among other distinctively human characteristics. How did these evolutionary developments prepare humans to be *capax Dei* by nature, the only embodied form capable of an ultimate supernatural destiny? And can St. Thomas Aquinas, who clearly taught the immediate creation of both Adam's body and soul, shed any light on this question? This essay will argue that Thomas does offer insights that help to understand how, in God's providence, human evolution was directed toward an eschatological end, foreshadowed in the state of original justice of the first parents. In the evolution of human beings, God prepared the human body for the infusion of a rational soul capable of grace and deification, and so with the potential for incorruptibility and the ultimate destiny of resurrection.

1. Evolution of the *imago Dei*

Pope St. John Paul II, in his 1996 "Address to the Pontifical Academy of Sciences," affirms Pope Pius XII's statement in *Humani Generis* that even if the human body has evolved from preexistent forms, human "souls are immediately created by God."[2] Therefore, John Paul II observes, while there may be physical continuity in the process of biological evolution, in the case of humans, "we find ourselves in the presence of a difference in ontological order, an ontological leap, one could say." The leap he refers to is not a physical one measurable by scientific observation, but "the moment of transition to the spiritual," which "is not the object of this kind of observation," although science can discover "a very valuable series of signs indicating what is specific to the human being."[3] In support of the pope's statement, Paul Flaman and others argue for "a gradualist approach to biological evolution" of the human body with an "ontological leap" in God's creation and infusion of the first human (spiritual) soul, a leap that would allow for genuine moral agency.[4]

---

2. Pope Pius XII, Encyclical Letter *Humani Generis* (August 12, 1950), 36.

3. Pope John Paul II, John Paul II, "Address to the Pontifical Academy of Sciences (October 22, 1996)," in *Papal Addresses to the Pontifical Academy of Sciences 1917–2002* (Vatican: Pontifical Academy of Sciences, 2003), 6. My translation. The pope continues, "But the experience of metaphysical knowledge, of self-reflection, of moral conscience, freedom, or again, of aesthetic and religious experience, falls within the competence of philosophical analysis and reflection, while theology brings out its ultimate meaning according to the Creator's plan."

4. Paul J. Flaman, "Evolution, the Origin of Human Persons, and Original Sin: Physical Continuity with an Ontological Leap," *The Heythrop Journal* 57, no. 3 (2016): 574–75, 580.

1.1. A "Well-Prepared" Body

Thomas Aquinas, of course, held the traditional position based on his reading of Genesis that both the body and soul of Adam were immediately created, with the body being formed by God out of the preexisting matter of dust but not from any preexisting body.[5] The proposal of biological gradualism with an ontological spiritual leap of rational ensoulment posits the immediate *ex nihilo* creation of the soul in the first humans, but not an immediate bodily creation; rather, a bodily change would take place through the generation of these first humans with new traits, although such traits would not necessarily have been significant enough immediately to constitute a biological difference in species (here defined as one that would constitute a barrier to interbreeding).[6] It can be argued, though, that on Thomistic principles, Adam and Eve—as the first truly human beings with rational souls—would have a new *nature* even if they were not a new biological species. Aquinas uses various definitions of "nature" in his works, but here I refer to the notion that, following Aristotle, "nature" primarily means a principle that directs the actions of a being to its determined end; a corporeal being's nature is composed of both form and matter, but its nature is determined primarily by its form as a principle of action.[7] So, Aquinas says, "the theologian considers human nature in relation to the soul, but not in relation to the body except insofar as the body has relation to the soul."[8] The infusion of a spiritual soul, making the first humans the *imago Dei* capable of being brought to eternal life, would truly be an ontological leap, a change in nature—even if within the same bio-

---

5. Thomas Aquinas, *Summa theologiae* (henceforth: *ST*) I q. 91.

6. Ernst Mayr first articulated this classic biological species concept in *Systematics and the Origin of Species* (New York: Columbia University Press, 1942). See his helpful retrospective discussion of the category of "species" in Ernst Mayr, "What Is a Species, and What Is Not?" *Philosophy of Science* 63, no. 2 (June 1996): 262–77. Travis Dumsday ("A New Argument for Intrinsic Biological Essentialism," *The Philosophical Quarterly* 62, no. 248 [July 2012]: 486–504) argues for the validity of moderate "intrinsic biological essentialism" (INBE), the currently-contested view that "biological taxa have fixed identity conditions, conditions which consist at least in part of intrinsic properties" (486), and that the occurrence of such new intrinsic properties may allow for the result of reproductive isolation and so a new taxonomic lineage (500). Before biological barriers to interbreeding were established between prehumans and the first human persons, even were there no geographical isolation, new intrinsic human properties (e.g., linguistic capacity) and the spiritual rational nature of human beings would arguably make it less likely that they would interbreed with nonrational prehumans. See note 9 below. For more discussion, see chapter 2 by Fr. Mariusz Tabaczek, OP, in this volume.

7. *Commentary on Aristotle's Physics* bk. 2, lect. 1–2.

8. *ST* I q. 75, prol.

logical species—to a nature with the new potential to be elevated by grace. As the human souls of Adam and Eve animated their suitably adapted bodies, those bodies—in comparison to those of their forebears and determined by this new form—would contribute to the composition of a new nature or principle of higher action, and so acquire an entirely new added potentiality and ultimate end.[9]

Debate continues about the proposition of biological gradualism with a leap of spiritual ensoulment, even among those who agree that God could have created human beings through an evolutionary process.[10] One question

---

9. Kenneth Kemp, in his helpful article, "Science, Theology, and Monogenesis" (*American Catholic Philosophical Quarterly* 85, no. 2 [2011]: 217–36) makes a similar claim in order to argue for the possibility of monogenesis within a larger interbreeding population. Drawing from the work of Andrew Alexander, CJ ("Human Origins and Genetics," *Clergy Review* 49 [1964]: 344–53), Kemp argues for distinction between humans as members of a biological (i.e., interbreeding), a philosophical, and a theological species. Kemp explains, "The philosophical species is the rational animal, i.e., a natural kind characterized by the capacity for conceptual thought, judgment, reasoning, and free choice," as a result of the possession of a rational soul created in each individual by God. This species is defined by its properties. On the other hand, "The theological species is . . . the collection of individuals that have an eternal destiny," because they have received in a "separate, free act of God," the offer of divine friendship (230). This species is defined by its potential destiny. Kemp's distinction between the philosophical and theological "species" separates the gift of God's offer of friendship from that of rationality, at least conceptually (230–31). My distinction between species and nature correlates more or less to Kemp's biological and theological species, but it seems clearer to me not to employ the term "species" in the latter case. By "species," I mean the group of biologically interbreeding animals with advanced but prelinguistic capacities (and so not yet fittingly disposed for rational souls). By "nature," I refer to the possession of infused rational souls by some of these beings, still within the same biological (interbreeding) species, but disposed by a linguistic adaptation to receive such souls. I argue below that all such individuals with a capacity for it would have an infused rational soul, not by any natural exigency, but by God's fitting ordination for those creatures so prepared by God's providential disposition (through evolution) of their matter. These creatures would now have fully human natures, in the sense that as new principles of operation, they would have new potential for supernatural action and destiny by the reception of grace. See also chapter 10 by Fr. Nicanor Austriaco, OP, in this volume.

10. Flaman presents a survey of recent opinions on this question that focuses on the views of Alan N. W. Porter in "Do Animals Have Souls? An Evolutionary Perspective," *The Heythrop Journal* 54, no. 4 (2013): 533–42; Denis O. Lamoureux, *Evolutionary Creation: A Christian Approach to Evolution* (Eugene, OR: Wipf & Stock, 2008); Benedict Ashley, OP, *Theologies of the Body: Humanist and Christian* (Braintree, MA: The Pope John XXIII Medical-Moral Research and Education Center, 1985, 2nd printing, 1995), 375–77; and Earl Muller, SJ, "Evolution," *New Catholic Encyclopedia*, Supplement 2009, A-I (Detroit: Gale in association with The Catholic University of America, Washington, DC, 2010), 312–23. For a wide-ranging, though substantially flawed, critical overview of the history of the Catholic Church's appraisal of theories of human evolution (with a skeptical evaluation of

at stake is how closely the ontological leap of spiritual ensoulment is correlated with some biological adaptation such that all those hominids whose bodies were "prepared" in that respect would henceforth receive the gift of a spiritual soul; another question is what adaptations that preparation would involve. Since the spiritual soul is immediately created by God, there can be no way in which it naturally emerges from or is even necessitated by some biological development in a strict sense (i.e., apart from the kind of "necessity" that is due to the ordination of divine providence).[11] However, it might be asked to what extent God's will to begin infusing spiritual souls into certain hominids at conception included a providential disposition of their matter such that they would be properly fitted to receive this new form. Looking at it from the perspective of God's loving plan to create the human race, God would fittingly cause through natural processes the evolution of a creature with the biological equipment, as it were, to support and dispose the higher operations

---

the magisterial authority of "'pro-evolutionary' ecclesiastical pronouncements," and by implication, of Catholic doctrine and evolutionary theory) see Michael Chaberek, OP, *Catholicism and Evolution: A History from Darwin to Pope Francis* (Brooklyn: Angelico Press, 2015), 307.

11. Although Thomas holds the common medieval theory of successive embryonic ensoulment, according to which a human embryo is not informed by a rational soul until it first passes through vegetative and sensitive forms, he makes a distinction between the causing of the rational soul and the prior vegetative and animal souls; the latter two exist "by the power of the semen," while the former is "introduced from without" ("Anima igitur vegetabilis, quae primo inest, cum embryo vivit vita plantae, corrumpitur, et succedit anima perfectior, quae est nutritiva et sensitiva simul, et tunc embryo vivit vita animalis; hac autem corrupta, succedit anima rationalis ab extrinseco immissa, licet praecedentes fuerint virtute seminis"). While the human body is produced by the seminal power as secondary instrumental cause under God's primary agency, the seminal power cannot produce, but disposes, for God's action in producing the human soul ("Corpus igitur hominis formatur simul et virtute Dei quasi principalis agentis et primi, et etiam virtute seminis quasi agentis secundi: sed actio Dei producit animam humanam, quam virtus seminis producere non potest, sed disponit ad eam"). *Summa contra gentiles* (*SCG*) 2.89. The underlying principle is that God alone can create the human soul, as a simple intellectual substance having God himself as its end (*SCG* 2.87). Karl Rahner examines the problem posed by the Church's teaching that the rational soul is created immediately by God, which seems to make it a miraculous supernatural event, undermining a (Thomistic) metaphysics of secondary causation that presupposes divine transcendence. Rahner's solution is to propose an understanding of creaturely operation as oriented toward self-transcendence, made possible by God, such that (in the case of parental generation, for example, by analogy with evolution), "the effect [of producing a whole human being with a rational soul] is not derivable from the essence of the creature acting and yet must be considered as effected by this agent." God, acting as the transcendent divine cause, "causes the operation of the creature which exceeds and transcends its own possibilities." Karl Rahner, *Hominisation: The Evolutionary Origin of Man as a Theological Problem* (New York: Herder and Herder, 1965), 98–101.

made possible by the infusion of a rational soul, and would also ordain to continue infusing rational souls into the descendants of these creatures in cooperation with the process of generation that passes on the human nature, as he does with every human person conceived.[12]

Even though Aquinas thought Adam was immediately created, he agrees that in creation, God fittingly gave Adam's body the best disposition for carrying out the operations of the rational soul, which is the body's proper proximate end, for the human body must be "suitably proportioned to the soul and its operations."[13] Identifying some traits that an evolutionary biologist would consider major hominid adaptations, Aquinas enumerates biological features of humans that proportion the body to intellectual operations: a refined sense of touch; more excellent interior sensitive powers than other animals (common sense, imagination, the estimative or cogitative power which collates the perception of singulars, and memory); the largest brain proportionately of all animals, providing "greater freedom of action in the interior powers required for the intellectual operations"; hands that are "becoming to the rational nature, which is capable of conceiving an infinite number of things, so as to make for itself an infinite number of instruments"; and an upright stature, so that a human "has his face erect, in order that by the senses, and chiefly by sight, which is more subtle and penetrates further into the differences of things, he may freely survey the sensible objects around him, both heavenly and earthly, so as to gather intelligible truth from all things."[14] Upright stature also

---

12. *ST* I q. 118, a. 2, ad 2 and ad 3. Thomas also states that human nature is passed on through generation in the context of discussing original sin (*ST* II–II q. 81, a. 1, ad 2). Flaman raises the objection that if the creation of the first human soul is tied too closely to a specific biological (genetic) state, then a deleterious mutation might be thought to result in loss of this gift, such that someone with, for instance, small brain capacity would be considered less human, or lacking in the dignity of personhood ("Do Animals Have Souls?" 576–77). However, from a Thomistic perspective, human nature is passed on by generation with God cooperating in the infusion of a rational soul, such that the descendants of human parents share fully in human nature regardless of any defect in operation for physical or developmental reasons; on this see, for example, *ST* I q. 100, a. 1; and Miguel Romero, "Aquinas on the *corporis infirmitas*: Broken Flesh and the Grammar of Grace," in *Disability in the Christian Tradition: A Reader*, ed. Brian Brock and John Swinton (Grand Rapids: Eerdmans, 2012), 86–123. For this reason, too, even though Thomas does not posit the immediate infusion of a rational soul, an embryo is still "human," with an internal finality that makes it develop toward a state apt for receiving the rational soul; *ST* I q. 118, a. 2. Also see *De Potentia* q. 3, a. 9; *SCG* 2.89; and Melissa Rovig Vanden Bout, "Thomas Aquinas and the Generation of the Embryo: Being Human before the Rational Soul" (PhD diss., Boston College, 2013), 180–81.

13. *ST* I q. 91, a. 3.

14. For the largest brain, see *ST* I q. 91, a. 3, ad 1; see also *ST* I q. 76, a. 5. For hands, see *ST* I q. 91, a. 3, ad 2.

allows greater freedom for the brain and hands to operate, and better allows for "speech, which is reason's proper operation."[15] Commenting on Aristotle's *Politics*, Aquinas explains elsewhere that human speech gives rise to sociality.[16]

For Aquinas, the intellectual acts of the spiritual soul (rational thought and willing) are not produced in any way from the action of the body, and yet human intellectual acts naturally depend upon the body's sensory perceptions and highly developed sensitive powers (due to a large brain, etc.) to provide the phantasms necessary for the intellectual operation of abstraction and for the active use of concepts.[17] The high quality of sensible knowledge possible through the corporeal organs of the human body is a kind of necessary material cause for intellectual knowing in this life.[18] This implies that truly human moral action also depends indirectly upon such a body well-proportioned to the soul. Indeed, Aquinas thinks that in the separated soul after death, without the body to provide phantasms, the will is immutable, fixed in its orientation at the time of death, and so no longer capable of moral action that would change its eternal destiny.[19] To the extent that human intellectual acts depend materially upon the sensitive powers arising from the body in this life, and given that the rational activity of abstract thought can only be the result of God's infusion of a rational soul and not an evolutionary development of the human body, such a body must nevertheless be properly disposed by the evolution of appropriate biological traits and capacities—a large brain, hands, bipedalism, speech—that proportion the body to the rational soul and its operations.[20]

---

15. *ST* I q. 91, a. 3, ad 3. Aquinas may be drawing this list of traits from his teacher Albert the Great's *De animalibus*, where Albert, in similar language, identifies these in various parts of the work as distinctive features of the human being as opposed to other animals. For instance, on the human mouth and tongue, see *De animalibus*, bk. 12, tr. 3, ch. 5. The best and most current edition of this text is *De animalibus*, Libri 1–12, ed. H. Stadler (Münster: Aschendorff Verlag, 1916–1920), 879–83.

16. *Commentary on the Politics* (bk. 1, ch. 1): "Nature gives speech to human beings, and speech is directed to human beings communicating with one another regarding the useful and the harmful, the just and the unjust, and the like. Therefore, since nature does nothing in vain, human beings by nature communicate with one another about these things. But communication about these things produces the household and the political community. Therefore, human beings are by nature domestic and political animals." Translation in *Thomas Aquinas: Commentary on Aristotle's* Politics, trans. Richard J. Regan (Indianapolis: Hackett Publishing Co., 2007), 17. See Aristotle, *Politics* 1.2.1253a7–18.

17. *ST* I q. 76, a. 1, ad 1 and a. 5 ad 2; q. 84, a. 7.

18. *ST* I q. 84, a. 6.

19. *SCG* 4.92–95; *De veritate* q. 24, a. 9, a. 10; *Compendium of Theology* bk. 1, chs. 174–75.

20. Kenneth Kemp provides an interesting appraisal of the perceptual complexity suitable for the infusion of rational souls by God, given different hypotheses for the evolutionary process leading up to this point. He notes, as I do, that the evolution of a being fittingly

1.2. Becoming "Sapiens"

Among these evolutionary developments, it seems there was one in particular that providentially prepared the bodies of the first humans for God's infusion of a rational soul. Aquinas's list of human characteristics (discussed above) identifies traits found not only in modern *Homo sapiens* but also in many of its hominid forebears, adaptations that distinguish them from their primate cousins in the fossil record. Early species like *Australopithecus afarensis* (3.5 mya) and *A. africanus* (some specimens dating to as recently as 2.0 mya) were at least partially bipedal, and the latter had a slightly larger cranial capacity; by the time of *H. erectus* around 1.5 mya, hominins were fully bipedal with a larger brain, human-like hands, and a distinctive tool industry. Yet it is not until about 200 kya that anatomically modern humans (*H. sapiens*) appear, and not until after 100 kya that humans (with some possible genetic contribution from their Neanderthal cousins) seem to make what the anthropologist Ian Tattersall has called a "great leap forward," exhibiting behaviors (such as artistic representation) that are related to the uniquely human capacity for symbolization. Tattersall suggests that this evolutionary leap took place around 100 kya with the emergence of human language, separating behaviorally modern *H. sapiens* from anatomically modern *H. sapiens*.[21]

Drawing from Tattersall as well as the work of the linguists Robert Berwick and Noam Chomsky, Fr. Nicanor Austriaco, OP, proposes that today all humans belong to a distinct subgroup of *H. sapiens* with the capacity for lan-

---

capable of receiving an infused rational soul in no way necessitates, in a natural sense, that God actually creates a rational soul for every such creature. Kemp, "God, Evolution, and the Body of Adam," in *Scientia et Fides* 8:2 (2020): 162–63.

21. Ian Tattersall, "The Great Leap Forward," *Weber: The Contemporary West* 28 (2011): 40–47; Michael Arbib, *How the Brain Got Language: The Mirror System Hypothesis* (New York: Oxford University Press, 2012); Agustin Fuentes, *The Creative Spark: How Imagination Made Humans Exceptional* (New York: Dutton Books, 2017); Agustin Fuentes, *Why We Believe: Evolution and the Human Way of Being* (New Haven, CT: Yale University Press, 2019). William Lane Craig has argued for an earlier appearance of fully human capacities, behavior, and language, and therefore the possibility that Adam was a member of *Homo heidelbergensis* >750 kya; see William Lane Craig, *In Quest of the Historical Adam* (Grand Rapids, MI: Eerdmans, 2021), 276–99. Kemp supports the plausibility of this hypothesis, in light of possible evidence for the rationality of Neanderthals, as well as the easier achievement of universal ancestry for all modern humans, "as Adam is moved further into the past": "Evolution, Adam, and the Catholic Church," *Logos* 26, no. 1 (Winter 2023): 36–40. Simon Gaine also favorably assesses the possibility that Neanderthals might be included in "theological humanity," and that, therefore, they might also have been redeemed by Christ: Simon Francis Gaine, OP, "Did Christ Die for Neanderthals?" *New Blackfriars* 102, no. 1058 (2020): 238.

guage as its distinguishing characteristic—the natural kind "*Sapiens*." Austriaco argues that "the capacity for language is intimately linked . . . with our rational capacity for abstract thought that Aristotle and Aquinas had identified as the specific difference of our species."[22] He points out that for Aquinas, the process of thought involves internal discourse, as in the formation of an interior word based on contemplation of the truth.[23] Austriaco proposes that human language capacity likely arose in one rare genetic event in only one individual, and was so adaptive that it quickly became established. Living within a biological population of *H. sapiens*, then, this first individual of the natural kind *Sapiens* could be the speaking and reasoning ancestor of all human beings.[24] In "classical scholastic language," Austriaco notes, this truly human person "would have been the first anatomical modern human to have evolved matter that is apt to receive a rational soul."[25]

It is important to note this last clarification; as we have seen, the incorruptible rational soul cannot be evolved *from* matter, nor (on a Thomistic account) can its acts of abstract thought and rational willing arise solely and directly from a biological operation. The human capacity for speech (due to the evolutionary development of the human brain) can dispose the body properly for the rational operation of the soul (i.e., abstraction and production of the interior word and love), can give it such a potential, but cannot be the actual principle of that operation. Rather, one could say that by evolution of the capacity for speech, God prepared the human body for the "ontological leap" of the infusion of a rational soul, which not only flowered in the "great leap forward" of human symbolic thought recorded in its archeological products, but made humans to the image of God.[26] To put it

---

22. Nicanor Pier Giorgio Austriaco, OP, "Defending Adam after Darwin: On the Origins of *Sapiens* as a Natural Kind," *American Catholic Philosophical Quarterly* 92, no. 2 (2018): 348. Austriaco refers to Robert C. Berwick and Noam Chomsky, *Why Only Us: Language and Evolution* (Cambridge, MA: MIT Press, 2016). Keith Frankish proposes a similar idea in a popular format ("Our Greatest Invention is Invention Itself," *Aeon Magazine*, June 24, 2020, https://psyche.co/ideas/our-greatest-invention-was-the-invention-of-invention-itself), which is based on the work of linguist Daniel Dor, *The Instruction of Imagination: Language as a Social Communication Technology* (London: Oxford University Press, 2015); and of Daniel Dennett, *Consciousness Explained* (London: Penguin Books, 1993).

23. Austriaco, "Defending Adam after Darwin," 349–50. Austriaco quotes Aquinas's *Commentary on John* (ch. 1, lect. 6) where Aquinas describes the process of abstraction. Aquinas himself draws from Augustine as well as Aristotle in his understanding of this process.

24. Austriaco, "Defending Adam after Darwin," 350–52.

25. Austriaco, "Defending Adam after Darwin," 351n45.

26. As noted above, the supposition here is that the evolution of linguistic capacity is a disposition in the logical not temporal sense; that is, it first happens in the same individuals

another way, the evolution of linguistic capacity in humans was the ultimate bodily disposition (in a logical sense, not a temporal one) for a nature capable of elevation by grace.

1.3. Beings of Word and Love

In his reflection on the creation account in Genesis, Pope Benedict XVI (as Cardinal Joseph Ratzinger) describes humans as "beings of word and of love, beings moving toward Another, oriented to giving themselves to the Other, and only truly receiving themselves back in real self-giving."[27] His thought, like Aquinas's, is rooted in an Augustinian understanding of the human person made to the image of God by virtue of the rational nature, capable like God of intellectual knowledge and love, and therefore able to enter into personal relationship with God and other human persons. As we have seen, Aquinas, drawing from Augustine, conceives of the *imago Dei* in linguistic terms; the rational creature is one who images the Trinity in which there is "the procession of the Word from the Speaker and the procession of Love connecting both," and this image is to be found especially "in the acts of the soul, inasmuch as from the knowledge we possess, by actual thought we form an internal word, and thence break forth into love."[28] The first humans were "beings of word and love" because the infusion of a rational soul animated their new linguistic capacity, patterning them after the Word in their intellect and Love in their will, so as to enable them to form an inner *verbum cordis* in the act of understanding truth, and to rationally desire and choose the apprehended good. Although every individual creature, and creation as a whole, manifests the divine goodness in various ways as participations in God's perfections, only in human persons among all corporeal creatures does God impress his personal stamp as the very exemplar of their nature—creating them as rational speakers who, in thinking, form an internal word by abstraction, and in rational willing, break forth into love.[29] The creation of the *imago Dei*, it might be said, is the greatest manifestation in the corporeal universe of God's

---

into whom God infuses a rational soul. Still, this raises the question of what capacities a nonrational and immediately prelinguistic human might possess. Presumably such a hominid would have a sophisticated ability to construct phantasms but not to abstract intellectual species from them; it would not produce an inner *verbum cordis* as do human beings made to the divine image.

27. Joseph Ratzinger, "Creation of the Human Being," in *In the Beginning . . . A Catholic Understanding of the Story of the Creation and the Fall*, trans. Boniface Ramsey, OP (Grand Rapids, MI: Eerdmans, 1995), 48.

28. *ST* I q. 93, a. 7.

29. *ST* I q. 6, a. 4; q. 44, a. 1 and a. 4.

will to communicate the divine goodness, producing a creature that is made capable of a share in the divine life itself.[30]

The evolution of *Sapiens* is therefore the ground of possibility for sanctification and even deification, and for a supernatural life to which irrational animals cannot be elevated. The ability to form an inner *verbum cordis* becomes deifying when, by grace, the image is assimilated in intellect (by wisdom) and will (by charity) even more perfectly to the Son and Holy Spirit, to the "Word . . . who breathes forth Love," so as to have God as the object of its knowledge and love.[31] Aquinas therefore thinks this elevation by grace bestows a "participation in the divine nature" that is truly trinitarian, making the rational creature an adopted child of God who is led by the Spirit toward beatitude as the principle of its own supernatural activity.[32] To know and love God by the infused gifts of charity and wisdom flowing from grace, and so "possess and enjoy" the indwelling trinitarian Persons, is to enter into a communion with God that can truly be called divine friendship.[33] By nature, and even more by grace, the human person shares in carrying out God's plan of divine providence by governing himself and others by rational activity, and so—from the creation of Adam—assumes the role and responsibility of stewardship over the rest of creation (Gen 1:28; 2:15).[34]

This ontological leap into spiritual existence would also bestow a radically new destiny on the bodies of human beings, informed by rational and immortal souls, and so capable of participating in moral action in this life and attaining final incorruptibility in the next. This means that the human body took on an entirely new potential in evolution, becoming the first material means by which God ordained that human beings should attain to immaterial realities and spiritual worship.[35] As will be discussed below, Aquinas thinks that, in the state of innocence, Adam did not need corporeal things like sacraments to perfect his soul because he was the recipient of the special preternatural gifts of infused knowledge and the perfect subjection of his soul to God and his body to his soul.[36] Adam would still worship God with body and soul,

---

30. On this, see Richard Conrad, "Humanity Created for Communion with the Trinity in Aquinas," in *A Transforming Vision: Knowing and Loving the Triune God*, ed. George Westhaver (London: SCM, 2018), 121–34.

31. *ST* I q. 43, a. 5, ad 2; q. 93, a. 8.

32. On Aquinas's theology of deification, see Daria Spezzano, *The Glory of God's Grace: Deification According to St. Thomas Aquinas* (Ave Maria: Sapientia Press, 2015).

33. *ST* I q. 43, a. 3; II-II q. 23, a. 1.

34. *ST* I q. 96, a. 1. Pope Francis reflects on this responsibility in his encyclical letter *Laudato Sí* (May 24, 2015), 66–75.

35. *ST* I q. 76, a. 5; II-II q. 81, a. 7; III, q. 61, a. 1.

36. *ST* III q. 61, a. 2.

however. Such subjection to God characterizes devotion—the internal act of the virtue of religion—and is expressed in sacrifice, among other external acts.[37] As a human being under the natural law, Adam would still exercise the virtue of religion through external and internal acts fitting to his embodied state, as did Christ himself.[38] Indeed, Adam had a body made for the worship of God.

The sacramental order became necessary after the fall and was fulfilled in the incarnation, which made possible the restoration and perfection of *Sapiens* as embodied rational speakers.[39] Aquinas argues that the Word, who is "the concept of eternal Wisdom, from whom all human wisdom is derived," fittingly united himself to human nature so that humans could be perfected in wisdom, which is their "proper perfection," as rational creatures.[40] In God's providence, the evolution of *Sapiens* was indeed the precondition for the incarnation itself. In the incarnation, Wisdom "prepared a body" for himself to take up and lay down as the Word made flesh. In his commentary on Hebrews 10:5, Aquinas writes that the body God "prepared" for Christ was made fit to be "a true sacrifice and a true oblation," offered up for sin in fulfillment of all sacrifices.[41]

Therefore, the evolution of *Sapiens* was the precondition for all the external and internal acts of human worship. To have a rational soul *and* a body—unlike angels—makes it possible for humans to offer themselves with devotion after the pattern of (or in anticipation of) the Word made flesh. As Ratzinger often emphasizes, human participation in the Logos is fulfilled in faith and *logike latreia*, "worship shaped by the word, structured on reason," spiritual worship conformed to the Word so as to "offer" one's body "as a living sacrifice, holy and pleasing to God" (Rom 12:1).[42] The Eucharist especially is the consummation of rational worship by embodied creatures:

37. *ST* II-II, q. 82, a. 1.
38. *ST* II-II q. 81, a. 7. Also see *ST* I-II, q. 101, a. 2: "Now the Divine worship is twofold: internal, and external. For since man is composed of soul and body, each of these should be applied to the worship of God; the soul by an interior worship; the body by an outward worship: hence it is written (Psalm 83:3): 'My heart and my flesh have rejoiced in the living God.' And as the body is ordained to God through the soul, so the outward worship is ordained to the internal worship. Now interior worship consists in the soul being united to God by the intellect and affections. Wherefore according to the various ways in which the intellect and affections of the man who worships God are rightly united to God, his external actions are applied in various ways to the Divine worship."
39. *ST* III q. 60, a. 2, a. 3.
40. *ST* III q. 3, a. 8.
41. Aquinas, *Super Heb*. ch. 10, lect. 1, no. 486–87; *ST* I-II, q. 102, a. 3.
42. Pope Benedict XVI, *Jesus of Nazareth: From the Entrance into Jerusalem to the Resurrection* (San Francisco: Ignatius Press, 2011), 80; Cardinal Joseph Ratzinger, *The*

This "word" that supplants the sacrificial offerings is no ordinary word. To begin with, it is no mere human speech, but the word of him who is "*the* Word," and so it draws all human words into God's inner dialogue, into his reason and his love . . . it is more than a word, because the eternal Word said, "Sacrifices and offerings you have not desired, but a body you have prepared for me" (Heb 10:5; cf. Ps 40:6). The Word is now flesh, and not only that: it is his body offered up, his blood poured out.[43]

In human evolution, God prepared a body for *homo* to become not only *sapiens* but "*adorans.*"[44]

Human beings, then, are created with a priestly role in creation that is most perfectly fulfilled by Christ, "our great High Priest" (Heb 4:14). With a body made for worship and informed by a rational soul, we stand at the interface between animal and spiritual, so that in us, material creation finds a voice with which to praise the Creator. To quote the seventh century Archbishop Leontios of Cyprus, "Through heaven and earth and sea, through wood and stone, through all creation visible and invisible, I offer veneration to the Creator and Master and Maker of all things. For the creation does not venerate the Maker directly and by itself, but it is through me that the heavens declare the glory of God, through me the moon worships God, through me the stars glorify Him, through me the waters and showers of rain, the dews and all creation, venerate God and give Him glory."[45] Woven into the web of life on earth by our evolution from primate ancestors, but endowed with spiritual life as the image of God, we are made to be priests and stewards of God's creation, and sharers in the eternal worship of heaven.[46]

Spirit of the Liturgy (San Francisco: Ignatius Press, 2000): "It is man, conforming himself to *logos* and becoming *logos* through faith, who is the true sacrifice, the true glory of God in the world" (67). On this topic, also see Roland Millare, "The Wedding Feast of the Lamb Has Begun: The Relationship between Eschatology and Liturgy in the Logoscentric Theology of Joseph Ratzinger"' (STD diss., Liturgical Institute, University of St. Mary of the Lake, 2018).

43. Benedict XVI, *Jesus of Nazareth*, 80.

44. Alexander Schmemann uses the term *homo adorans* to describe humanity's true identity before God in the world, which secularism denies. Secularism "is the negation of man as a worshiping being, as *homo adorans*: the one for whom worship is the essential act which both 'posits' his humanity and fulfills it." Alexander Schmemann, *For the Life of the World: Sacraments and Orthodoxy* (New York: St. Vladimir's Press, 2000), 118.

45. Apologetic Sermon 3, "On the Holy Icons" (Migne, PG 93.1604ab).

46. I am grateful to Richard Conrad, OP, for sharing ideas that inform this paragraph of my chapter.

2. God Does Not Take Back His Gifts: Original Incorruptibility and Final Resurrection

In being prepared for the infusion of a rational soul, the human body was also prepared for the radically new destiny of immortality given to the first parents, along with the other preternatural gifts that are part of the gift of original justice—integrity of the soul's powers and infused knowledge.. After the fall, with the loss of these gifts, the human body now subject to physical death was nevertheless still ultimately destined—unlike that of its prerational forebears—for the resurrection in eternal life. The scriptural teaching that "death entered the world" only after the fall "through sin" (Rom 5:12)—if this refers to biological as well as spiritual death, as Aquinas assumes—might seem hard to reconcile with the proposal for gradual biological evolution of the human body on scientific principles, since death is an integral part of the process of natural selection.[47] However, Paul is speaking of the death of Adam and Eve and their descendants in a postlapsarian state, presupposing their initial elevation to immortality. After the fall, biological death becomes a punishment for rational creatures who were at first uniquely preserved from it. If those first fully human parents are physically the product of gradual evolution from irrational creatures, though, the death of their ancestral pre-*Sapiens* hominids or that of any other creatures without a rational soul would not be excluded by Paul's claim; all such creatures would be subject to the natural processes of generation and corruption in evolution.[48]

Yet Paul's presupposition based on Genesis (2:17; 3:19)—that the first humans were initially exempt from but later subject to death—raises further questions from a purely metaphysical perspective because humans are uniquely composed of a material body and a rational soul. On the one hand, since corruption is natural to a living organism composed of form and matter, it seems that death would be natural for the first humans before sin, and so they must have been subject to it. On the other, since all humans have a rational soul, which in itself is subsistent, incorruptible, and therefore immortal, their death after sin seems unnatural or at least unfitting.[49] Does the Catholic tradition's teaching that the first parents were preserved from death before the fall by the preternatural gift of immortality mean that the first representatives of

---

47. *Sup. Rom.* ch. 5, lect. 3. For a discussion of this question in light of modern scholarship, see chapter 9 by Fr. Isaac Morales, OP, this volume.

48. I am grateful to Taylor Patrick O'Neill for his discussion of these points in his unpublished lecture, "St. Thomas Aquinas, Genesis, and Original Sin: On Prelapsarian Death and Macroevolution," delivered at Ave Maria University in February 2019.

49. See *ST* I q. 75 a. 6, on the incorruptibility of the soul.

human nature were actually living in an unnatural state? Or, after the fall, when this gift is lost, are death and corruption contrary to the nature of a creature with an immortal soul? In other words, is death natural or unnatural for human beings?

Aquinas addresses these questions in his commentary on Romans 5:12, where he argues that death is natural to human nature in one respect and yet unfitting in another. Because the matter of the body is "composed of contrary elements" necessary for the operation of the senses, it is "corruptible of its very nature."[50] Death is natural for human nature according to its intrinsic material principles. However, considering human nature from the viewpoint of "what divine providence provided it through original justice," death was not God's plan for human beings: "Divine providence planned [original justice] on account of the dignity of the rational soul, which, as it is naturally incorruptible, warranted an incorruptible body."[51] There is therefore a kind of internal tension between the principles of human nature—a material body and a rational soul—as the former is naturally corruptible and the latter naturally incorruptible. However, since nature derives especially from form, the incorruptibility of the soul takes precedence, as it were, in determining what is the most fitting state for the embodied rational creature, a state that nevertheless can only be attained with divine help.

Thomas puts this even more clearly in the *De malo*, where he answers the question of whether death and illness are natural to human beings:

> Death and dissolution are natural to human beings by reason of a necessity of matter, but immortality would befit them by reason of the form's nature. And yet natural sources do not suffice to provide immortality. Rather, a natural disposition for it indeed befits human beings by reason of their soul, and supernatural power fulfills it. Just so, the Philosopher says in the *Ethics* that we by nature have a disposition for moral virtues, but habits perfect them in us. And death and dissolution are contrary to our nature insofar as immortality is natural for us.[52]

Death is natural to us as rational *animals*, but immortality is in a sense natural to us as *rational* animals, although only potentially. Our soul naturally disposes us to immortality, but as Aquinas implies by his reference to the *Ethics*, this

---

50. *Sup. Rom.* ch. 5, lect. 3, no. 416. See also *QDaA.* q. 8, resp.; *In V Meta.* lect. 6, no. 833; *De malo* q. 5, a. 5. In *ST* I q. 91, a. 1, Thomas, drawing on medieval science, explains that it is necessary for humans to be composed of a balanced mixture of elements (fire, air, earth, and water) so as to have a refined sense of touch.

51. *Sup. Rom.* ch. 5, lect. 3, no. 416.

52. *De malo* q. 5, a. 5.

disposition must be made actual and lasting (like a habit) by a divine gift. In order to fulfill our potential for immortality of both body and soul, it is necessary for supernatural power to provide it.

In order to understand in what sense exactly Thomas thinks "immortality is natural for us," Robert Barry's explanation of the different ways Thomas employs the concept of nature is illuminating. Barry helpfully points out that for Thomas, the concept of human nature most fully includes not only "the elements of which humanity is composed [body and soul], in themselves or considered in the dignity of the highest powers of the soul," but also nature as the essence underlying human powers and operations, "which define the proper activity of a creature, and thereby its good," giving it the capacity to be rightly ordered and moved by God to its perfect good, the highest fulfillment of its rational powers.[53] That is, it is part of the essence of human nature to be *capax Dei* in its intrinsic principles of operation, and to require external supernatural elevation to perfectly order those principles so as to reach its highest good. In this way, grace, leading human persons to a beatitude exceeding the grasp of reason alone, is not natural in the sense of producing operations that proceed from the intrinsic principles of nature, but can be called natural in that it "moves the principles of intrinsic operation in the rational soul to the activity that is completely perfective of them."[54] Likewise, human beings were evolved for an immortality that would be natural to them even in this life, so long as they had remained perfected—as they were designed to be—by supernatural help.

2.1. Original Justice, the Preternatural Gift of Immortality, and the Fall

Aquinas's view, then, is that God, in his plan of divine providence for human bodily life, bestowed original justice on our first parents because it is God's intention that immortality should be natural for human nature as assisted by divine help, although the body is in itself naturally corruptible. Unlike the bodies of their irrational ancestors, the bodies of the first humans with rational souls were disposed to be elevated by divine power through those souls to a state of incorruptibility. Immortality, along with the first state of original justice experienced by both Adam and Eve, was God's intended state for human nature even in this life.

---

53. Robert Barry, "Original Sin and Pure Nature: What's the Difference, and What Difference Does It Make?" *Josephinum Journal of Theology* 25, no. 1 & 2 (2018): 5–7. Barry draws from the work of Lawrence Dewan, OP, "Nature as a Metaphysical Object," in *Form and Being: Studies in Thomistic Metaphysics* (Washington, DC: The Catholic University of America Press, 2006).

54. Barry, "Original Sin and Pure Nature," 8.

Aquinas explains in his commentary on Romans 5:12 that to overcome the natural corruptibility of the body of the first parents, "the divine power furnished what was lacking to human nature by giving the soul the power to maintain the body incorruptible."[55] Incorruptibility of the body is possible when the body is brought more perfectly under the dominion of the soul with the help of divine power, and this in turn is possible when the soul is subjected perfectly to God. Aquinas describes this prelapsarian state of original justice:

> This justice was a certain rectitude such that the human mind was under God, the lower powers of the soul under the mind, and the body under the soul, and all external things under man, so that as long as the mind remained under God, the lower powers would remain subject to reason, and the body to the soul by receiving life from it unfailingly, and external things to man in the sense that all things would serve him, and he would never experience harm from them.[56]

It was this intended state of divinely ordered rectitude that was lost by sin, so that man "lost the strength to control the lower powers [of the soul] as well as the body and external things," becoming "subject to death from intrinsic sources and to violence from external sources."[57]

Human biological death entered the world when rational creatures lost the strength that came from the divine help on which their capacities were naturally meant to depend for proper ordering to the good end because their soul was no longer subject to God. Postlapsarian humans were left to a disordered internal state in which the soul's lower powers rebelled against reason; because of this undue influence of their lower powers, they might act in similar ways to their prerational forebears who had only those powers. But now, because these humans were rational, those unruly powers uncontrolled by reason could incline them to acts with the character of sin and moral culpability. They would now be subject to a fate of mortality that could be called "unnatural" in light of God's plan for them to be immortal with divine help, though it was both natural and penal on the part of their bodies no longer fully subjected to their souls.[58]

The preternatural bodily gift of immortality (along with impassibility to external harm) thus properly depended on the soul's complete subjection to God by a gift of grace. In the *Summa theologiae*, Thomas explains that some-

---

55. *Sup. Rom.* ch. 5, lect. 3, no. 416.
56. *Sup. Rom.* ch. 5, lect. 3, no. 416.
57. *Sup. Rom.* ch. 5, lect. 3, no. 416. See also *ST* I q. 95, a. 1; *Compendium of Theology* bk. 1, 186–87; *De malo* q. 5, a. 1.
58. *ST* II-II q. 164, ad 1.

thing can be incorruptible in three ways: in its matter (as for the heavenly bodies), because of a perfect inherent disposition (as for the human body in the state of glory), or because of an external efficient cause. Prelapsarian humans were incorruptible and immortal in this third way, "not by reason of any intrinsic vigor of immortality but by reason of a supernatural force given by God to the soul, whereby it was enabled to preserve the body from all corruption so long as it remained itself subject to God."[59] Thomas argues in the *Summa theologiae* that Adam was created in (sanctifying) grace and that Adam's rectitude (resulting in the perfect subjection of his soul to God, his lower powers to reason, and his body to his soul and therefore his immortality, etc.) must have been dependent on that grace; otherwise, it would not have been lost by sin.[60] Here Thomas disagrees with others who hold that Adam was created in original rectitude before being given sanctifying grace; some hold that he would have had the preternatural gifts by a gift of grace to nature that was nevertheless not sanctifying grace.[61] Although there has been much debate as to whether Thomas thinks that the grace in which Adam was created was the formal or efficient cause of Adam's original justice (i.e., whether original justice was supernatural or natural), and whether his views on this developed over time, it seems clear that in the *Summa* Thomas thinks that this grace was sanctifying grace (*gratia gratum faciens*) and that it was the formal cause of Adam's immortality by ordering his soul to perfect rectitude.[62]

Thomas answers an objection that if prelapsarian immortality were due to grace, it would have been restored when grace was recovered by repentance

---

59. *ST* I q. 97, a. 1.

60. *ST* I q. 95, a. 1.

61. *ST* I q. 95, a. 1, ad 4. Here Thomas is disagreeing with an opinion held by the Franciscan school of Alexander of Hales in the *Summa fratris Alexandri* I–II no. 492, no. 505 (*Summa Fratris Alexandri siue Summa uniuersae theologiae—opus Alexandro moderante conflatum*): *prima pars secundi libri* (Rome: PP. Collegii S. Bonaventurae, 1928); and with Bonaventure, *Commentary on the Sentences* II d. 29 a. 2 q. 2.

62. Although Aquinas does not use the term *gratia gratum faciens* in *ST* I q. 95, a. 1 on Adam's creation in grace, in a. 4, he states that Adam's grace (and therefore charity) was the root of his meritorious action, which is true only of sanctifying (habitual) grace. In *ST* I q. 100, a. 1, ad 2, arguing that Adam's children would have been born with grace had Adam not sinned, Thomas says that the "root of original justice, in which man was made in rectitude, consisted in the supernatural subjection of the reason to God, which is *per gratia gratum facientum*." For an extended discussion on the development of Aquinas's views of the role of grace in original justice, as well as the related twentieth century Thomist debate, see David Houck, *Aquinas, Original Sin, and the Challenge of Evolution* (Cambridge: Cambridge University Press, 2020), especially chapter 2. On the latter debate, also see Cyril Vollert, "Saint Thomas on Sanctifying Grace and Original Justice: A Comparative Study of a Recent Controversy," *Theological Studies* 2, no. 3 (1941): 369–87.

(this would also apply to reception of grace under the new law by sacraments). Thomas explains that:

> This power of preserving the body was not natural to the soul, but was the gift of grace. And though man recovered grace as regards remission of guilt and the merit of glory; yet he did not recover immortality, the loss of which was an effect of sin; for this was reserved for Christ to accomplish, by whom the defect of nature was to be restored into something better.[63]

After the fall, grace restores to the individual soul justification, deification, and at least imperfect union with God by perfection of the divine image, but the graced human person does not return to the same state of original justice that the whole of human nature has been deprived of. Rather, some effects of this privation remain for one born with a corrupt nature, even after the healing and elevation of grace. The effects of original sin—weakness, ignorance, malice, and concupiscence—still persist to some extent, so that even one with the gift of habitual grace needs the continual help of actual graces to carry out the good against the "law of sin" in our flesh (Rom 7:25) that still seeks to make us captive.[64] Now that we are "slaves of sin," we are no longer able to avoid sin, nor even to do the good proportionate to human nature, without God's help.[65] The help of grace does enable us to avoid mortal sin by assisting the reason, but even under its influence we are still likely to sin venially because of "the corruption of the lower appetite of sensuality."[66] For postlapsarian humans, the effect of habitual grace is in a sense "imperfect inasmuch as it does not completely heal man."[67] Bodily defects stemming from the corruptibility natural to human beings (due to their corporeality) especially and evidently remain as a penalty consequent on the withdrawal of original justice, even after one receives the justifying grace of baptism.[68]

Why is this? Thomas in fact comments that baptism actually "has the power to take away the penalties of the present life, yet does not take them away in this life, but by its power they will be taken away from the just in the resurrection, when 'the mortal has put on immortality' (1 Cor 15:54)." Just as "God does not take back his gifts" of salvation (Rom 11:29), neither does he take back his gifts to human nature, but rather delays their full effects for

---

63. *ST* I q. 97, a. 1, ad 3.
64. *ST* I-II q. 85, a. 3; q. 109, a. 9; see *Sup. Rom.* ch. 7, lect. 4, nos. 588–89.
65. *ST* I-II q. 109, a. 2; a. 8, ad 3.
66. *ST* I-II q. 109, a. 8.
67. *ST* I-II q. 109, a. 9, ad 1.
68. *ST* I-II q. 85, a. 5; III q. 69, a. 3.

fallen humanity. All of the principles of human nature would remain the same in fallen *Sapiens*—bodies well-prepared for rational souls especially due to their capacity for speech, with those souls infused by God in each human person who would therefore still be *capax Dei*, but now with an unfulfilled disposition for immortality. The fall is not an "ontological leap" backward but a state of deprivation. The "penalties of the present life" result only from the lack of grace's ordering of human nature's principles perfectly in this life. While God could presumably have just started over rather than allowing Adam to pass on corrupt nature, in foreseeing the fall, he willed that afterward he would allow human nature to operate according to the internal tension of its natural principles while still offering the gift of grace that would, with human cooperation, ultimately raise them to the state of perfection intended for them originally.

Why was this divine ordination fitting? Thomas offers several reasons why it is reasonable that the grace of baptism does not take away bodily defects nor completely heal internal disorder in this life. They all revolve around the necessity to be conformed to Christ by meritorious cooperation with grace that will lead to eternal life. Incorporation into Christ by baptism makes it fitting for the baptized to be conformed to Christ, who had a passible body but was raised up to the life of glory. Likewise, "a Christian receives grace in Baptism as to his soul, but retains a passible body, so that he may suffer for Christ in it; yet he will eventually be raised up to a life of impassibility." The fight against concupiscence and other defects is "suitable for spiritual training," so that one will afterwards "receive the crown of victory." Finally, so that we do not have hope in Christ only for this life (1 Cor 15:19), we are not baptized in order to receive an impassible body now, but "for the sake of the glory of eternal life."[69]

Having a body that is passible and corruptible according to its natural corporeal principle makes it necessary for one to suffer, fight, and endure in dependence on Christ for future restoration. God's postlapsarian permission of the internal tension between body and soul and resulting disorder does not remove the human person's potential for ultimate integrity and perfection but requires struggle and resulting dependence on God's continual help in this life that leads, when one cooperates with grace, to spiritual growth suitable for "beings of word and love." By such willing struggle, graced rational creatures grow in charity and so in merit for eternal life, becoming more conformed to the Word and Love. After sin, human nature is more subject to weakness, especially because of disordered desires arising from bodily passions, but it is for this very reason that, proportionately, the good actions of fallen man are more meritorious than Adam's were before sin, "because a small deed

69. *ST* III q. 69, a. 3.

is more beyond the capacity of one who works with difficulty than a great deed is beyond one who performs it easily."⁷⁰

God accords to fallen humans the dignity of being instrumental causes in their own redemption through willing penance and loving sacrifice. While in baptism, the entire debt of eternal and temporal punishment for sin is removed for the one who has faith in Christ "by the power of Christ's Passion," and the penitent himself must offer satisfaction in the sacrament of penance for postbaptismal sin, a satisfaction that depends upon Christ's own but "shares in the power of Christ's Passion according to the measure of [the penitent's] own acts."⁷¹ When one turns back to God, the guilt of sin and the debt of eternal punishment are forgiven on account of Christ's superabundant satisfaction for the sins of the human race, but the remission of temporal debt that is personally due for inordinately turning toward material goods is only removed by "bearing punishment patiently with the help of divine grace."⁷² The willing acceptance of bodily suffering allows one to cooperate in satisfying for sin, but none of this is possible for fallen persons except through Christ—the second Adam—by being conformed especially by charity and obedience to him whose "body was prepared" for immolation, to wipe away sin and to become a "true sacrifice and a true oblation" in accordance with God's will (Heb 10:5–10).⁷³ Christ repairs in this life "what regards the person" (i.e., the guilt and debt of eternal punishment that deprives one of the beatific vision) but will not heal the penalties of sin that belong to the whole of human nature on account of its internal principles (such as death) "until the ultimate restoration of nature through the glorious resurrection."⁷⁴ Christ's willing satisfaction makes possible our own, just as his resurrection is the cause of ours, in body and soul.⁷⁵ The very reason that "we do not receive an immortal and impassible body at once," Thomas explains, is "so that we might suffer along with Christ," for "if we suffer with him, we may also be glorified with him" (Rom 8:17).⁷⁶

2.2. The Resurrected Body and Its Qualities

Thomas thinks that even Adam's earthly immortality would not have lasted forever if he had remained innocent, but eventually he would have attained

70. *ST* I q. 95, a. 4.
71. *ST* III, q. 69, a. 2; III, q. 86, a. 4, ad 3.
72. *ST* III, q. 86, a. 4, co. and ad 2.
73. *Sup. Heb.* ch. 10, lect. 1, no. 487.
74. *ST* III, q. 69, a. 3, ad 3.
75. Daria Spezzano, "'Be Imitators of God' (Eph 5:1): Aquinas on Charity and Satisfaction," *Nova et Vetera* 15, no. 2 (2017): 615–51. *ST* III, q. 56.
76. *Sup. Rom.* ch. 8, lect. 3, no. 651

the beatific vision and an eternal spiritual life and body in heaven.[77] One need not be a saint to be resurrected, however. Whether they will attain the vision of God or be reprobate, all human beings are destined for the reunion of soul and body in the resurrection; indeed, this resurrection will contribute to their eternal reward or punishment.[78] This follows from the very nature of the human being, which is not complete unless this union exists. Since the soul is incorruptible and cannot attain its final perfection without reuniting with the body, Aquinas thinks that the soul must be reunited with the body for the completion of human nature, and by divine power will finally make the body incorruptible.[79] Like death, resurrection can be said to be both natural and unnatural. Strictly speaking, it is miraculous, yet it is natural in a restricted sense, bringing about what is fitting to human nature as perfected by a supernatural gift intended by divine providence, even to the restoration of the numerically identical body possessed in this life.[80]

Resurrection restores to all the incorruptibility that was given to Adam by original justice, and for the blessed, it goes far beyond Adam's preternatural gifts. Aquinas argues that all will be restored to a state of incorruptibility and immortality, with a body free of all defects that arose from material causes—missing limbs will be supplied, the blind will see, and there will be complete freedom from illness and insufficiency. Because Christ satisfied for the sin of nature by assuming all of the defects of nature that flow from sin to the whole human race in common (apart from those incompatible with his perfection of knowledge and grace), all of the good of nature will be restored through Christ even to the reprobate by divine power.[81] Consideration of the tortures of the damned is not appealing to modern sensibilities, but for medieval theo-

---

77. *ST* 100, a. 2, q. 102, a. 4. After the fall, death pays the "debt of nature" owed on account of original sin in the flesh, so sin does not prevent the resurrection; *ST* III q. 69, a. 7, ad 3; *ST* supp. q. 75, a. 2, ad 4.

78. *Compendium of Theology* bk. 1, ch. 242.

79. *Compendium of Theology* bk. 1, ch. 151. *Sup. 1 Cor.* ch. 15, lect. 9, nos. 1013 and 1015.

80. *Compendium of Theology* bk. 1, ch. 154; *ST* supp. q. 75, a. 3.

81. *Compendium of Theology* bk. 1, ch. 158, 160, 176; *ST* III q. 14, a. 4. Aquinas disagrees with Augustine's doubt that the damned might retain physical deformities. He argues that "the dead will rise incorruptible" (1 Cor 15:52) because "in the resurrection the reparation of nature belongs to all, because all have communion with Christ in nature." Therefore, "whatever belongs to the reparation of nature is conferred entirely on [the damned] but what belongs to grace is conferred only on the elect": *Sup. 1 Cor.* ch. 15, lect. 8, no. 1010. Aquinas famously remarks that the resurrected will "rise at a perfect age, that is, thirty-two or thirty-three": *Collationes Credo in Deum* XIV, Latin text (Leonine edition) in Nicholas Ayo, *The Sermon-Conferences of St. Thomas Aquinas on the Apostle's Creed* (Notre Dame, IN: University of Notre Dame Press, 1988), 146. My translation.

logians it provides at least a test case for the logic of moral culpability and the effects of sin and the logic of divine justice. For the reprobate, who have freely persisted in malice against God until the end and whose will is forever fixed in the choice of evil, incorruptibility will justly mean that their bodies will always suffer punishment, yet without dissolution. Because they set all their affection on material rather than spiritual goods, their souls will not only be deprived of the vision of God but will "suffer the tyranny of material things," especially as they are spiritually "imprisoned" by fire.[82] In his sermons on the Apostolic Creed, Thomas identifies four qualities of the resurrected bodies of the damned; they will be filled with darkness, passibility, heaviness, and carnality.[83] The penalties of the damned make permanent in them the effects of the fall (except for physical death, which they have already experienced), in the sense that they are forever subject to internal disorder.

The souls of the blessed, who already enjoy the beatific vision, on the other hand, are confirmed in the good, fulfilling God's original intention for human nature by being once again and forever totally subject to God, although with an immediate knowledge and love even greater than that of Adam; they are made deiform by the light of glory that perfectly and immovably conforms them to the "Word, breathing forth Love."[84] Because of the immutability of their wills in subjection to God, their souls will have complete and unchangeable dominion over their bodies, which will be not only incorruptible but completely obedient to the soul, providing no obstacle to the soul's contemplation but sharing in the delight of the vision that overflows from soul to body.[85]

In line with the tradition, Aquinas assigns four "dowries" or special qualities of the glorified body that result from the beatified soul's perfect dominion over it, flowing in turn from the soul's perfect union with God. Unlike the body-disordering souls of the reprobate, the souls of the saints will impart to their resurrected bodies the qualities of impassibility, clarity, agility, and subtility.[86] Like other theologians, Aquinas drew on 1 Corinthians 15:42–44 as the scriptural referent for these qualities. In the *reportatio* of his scriptural

---

82. *Compendium of Theology* bk. 1, chs. 177–180.
83. *Coll. Credo in Deum* 14, Ayo, *Sermon-Conferences of St. Thomas Aquinas*, 148.
84. *Compendium of Theology* bk. 1, ch. 166; *ST* I q. 12, a. 5; *ST* I q. 43, a. 5, ad 2.
85. *Compendium of Theology* bk. 1, ch. 167. Because of the immutability of their wills, the state of the saints will be different from that of man in the state of innocence; the immortality of the resurrection cannot be lost (*ST* supp. q. 82, a. 1, ad 2).
86. *Compendium of Theology* bk. 1, ch. 168; *Coll. Credo in Deum* 14, Ayo, *Sermon-Conferences of St. Thomas Aquinas*, 148. For a discussion of Aquinas's treatment of the dowries in the context of tradition, see Caroline Walker Bynum, *The Resurrection of the Body* (New York: Columbia University Press, 1995): 232–37.

exegesis on this text, he explains that the body of the saints is "sown in corruption" in death but "rises in incorruption," not only imperishable but impassible. It is "sown in dishonor" because it is subject to miseries in life, but "'rises in glory,' which signifies clarity . . . for the bodies of the saints will be clear and shining." "It is sown in weakness," as an "animal body, which before death is weak and slow and not easily moved by the soul," but "'shall rise in power' because it will be so easily moved by the soul . . . that there will be no difficulty in moving it, which pertains to the dowry of agility." Subtility for Aquinas refers to the spiritual quality of the resurrected body such that it no longer needs animal functions but is entirely subject to the soul: "it is sown a natural body; it shall rise a spiritual body."[87] For Aquinas, God's intention for the immortality of rational embodied human beings cannot, in spite of sin and its deadly consequences, ultimately be thwarted. Divine providence—"because of the worth of the rational soul, which being incorruptible, deserved an incorruptible body"—provided immortality through original justice in the beginning of the human race, and will provide it through resurrection in its last end.[88]

Conclusion: The Glorious Telos of Evolution

Why did God bring about the biological evolution of *Sapiens*? Theologically the answer must be that God prepared the human body for the ontological leap of a transition to spiritual life not only in this world but in resurrected glory.[89] In God's providence, bipedalism, large brains, and especially the development of the capacity for language and symbolic thought prepared humans for the infusion of rational souls destined for eternal life. Now informed by a rational soul, these bodies would ultimately make the leap to immortality. Far

---

87. *Sup. 1 Cor.* ch. 15, lect. 6, nos. 980–88.

88. *Sup. Rom.* ch. 5, lect. 3, no. 416. All who are generated from the first Adam who was "of the earth and mortal" after sin bear the likeness of the earthly man, but for those who are conformed to Christ, the second Adam, "our body will be conformed to his body of radiance": *Sup. 1 Cor.* ch. 15, lect. 7, nos. 997–99.

89. It is perhaps necessary to clearly distinguish the position that the human body evolved in preparation for the infusion of the human spirit from the ideas of Pierre Teilhard de Chardin, who proposed that all of life on earth evolved toward the development of human spirit itself (i.e., "noogenesis") and that the process of evolution will culminate at last in a purely spiritual realization of the "Omega point," when the mind will be detached, "fulfilled at last, from its material matrix, so that it will rest henceforth with all its weight on God-Omega" (*The Phenomenon of Man*, trans. B. Wall [London: Collins, 1959], 288). De Chardin often writes in a mystical style that is unclear on specific points of doctrine, but he would seem to reject the teaching of *Humani Generis* no. 36 of God's immediate creation of every human soul.

from undermining the teaching that humans are spiritual beings created to attain glory, the data gained from studies of the gradual biological evolution of hominids can reveal God's goodness in preparing human beings in body and soul for such an exalted destiny, in harmony with the Catholic teaching that, made to the image of God, they are truly "beings of word and love." And even though, in line with tradition, Aquinas took literally the biblical teaching of the immediate creation of Adam from the dust of the earth, it seems likely that he would not reject the data of modern science that demonstrate the existence of prehominid forebears, and their evolution into anatomically and (eventually) behaviorally modern humans, as ways of understanding secondary causes in the "how" of human evolution.[90] Thomas would certainly have learned from the extensive biological research of his master St. Albert, who distinguished but did not oppose the methods of science and theology. For Albert, natural processes should be studied on their own terms (as to their "how"), without taking into immediate consideration the ultimate "how" and "why" of God's primary causality. Albert remarks in his *De caelo et mundo* that "in natural science it is not our business to inquire how God the Creator uses what he has created according to his free will to work miracles in order to reveal his power, but rather it is our task to inquire what can be done naturally in natural things according to the causes intrinsic to them." Yet, Albert thinks, we can still understand that divine providence works through natural modes of causation to bring about God's plan for creation.[91]

The ultimate "why" of human evolution is the creation of *homo adorans*—so that God should be worshiped and his goodness magnified not only by angels but also by the only corporeal creatures capable of singing his praise in *logike latreia*, who are in resurrected conformity with their great High Priest, the Incarnate Word, who shares their embodied nature. In the direct vision of God in heaven, Aquinas says, the bodies of the saints will no longer need to use figurative symbols of divine things by means of the senses, yet every bodily faculty will be flooded, by its total subjection to the glorified soul, with the experience of the joy of divine union:

---

90. For an opposing view, see Chaberek, *Catholicism and Evolution*: "It is certainly impossible to harmonize evolution, even the theistic variety, with the doctrine of St. Thomas Aquinas" (288).

91. Albertus Magnus, *De caelo et mundo* 1, tr. 4, ch. 10 (Editio Colonensis, Alberti Magni *Opera Omnia* ad fidem codicum manuscriptorum edenda apparatu critico notis prologemenis indicibus instruenda curavit Institutum Alberti Magni Coloniense [Münster: Aschendorff, 1951 seqq.] vol. 5.1: 103, v. 5–12), quoted in Benedict Ashley, OP, "St. Albert and the Nature of Natural Science," in *Albertus Magnus and the Sciences: Commemorative Essays, 1980*, ed. James A. Weisheipl (Toronto: Pontifical Academy of Mediaeval Studies, 1980), 83–84.

> For in the state of future bliss, the human intellect will gaze on the Divine Truth in Itself. Wherefore the external worship will not consist in anything figurative, but solely in the praise of God, proceeding from the inward knowledge and affection, according to Isaiah 51:3: "Joy and gladness shall be found therein, thanksgiving and the voice of praise."[92]

The joy and the voice of praise in the souls of the saints is the fruit of their charity, proceeding from an interior *verbum cordis* that fulfills their highest capacity for speech by making them the clear deiform mirror of the Trinity itself.

The praise of the saints will also glorify God's final creation of a "new heavens and new earth" (Rev 21:1) because the resurrection and establishment of all the saints in beatitude is, Aquinas thinks, the final perfection and consummation of the creation of the whole material universe, which now "'waits for the revelation' of the glory 'of the sons of God'" to be delivered from corruption and attain its final rest.[93] The saints' song of praise in their fruition of God is the ultimate priestly offering of the rational creature on behalf of creation, fulfilling the purpose of the whole universe to "show forth the divine goodness to the glory of God."[94] In his treatment of the six days of creation, Aquinas says two things are needed to attain this final beatitude of the saints—nature and grace. And "this consummation existed previously in its causes; as to nature, at the first founding of the world, as to grace in the Incarnation of Christ."[95] In the evolution of human nature, in preparing human bodies well-disposed for the ontological leap of ensoulment as beings of word and love capable of deification and immortality, God began to consummate his plan to bring the whole world through Christ to the glory of the new creation.

---

92. *ST* I–II q. 101, a 2.
93. *Sup. Rom.* ch. 8, lect. 4, no. 660 (see Rom 8:19 and 8:21); *Comp. Theology* bk. 1, chs. 169–71.
94. *ST* I q. 65, a. 2.
95. *ST* I q. 73, a. 1 corpus and ad 1.

Select Bibliography

Alexander, Andrew, SJ. "Human Origins and Genetics." *The Clergy Review* 49 (1964): 344–53.

Allen, Paul. "Evolutionary Psychology and Romans 5–7: The 'Slavery to Sin' in Human Nature." *Ex Auditu* 32 (2016): 50–64.

Austin, Christopher J. "Aristotelian Essentialism: Essence in the Age of Evolution." *Synthese* 194, no. 7 (2017): 2539–56.

Austriaco, Nicanor Pier Giorgio, OP. "Defending Adam After Darwin: On the Origins of *Sapiens* as a Natural Kind." *American Catholic Philosophical Quarterly* 92, no. 2 (2018): 337–52.

Barry, Robert. "Original Sin and Pure Nature: What's the Difference, and What Difference Does It Make?" *Josephinum Journal of Theology* 25, no. 1 & 2 (2018): 1–28.

Bergmann, Philip J., and Gen Morinaga. "The Convergent Evolution of Snake-Like Forms by Divergent Evolutionary Pathways in Squamate Reptiles." *Evolution* 73, no. 3 (2019): 481–96.

Berwick, Robert C., and Noam Chomsky. *Why Only Us: Language and Evolution.* Cambridge, MA: MIT Press, 2016.

———. "All or Nothing: No Half-Merge and the Evolution of Syntax." *PLoS Biology* 17, no. 11 (2019): e3000539.

Binmore, Ken. *Natural Justice.* Oxford: Oxford University Press, 2005.

Boulter, Stephen J. "Can Evolutionary Biology Do Without Aristotelian Essentialism?" *Royal Institute of Philosophy Supplements* 70 (2012): 83–103.

Brandi, Salvatore M., SJ. "Evoluzione e Domma: Erronee informazioni di un inglese." *La Civiltà Cattolica* 18, no. 6 (1902): 75–77.

Carl, Brian. "Thomas Aquinas on the Proportionate Causes of Living Species." *Scientia et Fides* 8, no. 2 (2020): 223–48.

Chomsky, Noam. *The Science of Language: Interviews with James McGilvray.* Cambridge: Cambridge University Press, 2012.

Cole-Turner, Ron. *The End of Adam and Eve: Theology and the Science of Human Origins.* Pittsburgh: TheologyPlus Publishing, 2016.

Conrad, Richard, OP. "Human Practice and God's Making-Good in Aquinas' Virtue Ethics." In *Varieties of Virtue Ethics*, edited by David Carr, James Arthur, and Kristján Kristjánsson, 163–79. London: Palgrave Macmillan, 2017.

———. "Humanity Created for Communion with the Trinity in Aquinas." In *A Transforming Vision: Knowing and Loving the Triune God*, edited by George Westhaver, 121–34. London: SCM, 2018.

Cory, Therese Scarpelli. "Is Anything in the Intellect That Was Not First in Sense? Empiricism and Knowledge of the Incorporeal in Aquinas." In *Oxford Studies in Medieval Philosophy* 6, edited by Robert Pasnau, 100–143. Oxford: Oxford University Press, 2018.

Craig, William Lane. *In Quest of the Historical Adam*. Grand Rapids, MI: Eerdmans, 2021.

Davison, Andrew. "'He Fathers-Forth Whose Beauty Is Past Change,' but 'Who Knows How?': Evolution and Divine Exemplarity." *Nova et Vetera* 16, no. 4 (2018): 1067–102.

De Haan, Daniel D. "Approaching Other Animals with Caution: Exploring Insights from Aquinas's Psychology." *New Blackfriars* 100, no. 1090 (2019): 715–37.

de Leguna, Theodore. "Stages of the Discussion of Evolutionary Ethics." *The Philosophical Review* 14, no. 5 (1905): 576–89.

de Queiroz, Kevin. "Different Species Problems and Their Resolution." *BioEssays* 27, no. 12 (2005): 1263–69.

———. "Species Concepts and Species Delimitation." *Systematic Biology* 56, no. 6 (2007): 879–86.

Devitt, Michael. "Resurrecting Biological Essentialism." *Philosophy of Science* 75, no. 3 (2008): 344–82.

———. "Historical Biological Essentialism," *Studies in History and Philosophy of Biological and Biomedical Sciences* 71 (2018): 1–7.

———. "Defending Intrinsic Biological Essentialism," *Philosophy of Science* 88, no. 1 (2021): 67–82.

———. *Biological Essentialism*. Oxford University Press, 2023.

Domning, Daryl P., and Monika Hellwig. *Original Selfishness: Original Sin and Evil in the Light of Evolution*. Hampshire: Ashgate, 2006.

Dulles, Avery, SJ. *Magisterium: Teacher and Guardian of the Faith*. Ave Maria, FL: Sapientia Press of Ave Maria University, 2007.

Dumsday, Travis. "Is There Still Hope for a Scholastic Ontology of Biological Species?" *The Thomist* 76, no. 3 (2012): 371–95.

Dupré, John. "On the Impossibility of a Monistic Account of Species." In *Species: New Interdisciplinary Essays*, edited by Robert A. Wilson, 3–22. Cambridge, MA: MIT Press, 1999.

———. *Humans and Other Animals*. Oxford: Clarendon, 2002.

Elder, Crawford L. "Biological Species Are Natural Kinds." *The Southern Journal of Philosophy* 46, no. 3 (2008): 339–62.

Ereshefsky, Marc. "Species." In *Stanford Encyclopedia of Philosophy*, edited by Edward N. Zalta. Article published July 4, 2002; last modified April 1, 2022. https://plato.stanford.edu/archives/sum2022/entries/species/.

Feser, Edward. *Five Proofs for the Existence of God*. San Francisco: Ignatius Press, 2017.

Finnis, John. *Natural Law and Natural Rights*. Oxford: Clarendon Press, 1980. Second edition published in 2011.

———. "Reflections and Responses." In *Reason, Morality, and Law: The Philosophy of John Finnis*, edited by John Keown and Robert P. George, 459–584. Oxford: Oxford University Press, 2013.

Fitzmyer, Joseph A. "The Consecutive Meaning of ΕΦ'Ω in Romans 5.12." *New Testament Studies* 39 (1993): 321–39.

FitzPatrick, William. "Evolutionary Theory and Morality: Why the Science Doesn't Settle the Philosophical Questions." *Philosophic Exchange* 44, no. 1 (2014): art. 2. https://soar.suny.edu/handle/20.500.12648/3279.

Flaman, Paul J. "Evolution, the Origin of Human Persons, and Original Sin: Physical Continuity with an Ontological Leap." *The Heythrop Journal* 57, no. 3 (2016): 568–83.

Foot, Philippa. *Natural Goodness*. Oxford: Oxford University Press, 2001.

Frey, Jennifer. "Neo-Aristotelian Ethical Naturalism." In *The Cambridge Companion to Natural Law Ethics*, edited by Tom Angier, 92–110. Cambridge: Cambridge University Press, 2019.

Gaventa, Beverly Roberts. "The Cosmic Power of Sin in Paul's Letter to the Romans: Toward a Widescreen Edition." *Interpretation* 58, no. 3 (2004): 229–40.

Grisez, Germain. *Christian Moral Principles*. Vol. 1 of *The Way of the Lord Jesus*. Chicago: Franciscan Herald Press, 1983.

Held, Lewis I., Jr. *Quirks of Human Anatomy: An Evo-Devo Look at the Human Body*. Cambridge: Cambridge University Press, 2009.

Hey, Jody. *Genes, Categories, and Species: The Evolutionary and Cognitive Cause of the Species Problem*. New York: Oxford University Press, 2001.

Hull, David L. "The Effect of Essentialism on Taxonomy—Two Thousand Years of Stasis." Pts. 1 and 2. *The British Journal for the Philosophy of Science* 15, no. 60 (1965): 314–26; 16, no. 61 (1965): 1–18.

———. "A Matter of Individuality." *Philosophy of Science* 45, no. 3 (1978): 335–60.

International Theological Commission. "Communion and Stewardship: Human Persons Created in the Image of God." In *International Theological Commission: Texts and Documents 1986–2007*, edited by Michael Sharkey and Thomas Weinandy, 319–51. San Francisco: Ignatius Press, 2009.

Jablonka, Eva, and Marion Lamb. *Evolution in Four Dimensions: Genetic, Epigenetic, Behavioral, and Symbolic Variation in the History of Life*. Cambridge, MA: MIT Press, 2014.

Jackson, Timothy P. "The Christian Love Ethic and Evolutionary 'Cooperation': The Lessons and Limits of Eudaimonism and Game Theory." In *Evolution, Games, and God: The Principle of Cooperation*, edited by M. A. Nowak and Sarah Coakley, 307–26. Cambridge, MA: Harvard University Press, 2013.

Jensen, Steven. *Knowing the Natural Law: From Precepts and Inclinations to Deriving Oughts*. Washington, DC: The Catholic University of America Press, 2015.

John Paul II. "Address to the Pontifical Academy of Sciences (October 22, 1996)." In *Papal Addresses to the Pontifical Academy of Sciences 1917–2002*. Vatican City: Pontifical Academy of Sciences, 2003.

Johnson, Mark. "St Thomas and the 'Law of Sin.'" *Recherches de théologie et philosophie médiévales* 67, no. 1 (2000): 80–95.

Joyce, Richard. *The Evolution of Morality*. Cambridge, MA: MIT Press, 2006.

Kemp, Kenneth. "Science, Theology, and Monogenesis." *American Catholic Philosophical Quarterly* 85, no. 2 (2011): 217–36.

Keown, John, and Robert P. George, eds. *Reason, Morality, and Law: The Philosophy of John Finnis*. Oxford: Oxford University Press, 2013.

Kertelge, Karl. "The Sin of Adam in Light of Christ's Redemptive Act according to Romans 5:12–21." *Communio* 18, no. 4 (1991): 502–13.

Kim, Hie Lim, Takeshi Igawa, Ayaka Kawashima, Yoko Satta, and Naoyuki Takahata. "Divergence, Demography, and Gene Loss along the Human Lineage." *Philosophical Transactions of the Royal Society B: Biological Sciences* 365, no. 1552 (2010): 2451–57.

Kitcher, Philip. "Biology and Ethics." In *The Oxford Handbook of Ethical Theory*, edited by David Copp, 163–85. Oxford: Oxford University Press, 2007.

———. *The Ethical Project*. Cambridge, MA: Harvard University Press, 2011.

Kitts, David B., and David J. Kitts. "Biological Species as Natural Kinds." *Philosophy of Science* 46, no. 4 (1979): 613–22.

Korsgaard, Christine. "Morality and the Distinctiveness of Human Action." In *Primates and Philosophers: How Morality Evolved*, edited by Stephen Machedo and Josiah Ober, 98–119. Princeton, NJ: Princeton University Press, 2006.

Lonergan, Bernard. *Insight: A Study of Human Understanding*. Toronto: University of Toronto Press, 1997.

Mahoney, Jack. *Christianity in Evolution: An Exploration.* Washington, DC: Georgetown University Press, 2011.

Marmodoro, Anna. "Aristotelian Powers at Work: Reciprocity Without Symmetry in Causation." In *Causal Powers*, edited by Jonathan D. Jacobs, 57–76. Oxford: Oxford University Press, 2017.

Martins, Pedro Tiago, and Cedric Boeckx. "Language Evolution and Complexity Considerations: The No Half-Merge Fallacy." *PLoS Biology* 17, no. 11 (2019): e3000389.

Mayr, Ernst. *Animal Species and Evolution.* Cambridge, MA: Harvard University Press, 1963.

—. *Populations, Species, and Evolution: An Abridgment of* Animal Species and Evolution. Cambridge, MA: Harvard University Press, 1970.

—. *Evolution and the Diversity of Life: Selected Essays.* Cambridge, MA: Harvard University Press, 1976.

—. *The Growth of Biological Thought: Diversity, Evolution, and Inheritance.* Cambridge, MA: Harvard University Press, 1982.

Mehler, Jacques, Peter Jusczyk, Ghislaine Lambertz, Nilofar Halsted, Josiane Bertoncini, and Claudine Amiel-Tison. "A Precursor of Language Acquisition in Young Infants." *Cognition* 29, no. 2 (1988): 143–78.

Midgley, Mary. *Beast and Man: The Roots of Human Nature.* New York: Routledge, 1995.

—. *Wickedness: A Philosophical Essay.* London: Routledge and Kegan Paul, 1984.

Moo, Douglas J. "'The Type of the One to Come': Adam in Paul's Theology." *Trinity Journal* 40 (2019): 145–64.

Muller, Camille. "L'Encyclique 'Humani Generis,'" *Synthèses: Revue mensuelle international* 5, no. 57 (1951): 296–312.

Newman, John Henry. *The Idea of a University.* London: Longmans, Green and Co., 1902.

Oderberg, David S. *Real Essentialism.* New York: Routledge, 2007.

Okasha, Samir. "Darwinian Metaphysics: Species and the Question of Essentialism." *Synthese* 131, no. 2 (2002): 191–213.

Phillips, Richard Percival. *The Philosophy of Nature.* Vol 1. of *Modern Thomistic Philosophy: An Explanation for Students.* Heusenstamm: Editiones Scholasticae, 2013.

Rahner, Karl. "The Theological Concept of *Concupiscentia.*" In Vol. 1 of *Theological Investigations*, translated by C. Ernst, 347–82. Baltimore: Helicon Press, 1961.

———. "Evolution and Original Sin." *Concilium* 26 (1967): 61–73.

———. "Brief Theological Observations on the 'State of Fallen Nature.'" In Vol. 19 of *Theological Investigations*, translated by Edward Quinn, 39–53. New York: Crossroad, 1983.

Ramage, Matthew J. *From the Dust of the Earth: Benedict XVI, the Bible, and the Theory of Evolution*. Washington, DC: The Catholic University of America Press, 2022.

Ratzinger, Joseph. *In the Beginning . . . A Catholic Understanding of the Story of the Creation and the Fall*. Translated by Boniface Ramsey, OP. Grand Rapids, MI: Eerdmans, 1995.

———. *The Spirit of the Liturgy*. San Francisco: Ignatius Press, 2000.

Rieppel, Olivier. "New Essentialism in Biology." *Philosophy of Science* 77, no. 5 (2010): 662–73.

Rosenberg, Alexander. *The Structure of Biological Science*. Cambridge: Cambridge University Press, 1985.

Ruse, Michael. "Biological Species: Natural Kinds, Individuals, or What?" In *The Units of Evolution: Essays on the Nature of Species*, edited by Marc Ereshefsky, 343–61. Cambridge: A Bradford Book, 1992.

Schreiner, Thomas R. "Original Sin and Original Death: Romans 5:12–19." In *Adam, the Fall, and Original Sin: Theological, Biblical, and Scientific Perspectives*, edited by Hans Madueme and Michael Reeves, 271–88. Grand Rapids, MI: Baker Academic, 2014.

Seyfarth, R. M., D. L. Cheney, and P. Marler. "Monkey Responses to Three Different Alarm Calls: Evidence of Predator Classification and Semantic Communication." *Science* 210, no. 4471 (1980): 801–3.

Sidgwick, Henry. *The Methods of Ethics*. 7th ed. London: Macmillan, 1907.

Simpson, George Gaylord. *Principles of Animal Taxonomy*. New York: Columbia University Press, 1961.

Singer, Peter. "Ethics and Intuitions." *The Journal of Ethics* 9 (2005): 331–52.

Sober, Elliott. "Evolution, Population Thinking and Essentialism." *Philosophy of Science* 47, no. 3 (1980): 350–83.

Spangenberg, Izak J. J. "On the Origin of Death: Paul and Augustine Meet Charles Darwin." *HTS Theological Studies* 69, no. 1 (2013): art. 1992.

Spezzano, Daria. "'Be Imitators of God' (Eph 5:1): Aquinas on Charity and Satisfaction." *Nova et Vetera* 15, no. 2 (2017): 615–51.

Sterelny, Kim, and Paul E. Griffiths. *Sex and Death: An Introduction to Philosophy of Biology*. Chicago: University of Chicago Press, 1999.

Számadó, Szabolcs, and Eörs Szathmáry. "Selective Scenarios for the Emergence of Natural Language." *Trends in Ecology and Evolution* 21, no. 10 (2006): 555–61.

Tabaczek, Mariusz. *Theistic Evolution: A Contemporary Aristotelian-Thomistic Perspective*. Cambridge: Cambridge University Press, 2024.

Tattersall, Ian. "The Great Leap Forward." *The Contemporary West* 28 (2011): 38–45.

———. "An Evolutionary Context for the Emergence of Language." *Language Sciences* 46B (2014): 199–206.

———. "At the Birth of Language." *The New York Review*, August 18, 2016. https://www.nybooks.com/articles/2016/08/18/noam-chomsky-robert-berwick-birth-of-language/

———. "Brain Size and the Emergence of Modern Human Cognition." In *Rethinking Human Evolution*, edited by Jeffrey H. Schwartz, 319–34. Cambridge, MA: MIT Press, 2018.

Tattersall, Ian, and Jeffrey H. Schwartz. "The Morphological Distinctiveness of *Homo sapiens* and Its Recognition in the Fossil Record: Clarifying the Problem." *Evolutionary Anthropology* 17, no. 1 (2008): 49–54.

Thompson, Michael. *Life and Action: Elementary Structures of Practice and Practical Thought*. Cambridge, MA: Harvard University Press, 2008.

Van Valen, Leigh. "Ecological Species, Multispecies, and Oaks." *Taxon* 25, no. 2/3 (1976): 233–39.

Vogler, Candace. "The Intellectual Animal." *New Blackfriars* 100, no. 1090 (2019): 663–76.

Wallace, Stan W. "In Defense of Biological Essentialism." *Philosophia Christi* 4, no. 1 (2002): 29–43.

Walsh, Denis. "Evolutionary Essentialism." *The British Journal for the Philosophy of Science* 57, no. 2 (2006): 425–48.

Wawrykow, Joseph. *The Westminster Handbook to Thomas Aquinas*. Louisville, KY: Westminster John Knox Press, 2005.

Weaver, David. "From Paul to Augustine: Romans 5:12 in Early Christian Exegesis." *St. Vladimir's Quarterly* 27, no. 3 (1983): 187–206.

Wilson, Edward O. *Sociobiology: The New Synthesis*. Cambridge, MA: Harvard University Press, 1975.

———. *On Human Nature*. Cambridge, MA: Harvard University Press, 1978.

Biographies

Nicanor Pier Giorgio Austriaco, OP, currently serves as professor of biological sciences and professor of sacred theology at the University of Santo Tomas (UST) in the Philippines. He earned his PhD in biology from MIT, where he was a fellow of the Howard Hughes Medical Institute (HHMI), and an STD in moral theology from the University of Fribourg. Fr. Austriaco is the principal investigator of the UST Laboratory for Vaccine Science, Molecular Biology, and Biotechnology, also known as the UST VaxLab, and the director of ThomisticEvolution.org. His first book, *Biomedicine and Beatitude: An Introduction to Catholic Bioethics*, was published by The Catholic University of America Press in 2011. It was recognized as a 2012 *Choice* outstanding academic title by the Association of College and Research Libraries. A second edition of the book was just published. Fr. Austriaco is a Balik Scientist of the Republic of the Philippines.

Robert Barry is a native New Englander who graduated with a BA in religious studies from Fairfield University. He studied systematic theology at Boston College under Rev. Matthew Lamb, writing his PhD thesis on Thomas Aquinas's *De malo*. Since 1996, he has taught in the Theology Department and in the Development of Western Civilization Program of Providence College. At different times, he has also served the college as chair of the Department of Theology, director of Graduate Studies in Theology, and as president of the Faculty Senate.

Brian Carl is associate professor of philosophy and director of the Center for Thomistic Studies at the University of St. Thomas in Houston, Texas. He earned his PhD in philosophy at The Catholic University of America with a dissertation entitled "The Order of the Divine Names in the Writings of Thomas Aquinas," and taught at the Dominican House of Studies in Washington, DC, before moving to Houston.

Richard Conrad, OP, gained a PhD in organic chemistry at Cambridge University. After joining the Order of Preachers, he studied philosophy at Blackfriars, Oxford, and theology at Oxford University and later at the Angelicum. He has taught a range of subjects at Blackfriars, Oxford, and at Maryvale Institute, Birmingham, including the Holy Trinity, fall-and-redemption, grace, and the sacraments. He was director of the Aquinas Institute at Blackfriars Hall in Oxford from 2014 to 2021.

Daniel D. De Haan is the Frederick Copleston Senior Research Fellow and Lecturer in Philosophy and Theology in the Catholic Tradition at Blackfriars and Campion Hall, University of Oxford. His research draws upon the thought of St. Thomas Aquinas to address contemporary issues in philosophical anthropology, moral psychology, metaphysics, and natural theology. He is the author of *Necessary Existence and the Doctrine of Being in Avicenna's Metaphysics of the Healing* (Brill, 2020), and "A Heuristic for Thomist Philosophical Anthropology: Integrating Commonsense, Experiential, Experimental, and Metaphysical Psychologies," *American Catholic Philosophical Quarterly*, 2022.

Simon Francis Gaine, OP, teaches in the faculty of theology at the Pontifical University of St. Thomas Aquinas in Rome (Angelicum). He is also the director of the Thomistic Institute and the Pinckaers Professor of Theological Anthropology and Ethics. He is a member of the International Theological Commission, the Pontifical Academy of St. Thomas, and a fellow of Blackfriars, Oxford. He is the author of *Will There Be Free Will in Heaven? Freedom, Impeccability and Beatitude* (T&T Clark, 2003) and *Did the Saviour See the Father? Christ, Salvation and the Vision of God* (T&T Clark, 2015).

Raymond Hain is associate professor of philosophy and associate director of the Humanities Program at Providence College in Providence, Rhode Island. His research interests include ethics (especially St. Thomas Aquinas), applied ethics (especially medical ethics and the ethics of architecture), Alexis de Tocqueville, and philosophy and literature. He is the editor of *Beyond the Self: Virtue Ethics and the Problem of Culture* (Baylor University Press, 2019)

Isaac Augustine Morales, OP, is associate professor of theology at Providence College in Providence, Rhode Island. He is the author of *The Spirit and the Restoration of Israel: New Exodus and New Creation Motifs in Galatians* (Mohr Siebeck, 2010) and *The Bible and Baptism: The Fountain of Salvation* (Baker Academic, 2022). He is also coeditor of *A Scribe Trained for the Kingdom of Heaven: Essays on Christology and Ethics in Honor of Richard B. Hays* (Fortress Academic, 2021) and *The Future of Catholic Biblical Scholarship: Marie-Joseph Lagrange and Beyond* (Eerdmans, 2024).

Daria Spezzano is associate professor and chair of theology at Providence College in Providence, Rhode Island. She holds a PhD in theology from the University of Notre Dame, a master's in liturgical studies from the Liturgical Institute, and an MPhil in biological anthropology from Yale University. Her book, *The Glory of God's Grace: Deification According to St. Thomas Aquinas*, was published by Sapientia Press in 2015. She has published scholarly articles in *Nova et Vetera*, *Cistercian Studies*, *Journal of Moral Theology*, and *The Thomist*, and chapters in several edited volumes, including *Reading Job with St. Thomas Aquinas* (The Catholic University of America Press, 2020), *Thomas Aquinas, Biblical Theologian* (Emmaus Academic, 2021), *Thomas Aquinas and the Crisis of Christology* (Sapientia Press, 2021), and *Thomas Aquinas as Spiritual teacher* (Sapientia Press, 2023).

Mariusz Tabaczek, OP, is a friar preacher, professor of theology, and member of the Thomistic Institute at the Pontifical University of St. Thomas Aquinas in Rome. He is the author of *Emergence: Towards a New Metaphysics and Philosophy of Science* (University of Notre Dame Press, 2019), *Divine Action and Emergence: An Alternative to Panentheism* (University of Notre Dame Press, 2021), and *Theistic Evolution: A Contemporary Aristotelian-Thomistic Perspective* (Cambridge University Press, 2024).

Index

A

Acta Apostolicae Sedis, 126–27, 140
Adam, 3, 6–8, 116, 123, 125, 126, 130, 132–33, 135–39, 143–45, 149, 157–63, 169–71, 177–78, 189–91, 193–201, 207–8, 219–20, 222–26, 234–35, 244, 247–48, 254, 256–59
   body of, 116, 130, 131, 132–35, 137, 141, 242
   descendants of, 149, 167, 194, 200, 201, 207, 220
   historical, 200, 225–27, 229, 231, 233, 235, 244
   lineage of, 197–99
   preternatural gifts of, 247, 250–257, 258
   sin of, 116, 158, 206–8, 211, 214, 221–22, 226
   transgression of, 116, 219, 221–22
   See also
affections, 165, 248, 259, 262
agency, 57–59, 103, 207
agent intellect, 68, 232
Albertus Magnus, St., 261
Alexander VII, Pope, 122, 129
Alexander, Andrew, 139, 240
altruism, 95, 97, 164, 185–87
Aquinas, St. Thomas, 2–5, 43–48, 50–64, 67–69, 71, 76, 81–84, 86, 98–99, 104, 116, 122, 129, 144–46, 149–57, 159–63, 165–67, 169–80, 183–84, 186–90, 192–94, 196, 198–200, 203, 207–9, 220, 224, 231, 235, 238–39, 241–43, 245–48, 250–62
   cosmology, 59
   embryology, 79–80, 83–84
   original sin and, 201
   psychology, 145
Aristotelian Essentialism. *See* essentialism
Aristotelian ethics, 100, 108
Aristotelian naturalism, 97–98
Aristotle, 27, 44, 46–54, 61–65, 71, 73–74, 77, 98, 100, 231, 243, 245.
art, 52, 58, 96, 162, 205

Augustine, St., 56, 156, 178–79, 205, 207–9, 221, 224, 245–46, 258
Austriaco, Nicanor Pier Giorgio, OP, 43, 91, 116, 146, 149, 226, 240, 244–45
Avicenna, 54, 68, 77

B

baptism, 125, 160, 210, 213, 215, 255–57
Barry, Robert, 164, 7, 252
beatitude, 180, 183–84, 186, 189, 247, 252, 262
behavior
   altruistic, 95, 114
   symbolic, 148, 228, 230
Benedict XVI, Pope, 140, 246, 248
Berwick, Robert C., 228–35, 244–45
biological essentialism, 27, 239
biological gradualism, 239–40
biological species concept (BSC), 17, 22–24, 239
blood, 50, 63, 249
BSC. *See* biological species concept

C

Carl, Brian, 4, 71, 91, 132, 159
Catechism of the Catholic Church, 2, 5–6, 8–9, 117–18, 134, 136, 140–41, 157, 191, 208, 225–27
Catholic Church, 2, 5–6, 8–9, 115, 117–19, 121, 123, 125, 127, 129, 131, 133–37, 139–41, 154, 157, 208, 225–26
Catholicism, 136, 139, 241, 261
causal powers, 71–73, 91, 111, 155
Chaberek, Michael, OP, 43, 48, 241, 261
chance, 2, 33, 53, 62–64, 73, 173, 237
character, 5, 14, 23, 35, 43, 48, 163, 188, 253
Chesterton, G. K., 156, 205
Chomsky, Noam, 228–35, 244–45
Commentary on Aristotle's Metaphysics, 53–54, 65, 189, 196
Commentary on the Sentences, 199
common origin, 126, 189

275

Compendium of Theology, 65, 145, 243, 253, 258–59
concepts, 12–13, 18, 20–21, 106–9, 112, 144, 146, 153, 232, 243, 248, 252
   abstract, 163, 232
   universal, 145–46
concupiscence, 143, 183–84, 190, 200, 202, 212, 255–56
Conrad, Richard, OP, 6, 43, 91, 152, 166, 171, 247, 249
convenientia, 149, 159–60, 164
cooperation, 58, 164, 170, 185–86, 242
corruption, 49–50, 53, 70–71, 77–79, 83, 85, 170, 250–51, 254–55, 262
cosmos, 5, 38, 49, 62, 66–68, 71, 73–84, 86, 88–91, 153, 155, 196
couple
   first, 125, 139, 182–85, 191
   original, 6, 178
creation, 1–2, 4, 6–7, 9, 11, 47–48, 64, 67, 116, 129–30, 134–35, 142, 179, 184, 194, 238–39, 242, 246–47, 249, 261–62
   immediate, 128–29, 132, 137, 238, 260–61
   special, 89, 132

D

Darwin, Charles, 1, 5, 8, 13–15, 18, 23, 38, 93–95, 98, 205, 225, 227, 229, 241, 245
dator formarum, 68, 81, 84, 86–88
death, 7, 9, 13, 18, 26, 29–30, 41, 116, 123, 143, 145–46, 153–54, 157–58, 171–72, 174–75, 183–84, 186, 190, 205–15, 217, 219–24, 226, 243, 250–51, 253, 257–58, 260
   natural, 211, 223
   origin of, 205
   physical, 7, 158, 209, 221–22, 250, 259
   total, 209
Decaen, Christopher A., 70, 79
De Haan, Daniel, 4–5, 43, 73, 79, 132, 145, 147, 159, 218
demons, 55, 58
Devitt, Michael, 23, 28–30, 39, 111, 113
divine providence, 67, 74, 241, 247, 251–52, 258, 260

Domning, Daryl, 185–87
Dumsday, Travis, 27, 32–33, 39, 41, 93, 110, 239

E

Ecological Species Concept (ESC), 17–18, 22–25
eduction, generative, 67, 77–78
efficient cause, 45–46, 104, 254
embryology, 79, 87
emergence, 44, 67, 76–77, 117, 185, 191, 217–18, 229, 232, 244
Ereshefsky, Marc, 14–15, 18–23, 25–26, 35, 41
ESC. *See* Ecological Species Concept
essences, 3, 11, 17, 24, 26–34, 36, 38–41, 69, 71, 200, 228, 241, 252
essentialism, 3, 11–13, 15–17, 19, 21, 23, 25–29, 31, 33, 35, 37–41
   Aristotelian, 13, 27, 31, 38
   Aristotle, 38
   biological, 12, 28, 30–31
   definition of species, 12, 16, 34
   evolutionary, 13, 32, 38–39
   intrinsic, 27, 239
   new, 26–27, 30
   real, 13, 24–25, 33–34, 36, 40
essentialist species concept (EssSC), 12, 17, 25, 27–28, 30–39, 41
EssSC. *See* essentialist species concept
Ethical Realism, 96–97
ethics, 5, 93–100, 104–6, 108, 110, 113, 251
Eve, 3, 6, 8, 116, 126, 130, 132, 139, 149, 177, 182, 225–27, 229, 231, 233, 235–36, 239–40, 250, 252
   body, 130, 132–33, 135
   mitochondrial, 177
   sin, 214
evolution, 1–5, 9, 11–15, 18, 24–27, 36–39, 41–42, 66–67, 75–76, 86–87, 93–98, 115–18, 126–27, 129–34, 136–43, 173–75, 177–78, 185–86, 191–92, 225, 229–31, 235–38, 240–41, 243–45, 247–50
   adaptive, 32
   body's, 134, 136
   convergent, 4, 36

evolutionary biology, 5, 11–13, 35–36, 93–101, 103–5, 107, 109–14, 189–90, 225, 237
  contemporary, 8, 12, 34, 41–42, 226
evolutionary species concept (EvoSC), 20–21
evolutionary synthesis, modern, 11, 13, 15, 36
evolutionary theory, 3–8, 22, 99, 111, 134, 177, 203, 241
EvoSC (evolutionary species concept), 20–21

F
faith, 6, 115–20, 125–28, 130–31, 134–35, 138, 141–42, 145, 161–62, 248–49
Fastiggi, Robert, 117, 145, 208
Finnis, John, 99–105, 112–13
first parents, 6, 9, 130, 137, 178, 188, 190, 192, 208, 224–27, 236, 238, 250, 252–53
fittingness, theological, 235
Fitzmyer, Joseph A., 206–7, 221–22
FitzPatrick, William, 96–99
Francis, Pope, 241, 247
Frey, Jennifer, 109
Fuentes, Agustin, 244

G
Galatians, 217
Ganoczy, Alexandre, 174
Garrigou-Lagrange, Reginald, OP, 138
Gaventa, Beverly Roberts, 215, 217–18
generation, 22–23, 40–41, 47–53, 55–60, 62–64, 70–71, 77–79, 82–84, 90, 139, 162, 167, 177–78, 193–96, 198, 201–2, 239, 242
  active power of, 198
  animal, 45, 49–50
  bodily, 161, 196
  cause of, 60–61
  natural, 71, 84, 86, 137, 178
  process of, 193, 242
  substantial, 50, 68
  univocal, 44–45
George, Marie, 226, 232
Ghiselin, Michael T., 14, 19, 25, 26

glory, 9, 91, 145, 154, 174, 197, 247, 249, 254–56, 259–62
goodness, 64, 102–3, 105, 152, 154, 157, 179, 261
grace, 6–7, 9, 76, 84, 122–25, 133, 143–45, 153, 155, 160–61, 163–65, 167, 169–71, 174–75, 182, 184, 189–90, 192, 194–97, 199–204, 210, 218–21, 238, 240, 242, 246–47, 252–56, 258
  deification and, 9, 238
  divine, 121, 190, 257
  freedom and, 76, 84, 122, 133
  gift of, 7, 190, 192, 199, 253–56
  habitual, 255
  original justice and, 7, 186, 190–92, 194–95, 197, 199–200, 204
  sanctifying, 7, 144, 167, 182, 184, 186, 188, 190, 194–98, 201, 254
  supernatural, 125, 139, 154–55, 162, 166, 171, 184
  unmediated, 193, 203
grace of original justice, 7, 186, 190–92, 194–95, 197, 199–200, 204
gratia gratum faciens, 144, 254
Griffiths, Paul E., 18, 26, 29–30, 37
Grisez, Germain, 99, 140

H
Hain, Raymond, 5, 43
Half-Merge, 234–35
Historical Adam. *See* Adam
Historical Biological Essentialism, 29, 111
homeostatic property cluster (HPCSC), 12, 17, 34–35, 39
hominids, 116, 233, 241, 246, 250, 261
hominins, 147, 151, 164, 175, 177, 188, 190–92, 244
  prehuman, 143–44
homo adorans, 249, 261
homo sapiens, 8, 111–12, 116–17, 144, 148, 177, 186–87, 226–28, 233–36, 244
  recent origins in Africa, 177
Houck, Daniel W., 177–78, 184, 199, 254
HPCSC. *See* homeostatic property cluster
Hull, David L., 17, 19–20, 25–26, 28
human condition, 143–44, 160, 197, 201, 222

human evolution, 4–5, 9, 115, 201, 227–28, 231, 237–38, 240, 249, 261
Humani Generis, 6, 126, 135–40, 147, 178, 189, 196, 198, 202–3, 238, 260
human language, 146, 150, 161–62, 168, 173, 229–31, 233–34, 244
  appearance of, 233–34
  hierarchical structure of, 230
human nature, 5, 7, 95, 98–100, 103–6, 110, 112–14, 124, 160, 175–76, 179, 182–86, 188–201, 203–4, 239–40, 242, 248, 251–53, 255–59
  accounts of, 105–6, 176
  parts of, 11–12, 106, 140, 246, 249
  principles of, 7, 184, 190, 197, 199, 251, 256
  transmission of, 190, 193, 203
human origins, 3, 6, 8, 115–16, 118–20, 123, 125–26, 129, 131, 139, 142, 144, 177–78, 191, 224
humans
  archaic, 227
  biological, 149, 203
  first, 3, 6, 143–44, 154–56, 161–62, 165, 168–69, 171–72, 201, 239, 244, 246, 250, 252
  modern, 177, 188, 227–28, 230, 233, 238, 244, 261
human soul, 117, 119, 128, 130, 132–33, 139, 145–46, 184, 193, 200, 240–41, 260
hybridization, 44, 47–48, 63, 82
hylomorphic, 33, 36, 41, 66, 68
  species, 81, 89–91
  substances, 5, 66, 68–74, 76–82, 88–90
  systems, 73–74, 76
  theory, 34
hylomorphism, 33
  doctrine of, 69

I
ignorance, 29, 102, 184, 186, 190, 255
Immaculate Conception, 120–23, 125, 129, 134, 141
immortality, gift of, 124–25, 143, 154, 174, 250–60

INBE. *See* intrinsic biological essentialism
inclinations, 100–101, 103–6, 113, 141, 167, 184, 187, 226
  rational, 100
incorruptibility, 9, 238, 250–53, 258–59
infallibility, 118–20, 128
infusion, 9, 146, 149–50, 168, 191–96, 232, 238–39, 242–46, 250, 260
insight, 67, 75–77, 162
intellect, human, 103, 262
Intelligent Design, 9
International Theological Commission, 8, 142
intrinsic biological essentialism (INBE), 27, 30, 111, 239
intrinsic properties, 16, 32, 111–12, 239
intrinsic species concepts (ISCs), 12, 16–17, 19, 21, 25, 27, 34–36

J
Jaworski, William, 73–74
Jensen, Steven, 99, 103–5, 113
John Paul II, Pope St., 2, 115, 133–35, 140, 238

K
Kemp, Kenneth, 126, 139, 149, 189, 196, 198, 240, 243, 244
Kitcher, Philip, 3, 15, 21, 25, 29, 97–98, 114
knowledge, 13, 45, 99–102, 110, 112–14, 160–61, 164, 169–71, 175, 205, 246–47, 258
  infused, 154, 161–62, 169, 247, 250
  practical, 5, 99, 103–5, 110, 167
Koons, Robert C., 43, 62, 73, 74

L
language, 8, 26, 46, 106–7, 109, 140, 145, 167–68, 192, 210, 215–16, 219–20, 226, 228–35, 243–45, 260
  brain enabled for, 150, 233–35
  capacity for, 8, 226, 228–29, 231–35, 244–45, 260
  emergence of, 230
  evolution of, 233–35
  fiigurative, 6, 135–36, 225
  human, 146, 150, 161–62, 168, 173, 229–31, 233–34, 244

spontaneous invention of, 231
Lennox, James G., 38
life, origins of, 1–2, 33
linguistic capacity, 233–34, 238–39, 245–46
Lonergan, Bernard, 67, 75–77, 82, 84

M
MacIntyre, Alasdair, 113
maggots, 80, 83–84
magisterium, 118–24, 127, 129–31, 133–34, 137, 141–42
   extraordinary, 118, 121, 124–25, 128, 134
   ordinary, 6, 119, 121, 123–24, 126, 129–31, 134–36, 141–42
   papal, 121–22, 126, 131, 141
   universal, 118, 123, 128, 132, 137
Marmodoro, Anna, 58, 72–73
Martyn, Louis J., 217
matter
   disposed, 55, 63
   preexisting, 128, 130, 239
   primary, 33, 38
Mayr, Ernst, 14–18, 26, 29, 37–38, 237, 239
McInerny, Ralph, 43
McMullin, Ernan, 67
Merge, 230, 233–34, 236
   Internal, 234
   operations of, 230, 234
Midgley, Mary, 95–96, 151–52, 164
Mishler, Brent D., 14
monogenism, 6, 8, 136–42, 149, 189, 197–98, 240
   moral, 189, 203
Morales, Isaac Augustine, OP, 7, 116, 158, 210, 250
morality, 95–98, 102, 104, 110
Muller, Camille, 139

N
Natural Goodness, 98, 103, 108
natural kinds, 3, 8, 11, 16–17, 20, 22, 25, 27–28, 30–31, 33–35, 38, 41, 111–12, 226–28, 232–34, 240, 245
   biological, 30
   traditional, 93
natural law, 3, 74, 98–99, 103–4, 110, 114, 164–66, 171, 248
natural law ethics, 5, 99, 103, 109
neanderthal, 164, 244
Newman, St. John Henry, 156, 205
New Natural Law Theory, 99–100
nominalism, 12–13, 15

O
Oderberg, David, 13, 23–25, 33–36, 39–40, 74, 93
operations, 67, 73, 76, 112, 122, 183, 188, 190–91, 193, 196, 230, 234, 240–43, 245, 251–52
original justice, 7, 9, 124, 159, 179, 182–86, 188–92, 194–200, 204, 209, 224, 238, 250–55, 258, 260
original righteousness, 124–25, 136, 139, 195–96
Original Selfishness, 185, 187
original sin, 7, 123, 136–40, 143–44, 157–58, 167, 170, 174, 177–79, 181–201, 203, 205–8, 212–13, 218–19, 221, 225–26, 238, 242, 250, 255, 258
   condition of, 7, 185, 189–92, 197, 199
   decree on, 157
   doctrine of, 137, 178, 186, 197, 205–7
   evil and, 185
   inherited, 137
   original death and, 219
   polygenism and, 136, 139
   pure nature and, 178, 252
   state of, 158, 182, 184, 186–88, 190–92, 197
   St. Augustine and, 206
   St. Thomas Aquinas and, 201
   transmission of, 137–38, 177–79, 181–85, 187, 189–93, 195, 197, 199, 201, 203, 208
   wounds of, 184, 212
   See also Adam: sin of
origin of death. *See* death: origin of
origins of life. *See* life, origin of

P
Paul, St., 153, 205–7, 209–24, 250
   See also Romans, Letter to

INDEX

perfection, 43, 46, 57, 68, 76, 78, 82, 105, 152, 180, 183, 195, 232, 246, 248, 255–56, 258
   final, 258, 262
Phenetic Species Concept (PSC), 12, 17, 34–35
Phylogenetic-Cladistic Species Concept (P-CSC), 17–18, 20, 23–26
Pius IX, Pope, 118, 125, 130, 167
polygenism, 6, 8, 136–38, 140–42, 178
   inclination to, 141
   original sin and, 136, 139
   single-population, 140
Pontifical Academy of Sciences, 2, 126, 133–35, 140, 238
Pontifical Biblical Commission, 131–32, 135
Population Structure Species Concept (PSSC), 17–18, 24
powers, 2, 34, 43, 47, 50, 53–62, 64, 66–76, 79, 84, 115, 170, 180, 183–84, 186–88, 190–91, 194–95, 198, 218, 253, 255, 260–61
   active, 47–48, 52, 64, 198
   concupiscible, 187, 193
   divine, 178, 199, 252–53, 258
   explanatory, 102, 112
   generative, 82–84
   natural, 58–60, 67, 91, 172
   passive, 72, 74
PPC. *See* principle of proportionate causality
preternatural gifts, 152, 154, 160, 163, 168–69, 184, 189–90, 250, 254
   immortality, 250, 252
   integrity, 154–55
Principle of Cooperation, 185
Principle of Proportionate Causality (PPC), 4–5, 43–45, 56–57, 60, 63–64, 66, 68, 82–88, 91
proportionate matter, 146, 151, 155
PSC. *See* phenetic species concept
punishment, 158, 182, 188–89, 191–92, 197–99, 208–9, 214–15, 219–20, 250, 257–59

R

Rahner, Karl, SJ, 140–41, 144, 147, 158, 160, 163, 166, 202, 241

rational soul, 9, 68, 81, 89, 145–50, 155, 158–59, 168, 175, 191–96, 203, 238–46, 248–52, 256, 260
   immaterial, 68, 82, 89
   infused, 149, 159, 240, 244
relational species concepts (RSCs), 12, 16–22, 25–26, 29, 36, 39
reproduction, 22, 44, 50, 53, 60, 63, 79, 103, 129, 173, 195
resurrected bodies, 257, 259–60
Richards, Richard A., 15, 21
Romans, Letter to, 7, 116, 158, 205–24, 248, 250–51, 253, 255, 257, 260, 262
   death in, 206, 210, 214
   punishment for sin in, 215

S

salvation, 135, 141, 197, 202, 210, 219, 235, 255
sanctifying grace, 7, 144, 167, 182, 184, 186, 188, 190, 194–98, 201, 254
Schwartz, Jeffrey H., 147–48
selfishness, 185–87, 192
Simon Francis Gaine, OP, 5–6, 8, 141, 158, 244
sin, 6–7, 123–24, 137, 141, 143–44, 154, 158, 160, 165, 167, 171–72, 174, 177–83, 185, 188–90, 192–93, 195–202, 205–26, 248, 250, 253–60
   actual, 167, 170–71, 182, 207
   evolution and original, 140, 202
   human, 185, 198
   original. *See* original sin
   primal, 182
slavery, 211, 218
solidarity, 153, 155, 160, 208
soul, 8, 50, 56, 62, 81, 117, 119, 123, 125, 127–30, 133, 137, 139, 145–48, 153, 157–58, 160, 172, 175, 182–84, 189, 192–95, 198–99, 202, 208–9, 222–23, 232, 237–40, 242–43, 245–48, 250–62
   animal, 56, 146, 241
   body and, 127, 237, 248, 258
   human, 117, 119, 128, 130, 132–33, 139, 145–46, 184, 193, 200, 240–41, 260

immaterial, 132, 139, 191
immortal, 129, 139, 145, 151, 183, 247, 251
rational, 9, 68, 81, 89, 145–50, 155, 158–59, 168, 175, 191–96, 203, 238–46, 248–52, 256, 260
sensible, 56, 61–62
sensitive, 56–57, 79, 193
spiritual, 128–29, 142, 191, 239, 241, 243
substantial form and, 81
vegetative, 56, 79
speaking primates, 231–33, 235–36
speciation, 12, 14–15, 23, 36, 41
species, 1–3, 7, 9, 11–41, 44–45, 47–49, 51–54, 56–57, 60, 63, 65–66, 68, 70, 82–83, 85–86, 90, 93, 95, 98, 107–11, 116–17, 126, 132, 139, 143, 145, 147–49, 164, 168–69, 187, 196, 231, 237, 239–40, 245
biological, 3, 8, 12, 15, 23, 27–28, 32, 34–35, 37, 109, 116–17, 226–28, 233–35
concepts, 3, 12, 14–26, 29, 34–36, 107, 112
defining, 12, 29, 37, 41
evolution of, 38
new, 41, 47–48, 63–64, 82, 159
origin of, 1, 13–14, 65–66, 90, 93, 132, 239
particular, 17, 19, 29, 35
theological, 149, 189, 240
species concepts, 3, 12, 14–26, 29, 34–36, 107, 112
biological, 17
classic biological, 239
cluster, 35
ecological, 17–18, 22
intrinsic, 12, 16, 25
phylogenetic, 22
population structure, 13, 17–18
relational, 12, 16
speech, 126, 128, 229, 231, 243, 245, 256, 262
Spezzano, Daria, 9, 145, 149, 155, 247, 257
spiritual death, 8, 211, 213–14, 220–24, 250

spontaneous generation, 44, 47, 49–50, 53–54, 59, 63, 84
state of original justice, 9, 184, 209, 238, 255
substances, 4, 33, 58, 69–71, 74–79, 83, 86–89, 91, 129, 179–80
existing, 68, 89
intellectual, 56–57, 241
novel, 77, 85, 89
separate, 56–60
vegetative, 65, 80, 83
substantial change, 38–39, 50, 55, 58, 66, 69–70
substantial forms, 12, 17, 32–33, 36, 38, 40, 58, 68–71, 73–74, 77–83, 86, 89–90, 145–46, 193
supernatural gifts, 125, 155, 160, 196, 258

T
Tabaczek, Mariusz, OP, 3, 16, 38, 43, 67, 91, 93, 117, 143, 239
Tattersall, Ian, 148, 228, 230–31, 233, 244
ThomisticEvolution.org, 1, 9, 43, 91
tradition, 6, 99, 113, 115, 127, 143, 153, 157, 162, 167, 171, 174, 205, 208–9, 259, 261
Trent, Council of, 123–26, 136, 157–59, 196–97, 207–8, 215
Decree on Original Sin, 123

V
virtues, 16–17, 27, 30–31, 33, 54, 61–62, 86–87, 89, 98–100, 108, 110, 114, 144, 151, 153–54, 160, 163–64, 166–67, 169, 171, 176, 183, 195, 209, 246
acquired, 79, 166, 169
infused, 153, 155, 165–66, 169
roots of, 163–65
theological, 153
vocal communication, 230, 232

W
wisdom, 149, 155, 191, 235, 247–48
worship, 248–49

Z
ἁμαρτία, 216–17